Remapping Second-Wave Feminism

Remapping
Second-Wave Feminism

The Long Women's Rights
Movement in Louisiana, 1950–1997

JANET ALLURED

The University of Georgia Press
Athens

© 2016 by the University of Georgia Press
Athens, Georgia 30602
www.ugapress.org
All rights reserved
Designed by Kaelin Chappell Broaddus
Set in 10/13 Kepler Std by Graphic Composition, Inc., Bogart, Georgia

Most University of Georgia Press titles are
available from popular e-book vendors.

Printed digitally

Library of Congress Cataloging-in-Publication Data
Names: Allured, Janet, author.
Title: Remapping second-wave feminism : the long women's rights movement in Louisiana,
 1950–1997 / Janet Allured.
Description: Athens : University of Georgia Press, [2016]
Identifiers: LCCN 2015047526| ISBN 9780820345383 (hardcover : alk. paper) |
 ISBN 9780820350042 (e-book)
Subjects: LCSH: Second-wave feminism—Louisiana—History. | Feminism—Louisiana—
 History—20th century. | Women's rights—Louisiana—History—20th century. |
 Women—Louisiana—Social conditions—20th century.
Classification: LCC HQ 1438.L8 A45 2016 | DDC 305.420976309/04—dc23
 LC record available at http://lccn.loc.gov/2015047526

To my family and to the Louisiana women

who shared with me their life stories and their passion

for making the world a better place.

CONTENTS

ACKNOWLEDGMENTS

This book would not have been possible without the help and financial support of a considerable number of entities, institutions, and individuals. The university where I have taught since 1989, McNeese State in Lake Charles, is classified as a teaching institution. Providing me with occasional relief from my four-course-per-semester workload allowed me to pursue research and find the time necessary to put it together in coherent form. I am grateful for the sabbatical year of 2007–8, and the leave time in 2012 made possible by a Board of Regents Award to Louisiana Artists and Scholars (ATLAS), the first ever awarded to a faculty member at McNeese. Jeannie Robertson and Janet Woolman in the Office of Research Services provided invaluable guidance throughout that process. Another leave allowed me to accept a yearlong position as a visiting scholar at Newcomb College Institute in 2013–14. Without the assistance of Newcomb director Sally J. Kenney, Newcomb archivist Susan Tucker, Laura Wolford, and the rest of the staff there, this book would never have seen the light of day.

I also benefited from funds established for the support of faculty research at McNeese, particularly the Evelyn Shaddock Murray Professorship in History and the Violet Howell awards. The Hardtner family deserves special recognition for its beneficence. Sisters Violet Hardtner Howell and Juliet Hardtner (1918–96), born in Alexandria, Louisiana, were daughters of Henry E. Hardtner, a lumberman known as "the father of modern forestry" in the South. Violet, married with three sons of her own, took in and raised Juliet after both her parents died while Juliet was still a teenager. Juliet graduated from Goucher College in Baltimore, Maryland, and became a lieutenant in the navy during World War II. A member of the WAVES, she was awarded the American Defense and the World War II Victory Medal ribbons. After the war, she left the service and moved to New York City, surrounding herself with a circle of intellectuals and close friends. An independent soul, she never married and became a patron of female artists and scholars. She moved back to Lake Charles in 1990 to live her last years near her family. Since she had no children, she decided to donate her substantial fortune entirely to charity, especially to causes that benefited women and education. The Episcopal Church of the Good Shepherd in Lake Charles, Louisiana, and the associated school, the Bishop Noland Episcopal Day School (EDS) benefited, and so, too, did McNeese. Violet Howell and Violet's son, William D. "Billy" Blake, ensured that Juliet Hardtner's final wishes were carried out and that her endowments are dedicated to supporting faculty research and publication on women. I received quite a few of both awards over the years, and those grants made it possible for me to tell the previously unknown story of Louisiana warriors for gender justice. I think both Violet Howell and Juliet Hardtner would be pleased with the result.

No research project of this magnitude is ever accomplished without the expertise and guidance of librarians and archivists. I owe my biggest debt of gratitude to Susan Tucker, longtime archivist at Newcomb, who in many ways inspired this work. She and Beth Willinger had a vision of Newcomb College as a repository for Gulf Coast women's history, and in the 1990s, Tucker began collecting documents from second-wave feminists. Around 2000, she and the Newcomb staff sponsored a series of symposia on the subject. The subsequent web display caught my attention, just in time for my sabbatical year of 2007–8. I knew immediately that I had found the subject that would become my next academic monograph. Susan retired from Newcomb in 2015, but the archive will be her lasting legacy and is now in the good hands of Chloe Raub, who picked up where Susan left off and assisted me as I made the final touches on the manuscript. Leon C. Miller, head of Tulane's Louisiana Research Collection, and his able assistant, Sean Benjamin, deserve special attention for recruiting, cataloging, and conserving an important collection of New Orleans women's history materials (some of which were salvaged from Katrina's flood waters and freeze-dried in order to preserve them). Art Carpenter and Trish Nugent in the Special Collections Department of Loyola University allowed me to sift through the papers of Janet Mary Riley before they were processed. Laura L. McLemore, head of Archives and Special Collections at the Noel Memorial Library at LSU–Shreveport, and Florence Jumonville, who presided over the Louisiana Room in the Earl K. Long library at UNO for many years, proved equally valuable. Jean S. Kiesel, librarian at the Louisiana Room, helped enormously with photo selections from the wonderful Ollie Osborne collection. The papers of Acadiana feminist Ollie Osborne were collected and deposited by Vaughan Burdin Baker, who understood the importance of women's archives. Finally, the capable assistance of librarians at McNeese also made this book possible. Jessica Hutchings, Walt Fontane, Pati Threatt, Janet Woolman, and David Guillory as well as the many library staffers who invariably delivered efficient service with a smile made long-distance research not only possible but fun.

Preserving documents in the midst of the storms that regularly befall the Gulf Coast is not an easy task. Many people whose stories I wanted to tell had no documents left to give me. I relied instead on their recollections, which often required many hours of face-to-face interviews and follow-up emails and phone calls. I am exceedingly grateful to those movement participants (listed in the appendixes) and to their family members who gave of their time and willingly shared their stories with me. Occasionally, they were able to recover a few dusty documents from someone's attic. Those, too, have been deposited at Newcomb.

I owe great debts to the scholars who, with no thought of reward or compensation for themselves, read and commented on conference papers, chapters, and drafts of the manuscript. Like me, they sought only that the final product be accurate. For their invaluable insights I thank Sara Evans, Alecia P. Long, Pamela Tyler, Harold L. Smith, Ellen Blue, and Marjorie Spruill; Michelle Nickelson, Joan Johnson, Gail S. Terry, Linda Sturtz, and others at the Newberry Library seminar on women and gender; scholars of the Delta Women Writers colloquium; and my smart and supportive colleagues at McNeese: Derek Blakeley, Michael Crawford, Philippe Girard, Martha Hoskins, Bobby Keeling, Michael T. Smith, and Rachel Williams. Amanda Ogea, a McNeese graduate who will likely become a published writer herself soon, offered excellent feedback on the introduction. Megan Taylor Shockley at Clemson University, while hard at work on her own history of second-wave feminists in Virginia, read a draft of the entire manuscript and offered sage comments. I am deeply thankful to them all.

Several members of the Delta Women Writers' workshop deserve special thanks. The founding mothers of that informal "southern Berks" are Elizabeth Anne Payne, the first historian of women's history at the University of Arkansas, who mentored me as I churned out a dissertation in the field of rural women's history in 1988, and Elizabeth "Betsy" Jacoway, an independent scholar near Little Rock, Arkansas. Betsy encouraged me when I, as a PhD student in the 1980s, wrote an early overview of Arkansas women's history for *Behold! Our Works Were Good*, a traveling exhibit that Betsy saw through to completion. Both of these women taught me a new respect for the role of liberal southerners in advancing social justice. Both also read very early rough drafts of more than one of these chapters and, with southern grace and warmth, offered editorial help as well as insightful criticism. Tulane professors Sylvia Frey and Emily Clark not only asked probing questions but also offered kind reassurance to a writer struggling to find the appropriate voice. To all these women, I offer heartfelt thanks.

A number of writers and professionals directed me to sources and even mailed materials that I might never have located without their help. There are more of them than I can name here, but I want to thank a few whose assistance was particularly valuable. Patsy Sims, Joan Kent, and Betty Anding, reporters who covered women's issues for the *New Orleans States-Item*, in 1971 wrote an award-winning series on illegal abortion practices in Louisiana. Sims and Kent alerted me to the series, and Sims sent me original copies, which I greatly appreciated because the *New Orleans States-Item*, unlike the *New Orleans Times-Picayune*, is not digitized. Their reporting provided invaluable information that would otherwise have been lost to history. Rose Norman, general editor of the Southern Lesbian Feminist Activist Herstory Project, and artist Robin Toler introduced me to the issue of *Sinister Wisdom* that examined southern lesbian history and assisted my search for literature on the landdyke movement in the South. Cheryl Kirk-Duggan, an expert on womanist theology who, as it happens, grew up in the southern industrial town where I live, Lake Charles, supplied a bibliography and advice on womanism. As I was almost ready to submit the manuscript to the press, Barbara Jo Brothers sent me a stack of materials about Sister Fara Impastato, a New Orleans feminist who deserves far more attention than I was able to include at the last minute. Fran Bussie welcomed me into her home for interviews and cheerfully answered my follow-up emails and phone calls. In addition to pointing me to her papers in the Louisiana State Archives, Bussie handed me photos and documents from her own storage bin. Others who assisted me in a like manner are acknowledged in the footnotes.

I cannot thank the University of Georgia Press's editorial team enough for their warm encouragement and professional assistance during the almost ten-year-long production of this book. Nancy Grayson, who stayed with me through two major hurricanes as I pulled together and coedited volume 1 of *Louisiana Women*, also fostered this project before she retired as editor-in-chief. Mick Gusinde-Duffy, Beth Snead, Jon Davies, John Joerschke, and my copyeditor, Barbara Wojhoski, have buoyed my spirits, answered my questions, and corrected my mistakes with patience and grace. This book has been immeasurably improved by their suggestions.

Saving the most important to the end, I wish to acknowledge some personal debts as well. Jessica Hutchings and Janet Woolman, indispensable colleagues at McNeese, also became loyal friends. Their unwavering good cheer, dependable companionship, spirited conversations, and occasional gardening and cooking assistance, so very welcome after an exhausting week at work, kept me going when giving up might have been easier. Susan Tucker and Clay Latimer not only assisted in locating sources but also graciously opened up their homes, putting me up for days at a time while I conducted research in New Orleans. I consider them collaborators in this research project as well as friends. They shared meals and accompanied me to events, introduced me to people who could serve as sources, offered encouragement, and answered my innumerable questions at a moment's notice. Jody Gates and Marilyn McConnell let me stay overnight in their wonderful home that abuts Tulane University. Sue Laporte and I shared many meals together as we bandied about memories and ideas. Karissa Haugeberg, my suite mate in Caroline Richardson Hall and now the American women's historian at Tulane University, read portions of the manuscript, allowed me to bounce ideas off her, and provided after-work conviviality and relaxation on numerous weekends in New Orleans. I value the friendship of all these women still.

Finally, I wish to acknowledge the sacrifices made by my dear, patient husband. David Edwards has supported me in numerous ways through frequent absences and weathered those periods when the stress of trying to write a magnum opus while juggling a four-four course load almost proved too much. Any rewards that may accrue from the final product belong to him as well as to me. Any mistakes or stumbles are mine alone.

Remapping Second-Wave Feminism

"To My Yankee Friends"

Southern Feminism, Northern Imperialism,

and National Historiography, 1965–present

In 1971, a feminist organization called Tulane Women for Change sponsored a talk by Robin Morgan, who was on tour promoting her newly released (and now classic) edited volume *Sisterhood Is Powerful: An Anthology of Writings from the Women's Liberation Movement.* Morgan's appearance rankled some New Orleans women's liberation activists because, as one of them, Sandra "Sandy" Karp, said, "We didn't need anyone to tell us how to be feminist."[1] Even though Karp was originally from the North, she resented Morgan's appearance and was insulted by her authoritarian air. Karp considered the newly invigorated feminist movement in New Orleans, which she helped to energize and shape, her own and thought of it as unique to her adopted city.[2]

Though born in the North, Karp identified with New Orleans because it was the first place she had lived where she encountered like-minded women who helped her develop both a feminist and a lesbian identity. She had moved there in the summer of 1969 to enter graduate school on a scholarship at Tulane University.[3] When she arrived, several consciousness-raising groups were already meeting in the city. She affiliated with Amazon Tribe, "a very mixed group of white women students, teachers and housewives" interested in women's liberation. With the Amazon Tribe women, Karp felt comfortable coming out as a lesbian feminist and a socialist. She became active in what the participants referred to as the Autonomous Women's Movement (roughly, the radical wing of the feminist movement) in New Orleans. She cofounded Sisters Helping Sisters, an abortion referral service that operated both before and after *Roe v. Wade,* the Supreme Court decision legalizing abortion. When women called the

Sisters Helping Sisters hotline, the phone rang at a women's center that Karp and her friends operated from a rented apartment in New Orleans's Irish Channel district. Karp also worked with poor women, white and black, in the welfare rights movement, and in 1980 she helped to organize a Take Back the Night march in New Orleans. These activities were precious to her, an integral part of her sense of self. The camaraderie and support she found among her fellow activists, as well as her belief that she was undermining the city's old boys' culture, made New Orleans feel like her real home.[4]

Sandy Karp counted among her close friends Phyllis Parun, a New Orleans native. A radical socialist who at the time identified as lesbian, Parun was a skilled grassroots organizer, who, like Sandy, resented outsiders taking credit for the movement in New Orleans. Though most of the women in New Orleans's small, grassroots women's rights movement were southern, some had come from outside the region intent on teaching Louisiana women about feminism. Parun and the other natives hated that condescending Yankees saw them as benighted and backward. Northerners had a responsibility to analyze and control their chauvinism toward southerners, she argued in a 1971 position paper titled "To My Yankee Friends." "We do not wish to be patronized by your northern arrogance," Parun told them in no uncertain terms.[5]

That Sandy Karp considered New Orleans her home is somewhat puzzling, for several of her identities marked her as an outsider in the South: she was a socialist, a Jew, and a lesbian. At the same time, these markers helped her to sympathize with southerners in their dealings with arrogant northern feminists. Jews and lesbians knew what it was like to be marginalized in a women's movement that was on the whole homophobic and culturally Christian.[6] And socialists certainly felt oppression in the United States. Because of their "otherness," women like Sandy Karp and Phyllis Parun could see that most white feminists were blind to their own roles as oppressors. That assessment extended to northern women's attitude toward southern women. Critiques of colonialism and imperialism were common among the New Left at the time. Parun fought "isms" of all kinds, including North American chauvinism (objecting, for example, to the United States claiming the term "America" for itself) and "Yankeeism," by which she meant the supercilious attitude of northern liberals who held that southerners were unschooled simpletons with little political savvy and no leadership skills.[7] Parun and Karp's stance against their Yankee friends, then, was consistent with radical feminism's position against colonialism in all forms, domestic and foreign.

Anti-Yankee sentiment was not peculiar to southern feminists. African Americans in the black freedom struggle had for years voiced resentment of northern white liberals who came south to assist the movement. The northerners assumed that they should hold leadership roles because southerners needed help organizing and running a movement. This eventually led to deep fissures in the civil rights movement. In the same way, many southern feminists resented northern women who pontificated to them. Southern women activists of all ethnicities believed they could teach northern women a thing or two about organizational strategies and theories of oppression rather than the other way around.

The two movements—civil rights and women's rights—were inextricably linked in place and time and in many operational ways. Before we explore that idea further, however, an explanation about the subtitle, "the long women's rights movement," is in order. When modern feminists began to refer to their foremothers in the suffrage movement as the "first wave" in order to distinguish their own generation's activism as a separate "second wave," it was a bit of a misnomer because progressive women had remained active in less noticeable ways during the interim.[8] Their activism between 1920 and 1960 is the subject of chapters 1 and 2. Some historians have critiqued the wave metaphor as too restrictive because it conceptualized feminism from the perspective of white women.[9] It is better, they (and I) argue, to think of a "long women's rights movement," borrowing a phrase Jacqueline Dowd Hall used to describe the civil rights movement before the 1950s. Yet the term "second-wave" remains useful in describing the renewed burst of grassroots service and political activism in the 1960s and 1970s. Thus I use it interchangeably with "modern women's rights movement" throughout this book.[10]

One purpose of this book is to encourage the full and complete telling of the story of second-wave feminism in the South. My primary research covering Louisiana, read alongside work published about the movement in other southern states (discussed later), shows that the South had a vigorous, defiant, and persistent cadre of committed feminists who supplied the national organizations with both ideas and personnel. Feminism, in other words, was part of a regional movement against social injustice that southerners of all ethnic backgrounds initiated and energized. Louisiana, in fact, has a long history of oppositional social movements on which second-wave feminists built.

Politically, Louisiana resists categorization, manifesting both a profound conservatism and a long tradition of radical protest. In this state, politicians from white supremacists such as Murphy J. Foster and Leander Perez to demagogues such as Huey and Earl Long and Edwin Edwards have claimed the mantle of "reformers." The term "grandfather clause" (which allowed whites a loophole to register to vote while disfranchising blacks) originated in Louisiana, and the state was the site of *Plessy v. Ferguson,* an unsuccessful challenge to the state's racial segregation laws (the U.S. Supreme Court determined that racial segregation did not violate the Fourteenth Amendment so long as facilities provided were "separate but equal"). The men who backed Homer Plessy's challenge to the state's Separate Car Act were mixed-race, French-speaking Catholics, frequently referred to as Afro-Creoles. Classified by the census as free people of color before the Civil War, they were the product of Louisiana's unique mixed-racial heritage, which in turn resulted from its long history as a colony, first of France and then Spain. The frequent sexual liaisons between wealthy white men and black and Indian women had produced the largest and wealthiest group of free people of color in antebellum America. While these people could also be exploitative—some owned slaves—by the late nineteenth century they had sufficient material and educational resources to push a legal challenge all the way to the Supreme Court. They recruited Homer Plessy, an octoroon—in New Orleans parlance, a person who was one-eighth black—to their cause.[11] When Plessy boarded the "whites only" car of the East Louisiana Railroad number 8 train at the Bywater station in New Orleans, he committed one of the first acts of civil disobedience to challenge the second-class citizenship of African-descended people.[12] Though they lost that case and, as a result, also lost a good deal of momentum, a later generation of black citizens of Louisiana took up that fight. One of them was A. P. Tureaud, an Afro-Creole and the chief lawyer for the National Association for the Advancement of Colored People (NAACP) in Louisiana. From the 1920s onward, Tureaud worked closely with the national NAACP and its legal team, led by Thurgood Marshall, in pushing forward cases against school segregation and unequal pay for teachers. Likewise, many black teachers, male and female, worked for civil, economic, and political equality for black citizens of Louisiana.[13] White and black Populists in the 1890s had also sought to overturn the corrupt one-party rule of the white supremacist Bourbon Democrats, and unions had long worked toward economic justice goals. White and black women were active in these change-seeking campaigns from the beginning, and the fight against gender injustice that took inspiration from the black freedom movement was no different.[14] Thus, Louisiana, like the rest of the South, had a history of oppression—of races and classes and women—but at the same time a history of resistance to that oppression. Out of the tradition of oppositional movements came feminism.

History of Second-Wave Feminism

Factors outside the South also helped reinvigorate the feminist movement. Women in labor unions all over the United States pushed for equal pay and equal opportunity long before the independent feminist movement appeared in the mid-1960s. Historians of "labor feminism" have revealed how working-class

women's efforts on behalf of workplace justice foreshadowed and also disseminated modern feminism. Labor historians have shown that working women
had begun agitating for economic justice (sometimes alongside men of their
own ethnicity and class) as far back as the 1930s. Labor feminists became conscious of gender inequities on the job, and working-class women, who did not
have the luxury of depending on the "family wage," agitated for the Equal Pay
Act of 1963 and the establishment of the Commission on the Status of Women
(PCSW) by President Kennedy (and the subsequent state commissions).[15] Cell 16
in Boston, the Chicago Women's Liberation Union, New York Radical Women,
Betty Friedan's *The Feminine Mystique*, and the PCSW all helped to galvanize
a national movement. All over the country in the early to mid-1960s, women
began coming together to discuss their dissatisfaction with modern American
society and its rigidly defined gender roles in loose-knit consciousness-raising
(CR) groups. Some of the first cities where these CR sessions took place were in
the South, a result of southern women's work in or close proximity to the black
freedom struggle raging around them.

One reason that Louisiana has not received the credit it deserves for nurturing modern feminism is that as the grassroots women's liberation movement
spread outside the region, its origins often became unrecognizable. This transformation of the movement created misconceptions about Louisiana (and the
South more generally) as homogenously conservative and staunchly antifeminist. Yet many nonsouthern activists derived their feminist consciousness from
southern women, black and white, in the 1950s and 1960s. Northern women
got to know southern women and their particular forms of resistance while
living in the South, perhaps as students or as participants in the civil rights
movement, or they encountered southern women after they moved north.
Furthermore, many white women who influenced the national movement also
developed feminist insights as a result of participating in women's liberation
groups in New Orleans. Among them were Dorothy "Dottie" Zellner, Kathy Barrett, Cathy Cade, Peggy Powell Dobbins, Suzanne Pharr, and Moira Buckley
Ambrose, wife of historian Stephen Ambrose. Kim Gandy, a native of Bossier
City, Louisiana, joined the National Organization for Women (NOW) in New Orleans in 1973. In 2001, she became its national president.[16]

Southern feminists were easy to overlook because they seldom appeared
or acted like the stereotype that dominated the popular imagination. Because
direct confrontation with the powers-that-be could be economically ruinous
or even deadly, they tended to behave with decorum. Women in Louisiana
who challenged the status quo often found it difficult to get or to keep employment in the occupations of their choosing. If they were married, their husbands
might have experienced economic reprisals. This is one factor that accounts

for the high percentage of lesbians in the movement: they were unattached to men who might have suffered because of their activism. Southern women who adopted feminist goals, then, were mindful of the ever-present possibility of retaliation and thus had a tendency to glove their defiance in respectability. African American women, who were quite familiar with the violence that had greeted many of the civil rights workers in the South, understood that any kind of activism could put them and their families in danger. Black feminists, then, were even more likely than white feminists to present themselves in a respectable manner. Southerners' tendency to shun ostentation or "shock and awe" and to behave with propriety caused observers to miss the revolutionary nature of their protests. Spotting these "stealth feminists" can be difficult.[17]

The prevailing image of a feminist was either a shrill, angry, radical leftist Yankee from a big city like Chicago, New York, or Boston, or a promiscuous Left Coast hippie living in the San Francisco Bay area. Those gendered images (no man is ever described as "shrill") connoted a woman who was not only unladylike but even unpatriotic. The term "feminist" implied women who rejected traditional notions of respectability and probably men, too. Some feminists fit that model, but to focus on those few to the exclusion of all others distorts the meaning of the term. In reality, there were many types of feminists, and most were not of the radical variety.

Most feminists in Louisiana, as liberals, had no interest in overthrowing capitalism. They asked little more than that the state and the nation uphold its promise of equality of opportunity for women of all races and ethnicities. New Orleans had a small cadre of radical young feminists, predominately lesbian, whose drive to create womansafe spaces helped initiate women's centers and the antiviolence movement in that city. Their youth gave them freedom to experiment with clothing styles, too, but for the most part, Louisiana feminists, black and white, wore fashionable attire, worked as middle-class professionals in a service career, and were married to like-minded men. "White glove" activists pursued female empowerment through women-run organizations interested in advancing women's rights. Some were heterosexual, some sexually fluid, but regardless of their sexual orientation, Louisiana feminists were, for the most part, well-educated, well-groomed professionals who eschewed the countercultural styles of their more radical sisters.

What Is a Feminist?

In the 1960s, as the new feminist movement sought to define itself, factionalism and bitter feuds erupted around what constituted appropriate feminist behavior and ideas. Since the 1970s, however, feminists have adopted a more expansive, inclusive, and pluralistic view of what constitutes feminism. While acknowledging that many types of people perform acts of feminism, sometimes randomly, throughout their lives, I use the term "feminist" in this book to describe someone who works on behalf of legal, social, and political equality for women of all backgrounds, and not just for personal gain or career opportunities. Barbara Smith, a leading black feminist theorist, described this well when she said that "feminism is the political theory and *practice* to free all women: women of color, working-class women, poor women, physically challenged women, lesbians, old women, as well as white economically privileged heterosexual women. Anything less than this is not feminism, but merely female self-aggrandizement."[18] The key word in her definition is "practice." There may have been many closet feminists in Louisiana, but if they did not act on their beliefs in a public way, their story cannot be told in an academic history. Those women, black and white, who joined single-sex organizations or centers, who spoke out and took action on behalf of women, and who are thus documented in newspapers or in other written sources are those whom I identified and interviewed, whenever possible, so that I could tell their stories.[19]

Because there are many misconceptions about feminism, perhaps especially in the South, I want to quote Virginia Methodist Mary King's description of what the movement meant to her. In a 2007 interview, King said:

> Feminism is the emancipatory project for women and it is inclusive of all women; there are no exclusions inherent in it. It is inherently pluralistic. That's not advocating one way of being; it is a doctrine of choice. A doctrine that says every woman has a right to be as she chooses and that she has an equal claim to humanity as [does] any other human being, and inherent to that is a profound respect for equality. There is also no demand for conformity, but [a recognition] that there will be . . . thousands upon thousands of manifestations of what emancipation means for women. So I would say that it is inherently respectful of all races, of all creeds, of all systems of thought, of all walks of life, of all belief systems, of all priority systems. It is inherently the right of a woman to navigate her way through life and become who she believes she would like to be.[20]

King's is an ethical, almost utopian vision that imagines a society where all people can, in Thomas Jefferson's words, "pursue happiness." In that sense, while global theories and movements against oppression have informed the modern women's movement in many ways, second-wave feminism in the United States is also based on quintessentially American ideals.

King's understanding of feminism evolved, as did most women's, from the first dawning of feminist awakening in the 1960s until she gave that interview in 2007. Perhaps most importantly, her more mature definition of feminism now includes women of color and women in other countries. (Interestingly, as we will learn in chapter 3, she first developed a feminist consciousness because she wanted to reach out to women of color.) Though women of color were on the founding board of NOW and other national political organizations, their relationship with white feminists, nationally at least, was a rocky one.

Feminists of Color and Intersectionality

For women of color, the label "feminist" was even more fraught with negative connotations than it was for white women. Black women faced intersecting oppressions—gender, race, and class—not just in society but also within movements for liberation. Thus they struggled with multiple identities and loyalties. Like white men, black men often saw feminism as an attack on them. African American males had enough trouble gaining white respect; the last thing they wanted was women in their communities airing their dirty laundry, as it were. At the same time, women of color believed that "they needed to express solidarity with black men in the struggle against racism." Rupert Richardson, an African American woman from Lake Charles, Louisiana, who served as president of the state and national NAACP in the 1980s and 1990s, recognized that black men sometimes resented the call for gender equality: "Unfortunately, the world has a pecking order. Black men adopt the idea of a pecking order and feel like they have to be superior to somebody, and unfortunately, that becomes black women. A rivalry sets in. But we should not see each other as rivals. That may be because when affirmative action was new, employers were quick to hire a black female because they thought they could satisfy the federal requirements (killing two birds with one stone). But we were supportive of our men and began to pull the men in."[21] Feminists of color in Louisiana found ways to successfully navigate competing loyalties. Rather than prioritizing one cause over another, they instead worked to end both gender and racial oppression simultaneously, and some, like Sibal Taylor Holt, the first African American woman to head a state AFL-CIO organization, also took on class oppression.

While the writings of northern black feminists often excoriated white feminists for their failure to understand how racism, sexism, and classism intersected in their lives, African American author and theoretician (and Kentucky native) bell hooks pointed out that, in the 1970s, "for every black anti-feminist article, there existed a pro-feminist black female position."[22] In other words, not all black women rejected feminism as a whites-only movement. Hooks explained in 1981 why she was proud to claim the label "feminist": "To me feminism ... is a commitment to eradicating the ideology of domination that permeates Western culture on various levels—sex, race, and class, to name a few—

and a commitment to reorganizing U.S. society so that the self-development of people can take precedence over imperialism, economic expansion, and material desires."[23] Linking multiple oppressions under one rubric of "the ideology of domination" was a major contribution that women of color made to feminist theory. Thus, though there was tension between white and black women, often, and perhaps particularly in the South, they managed to develop alliances that benefited both groups. (Political alliances across the color line in Louisiana are explored in chapter 8.)

Some scholars have argued that U.S. feminism, far from being a white invention, may well have begun among black women. Historians Johnetta Cole, Beverly Guy-Sheftall, and Patricia Hill Collins contend that black women invented feminism in the Student Non-Violent Coordinating Committee (SNCC).[24] Other scholars see black feminism as emerging alongside white feminism(s) and not derived from it. Rosalyn Baxandall identifies two groups that have the hallmarks of feminist organizations that were unconnected with the civil rights movement, Mothers against Working, a group of two hundred poor black and white women in San Francisco that began in 1965, and a Mount Vernon/New Rochelle group of primarily African American women that formed in 1960 as an outgrowth of Planned Parenthood. Benita Roth, a historian of African American feminism, says black and white feminist movements "were linked in a crowded, competitive social movement sector, and there were mutual and complicated relationships between feminist activists from different racial/ethnic communities."[25] Women of color helped to develop notions of anticolonialism that feminists found so useful. For a brief period after World War II, black women had organized internationally not only around the issue of white supremacy but also around matters concerning women's oppression, though this effort was ultimately thwarted by anti-Communist politics. Inspired by the earlier movements and seeking to know their own heritage, a delegation of SNCC women toured Africa during fall 1964. Indeed, the Black Women's Liberation Committee, founded by Frances Beal, represented one of the new directions for SNCC in the post-1966 period. Beal later founded the Third World Women's Alliance, indicating again the importance of the transnational movement of ideas.[26]

Black women in the United States, in other words, were integral to the development of feminist theory. Yet most African American theoreticians wrote from outside the South, and their view of feminism may have been quite different from that of southern activists of color who remained in the region of their birth. It is hard to know for certain, because southern black women typically did not write about or publish theories of intersectional oppression. In a region as poor and underresourced as the South, most activists' time and energy went into doing rather than writing.

Additionally, black women in the Louisiana movement (and probably else-where in the South) often worked singly, rather than in groups, toward femi-nist goals. Their primary collective activity was on behalf of their race, so they joined white independent feminist organizations in relatively small numbers. Yet because they often did not inhabit woman-only spaces, it is easy for histo-rians to miss southern feminists of color (a point that speaks to white women's narrow construction of feminism). African-descended women worked with white-dominated feminist groups, but they also worked within mixed-gender organizations; thus, it is important to broaden our focus and look for African American feminists in interstitial spaces. As historian Becky Thompson notes, "Those organizations that confront gender, race, sexual, and class oppression, whether named as 'feminist' or not, need to be considered as integral to multi-racial feminism."[27]

African American theorist Alice Walker believed that black women's identity was sufficiently different from white women's that it needed its own descrip-tion, so she coined the term "womanist" in 1982 to describe an assertive black woman. A loose translation of the term could be "black feminist," but "femi-nist," as we have seen, was a term that many black women would not choose for themselves. Womanists did not work solely on behalf of feminist causes. Instead they worked for the benefit of the entire race. To Walker, a womanist is "committed to survival and wholeness of entire people, male and female. Not a separatist."[28] If Louisiana is any guide, southern black women were of a dif-ferent sort than the more famous and oft-studied feminists of color elsewhere in the country. The earliest black feminist organizations in the United States emerged on the East Coast and were inspired by the black power movement: the Third World Women's Alliance (1968), mentioned earlier, and the National Black Feminist Organization (1973). But black women who advocated feminist goals in the South, it appears, were not much interested in separatism of any kind, either racial or gender. They were generally more bourgeois in manners and in goals than their northern counterparts, and most were educators of one type or another, either teachers in elementary and secondary schools or profes-sors at historically black colleges or universities (HBCUs), of which there were several in Louisiana.[29] Chances were that Louisiana black women activists par-ticipated in a number of social service or community uplift organizations, start-ing with their church, which was most likely Catholic, Baptist, or Methodist, the three largest denominations in Louisiana. They might have found strength and networking opportunities through the National Association of College Women (which in 1974 became the National Association of University Women), the black counterpart to the American Association of University Women; one of the black service-oriented sororities; the Urban League; the Young Women's

Christian Association (YWCA); and/or in neighborhood improvement associations.[30] National polls also showed that African American women routinely supported efforts to improve women's status in higher percentages than did white women. Statistics like these show that black women were sympathetic to feminism even if they did not have time or resources to commit to organizing on its behalf. They supported it in their own ways, through their own organizations.[31]

Some authors have interpreted feminism in the 1960s as a search for identity or authenticity among a generation of young people, a psychological explanation, in essence. What I offer is a historical answer to a question that I have considered for many years now: how is it that the region of the country best known for its conservative politics and social hierarchies of class, race, and gender incubated a revolution in gender roles? Only by looking at the long history of grassroots activism among southerners, black, white, and—especially in Texas—Chicana, can we fully understand the genesis of second-wave feminism. Many progressive activists in the South believed that overturning rank injustices in the social order was a responsibility they owed to God. For southerners who came from liberal religious faith traditions that had long demanded equality of opportunity for oppressed people, the drive for gender equality was right, fit, and just.

Emphasizing the South's failure to ratify the Equal Rights Amendment (ERA), as many previous historians have, blinds us to the often transformative successes of southern feminists. In Louisiana, even conservative women, some of whom vigorously opposed the ERA, welcomed a new role for women in society and proclaimed their support for gender equality. In other words, the paradigm shifted thanks to feminism. Louisiana feminists resolutely challenged white male hegemony and won significant victories as a result. They developed alternative political organizations and counterinstitutions that defied the patriarchal lock on power and new ideologies that changed deeply entrenched assumptions about women's social and political role. The movement to achieve gender equality in Louisiana was perhaps smaller in numbers and in scope than those in New York, San Francisco, Boston, and Chicago, but the women involved were just as active in lobbying for passage of the ERA and in establishing counterinstitutions such as feminist newspapers, battered women's shelters, rape crisis hotlines, and women's centers and collectives. With the help of the federal courts and federal laws, they pried patriarchal privilege out of the hands of the old boys' club and achieved gender neutrality in the law, if not always in practice. Imperceptibly at first, they changed the nature of the debate about women and minorities in what was otherwise a profoundly conservative state.

Those of us who study feminism in the South have discovered that the traditional labels—"cultural" versus "lesbian" versus "politicos"—developed by academic historians and sociologists to categorize feminists seldom applied in this
region. Where the movement was fairly small and beleaguered, as in Louisiana,
women tended to join forces and work together, although not always smoothly
or without confrontation. Historian Alice Echols defines cultural feminism as
"a countercultural movement aimed at reversing the cultural valuation of the
male and the devaluation of the female." In Louisiana, virtually all feminists
sought this goal, and Doug Rossinow also notes in his study of New Left movements in Austin, Texas, that cultural feminism was not antagonistic to political
feminism but in fact was conducive to and supportive of political activity.[32]

Louisiana feminists did not have the same philosophies, goals, or strategies, but they cooperated on many major initiatives. Lesbian feminists in
New Orleans led NOW branches and worked on domestic violence and rape
crisis hotlines, while NOW women organized zap actions (direct actions) and
women's music festivals. The Independent Women's Organization, a group of
Democratic New Orleans uptown matrons connected with well-to-do families, assisted feminists who came from far more humble circumstances and
lacked advantageous social networks. The common cause of feminism created
a vehicle for overcoming class, racial, and philosophical barriers. Taking a long
view of the movement minimizes the personality clashes and divisions over
ideology and sexuality and emphasizes instead cooperation across ideological,
class, and racial lines.[33]

Historiography of Second-Wave Feminism

Highlighting the positive role of lesbians in the movement is another way in
which this book rounds out the history of the second wave. In 2014, the lesbian journal *Sinister Wisdom* put out a special issue titled *Southern Lesbian-
Feminist Herstory, 1968–1994*, in which the editors argue that southern lesbian
feminists have been largely ignored by scholars: "The achievements of southern lesbian-feminists have been disregarded. At best, the existence of southern
lesbian-feminists has been marginalized; at worst, southern lesbian-feminists
have been stereotyped as dependent, racist, uneducated, unsophisticated,
phony, and slow. We have been the butt of disrespectful jokes. . . . We have not
been considered to be capable of independent radical activism by some of the
more important lesbian-feminists of the times. Among our own, however, in
the places where we lived, southern lesbian-feminists were movers and shak-
ers." My research helps revise those negative stereotypes and reveals that lesbians were vital to the movement's successes in Louisiana.[34]

Southerners have been overlooked in the historiography of the second wave in part because they did not have access to national media outlets and major publishing houses as did women in many northern or West Coast cities. Though the newspapers in their towns may have reached large numbers of subscribers in the region, they had little or no national circulation compared to, say, the *New York Times* or the *Wall Street Journal*. As a result, southern activists received little notice, and a "bicoastal" bias that privileged the history of the urban North and West emerged.

Southern feminists disseminated their ideas primarily through mimeographed memos and manifestos that they distributed among themselves and elsewhere in the country.[35] Yet the earliest feminist publications, produced in the North and the West, contained almost nothing from the South, even though southern women generated influential critiques of racial and gender hierarchies. Of the thirty-three memoirs in *The Feminist Memoir Project: Voices from Women's Liberation*, produced in New York in 1998, only one very brief entry is written by a native-born southerner, Minnie Bruce Pratt (a lesbian feminist).[36]

The first academic historian to try to insert the South into the dominant bicoastal narrative was South Carolina native Sara Evans, a Methodist minister's daughter active in the student Christian movement and the black freedom and feminist movements. She described this journey in her dissertation, which she published in book form as *Personal Politics: The Roots of Women's Liberation in the Civil Rights Movement and the New Left*. Concerned about the top-down and northern-oriented early histories of the movement appearing on the bookshelves, Evans highlighted the religious motivations of southern whites involved in civil rights who subsequently became "founding mothers" of the women's liberation movement.[37] Evans rightly shifted the origins of feminism away from the North to the black freedom movement of the South, but she then turned her attention away from the South and onto those women who moved north. Likewise, most work since then has kept the focus on activists living in the major cities of the Northeast, Midwest, and West Coast.[38]

While the lack of documents sometimes caused bicoastalism and Yankeeism, scholars have discounted the region's feminist activity also because southern states either did not ratify the ERA or rescinded their ratification if they did (except Texas, where rescission failed).[39] The ERA, proposed in 1923 by the National Women's Party and passed by Congress in 1972, never secured the required approval of three-fourths of the states that would allow it to become part of the U.S. Constitution. This loss was a bitter pill for the legions of feminists nationwide who had devoted many years and much energy attempting to persuade state legislatures to approve its ratification. Participants wrote most of the first histories of the movement, and their resentment of the South colored their interpretations of southern feminism. The devastating loss of the ERA due to the opposition of defiant, states-rights southern legislatures blinded observers to the roots of feminism in the Deep South.

Donald G. Mathews and Jane Sherron De Hart did an in-depth analysis of North Carolina to try to understand why that state failed to ratify the ERA. Theirs was the first book-length study to focus on a southern state, and they conducted their research—consisting of interviews and observations of hundreds of participants (proponents and opponents of ERA) as well as archival research—over the course of eleven years while the wounds from the battle were still fresh. Mathews and De Hart showed that in North Carolina (and presumably all other southern states), feminist rhetoric was tied to race, still an extremely divisive issue where whites, bound by historic prejudices, were unwilling to accept a new racial order imposed on them by federal laws and court rulings. The authors helped explain not just the philosophical positions of both sides in the ERA fight but also why the South was exceptionally resistant to ratifying the ERA. This immensely valuable book nonetheless foregrounded a feminist failure. By focusing so intensely on the ERA, they (like others at the time) gave the impression that the ERA was the be-all and end-all of the modern feminist movement.[40]

A growing body of recent scholarship has focused on second-wave feminism at the local level and has helped to broaden that focus. Stephanie Gilmore's *Groundswell: Grassroots Feminist Activism in Postwar America* examines local NOW chapters in three cities, Memphis; Columbus, Ohio; and San Francisco. Gilmore shows that in Memphis, NOW, because it was the only explicitly feminist organization in town, tended to be the vehicle for feminists of many different varieties who lacked sufficient numbers to establish their own institutional or bureaucratic homes. This same phenomenon existed in most cities in Louisiana as well.[41]

Gilmore's book is typical of much of the newer work on second-wave feminism in that she picked three cities and used them as microhistories to represent different regions of the country. Likewise, Melissa Estes Blair's recent book, *Revolutionizing Expectations*, focuses on women's organizations in Durham, Denver, and Indianapolis, with an eye to showing that many traditional women's groups contributed to feminism, too, and not just the overtly feminist organizations such as NOW. That, too, is something that my research into Louisiana women led me to conclude and is the subject of chapter 1.[42]

Unlike many of the national histories of feminism in the United States, which presume a universalism about the movement and thus do not engage with the local setting, Anne M. Valk analyzes the peculiarities of geography in her well-received 2008 volume, *Radical Sisters: Second-Wave Feminism and*

Black Liberation in Washington, D.C. The nation's capital had a number of distinctive characteristics that made its feminist movement unique. Because so many national organizations were headquartered there, it had an unusual mix of activists from all over the country. Also, because the district had limited political autonomy, the fights there were different. Elsewhere, activists battled state legislators, but in Washington, activists were as likely to be working on national agendas as local ones. Valk's definition of the word "feminist" includes all women who sought to "elevate women's status in their own communities and in the larger society through movements for economic justice and black liberation." Such an inclusive definition expands the view to include many women, most importantly black and poor women, who are often seen as tangential to the movement, or at least not particularly engaged with it. Thus she incorporates women who may have been active in welfare rights but who may not have joined an independent women's organization such as NOW. Not only did feminism cross both racial and class boundaries; it also continuously adapted and evolved. Valk shows the interconnectedness and mutual reliance of groups that may be termed "black feminist" with those traditionally understood as "white feminist."[43]

Florida, like Louisiana, was one of the key southern states that helped produce the modern feminist movement. Carol Giardina, a participant in the Florida movement, provides compelling evidence for the pivotal role that the university town of Gainesville played in originating the women's liberation movement. Noting the influence of black women in the creation of feminist thought, Giardina traces the intellectual and experiential threads that informed one of the earliest writings of the women's liberation movement, "Toward a Female Liberation Movement," also called "The Florida Paper." Coauthored by Judith Brown, who eventually left her husband and came out as a lesbian, and Beverly Jones, the authors also founded Gainesville's Women's Liberation, one of the first such groups in the nation. Both Carol Hanisch and Kathie Sarachild moved to Gainesville to join this group. While there, Sarachild wrote the first pamphlet on feminist consciousness-raising, and Carol Hanisch wrote the famous essay "The Personal Is Political" (discussed in chapter 3). There was a good deal of lesbian feminist activism in Gainesville as well.[44]

Florida women are also the subject of articles by Joan S. Carver, "The Equal Rights Amendment and the Florida Legislature," and Kimberly Wilmot Voss, "The Florida Fight for Equality: The Equal Rights Amendment, Senator Lori Wilson and Mediated Catfights in the 1970s." Voss's is a fascinating exploration of media depictions of women on both sides of the ERA fight in Florida.[45]

In *Texas through Women's Eyes*, Judith N. McArthur and Harold L. Smith examine the long women's movement, going back to the first wave of the early twentieth century. Texas was unusual among southern states in that it passed a state Equal Rights Amendment in the 1950s, long before any other southern state took up the issue. Texas was also one of two former members of the Confederacy that ratified the federal ERA in 1972 (the other being Tennessee), and it was the only one where rescission efforts failed. Nancy Baker analyzes the reasons for this in her work on Hermine Tobolowsky, the "mother of the Equal Rights Amendment in Texas."[46]

Texas was also the only southern state with a substantial Latina population in the twentieth century, and MacArthur and Smith document feminism within both the Hispanic and the African American communities. The Lone Star State was home to the International Women's Year conference in 1977, the Farah Manufacturing protest of the 1970s, and the case of *Roe v. Wade*, the U.S. Supreme court decision that overturned states' restrictive abortion laws in 1973. Texas straddled the line between western and southern, a fact that Sarah Weddington (the lawyer for Jane Roe) found important in understanding the uniqueness of the women's movement in the state. Smith's article about Casey Hayden in *Texas Women: Their Histories, Their Lives*, as well as his book, connects Texas women involved in the civil rights movement with the rebirth of feminism.[47]

That graduate students are beginning to take notice of feminism in the South is heartening. Katarina Keane's dissertation, "Second-Wave Feminism in the American South, 1965–1980," which appeared in 2009, opens up new areas of research for historians of the second wave. Keane picked a few southern cities—Atlanta, Georgia; Chapel Hill-Durham, North Carolina; and Austin and Dallas, Texas—to get a sense of women's activism below the Mason-Dixon Line. Examining women's independent feminist organizations, feminist business enterprises, and legal cases that arose in the South, she makes a case for southern women's inventiveness, though as with most other such studies, she finds that the shape of the movement was not much different in this region than it was elsewhere. Also, Laura Foxworth's 2011 master's thesis focuses on feminists' attempts to get the ERA ratified in South Carolina.[48]

Much of the historiography on second-wave feminism in the South comes in the form of journal articles and essays in compilations. Essays about feminism in Arkansas emanated from the flagship university in Fayetteville, in the northwest corner of the state in the Ozark Mountains. My first published paper, a product of a graduate school seminar with David Edwin Harrell at the University of Arkansas, discussed the rhetoric of competing religious views during the ERA battle in Arkansas. Janine A. Parry, a political scientist, analyzed the local women's commissions in "'What Women Wanted': Arkansas Women's Commissions and the ERA." Research completed by Anna M. Azjicek,

Allyn Lord, and Lori Holyfield uncovered not just the role of the University of Arkansas in the rebirth of feminism in that state but, perhaps even more importantly, reveals that the aptly named "Natural State" proved an attractive draw for "landdykes"—lesbians who became part of the back-to-the land movement and founded "intentional communities," otherwise known as communes. In Arkansas hill counties, the rugged, isolated, largely inaccessible (and therefore inexpensive) land proved fertile ground for lesbians seeking female-dominated spaces and alternative, self-sufficient lifestyles. While the lesbian intentional communities in the northern and northwestern states, particularly Oregon, have gotten a fair amount of attention, a high percentage of the land-dyke communes were in the South, and their history remains largely unwritten. Grounded in ecofeminist philosophies, woman-only communes rejected patriarchal notions about domination of nature and other humans and sought to live in harmony with "the sacred female power" of Mother Earth. Casting off hierarchical structures of governance associated with patriarchy, they sought decision making by consensus. The founding of intentional communities by feminist lesbians is an aspect of second-wave feminism in the South that begs for a book-length academic study.[49]

The volumes in the University of Georgia Press's histories of women in southern states are also making inroads toward conceptualizing the history of women activists in the post–World War II period.[50] "In the Mainstream: Mississippi White Women's Clubs in the Quest for Women's Rights in the Twentieth Century," by Martha Swain, concentrates primarily on the years before the battle for the ERA. Swain, a native of the Magnolia State and a trailblazer in her own right, argues against the idea of southern exceptionalism, concluding that Mississippi women's clubs were "no more progressive or regressive than . . . in most other states." For women in the traditional organizations, such as the Mississippi Federation of Women's Clubs, the League of Women Voters, the American Association of University Women, and the Business and Professional Women, the ERA was less important than equal access to education, improved sanitation and health care, and fair workplace treatment. Indeed, Mississippi was the only state where the ERA never got to the floor of the legislature for a vote. But the older women's groups, as well as newer ones, took up issues that concerned both generations of women, including child and spousal abuse, child care, family planning, mental health, and self-protection. Feminists continued their activism on behalf of those issues, despite (or perhaps because of) the defeat of the ERA. In other words, concentrating on the battle for the ERA misses much feminist activism that predated the push for ratification and continued after the amendment's defeat in 1982. In that same volume, Marjorie Julian Spruill examines second-wave feminists and their opponents in an article focusing on conservatives' takeover of the International Women's Year conference in Mississippi.[51]

Spruill, who is working on a comprehensive history of the rise of the feminist movement and its conservative opposition, also has an essay in volume 3 of *South Carolina Women: Their Lives and Times* that tells the story of five self-identified feminist activists, four white and one black, who lived and worked in Columbia, the state capital. Spruill continues the trend of looking beyond the ERA to identify areas where feminists made progress: on issues of rape and domestic violence and in raising awareness about the new federal laws and demanding their enforcement (sometimes through lawsuits), especially in opening up avenues to employment. Like Louisiana women, feminists in the Palmetto State resented the condescending attitude of Yankee feminists. As southerners, they had far bigger obstacles to overcome than those faced by women in northern states, and they were proud of what they managed to accomplish despite some very long odds.[52]

Megan Shockley conducts a similar examination of the Old Dominion in the final chapter of *Changing History: Virginia Women Through Four Centuries*. Shockley admits that conservatives in the Virginia legislature defeated nearly every reform sought by feminists and that progress in women's equality was generally the result of federal legislation, but she also praises the many courageous activists who fought despite enormous opposition. Among the women she profiles are those who initiated legal challenges to patriarchal privilege. Unlike legislative battles, this tactic, with the help of the federal government and courts, was far more likely to succeed.[53]

In the border state of Kentucky, the trials and tribulations of Martha Layne Collins, the commonwealth's only woman governor, gets evenhanded treatment from author John Paul Hill, who "illuminates the difficulties that women in general, and women in the conservative South in particular, faced in their attempt to gain personal freedom and political power in the 1970s, 1980s, and onward." Carol E. Jordan examines the history of the anti–domestic violence movement (discussed in chapter 4) in *Violence against Women in Kentucky: A History of U.S. and State Legislative Reform*.[54]

Another aspect of the historiography of second-wave feminism where this book makes an important contribution is in the field of religion. Early scholars of women's history focused on women's political and legal gains and cast the actors' public lives in a secular light. More recently, women's historians have discovered evidence that points to the religious origins of much of the reformism of the nineteenth century, including but not limited to women's rights. (Abolition, temperance, and prison reform were among the others.) Scholars of the second wave have been slower to follow this trend, but as more women have entered the clergy and as laywomen have been emboldened by feminist rhetoric, they have begun to write about their religious experience, too. The religious bases of the New Left have been well documented by Doug Rossinow in *The Politics of Authenticity* (1988), which discusses the movement in Austin, Texas, and in Sara Evans's now-classic *Personal Politics* (1979). Susan Hartmann and Bettye Collier-Thomas have also foregrounded the role of religion in both civil rights and feminism. The work of southern feminists against racial and gender bias within their faith traditions and in society at large may be unique to the South and may help to explain why this aspect of modern feminism has been overlooked by most scholars of the second wave—because it was associated with that part of the feminist movement that northern-oriented scholars neglected to study.[55]

Whether motivated by a religious ethic or not, the South's feminist activists worked toward gender equality in the law, in society, and in marriage; in employment and in financial credit; and in churches and synagogues. This book provides some of the missing pieces of post–World War II women's history by documenting how Louisiana was a key incubator of the modern women's rights movement. It introduces a southern element into an overwhelmingly northern- and western-dominated narrative, showing that modern feminism had a vast popular base around the country; that it was not a Yankee invader; and that, although the federal government and the courts were important allies in the fight for gender equality, feminism had its own local basis of support and was not imposed by Washington, D.C. It highlights the importance of liberal religious denominations, Christian and Jewish, in initiating and sustaining women's commitment to gender equality. And, finally, it shows that regional differences were perhaps most apparent in the way African-descended women in Louisiana worked toward feminist goals. Whereas in the North, feminists of color were spurred by black nationalism, in Louisiana they were far more likely to be influenced by their faith commitments, their unions, or their commitment to other social justice or civil rights organizations. Southern feminist ideologies and tactics were not remarkably different from those of the North, though there was less flagrant radicalism. Given the extremely conservative and powerful infrastructure that opposed them, southern feminists were sometimes less successful than their counterparts in the North or in the West.

Methodology and Theory

Louise A. Tilly said many years ago that women's history is distinguished from most other history in that it has been "movement history; to a large degree, it has been written out of feminist conviction." Whether or not women's historians are members of feminist organizations, "their work has been shaped by the feminist social movement of the 1970s and 1980s."[56] That certainly describes me and is one reason that I spent almost ten years researching and writing this book. My home, Lake Charles, Louisiana, is the site of McNeese State University, which I attended as an undergrad and then returned to as an assistant professor in 1989 following graduation from the University of Arkansas in 1988. My dissertation focused on rural women in the Arkansas Ozarks and out of necessity used a great deal of oral history as source material before the method had become commonplace among historians. Once at McNeese, I took over a course in American women's history and discovered that relatively little academic work existed on the history of Louisiana women. Together with Susan Kelso, director of the theater program, I received approval for a women's studies concentration in 1999 and began looking for readable but also rigorously academic material on Louisiana women's history appropriate for an undergraduate college classroom. Finding only a few monographs, most of which had been published within the past decade, I sought contributors for a book that ultimately became *Louisiana Women: Their Lives and Times*, a collection of minibiographies encapsulating a bit of what we knew about Louisiana women's history and encouraging further research among authors, doctoral students, scholars, and readers.[57]

When I began the research for this project in 2007, I discovered to my horror that many who had been activists in the movement for gender or racial equality in Louisiana had lost their private archives in the hurricanes that swept through the state in the early twenty-first century, most famously Hurricane Katrina in 2005. To fill the gaps, I have relied on oral histories. Those who shared with me their time and their documents inevitably get more space than women whose stories were lost due to death or destruction. That is not an attempt to diminish the importance of those unfortunates. It is, however, a reminder that the historian's craft relies heavily on written documents. Where those are lacking, writing the personal or even the public history of relatively anonymous people is much more difficult. Keeping the focus on the major actors, I went where their stories and related documents led me. With the goal of encouraging a broad audience, I refrain from using academic jargon, including that which is common to feminist theory, in favor of highlighting the historical, geographic, personal, and intellectual connections among actors.

Individual women's life histories illuminate the themes and arguments of each chapter because I was curious about how and why activists in Louisiana decided to embrace a cause that carried a great deal of social opprobrium and that caused them to butt heads repeatedly with a powerful and better-financed opposition. Using a feminist approach to writing their biographies, I started with the premise that the personal is political, that women's private lives shape their public personas. A feminist approach presumes, too, that gender and personality development result from the influence of culture and society and rejects the older, essentialist view that female characteristics are genetic and unalterable. Yet while culture scripts gender norms that people internalize and perform, people also "individuate" those norms, rewrite those scripts, and bring about historical change. Feminists developed an oppositional consciousness that allowed them to challenge the cultural landscape. Seeking to locate the causes of that development, I investigated their physical and intellectual experiences. A feminist historian foregrounds the impact that gender and sexuality have on women's life choices, but always with an eye on the historical cultural context. Biography helps us understand historical periods and places, for the goal of the historian is always to contextualize and interpret our subjects' lives. Biography also allows readers to empathize with the subjects and hopefully provides role models for younger readers.[58]

The criteria for highlighting a woman's personal history is that her years of feminist activism occurred primarily in Louisiana. Some women, like Sandy Karp, may have been born and raised in the North, but most were southerners; not all were native Louisianans. Lynn Miller is a good example. Founder of the Women's Liberation Coalition, the Women's Center, and the Gay Liberation Front in New Orleans, Miller left the city for the mountainous regions of the South in the early 1970s, burned out and ill from "hay fever." Nevertheless, though she left the state while still quite young, she meets the criteria for women profiled in this volume because her involvement left a permanent mark. I also include Louisiana native Kim Gandy, who combined her law practice with feminist activism for ten years before moving up into the hierarchy of the National Organization for Women, leaving the state, and subsequently becoming a national leader in the anti-domestic violence movement. I did not include Baton Rouge native Ti-Grace Atkinson, a well-known figure in radical feminism, because she left before she identified as a feminist and never lived in the Bayou State again. Women who helped to craft and define feminism in Louisiana, whether or not they were native to the state, are the protagonists in this story. Furthermore, these women have been ignored and invisible for too long, and I want to honor them by telling their stories. Few of them are famous, but they may all rightly be regarded as feminist heroes.

It was quite a challenge deciding where to locate each woman's primary biography because their lives seldom fit neatly into one compartment. Thus, Vaughan Baker is introduced in chapter 2, where the religious background of many feminists is discussed, but her full biography opens chapter 6 as a segue into the discussion of the role of universities and academics in the movement.

Likewise, Clayton "Clay" Latimer's biography appears in chapter 1 in the context of the Women's International League for Peace and Freedom, but most of Latimer's feminist work is covered in later chapters. Louisiana feminists' lives are sometimes difficult to categorize.

This book delves into the movement of people and ideas across the Atlantic world and probes the history of several generations of women in order to explicate both the secular and the religious origins of second-wave feminism in a Gulf Coast state. The first section, encompassing chapters 1 through 3, takes a bird's-eye view. This wide perspective enables us to see, first, that the women's movement began well before the mid-1960s and, second, that feminist ideas developed in part because of the international interchange of people and ideas across regional, national, and international boundaries.

The first chapter joins the new scholarship on the second wave in examining organizations that served as springboards to feminism, some of which were decades old. Proto-feminist in that they advanced the cause of women, they laid the groundwork by providing training, experience, and organizational skills to women who would go on to launch a revolution against gender inequality. In the traditional academic narrative of the second wave, the independent feminist organizations that emerged in the 1960s and 1970s—from radical women's liberationists to the more centrist National Organization for Women—received all the attention, thus stealing the limelight from the earlier single-sex groups.

The second chapter focuses on faith traditions as the source of feminist consciousness for many Louisiana women. When I began this research, it did not occur to me to look for or ask my sources about the influence of the faith of their upbringing on their social justice work, but over and over again it popped up. Religious teachings were not important for everyone profiled in this book, but even some women who had left the denomination of their upbringing (or "decommitted") recalled how they had been influenced by the social justice ethic they learned in Sunday school, in church-affiliated youth groups, and/or from devout parents. Christian and Jewish denominations with international roots and a history of missionary work (especially Methodist, Lutheran, Episcopalian, and Reform Judaism) produced the most liberal activists in the postwar period. Few if any Louisiana feminists, unsurprisingly, came from conservative denominations. Raised Methodist myself, I converted to the Episcopal Church as an adult, and I have no doubt that this accounts for my own strong beliefs in social justice as well.[59]

Chapter 3 examines the ideologies current in the 1950s and 1960s, especially existentialism and the philosophy of otherness, that influenced some of the early southern feminists and follows the circulation of these ideas around the Atlantic world. Contact with African Americans as well as transatlantic connections (some of them religious) in Texas, Louisiana, and Florida produced some of the nation's first feminist ideas and grassroots feminist meetings. The point is that these southern women developed feminist insights independently of anything going on in the North.[60]

The second part of the book focuses more narrowly on Louisiana. Chapter 4 examines the various sources of the antiviolence movement in the state. Though it was gendered everywhere, meaning that the activists sought to stop violence against *women*, only in New Orleans did radical lesbians play a significant role. Elsewhere, it often involved men and women affiliated with churches and YWCA chapters. Such is the nature of grassroots movements: they tend to have local peculiarities arranged around the specifics of place.

Chapter 5 discusses abortion practices in Louisiana during the twenty years before abortion was legalized in 1973 by the U.S. Supreme Court's *Roe v. Wade* decision and explodes the popular myth that abortion has always been reviled and denounced in the Bible Belt. In fact, the desire to provide women with safe abortions and the movement to overturn criminal abortion laws had support from a wide swath of the population, including religious leaders. Some of the clergy at campus-based churches or ministries in Louisiana were part of an organized movement, the Clergy Consultation Service on Problem Pregnancy, that assisted women in getting safe, if illegal, abortions.

As those campus ministers exemplify, colleges and universities were integral to the feminist movement in Louisiana. Chapter 6 discusses the role of the state's institutions of higher education in nurturing and sustaining feminist activism and also details how feminists changed the universities and their curricula by creating women's studies programs and woman-focused archives.

Chapter 7 examines the many faces and facets of feminism in Louisiana, focusing primarily on the high visibility of lesbians in the New Orleans movement. Though it caused some dissension in the ranks, for the most part, the Louisiana movement suffered much less division over that issue than has been described elsewhere, and much less than the movement confronted nationally in the 1960s. Over time, the factions largely disappeared, and feminists in Louisiana collaborated far more than they competed with each other.

Second-wave feminism as a whole was predominately white and middle class, but perhaps less so in Louisiana than elsewhere because Louisiana was a poor state with a multiracial heritage going back to the colonial period. Chapter 8 discusses how and why African American and Hispanic women, particularly through labor union affiliation, forged alliances with white, middle-class Louisiana feminists, particularly as they lobbied in Baton Rouge for the ratification of the ERA. The number and significance of black women in Louisiana feminism calls into question the notion that feminism in the United States was everywhere unwelcoming to women of color. The South, in fact, may have presented greater opportunity for working across the color line than did other parts of the country.

Given the stubborn opposition of male-dominated legislatures to gender equality, lawsuits challenging gender discrimination often had more far-reaching effects than legislation resulting from political compromise. Chapter 9 highlights those aspects of the movement that depended heavily on the assistance of female lawyers, showing how lawsuits and the attorneys who filed them impacted women's rights in several southern states. Attorneys assisted the movement politically, too, fashioning legislation that feminist leaders sought and even forming a network to hire a female lobbyist to work full-time on behalf of women's issues in Baton Rouge.

The epilogue shows how women profiled in this volume carried feminism into their lifelong careers or other forms of activism and highlights both the successes and the limitations of the reforms that Louisiana feminists achieved. It suggests areas where women and men born after the years covered in this book might take up where the older generation of feminists left off.

This is not a definitive history. It is only part of the story and undoubtedly I have made errors of commission as well as omission. My objective is to spark a discussion, hopefully a national rather than a regional one, about the role of the South in originating and fueling one of the more important national and international movements for change in modern history.

CHAPTER 1

"Me? A Feminist?"

Proto-feminist Women's Organizations and the

Long Women's Rights Movement, 1950–1967

In the mid-1970s, the Louisiana Federation of Business and Professional Women's Clubs (La. BPW) placed an advertisement with the headline "*Me? A Feminist?*" in newspapers around the state. The purpose of the ad was to "educate men and women to the meaning of feminism, minimize the hostility some people feel toward the women's movement, and create an atmosphere more receptive to ratification of the Equal Rights Amendment." The text tried to normalize a term that, by the mid-1970s, carried terribly negative connotations, one that conjured up images of a woman who was antimale, antifamily, antimarriage, and probably a Communist.

To counter the popular perception, the ad asked:

Do you think men and women have equal talents, abilities, and potentials?
  Then you're a feminist.
  Do you think men and women should receive equal pay for equal work?
  Then you're a feminist.
  Do you think women who spend their lives making a home for their families deserve respect for the job they're doing?
  Then you're a feminist.

The two thousand or so members of the Louisiana BPW—businesswomen, college professors, teachers in public and private schools, among others—hoped that this ad would convince the average voter that feminism was nothing to be feared and that ratification of the ERA fit squarely within the much-celebrated mainstream ideals and traditions of the United States.[1] Although that endeavor did not succeed, and Louisiana never ratified the ERA, the ad copy illustrates that not all feminists belonged to self-identified feminist groups, and that in fact many traditional organizations like the BPW not only supported feminist goals but allied with avowedly feminist groups such as NOW. The BPW was, in fact, one of many women's associations that served as a springboard for the resurgent feminist movement of the 1960s and 1970s.[2]

Since at least the 1990s, historians have been expanding the definition of what constituted feminist work and in the process have made the case for extending the chronology of second-wave feminism back to the 1950s and perhaps even earlier. World War II and the Cold War created a new set of circumstances that increased women's participation in clubs and associations and pushed them toward civic activism. Progressive women in the 1950s, historian Susan Lynn recaps, "promoted a variety of causes: an expanded welfare state, a powerful labor movement, a strong tradition of civil liberties, the principle of racial equality, and a new international order in which nations would share economic resources more equitably and negotiate disputes through the United Nations. They worked along a variety of fronts within peace, civil rights, religious, and women's organizations, and in the case of working-class women, in labor unions."[3] Lynn documents the work of progressive women in all-female as well as in mixed-sex organizations, but in Louisiana, for white women anyway, the most proto-feminist organizations were all-female. Proto-feminist associations viewed their work through a gendered lens that distinguished them from women's organizations whose goal was to serve the larger community, such as the Junior League; The Links, Inc. (the black equivalent of the Junior League); and the black sororities. These single-sex organizations, dedicated not so much to creating opportunities for women as to ameliorating problems in the larger communities of which women were a part, were far less likely to supply personnel to the independent feminist movement than were the BPW, the League of Women Voters (LWV) and its black counterparts (for example, the Louisiana League of Good Government), the Independent Women's Organization (IWO), the Young Women's Christian Association, and the Women's International League for Peace and Freedom. (The National Council of Jewish Women, equally as important, will be covered in the next chapter about women's religiously affiliated associations.) The traditional "women's jobs" created by the first wave, especially social work, also provided a cadre of women activists, black and white, to second-wave feminism in Louisiana, thus linking those two waves.

Civic-minded women of the 1950s and early 1960s who joined groups such as the Parent Teacher Association (PTA) and the LWV adopted the cultural values of the bourgeoisie. Black or white, they typically wore hats and gloves, were well coiffed and well spoken. They seldom challenged dominant gender roles and held values only slightly left of center. Yet they pushed the envelope in various ways that prefigured the overt feminism of the 1960s.

Preexisting liberal women's groups and associations such as the BPW developed networks and progressive ideas on which second-wave feminism built. The women's rights movement was by no means confined to the few small, poorly financed, and often transitory independent organizations such as NOW and the Women's Political Caucus. Instead, the foundations of feminism in Louisiana rested on a broad base of established women's groups that counted among their members many traditional-looking—but forward-thinking—southern women, black and white.

While chapter 2 will examine the religious roots of second-wave feminism in Louisiana, the associations described in this chapter are mostly secular—with the exception of the YWCA—and are typically civic in nature. To personify and concretize the themes of the chapter, and to provide a taste of what feminism in Louisiana looked like in the early to mid-1960s, I highlight the lives of one or two members of each organization. Most were born before World War II, usually in the 1930s, so I refer to them as "older" feminists to distinguish them from the younger women of the 1960s generation who were born ten or more years later. Notably, the older women may have been black, white, or mixed-race. Ironically, racial segregation—state law until the mid-1960s—had the advantage of providing leadership opportunities for women of color in their own all-woman organizations.

Examining why a recognizable mass grassroots movement took shape in the mid-1960s rounds out the last quarter of the chapter. The 1964 Louisiana Commission on the Status of Women played a part in generating a new feminist wave, as did the women's peace movement, which had a long history of progressive activism. Since the early part of the twentieth century, women peace advocates had critiqued militarism, conquest, and colonization of other lands. In the 1960s, they broadened that critique to include violence, conquest, and colonization directed against women in the home, in public spaces, at work, or in society at large. The United States' participation in the Vietnam conflict swelled the ranks of the antiwar movement in the mid-1960s, and female "peaceniks" (as they were often derisively called) were drawn to the new CR sessions that birthed the grassroots women's movement at about the same time.[4]

Voter Education Organizations

For white Louisiana women, the most significant organization that produced a cadre of engaged civic activists, at least in terms of numbers, was the League of Women Voters. Formed in 1920 after women in the United States won the right to vote, it had a slow start in Louisiana, which, like most southern states, did not ratify the woman suffrage amendment (the Nineteenth). Kate and Jean Gordon, two suffragists from New Orleans, white social reformers during the Progressive years, campaigned against the federal Anthony Amendment on racist grounds, arguing that only states had the right to grant suffrage—a stab at the Fifteenth Amendment, which had granted freed slaves the right to vote.[5] However, once the Nineteenth Amendment became part of the federal constitution, all states, even the nonratifying ones, were required to follow it. In the wake of the suffrage victory, the National American Woman Suffrage Association transformed itself into the League of Women Voters with the mission of educating women about exercising their newly won right. Though it did not endorse candidates and remained strictly nonpartisan, the LWV encouraged advocacy on many different issues, not just those involving women. It thus trained many progressive activists, among them Evelyn Daniel Cloutman of Lake Charles, Louisiana.

Born in Kentwood, a small town in rural east Louisiana, in 1918, Evelyn Daniel was of the generation who found the LWV an attractive progressive organization, in part because it was the only one available. Daniel graduated from segregated public schools in Kentwood, and from there went to the whites-only flagship university, Louisiana State University (LSU) in Baton Rouge. (Southern University, the historically black public counterpart, sat on the outskirts of Baton Rouge, a geophysical reminder of the second-class citizenship of African Americans living in a white-ruled society.) After acquiring a BS degree and teacher certification, Evelyn moved in 1938 to Lake Charles, an industrial city of seventy thousand people about thirty miles from the Texas border, where her father managed a lumber company. Within a few months, she married fellow teacher Edward B. Cloutman Jr. Because the Calcasieu Parish School Board's policy forbade the employment of married women, her contract was not renewed, although her husband, needless to say, did not suffer the same fate.

The practice of firing either married or pregnant women was customary in the United States at the time. The shortage of labor during World War II caused many school boards to abandon the policy, but even after the war, it continued in some Louisiana parishes, which explains why many female teachers remained single their entire lives, often living together so that they could share expenses. Clearly, for some women, giving up families of their own to live alone or with another woman was preferable to watching one's investment in higher education evaporate upon marriage.[6] For Evelyn Cloutman, however, being fired for no reason other than that she was female was a "click" moment—an epiphany when she realized that women suffered from socially imposed disabilities that men did not.

Evelyn Cloutman was of the demographic cohort—Cold War–era baby-boom parents—described by Betty Friedan in *The Feminine Mystique* (1963). Friedan's book arose out of a survey she conducted of her Smith College classmates documenting the malaise felt by many contemporary housewives who otherwise lived a supposedly ideal life in middle-class America. Some women who had retired to a life of conventional domesticity, especially if they had more than a high school education, found themselves feeling unfulfilled, depressed, and restless in their "comfortable concentration camp" of a three-bedroom home in the suburbs. For them, the book struck a chord.[7] But though she lived in a ranch-style house in a nice subdivision of Lake Charles, Evelyn Cloutman was not one of the discontented housewives Friedan described, and Friedan's book was unimportant to her dawning feminist awareness. To the contrary, Cloutman's husband supported her career ambitions. Evelyn bore four sons within five years, yet went back to school to get another degree, this time in social work, while her children were young. Social work was one of very few white-collar careers open to college-educated women at the time; teaching, nursing, library administration, and clerical work were others. The demand for social workers was so great that Cloutman could be reasonably certain she would not be fired because she was the wrong gender, or because she was married.

Working for the Department of Child Welfare as a caseworker, Cloutman saw many women and children, both white and black and nearly all poor, trapped in homes with abusive fathers and/or husbands, with little recourse. The injustice she witnessed in the courts as well as in those homes produced more "click" moments that moved her to action. Feeling as though her work was palliative, she determined to bring about more fundamental changes in the system—institutional, legal, and cultural changes. Possessed of greater opportunities and a broader vision of equality than women of the earlier first-wave suffrage movement, Cloutman joined the local chapter of the LWV. The league was the closest thing to a feminist organization in town and had a reputation for successful lobbying. From her research and experience in the league, Cloutman learned how the entire system "was tilted against women." The league meetings were held at her church, University United Methodist, and many members of the church joined her in membership. Cloutman's faith made her believe that eliminating the oppression of women "was just the right thing to do. God did not favor men over women, but the state of Louisiana did." In the early 1970s, she became president of the local LWV chapter. The league gave her skills and the network that allowed her to put her convictions to work: she lobbied the local legislative delegation in support of ratification of the ERA and committed herself to a variety of social justice and civic-improvement causes.

She cofounded the Calcasieu Parish Battered Women's Shelter (later called Oasis: A Safe Haven for Survivors of Domestic and Sexual Violence), the second domestic violence shelter in the state, in 1979. The board she assembled provided money, permits, housing, land, and leadership for the new shelter, and included men and women of different faiths, Catholic, Protestant, and Jewish.[8] This collaboration among different groups, many of which were not normally associated with feminism, is typical of how feminist goals were achieved in Louisiana.

The LWV, a powerful and important venue for early feminist activism, has never quite recovered from the stigma conferred upon it by Betty Friedan, who scoffed at its afternoon teas (connoting women who did not work and therefore represented a bygone era). For young student activists in the 1960s, the league conjured up unappealing images of dowdy straight women married to businessmen who played by conventional rules. Yet, despite its shortcomings, this group served as an important bridge and training ground for progressive public activists between the first wave of suffrage and the reinvigorated feminist movement of the 1960s and 1970s. Many league members would not have referred to themselves as feminist (although Cloutman did), for the word fell into disuse after World War I, but they nonetheless advocated some of the same issues that younger women of the second wave later took up.[9]

The league was especially important for women's political activism in the South, where few alternate independent women's organizations existed.[10] League actions taught women how to influence politicians at every level of government (local, state, and national) through effective testimonials and lobbying, either in person, in the media, or by mail. The league generally supported progressive policies regardless of whether they were "women's" issues. For example, though it followed Louisiana law and remained segregated until the mid-1960s, the all-white LWV members in New Orleans worked with other organizations—primarily a new one called Save Our Schools—to oppose continued segregation and the city's attempts to close public schools.[11] League members were disproportionately represented at the International Women's Year conferences held in Baton Rouge and Houston in 1977, and some league members went on to enter politics themselves. Willie Mount of Lake Charles, for example, president of the local LWV chapter, became the first woman mayor of her city in the 1990s and the first woman state senator from southwest Louisiana.[12] (It is startling how many of this first generation of female political activists had first names that either sounded male or were gender neutral, for example, Willie Mount, Clay Latimer, George Ethel Warren, Rupert Richardson, Clarence Marie Collier, Shirley Marvin, Ollie Osborne, Pat Evans, and Robbie Madden.)

Evelyn Cloutman is typical of native-born Louisiana feminists of her generation, many of whom, like her, were white, well-educated career women, practicing members of mainstream religions, and mothers. They often held service-oriented jobs traditionally defined as "women's work." A significant percentage, also like Cloutman, worked in the welfare department as social workers. Due both to their religious convictions and to their exposure to people less advantaged than they, these white women recognized the burdens of poverty and dark skin in southern society. Thus they took tentative steps toward sisterhood across the chasm of race, challenging customs, laws, and perceptions of machismo that pitted black and white women against each other throughout this state.

Though state laws made it illegal for blacks and whites to meet as equals (for example, in each other's living rooms), or to eat together (making restaurant meetings impossible), the LWV in Lake Charles admitted its first black member, Bernardine Brothers Proctor, in 1964, testing local practices, laws, and customs. Proctor's paternal grandmother was a penniless free black refugee from Saint-Domingue (Haiti) who raised five children on her own after her husband died. One of those children, Adam Brothers, Bernardine's father, had only a first-grade education. Bernardine's mother, Lenora Alex, from the small town of Opelousas in southwest Louisiana, had a sixth-grade education, not unusual in early twentieth-century Louisiana, when high schools for blacks were frequently unavailable in small towns. (Bernardine's father joked that he had "married up.") Both parents worked hard, her mother as a seamstress and her father as a carpenter, and they taught their five children to do the same. Trading their skills for a piano and lessons for the children, Bernardine's parents encouraged her musical and artistic talents. She began playing the organ for her church, Sacred Heart Catholic Church in Lake Charles, at the age of fourteen. She and her four siblings all became highly successful and brokered a number of "firsts" for African Americans in southwest Louisiana. Bernardine graduated from Xavier University in New Orleans, the only Roman Catholic university for African Americans in the country, and taught school before working for the U.S. Navy as a clerk during World War II in Washington, D.C. While there, she watched as less-qualified whites were promoted around her. With the encouragement of the staff at the nearby federal office of the Fair Employment Practices Commission, she stood up to her superiors and got promoted to the job she sought. She moved back to Lake Charles in 1951, continued working, and eventually earned an art degree from McNeese State University. Having no children of her own, she devoted her life to civic activities. She and Evelyn Cloutman became acquainted through the LWV and developed great respect for each other.[13] The league brought them together and facilitated a cross-racial alliance that benefited all women in the community, regardless of their ethnic background. Proctor and Cloutman became friends and compatriots in a number of progressive causes, including the founding of the Calcasieu Women's Shelter.

The New Orleans chapter of the LWV (hereinafter LWVNO) had begun trying to racially integrate in the 1950s, but the state repeatedly threw barriers in its way.[14] Frustrated with the slow pace of progress and eager to begin mobilizing the growing black electorate, women of color in New Orleans formed organizations parallel to the LWV. In the 1960s, as Louisiana blacks challenged legal disfranchisement in the courts, New Orleans black women formed the Metropolitan Women's Voters' League to assist voter registration drives in black neighborhoods.[15] This organization served much the same function for women in black communities as the LWV did among whites. So, too, did the Louisiana League of Good Government (LLOGG), founded in 1963 by a group of African American teachers led by Sybil Haydel Morial.

Born in 1932, Sybil Morial is representative of a generation of black women leaders born before World War II who utilized a strategy of racial uplift dubbed by historians "the politics of respectability." This term, coined by Evelyn Brooks Higginbotham to describe the work of the Women's Convention of the Black Baptist Church during the Progressive Era, has been used repeatedly by historians of African American women to describe both a racial and a class dynamic. Reviewer Paisley Jane Harris summarized it this way: "The prevailing interpretation suggests that the politics of respectability undermined the rigidly scientific nature of racial categories, but generally tended to reinforce status distinctions within the African American community. These distinctions were about class, but they were defined primarily in behavioral, not economic, terms. By linking worthiness for respect to sexual propriety, behavioral decorum, and neatness, respectability served a gatekeeping function, establishing a behavioral 'entrance fee,' to the right to respect and the right to full citizenship." While respectability was a strategy by which "African Americans claimed equal status and citizenship during the Progressive Era, it continued to be an influential basis for claiming rights through the civil rights era and beyond."[16] Most black women leaders in Louisiana fit this model. This is certainly true of Sybil Haydel Morial, whose primary commitment was to the African American community and who, like Mary McLeod Bethune before her, founded or assisted organizations that empowered African American women in particular. Sybil and her husband, attorney Ernest "Dutch" Morial, first became famous in New Orleans for their civil rights activism decades before his election as the city's first black mayor in 1973. In the 1970s, several of the all-women organizations of which she was a member chose to support feminist causes as well.

Sybil and "Dutch" (as he was familiarly known) were both born in New Orleans's Seventh Ward, a huge, cone-shaped, ethnically diverse, socioeconomically mixed neighborhood that was home to many Roman Catholic Creoles of color.[17] Though her husband's family was poor, Sybil, like most black women leaders in Louisiana, came from a family of well-educated professionals. Her father, Clarence Haydel, went to Straight (later Dillard) University in New Orleans, a private HBCU, and from there to Howard University in Washington, D.C., for a medical degree. A surgeon, Sybil's father cofounded, with other black doctors, Flint-Goodrich Hospital in 1933 to serve African Americans in New Orleans. Sybil's mother, Eudora Arnaud Haydel, was a teacher, the most common profession for educated women of color. Like other Louisiana teachers, Eudora Haydel had been forced to quit teaching school when she married. Still, she encouraged her two daughters and one son to get advanced degrees and pursue careers. These values marked the Creole middle class in Louisiana: hard work and educational achievements along with impeccable manners and deportment. Sybil thus had advantages over many other African Americans in Louisiana. The Haydels' comfortable home in the Seventh Ward hosted social and educational events in the community and provided lodging for famed black artists and visiting lecturers, who, because of discriminatory laws, could not otherwise find decent lodging in New Orleans. Thus, Sybil had exposure to a variety of ideas in her home, at the two black universities (Xavier and Dillard) where the family frequently attended concerts and lectures, and when she traveled with her parents to conferences.

After attending Catholic elementary schools in New Orleans, Sybil Haydel graduated from Xavier Prep (a black Catholic high school) at fifteen, earned a degree from Boston University College of Education in 1952, and for several years was the only black schoolteacher in Newton, Massachusetts, public schools. She described this as an exceptionally good experience and said that she might never have come back to Louisiana except that she fell in love.

Sybil and Dutch Morial met during one of her summer vacations in New Orleans at an event she helped to organize: the "Great Books" club, a reading and discussion group she held for blacks because they were not allowed to enter the public library. She recalled, "This was right after the *Brown* decision had come down. It was in June 1954; we conversed about that and we were very excited about it. We fell in love talking about the possibilities that lay before us." They married in 1955. Dutch Morial was an attorney in practice with A. P. Tureaud, the leading civil rights attorney in Louisiana and another Creole of color who lived in the Seventh Ward. Tureaud was the principle attorney for the NAACP, and Morial assisted him in his antidiscrimination lawsuits. The Tureauds and the Morials were "in the company of legal giants like Thurgood Marshall [later appointed the first African American justice of the U.S. Supreme Court]. I was home with two babies," Sybil said. "I wanted to be involved, too! I joined the Urban League [women's] guild so I could be active in change, too." When she could not be admitted to the LWV because of Jim Crow laws, Sybil, with seven other teachers, founded the Louisiana League of Good Government (LLOGG).[18] She explained, "We set up voter education workshops in several black neighborhoods to help them pass citizenship tests so they could vote, including figuring out how to put down their age in years, months and days [as required by state law at the time—an attempt to thwart black voting rights]!" The LLOGG integrated after the Civil Rights Act of 1964 outlawed racial segregation, but it always remained primarily black. By remaining separate from the LWV, it offered black women the opportunity for leadership. Borrowing a technique of the league's, it sponsored candidates' forums. After the Voting Rights Act of 1965, its forums included both black and white candidates for office. The LLOGG sponsored a membership luncheon every year with a nationally prominent black woman speaker, thus exposing local audiences to outside ideas and making them feel that their efforts in New Orleans were worth continuing.[19]

Meanwhile, Sybil Morial went back to work in New Orleans's public schools. She became involved in civil rights when in 1956 the State of Louisiana, in an effort to break the back of the NAACP, prohibited any teacher from advocating integration of the schools or being a member of any organization that advocated integration (as the NAACP had been doing for years). Teachers made up the bulk of the NAACP's membership. This threat to their livelihood meant that the NAACP would likely fold. Sybil filed a successful lawsuit challenging the state, with Dutch Morial, then president of the New Orleans NAACP chapter, serving as lead attorney.[20] At a time when the leaders of civil rights initiatives were sometimes murdered (as was Medgar Evers and many others in Mississippi) or their houses bombed (as was Martin Luther King's home in Birmingham), putting one's name on a lawsuit required a great deal of courage. Not only did she risk losing her job, but the Morials also received menacing phone calls in the middle of the night and even death threats. Fortunately, no harm came their way.

Like many successful, well-educated women of color, Sybil Haydel Morial joined and often served as a board member of many organizations. In addition to LLOGG, she spent a great deal of her time assisting the United Fund (the black equivalent of the United Way) and Alpha Kappa Alpha, a service-oriented sorority. When LWVNO finally desegregated in 1963, Morial happily became one of the first women of color to join, primarily because she wanted to work on the education committee to improve public schools. She also joined her mother, Eudora Haydel, in The Links, Inc., the African American equivalent of the Junior

League, where she served as president for four years.[21] The Links, like the Junior League, was exclusionary, which speaks to how the "politics of respectability" involved a classist element, as well.

Yet, like many women of color, Sybil combined her community service work with full-time employment.[22] Following a short hiatus when her children were little, she went back to work, this time at Xavier University of Louisiana, where she remained for twenty-eight years. Sybil Morial's high-profile civic activity created a constituency among people of color that helped her husband's political career. In 1978, Ernest Morial became the first black mayor of New Orleans.[23] As New Orleans's first lady, Sybil considered herself and her husband "a team," noting, "We've always been supportive of each other."[24] Well-educated, heterosexual, married, and the mother of several baby-boom children, Sybil Morial exhibited characteristics typical of the white-gloved feminists of this older generation in Louisiana.

Several of the organizations that Sybil Morial joined or led went on record in support of the ERA and other feminist-initiated legislation, among them the LWV. Though the league was strictly nonpartisan, its positions, especially after 1965, aligned with those of the independent women's movement. In fact, conservative groups that targeted other progressive organizations and civil rights groups trotted out the same criticism of the LWV, saying that it was an "international conspiracy" that sought to subvert American ideals. Human Events, a conservative organization founded in 1944, called its tactics "reprehensible" and said that the national LWV board "brainwashed" its membership on national and international issues. The league's support of the United Nations particularly invoked the ire of the right wing, which hated that "the League's National Board concluded arbitrarily that 'the interests of the United States are best served by a foreign policy based on the principle of international cooperation.'" The LWV, in Human Events' view, was not sufficiently anti-Communist. That it did not encourage its members to study Communism and published no material on the subject made it instantly suspect. Also suspicious was that it worked closely with organized labor, including the AFL-CIO's Committee on Political Education and "other Democratic-biased union adjuncts." The LWV, this group concluded, was "markedly left-of-center."[25] Given that the national, state, and local LWV chapters typically worked toward passage of legislation sought by self-professed feminist organizations, this statement rings entirely true.

The 1960s and 1970s were the heyday years for the LWV. Its membership dropped off dramatically as more women entered the workforce and no longer had time to attend luncheons or devote to the many responsibilities that league membership required. Its nonpartisan stance hampered it in the 1980s, when members abandoned it in favor of political organizations affiliated with the major parties or those committed to supporting certain candidates. But during the years while conditions were favorable to its mission and organizational structure, the league was an invaluable training ground for feminist political activists.[26]

Unlike the LWV, which did not endorse candidates, the Independent Women's Organization existed for the express purpose of exposing and defeating corrupt politicians, particularly those associated with former governor Huey P. Long and his machine. Elite white women in New Orleans, indignant at the corruption revealed by federal indictments of Long and his crowd, began speaking out in the 1930s against the cigar-smoking, heavy-drinking, back-room-deal-making men who ran Louisiana, and they formally organized the IWO in 1946. Having seen firsthand the way men ran the state (very badly, in their view), they decided that women could do a better job. They became involved in a variety of good-government issues, supported public-school reform, and integrated their group in the 1960s. The IWO's foray into the dirty, male-dominated world of electoral politics convinced members that women needed more power. Though they would not have publicly self-identified as feminist, many joined organizations that lobbied for the ERA and other pro–women's rights causes. The IWO's Margaret Polk "Pokey" McIlhenny (married to Paul McIlhenny of Tabasco hot sauce fame), for example, formed cross-class alliances in New Orleans to support women's rights efforts. She cofounded Women in Politics, an organization designed to get more women elected in Louisiana, and furnished considerable resources to ERA United.[27] When the ERA debuted in the Louisiana legislature in May 1972, the IWO was one of the first organizations to endorse it.[28] Women's participation in all-woman organizations devoted to civic improvement and to cleaning up corruption, then, often led them straight to support for feminism.

The YWCA

Another progenitor of second-wave feminism was the Young Women's Christian Association (the YWCA, or YW for short). An entirely female-led organization founded in the mid-nineteenth century, the YW had always been dedicated to empowering women, especially working women. The female leaders of the YW in the early twentieth century formed industrial clubs as well as associations on college campuses for girls, emphasizing, in addition to Bible study, direct action on social and economic issues. For decades, "the YWCA inspired a strong ethical concern in several generations of young women" and prepared young women—black and white—to become leaders for social justice issues. Thus, for more than half a century before the second wave emerged and the YWCA became a critical site of support for that movement, girls and women at the Y developed a culture of resistance to mores that they judged to be inharmonious with the Y's Christian ethics. Most importantly in the South, the YWCA's push toward interracialism, well ahead of its time, was a catalyst for feminism in the 1960s.[29]

Interracial efforts emerged from black women at the segregated "branch" YWCAs. The first black YWs opened in the North in the 1890s. After the turn of the century, the national board authorized segregated Ys in the South but—to the irritation of the African American women involved—put them under the supervision of white women. Lugenia Burns Hope of Atlanta (whose husband, John Hope, became president of Atlanta University) pushed the national YWCA to change that policy, saying that she represented hundreds of thousands of black women in the South in doing so. Through her efforts, black YWCA leaders entered into dialogue with white women and began educating "white colleagues about racism" and guiding the organization "toward a greater commitment to racial equality," as historian Bettye Collier-Thomas points out in her book on religion and black women's progressive reform efforts. "At each crucial juncture in the YWCA's progress toward racial integration, black women took the lead, pressing for an interracial conference in 1915, demanding that the Southern Student YWCA integrate at the leadership level in the early 1920s, pushing for racial integration in community YWCAs during the years of World War II, and providing important leadership in the struggle to implement the Interracial Charter after the war."[30] The Interracial Charter, a thirty-five-point program that included racial integration on the boards and staff and in all YWCA activities, "was by far the most far-reaching action taken by any organization in the United States," Collier-Thomas asserts. Historians, as well as the YMCA itself, generally concur that the YWCA was ahead of its male counterpart, the YMCA, in advancing race relations. Historian Susan Lynn considers the dialogues between white and black women that were part of the process of implementing the Interracial Charter as a precursor to the women's rights movement's "personal is political" slogan. [31]

Black women's insistence on running their own YWCA branches paid off in that it allowed them to hone management and oratorical skills. Among those for whom the YWCA was a catalyst for their leadership in liberation movements are Ella Baker, Pauli Murray, and Dorothy Height, whose life's work influenced both black and white organizers of the second wave. The following brief sketches of their lives, while woefully inadequate to convey the richness of their work, introduce them in the context of their religious and social justice training at the Harlem YWCA, that institution of black female agency, in the 1920s. All three women were born in the South but educated in the North. Ella Baker, born in North Carolina, acquired her college degree and many years of organizing experience in the North. A founder and coach of SNCC, in the 1960s Baker "traveled around the south conducting workshops for the Y" that had as their goal fostering greater understanding between the races.[32] Pauli Murray, originally from North Carolina, graduated from Howard University and then earned a law degree from the University of California, Berkeley. Long before President Kennedy appointed her as a member of the President's Commission on the Status of Women (PCSW, discussed later), she had identified a system of discrimination against women that she labeled "Jane Crow." One of the founding members of the Congress of Racial Equality (during World War II) and the National Organization for Women (in 1966), Murray went on to a long and illustrious career as a champion of racial and gender justice. She was a driving force behind the passage of the Equal Pay Act in 1963 and was largely responsible for ensuring that Title VII of the Civil Rights Act of 1964 retained a provision prohibiting discrimination on the basis of sex.[33]

Dorothy Height, like Pauli Murray, made lasting contributions to both the black freedom movement and to second-wave feminism. Born in Richmond, Virginia, in 1912, Height attended schools in the North and, thanks to a scholarship, earned two degrees from New York University. After graduation, she joined the staff of the Harlem YWCA in 1937, where she met Mary McLeod Bethune, the founder of the National Council of Negro Women (NCNW). Height had become a leader of the United Christian Youth Movement of North America in 1933, and in 1939, she became executive director of the Phyllis Wheatley YWCA in Washington, D.C. As an executive member of the national YWCA's staff, she supervised the implementation of the Interracial Charter, adopted at a national convention in 1946, and founded the Y's Center for Racial Justice. In 1958, after years of working as a volunteer, she became president of the NCNW, a position she held until 1998. Her high profile as a leader among black women earned her an appointment to President Kennedy's Commission on the Status of Women in 1961. In the mid-1960s, she and Polly Cowan, a white NCNW board member, organized "Wednesdays in Mississippi" (WIM), a program that flew interracial interfaith teams of middle-aged, middle- and upper-class northern women into Mississippi on Wednesdays to meet with black and white women. Sponsored by the NCNW and with participation by the YWCA and several other religious women's organizations, the members of the WIM teams presented a "respectable appearance and quiet approach [that] enabled them to open lines of communication between black and white Mississippi women and build bridges of understanding across region, race, and religion." The first person Height and Cowan contacted in Jackson, Mississippi, to help them find local women receptive to meeting with them was Barbara Ann Barnes, the director of the white YWCA. Height also served on the National Council of Churches governing board and was a cofounder of the National Women's Political Caucus, along with Betty Friedan, Gloria Steinem, and Shirley Chisholm.[34] The influence of Height, Murray, and Baker on antiracism and feminism in Louisiana was indirect, but they are good examples of how the YW as an institution trained women for social justice work.

The profiles of these three women illustrate the frequent crossover of membership in organizations dedicated to advancing equality. A well-educated black woman was likely to serve on multiple boards at one time and thus to influence multiple groups of people. At the local level as well as the national, organizational boundaries were permeable; groups and organizations overlapped and cross-fertilized one another. A good example is George Ethel Warren (George was a family name that her parents had committed to bestowing on their next child regardless of its sex), a community activist in New Orleans's predominately African American Lower Ninth Ward, where she and her family lived for forty years. A member of the LWV, she was also a board member of the New Orleans YWCA, the NAACP, and president and founder of the Citizen Voter Education Association, a nonpartisan organization dedicated to increasing voter participation but also to holding politicians accountable "to the people." Warren considered herself a feminist (though she did not typically use that term) and joined a local NOW chapter. She worked with Total Community Action, the New Orleans Metropolitan Household Technicians, and the PTA; she conducted prison ministries and chaired the workshop on Women in Crisis at the International Women's Year conference in Baton Rouge in 1977. Though she was a member of and served on the board of literally dozens of community organizations, the NACW and the NCNW were not among them, even though chapters existed in both Baton Rouge and New Orleans.[35] Few if any of the black women who joined the ranks of the feminist movement in Louisiana were members of either group, indicating that those associations were less important in producing a feminist consciousness than was the YWCA.

One black woman whose interracial work at the YW led to her support for the feminist movement is New Orleans native Louadrian Dejoie Reed. Born and baptized a Catholic with a French Creole surname in 1938, Louadrian Dejoie was active in the Claiborne Street YW from the time she was a little girl in the "pigtail" group.[36] This YW functioned as a community center for African Americans in the neighborhood and hosted a variety of happenings, she remembered, including wedding receptions and other kinds of parties or events, partly because it was a large, safe, well-maintained, and often-used space. While in college at Dillard University in New Orleans, she served on the national board of the young adult program of the YWCA and traveled to Washington, D.C., for national meetings. Southern regional meetings, held in Atlanta on the campus

of Spelman College, were segregated according to state law, but national meetings were integrated. Thus, in Washington, she met people from all over the
country, and as a result developed a broad, national vision for the possibility of
change. She also learned how to organize, as her group developed policies and
procedures to encourage the participation of more young people in the organization. Reed credits the YWCA's influence for her later years of feminist activism. She became one of the first African American women in several feminist
organizations in New Orleans, including the National Women's Political Caucus
and the IWO.[37]

Though the Interracial Charter adopted at the national level guided local
YWCAs, Louisiana's Jim Crow laws made integrated meetings difficult. The
YWCA in New Orleans had 871 black members with "full electoral status," but in
order to comply with the state's segregation laws, those women were not permitted to attend any meeting that included food nor were they allowed to use
the white YWCAs recreational facilities. Nonetheless, Shannon Frystak, a historian of the New Orleans YWCA's desegregation process, has concluded that
"the YWCA's commitment to interracial membership contributed to its having
a more progressive-minded membership than did organizations like the LWV."
Indeed, it was so progressive that an ultra-right-wing group, the Constitutional
Education League, in 1948 accused the national YW of being a Communist front
organization.[38]

Not every YWCA in Louisiana was as progressive as the one in New Orleans,
however. In the state capital, Baton Rouge, a far more conservative city than
New Orleans, the YWCA refused to integrate even after the passage of the Civil
Rights Act of 1964. There, the white YW held a meeting to which the women
from the branch Y (the Maggie Nance Ringgold Unit) were invited but were not
allowed to vote. The women in charge decided to disaffiliate from the YWCA
and change their organization's name to the YWCO. The black women and the
white women who disagreed with the decision got together and created a new,
integrated YWCA. Nina Pugh, one of the white women, had a cross burned on
her lawn. Earline Williams, who was black, became president of the new YWCA.
She and Clarence Marie Collier (another African American woman about
whom we will hear more later on) initiated a lawsuit against the YWCO. That
lawsuit did not succeed, and the YWCO continued for many years.[39] That Collier
and Williams were willing to sue, however, indicates the fortitude and courage
that their membership in the Y had conferred on them.

To try to overcome their historic differences, white women in the reborn
YWCA developed Living Room Dialogues, whereby white and black women
came together in one another's homes to discuss issues of race. The reorganized YWCA strove for racial balance, and it incorporated the 1960s initiative into
a long-term program focusing on racial justice called the Dialogue on Race.[40]

If black women benefited from YWCA social justice activism, so too did many white women. Sandra "Casey" Cason Hayden and Mary King, two southern white women who worked with Ella Baker in the civil rights movement and who would play significant roles in SNCC, were both politicized through the YW. Casey Hayden recalled that at YW regional meetings (which were, recall, racially integrated), she "first came into contact with the personal feelings of young black people about segregation." Mary King said that the National Student YW for which she worked in Atlanta "was more enlightened and progressive than its male counterpart." The student organization had hundreds of thousands of adherents nationally and proved critical to the dawning social consciousness of many young women because, as Mary King explains, "the Student Y was frequently the only place on a campus where social-change issues were discussed."[41] As we shall see, YWCAs provided management, institutional support, and space for feminist initiatives in Louisiana, as well.

The YWCAs around the nation, then, were important both to the black freedom movement and to the renewal of the 1960s feminist movement. Many young women, white and black, learned to critique hierarchical social structures as a result of their work with the YWs and became committed to eliminating discrimination both within their own ranks and in the rest of society. This led the director of Atlanta's Y to proclaim in 1973 that "the YWCA was working for women's lib long before it was called that." Historian Melissa Estes Blair argues, too, that the YWCA in Durham, North Carolina, laid the foundations for 1970s feminist activism there. Perhaps because there were so few other independent progressive institutions led by women in the South, the YWCA became a vehicle for gender as well as racial justice. Out of Christian progressivism came momentum for multiple fundamental changes.[42]

Because its pre–Civil Rights Act interracial activities gave the YWCA a reputation as one of the more enlightened institutions in the South (or "communistic," in the eyes of its critics), it was logical that when left-leaning women's liberationists looked for a site for the first International Women's Day celebration to be held in Louisiana in 1970, they received permission to hold it on the grounds of the newly integrated YWCA on St. Bernard Avenue in New Orleans.[43] International Women's Day originated with the socialist left in the early part of the twentieth century but was discontinued in the United States in the face of successive Red Scares (though it continued to be celebrated in socialist nations). In 1969, Berkeley Women's Liberation revived the tradition, and Berkeley feminist Laura X spread the word around the country.[44] The following year, New Orleans was among thirty cities in the United States celebrating International Women's Day. The holiday in the United States commemorated a 1918 strike of New York City garment workers demanding better working conditions and equal rights. Linking themselves to the previous wave and to working-class feminism—but not to the Communist Party—black and white women in New Orleans joined forces to launch a renewed effort on behalf of women's rights. The purpose of the meeting was to explore ways for women to win full equality and liberation as individuals. The *Louisiana Weekly* (an African American–owned and operated newspaper) ran several stories on the event, noting that it included workshops on the family, women's history, women on welfare, working women, and women in the media (led by Darlene Fife and Rae Mathews). Even though many of the organizers had no children themselves, the advance publicity noted that day care would be provided. This was the first of many International Women's Day events in New Orleans, which women of diverse social and ethnic backgrounds attended.[45]

As had happened at the YWCA, white women learned a great deal from African American leaders and took those lessons with them into new movements for social justice. Bernice Johnson Reagon has called civil rights the "borning" movement because it produced so many others.[46] Susan Lynn argues that "the issue of racial equality gradually became a litmus test for progressive activists, a core issue for those concerned with social justice."[47] Civil rights activity emanating from black communities forced progressively minded white women to come together to defend public schools. In 1960, white women in New Orleans formed Save Our Schools (SOS) at the instigation of Rosa Freeman Keller (1911–97) and Gladys Cahn. Both women were members of the Urban League (an integrated organization), the LWV, and the YWCA. (Cahn was also a member of the National Council of Jewish Women, discussed further in the next chapter.) Rosa Keller, whose work for integration of public schools and libraries has been well documented, was aunt and mentor to another progressive activist, Mary Elizabeth Wisdom, always known as Betty.[48]

Rosa Keller and her niece Betty Wisdom were elite white women who modeled courageous behavior on behalf of the less advantaged. The women benefited from their connection to the Freeman family fortune, which came from interests in two southern companies, Delta Airlines and Coca-Cola. Betty was the daughter of William B. and Mary Freeman Wisdom, and the niece of the famous (or, to segregationists, infamous) federal judge John Minor Wisdom, whose rulings helped to end segregation in New Orleans. Betty Wisdom had one brief early marriage and no children. With no family to tend to and a family fortune to support her, she dedicated her time to assisting many left-leaning organizations, including the IWO, the ACLU, the New Orleans LWV (of which she was president for two terms), the Women's Intergroup Council of Greater New Orleans, Louisiana's Civil Rights Commission, New Orleans Human Relations Committee (a group appointed by the mayor to help ease racial tensions), VISTA (a War on Poverty organization), Alliance for Affordable Energy (a consumer group that advocated for lower energy costs to help the poor), and the Urban League. She was most famous locally for single-handedly saving Audubon Zoo from its status as an "animal ghetto" (as the newspaper called it) in the 1970s. Animal welfare dovetailed with her belief that women in her position were responsible for helping the powerless, be they poor working-class people or defenseless animals left in deplorable conditions in a run-down zoo. Her philosophy tended toward the maternalism of an earlier time, but both she and her aunt Rosa took what were for their time rather audacious stands on controversial social justice issues and thus provided a form of activist southern womanhood that younger generations of New Orleans women could follow.[49]

Some organizations that trained the next generation of women leaders were decades old, while others such as Save Our Schools were ad hoc, upstart, and evanescent. Some appeared so unthreatening that the casual observer would never have considered that they were training leaders who would eventually challenge patriarchy itself. Such is the case of the PTA, which was particularly important in launching the political careers of women of color. Through the PTA, black women protested the poor conditions of public schools and supported integration efforts in the early 1960s. In the PTA, they got to know people within their districts. If they had political skills and leadership instincts, becoming president of the PTA earned them reputations as people who could leverage the power structure. Dorothy Mae Taylor, the first black woman in the Louisiana legislature, got her start fighting the blatantly discriminatory practices of the New Orleans School Board and was elected PTA president of two schools simultaneously. A leadership role in the PTA provided experience, name recognition, and networks that launched some women into activism.[50]

Social Workers

Women like Dorothy Mae Taylor, Sybil Morial, and Evelyn Cloutman, who married and raised houses full of baby boomers while also maintaining professional careers and engaging in meaningful civic volunteerism, represent one type of mid-twentieth-century proto-feminist. Another was the professional woman who never married. The generation of women born in the decades after the Civil War and Reconstruction was the least likely to marry, because combining a career and motherhood, among white women at least, was frowned upon. (Another probable reason was the shortage of marriageable men due to Civil War casualties.)[51] Furthermore, before modern technology and labor-saving devices in the home became common, it was considered impossible for a (white) woman to be a successful wife, mother, and full-time worker. Even as late as 1939, the *Ladies Home Journal* published a story cautioning women against believing they could "enter engrossing and demanding occupations . . . and at the same time have happy and productive marriages." That was "an illusion." "One woman in a thousand can do it. And she is a genius."[52]

The woman who cofounded the Tulane School of Social Work, Elizabeth Wisner (1896–1976), is representative of that cohort of professional women born at the end of the nineteenth century who were likely to remain single. Elizabeth, the daughter of philanthropist Edward Wisner (for whom Wisner Boulevard in New Orleans is named), was born in 1896 and graduated from Newcomb College, a coordinate women's college within Tulane University, in 1914. She received her master's in social work from Simmons College in Boston and her doctorate in social service administration from the University of Chicago (1929), where she was influenced by Jane Addams, Edith Abbot, and Sophonisba Breckenridge, three women famous for their pioneering work in social reform. The women had become acquainted through their work at Addams's Hull House in Chicago, and together they developed and professionalized the new field of social work.[53] Furthermore, all of them, including Elizabeth Wisner, at one time or another advised Harry Hopkins, an aid to Franklin Roosevelt. Believing that the state had a responsibility to alleviate social welfare problems, they brought to him their considerable intellectual talent and personal experiences as he helped to craft the New Deal's social programs.[54]

None of those four women married. Rather than brave living alone (which was socially unacceptable and probably dangerous), they lived either in a house with many others (as Jane Addams did at Hull House) or in domestic partnership with another woman. The custom of educated single women living in pairs became common enough in the late nineteenth and early twentieth centuries to acquire a name: a "Boston marriage."[55] Regardless of whether these relationships included a sexual element, they presented an alternative to traditional heterosexual marriage, one that the public generally accepted. Though people may have gossiped about "odd girls," for the most part women living in partnership with each other were not stigmatized.[56]

Elizabeth Wisner had such an arrangement with her life companion, Florence Sytz. When Wisner returned to New Orleans from Chicago and became a member of the faculty of Tulane's newly founded School of Social Work, she recruited her companion, Sytz, to join her on the faculty. She and Florence bought a home together, where they lived their entire lives. Staying together through sickness and health, they also raised a relative's child, Mary White.[57] In all respects, the three females comprised a family. Wisner provided an example of a woman-identified woman who controlled her own career and rose through the ranks of male-dominated administration at a prestigious southern university. By all accounts, she was extraordinarily beautiful. Coming from a wealthy family and endowed with a decent inheritance, she could have had her pick of men, but instead she chose to live with another woman for whom she clearly had a great deal of respect and affection.[58]

Just as Jane Addams's Hull House developed an affiliation with the University of Chicago, the Tulane School of Social Work grew out of its relationship with Kingsley House, a settlement established in the Irish Channel of New Orleans in 1896 by Trinity Episcopal Church. Kingsley House, the first settlement house in the South, offered a variety of children's programs that provided the model for later kindergarten and after-school programs, as well as for NORD, the New Orleans Recreation Department. Though Kingsley House had been established by the pastor of Trinity Episcopal Church, its director was Eleanor McMain, the "Jane Addams of the South," who developed it into the largest and most influential settlement house below the Mason-Dixon Line. Since most people in the community surrounding Kingsley House were immigrant Irish Catholics, McMain transformed it into a nonsectarian facility so that it could serve everyone regardless of the person's religion.[59] Born in 1868 in East Baton Rouge Parish, McMain moved to New Orleans in the late 1890s to teach in the first kindergarten established in the state of Louisiana—at Kingsley House. In 1901, the never-married McMain became head resident, a post she held for the next thirty-three years. Like other settlement-house workers, McMain championed a variety of progressive reforms such as compulsory education and child-labor regulation. New Orleans was one of the filthiest and most disease-ridden cities in the world at the time, so Kingsley House residents formed the Anti-Tuberculosis League and worked to eradicate yellow fever by encouraging the use of screens in windows and cisterns. McMain also campaigned to improve public health services, which the city soon accomplished, to dramatic effect.[60] McMain collaborated with Wisner to found the Tulane School of Social Work, and Kingsley House served as the school's first campus. After the school moved to Tulane's campus proper, the students continued to get many hours of practical experience at Kingsley House. The women of the suffrage era, in other words, created an institutionalized vehicle for training social reformers of the future.

A brilliant administrator and successful academic, Wisner was appointed director of the School of Social Work in 1932, and in 1939 she became the first female dean in Tulane's history. She served in that position from 1939 until her retirement in 1958. Role model, mentor, and teacher, Wisner influenced many students. Even if they did not, in the end, become social workers, her students credited her with prompting them to become crusaders. Wisner, like many other female social workers of her generation, provided a powerful example of an unmarried woman professional who devoted herself to improving the quality of life for people far beneath her on the socioeconomic ladder.[61]

The next generation of woman-identified women at the Tulane School of Social Work included Sarah Elizabeth "Bette" Hugh, who worked with the Red Cross, and Mildred Fossier, who is best known for her environmental work. (Hugh was also involved in the anti–domestic violence movement, discussed further in chapter 4.) By the time Hugh and Fossier became professionals in the 1940s and 1950s, lesbianism had been pathologized; it was in their interest to hide the intimate nature of their partnership from all but their closest friends. They were, however, among those who pushed the envelope a bit in the 1970s by cofounding the Gertrude Stein Society, an organization of gay men and lesbians in New Orleans who wanted intellectual alternatives to the bar scene. Examples such as these inspired many women in New Orleans who embraced a lesbian feminist identity.[62]

Through all-woman organizations like the LWV or educational institutions such as the Tulane School of Social Work or in churches (as we shall see in chapter 2), older women demonstrated new ideals of southern womanhood. While the younger generation often scoffed at the respectability of their seniors, there were overlapping areas of agreement and a great deal of intergenerational transfer from older women to younger. This information sharing and the modeling of feminist lifestyles served an important function from the 1920s to the 1960s, a time when almost no women's history had been written and what did exist was seldom taught in schools. As historian Stephanie Coontz puts it, during the New Deal (1930s), World War II (1940s) and the extremely conservative Cold War period (1950s), feminism lost its "public face."[63] Young women interested in reform learned about activism from the elder women who led by example.

Liberal movements by definition build on and borrow from one another (a measure of their relative moderation), often unaware of the work that preceded them. There is, activist Mary King has said, a process of "transference, transmittal, application" of insights gained by one struggle for justice that participants apply to another.[64] "White glove" feminists plugged away between the two waves, meeting each other in various groups and movements (although usually not across the color line until after 1965), incrementally pushing institutions toward change.

Then, suddenly in the mid-1960s, a reinvigorated feminist movement burst forth. Why? In part, it occurred because conditions changed, forcing a reconfiguring of old mores and values. The Great Depression and World War II had propelled many women into the workforce, and unlike previous cohorts of women who worked outside the home, a substantial number of these women were married. Everywhere in the United States, the percentage of women who worked climbed rapidly during the 1950s; more and more frequently, not only were they married, but they had children, since this was height of the baby boom. By 1970, following the national trend, 55 percent of Louisiana women who worked were married, and many were also mothers; 43 percent of all Louisiana women with children of school age worked outside the home. Many of them were African American women who generally worked out of necessity, most commonly as domestics in the homes of white women.[65]

Yet working women remained confined to dead-end jobs that paid little, regardless of their educational achievements. The percentage of women in the highly skilled professions (e.g., scientists) actually dropped between 1950 and 1960. White-collar occupations available to women were mostly the poorly paid ones of teaching and nursing. As a result, most women worked long hours for meager salaries that were well below the federal poverty level.[66]

At the same time that well-paying jobs were unattainable for most women, the educational attainments for Louisiana women ironically increased, as the women profiled in this chapter illustrate. Colleges in Louisiana welcomed women, at least at the undergraduate level (professional and graduate schools routinely discriminated against women), but black women's educational achievements lagged far behind those of white women.[67] Financial necessity prevented most black women from achieving a higher education. The young black women who attended HBCUs in the state—Xavier, Dillard, Grambling, SUBR, and SUNO—to attain degrees that afforded them professional stature represented a tiny fraction of the population. Yet many civil rights workers were students in these schools, and it was not uncommon for leaders of the women's movement to be employed as professors.[68]

In *The Feminine Mystique*, Betty Friedan notes that education became a psychological burden when women could not gain fiduciary reward from it. In 1970, the median earnings of women workers in Louisiana were only half those of men workers.[69] Educated women noticed, and the difference created friction, anxiety, and frustration. Furthermore, because education presumably prepared the graduate for meaningful work, if an educated woman married and spent most of her twenties and thirties raising children, she sometimes became depressed. Her education raised expectations and notions about what might be possible, but socially constructed gender norms made her feel guilty for expecting anything more. Conflicted, guilt-ridden, frustrated, or just annoyed as they watched less-qualified men promoted over them, many women decided things had to change. Irritation—or anger produced by injustice—is a powerful motivator, but resources such as education and networks as well as the leisure time necessary to turn anger into constructive change are something middle-class women were more likely to have than women in lower socioeconomic groups.

In addition to rising educational levels, another structural change that prompted a renewed feminist movement was an increase in the divorce rate. Highly restrictive laws kept Louisiana's divorce rate lower than the national average for most of the century, but nonetheless it steadily ticked upward even before Louisiana passed a "no-fault" divorce law in 1975 that did not require one spouse to prove desertion or adultery on the part of the other.[70] No-fault divorce laws were not sought by feminists, though antifeminists often blamed them for the rising divorce rate. In fact, the move toward no-fault divorce was typically the result of male actions (legislators acting on the recommendation of the American Law Institute). The effects could be devastating, resulting in what Diane Pearce calls "the feminization of poverty." Divorced women could not rely on alimony and child support, even if the court had ordered their former husbands to pay. Thus women who needed to support themselves and their children wanted access to better education, better-paying jobs, and credit. Feminists did not want women left in the lurch; the solution to the problem of poverty among women was better opportunities and fair pay.[71]

Technological change inevitably reorganized people's lives and forced reconsideration of old mores. Modern conveniences like packaged food and inexpensive ready-made clothing and labor-saving devices such as dishwashers, washing machines, and vacuums, reduced the amount of time spent caring for home and family. Increasing access to birth control led to smaller families after 1964, when the baby boom officially ended, meaning fewer demands on a woman's time, especially as her children reached school age. These changes allowed for the possibility of furthering her education and advancing her career. Women also turned to abortions, illegal under most circumstances in the United States until 1970, when some states began to liberalize their abortion laws. Once fertility control became an option, women could envision putting their education to work by pursuing certain respectable "pink collar" careers (white-collar jobs that had become dominated by women), primarily teaching, social work, clerical work, and nursing. They might even become professors at a women's college or at a historically male university, as Elizabeth Wisner had done at Tulane. Space in the imagination opened up career ambitions as women realized they could postpone childbearing while they acquired an education and work experience or could cease childbearing once they had as many children as they wanted.

Thanks to technology, travel became easier and cheaper in the postwar period, allowing women to move about more freely. Many Louisiana feminist activists traveled extensively or were away from home as students. Phyllis Parun, for example, was tailed by the FBI at least in part because she traveled widely as she made contacts with other feminists. Her FBI file, ominous in its recording of completely legal and innocent activities, summed up its findings by saying "subject continues to associate with women's liberation activists in New Orleans. She traveled to Indianapolis, New York, London and Cardiff,

Wales, in the fall and winter of 1971 to visit feminists in those areas."[72] (The FBI surveilled Parun for two primary reasons: because she began a Marxist study group for women, and because she was lesbian. In the 1970s, homosexuality was still treated as a security risk by federal authorities.) With mobility, the pull of tradition and the family of origin receded.

Whether or not they had the language to articulate it, women were aware of the structural changes occurring around them. Old ideas that "a woman's place was in the home" were simply not relevant for most families anymore. While technology and the social organization of people's lives were clearly in flux, ideas and the laws and customs that followed them had not adjusted to the new technologies. This produced a cognitive dissonance and momentum for reform. Thus, as Susan Levine, a historian of the American Association of University Women, points out, "issues such as equal pay, day care provisions for working mothers, and the reform of credit laws regularly appeared on the legislative agendas of AAUW, the LWV, the BPW, and other organizations."[73] The resurgence of feminist activity in the 1960s sat atop a mountain of previous women's organizing experience, thrust up by the continental shifts of technology and the pressures of pent-up frustration at injustice in a country that prided itself on equality of opportunity.

Labor Feminism

Another wellspring of second-wave feminism came from women in labor unions, who had been agitating for workplace justice for decades. Labor union women had also been urging the establishment of a national commission to study the problems of women, both housewives and workers. Esther Peterson, a labor union lobbyist, saw her chance to push for just such a thing when newly elected president John Kennedy appointed her to head the Women's Bureau, a division of the U.S. Labor Bureau. Kennedy had won the election of 1960 over Republican challenger Richard Nixon by a razor-thin margin, and he owed his victory partly to the labor vote. Such a commission would be one way to repay them and the army of Democratic women who had put boots on the ground to help him win. Acting quickly after Kennedy took the oath of office in January 1961, Peterson mobilized a coalition of women from trade unions and liberal women's organizations and, with the help of her friend and former first lady Eleanor Roosevelt, urged Kennedy to establish the President's Commission on the Status of Women. He took her advice and appointed Eleanor Roosevelt as chair and Peterson as the executive vice-chair. Peterson in turn appointed to the commission and its committees an array of leading intellectuals, government officials, and leaders of labor unions and women's organizations. Because she believed that race and civil rights should be part of women's reform efforts, she appointed African American women, too. Among the eleven men and fifteen women on the commission were Dorothy Height and Pauli Murray.[74]

When it was released in 1963, the PCSW's report, titled *American Women*, generated front-page publicity (instead of being relegated to the society section, where news about women typically appeared) because it not only documented widespread sexism and discrimination but also called for expanding opportunities for women in education and employment as well as for giving working mothers social support and greater flexibility on the job. It suggested, additionally, that women should be paid the same as men for comparable work—something union women had insisted on for decades. That recommendation resulted in the Equal Pay Act of 1963, although its impact was far more limited than its supporters had wanted. Equally important, the mere existence of the commission emboldened women's groups to urge that similar commissions be set up at the state level. By 1967, all fifty states had done just that.[75]

Louisiana Commission on the Status of Women

Chief among those organizations agitating for the establishment of state commissions was the National Federation of Business and Professional Women (NFBPW), which had been seeking economic equality for women in the workplace since its founding in 1919. The NFBPW had a long history of collaborating with the Women's Bureau, and it worked with Esther Peterson to prepare guidelines for the presidents of the state commissions. The NFBPW had first endorsed the Equal Rights Amendment in 1937, but not until World War II did it and other women's organizations develop proactive platforms designed to make women's wartime employment gains permanent. The first Louisiana chapter was established in New Orleans in 1919, the year that the national organization was founded, and has been in continuous existence ever since. In the 1970s, it was the first statewide gender-segregated organization to endorse the ERA, and it consistently contributed money and personnel to ERA ratification efforts and other feminist causes.[76]

Following the national trend and at the urging of Louisiana's professional women, Governor John McKeithen established the Commission on the Status of Women (CSW) in 1964. To chair it, he appointed Baton Rouge native Ellen Bryan Moore, the only woman elected to a statewide office at that time. (She was registrar of state lands, a demanding position with significant responsibilities.) The twenty-nine members of the commission—twenty-one women and eight men from around the state—worked without compensation, not even reimbursement for travel expenses, for two years.[77] That they could afford to do this suggests that they were fairly well-to-do. Like the members of the BPW, they were all well coiffed, high-heeled, and respectably dressed. They were also white. Before the Voting Rights Act of 1965 restored the franchise to blacks, Louisiana politicians seldom paid attention to African Americans, and McKeithen had been elected on a segregationist platform in 1964. The commission's report, *Louisiana Women*, reflected the biases typical of white women in the 1960s South. It noted disparities in pay, income, and education between white and black women, as well as between rural and urban women, but—as might be expected from a document produced by white people appointed to an official commission during the age of Jim Crow—it offered no explicit racial analysis nor any programs specifically designed to alleviate the poverty of black women.[78]

The report summarized data documenting the unequal status of women compared to men in Louisiana and made recommendations for changes. Some of its proposals, such as affirmative action programs for women in the workforce, echoed those of the national PCSW. Taken as a whole, its recommendations were fairly progressive for the time. It advocated training and encouraging the employment of women in careers that were normally reserved for men; programs to educate and procure employment for welfare clients; expansion of the state's visiting-nurse program; centralization of state health services; increased funding for preventive health care; employment of school health educators; and the creation of a program to "teach population control," aimed at reducing the number of unwed mothers on welfare. Though they did not specify the contours of such a program, it was likely that they had in mind black women, who were disproportionately poor and, in the popular imagination anyway, were more likely than white women to be unwed mothers. As we will see in chapter 5, Governor McKeithen quietly supported the establishment of a pioneering family planning program targeting low-income women.[79]

Louisiana Women mirrored the national PSCW and most other states' commissions in not mentioning the Equal Rights Amendment (ERA). Part of the reason for establishing the PCSW in the first place had been to fend off calls for an ERA. Commissioners wanted to address women's grievances through avenues other than a blanket amendment, which in 1961 did not have the support of laboring women because it would invalidate protective legislation.

Many of the Louisiana commission's recommendations became law, including the one to make itself permanent. In 1972, an act of the legislature transferred the commission to the Louisiana Health and Human Resources Administration and changed its name to the Bureau on the Status of Women. Under the leadership of its energetic new director, Pat Evans, the bureau garnered consistent state funding and became a more powerful presence in Baton

Rouge than previously.[80] Though it took twenty years and a great deal of lobbying from both within and without the government, many of the commission's other recommendations also came to fruition: money for training women for nontraditional careers; Displaced Homemaker's Centers for women who had been out of the workplace while raising families; the removal of restrictions on women serving on juries; an end to protective legislation; an end to male control of community property; and licensing of day-care centers. By documenting inequality, the Commission on the Status of Women helped to define the problems women faced; by calling for solutions, it energized women's organizations; by garnering the imprimatur of the legislature and the governor who solicited and promulgated the report, it emboldened those women who wanted to see its recommendations enacted.[81]

Women in the Peace Movement

Throughout the twentieth century, feminists, feminism, and the peace movement were intertwined. While the antiwar movement of the 1960s is well known for having cultivated a generation of feminist activists, less celebrated in that role are the preexisting all-woman peace organizations. The largest, oldest, and arguably most important of those was the Women's International League for Peace and Freedom (WILPF), created after World War I by advocates of women's equality who had been active in the global suffrage movement. Aghast at the suffering, waste, and carnage of that war, hundreds of women met in 1919 in Zurich and elected Jane Addams the first president. Conservatives in the United States despised and distrusted both Addams and WILPF, believing that anyone with a goal of peace and disarmament was somehow disloyal, unpatriotic, or treasonous. The WILPF condemned both militarization and violence against women in the home and in society, which is perhaps what irked critics as much as feminists' call for world peace. The WILPF considered all forms of oppression morally reprehensible, and believed that eliminating one required attacking them all. Thus, in addition to advocating general disarmament, it also sought to create a world free of sexism, racism, classism, and homophobia; the guarantee of fundamental human rights; an end to all forms of violence: rape, battering, exploitation, and war; and economic justice within and among nations.[82] The platform appealed to feminists, who played a dominant role in this and other all-female peace organizations in the twentieth century.

The WILPF, then, introduced members to activism on several fronts. In New Orleans, Darlene Fife, who with Robert Head ran *NOLA Express*, an antiwar French Quarter rag, described the members of the WILPF in the mid-1960s as "primarily older women who were committed to peace and integration."[83] In other words, in this southern state where white supremacy still reigned, the WILPF's goals included the elimination of both war and racial injustice. Fife joined this organization as well as Women Strike for Peace (WSP). One of the organizers of the first International Women's Day celebration in New Orleans, Fife represents many young women who transitioned from the 1960s peace movement to the reinvigorated feminist movement.[84]

The WILPF's antiracist efforts in New Orleans attracted the attention of Clayton "Clay" Latimer, who joined it in the mid-1960s because she wanted to be part of a woman-led organization working to end racial segregation. "It was a gift to me that I found WILPF," she recalled. "It was such an early activist organization." A native of Montgomery, Alabama, Latimer had witnessed the Montgomery bus boycott in 1955, which helped her develop a social conscience and an awareness of discrimination against marginalized groups. After her parents died when she was a teenager, she moved to New Orleans to live with relatives. For one year she taught in a Catholic school in Folsom for biracial children who, due to their race, were not admitted to either the white or the black schools, a situation she found outrageous. Through Rev. Albert D'Orlando at the Unitarian Universalist Church in New Orleans and attorney Benjamin E. Smith of the Louisiana ACLU, who were working on antiracist efforts centered at D'Orlando's church, she met members of the WILPF.[85] "I was involved with desegregation efforts, but I wanted female leadership," she reflected. When a desegregation crisis occurred in Plaquemines Parish, just south of New Orleans, in 1966, Latimer along with other members of the WILPF stepped in to help. All the white teachers had quit the public schools in Plaquemines Parish following a federal desegregation order. Because they saw teaching as a female occupation, the Justice Department was looking for women to serve as substitute teachers for the students left without instructors and called the WILPF, whose reputation must have brought it to the department's attention. Latimer along with other members of the WILPF agreed to go (they were paid a salary). Although the press described them as "housewives," as though they were not working outside the home in any capacity, most of the women who went to Plaquemines Parish were highly engaged citizens who supported racial integration. Among them were Ruth and Mathilde Dreyfous.[86]

Jewish women deeply involved in antiracism in New Orleans, Ruth and Mathilde were among the white women who left their comfortable homes every day to become substitute teachers, a job for which they probably had never trained, in a rural parish run by an infamous segregationist, Leander Perez. Ruth Dreyfous, brother of ACLU and civil rights attorney George Dreyfous, had quit the NOLWV in 1948 out of frustration. She characterized it as "a pokey sort of organization" that could not take a stand on issues without "studying them to death." These were almost exactly the same sentiments express by Clay Latimer in a 2015 interview: The WILPF acted, she said, whereas the League "studied." Mathilde Dreyfous, George's widow, had cofounded the Louisiana branch of the ACLU with him in 1956 and was a noted civil rights activist in her own right. Unlike her sister-in-law, she remained committed to the NOLWV during the 1960s, overseeing its integration efforts, and was the first Louisianan to serve on the national board of the league. A generation older than Clay Latimer and a role model in many ways, Mathilde Dreyfous was involved in a number of progressive groups that presaged feminism.[87]

These were the kind of women willing to leave their comfortable middle-class lives in order to rectify a social wrong—liberal well-educated members of multiple civic organizations. Not all of them stayed at the job in Plaquemines the entire year, but Latimer did, giving her an immersive experience in direct action. The women of the WILPF as well as the other women with whom she worked that year taught her to serve justice by acting on behalf of others. This was a general principle she followed her entire life, but her heart lay in the pursuit of women's rights. She was unaware of any feminist activity in New Orleans until she heard about a rally in Audubon Park on St. Charles Avenue on August 26, 1972—a celebration of Women's Suffrage Day—sponsored by the New Orleans chapter of NOW. Latimer joined NOW that day, which was also her first day at Loyola University School of Law. After graduation, she used her law school training to become a leader in the fight for the ratification of the ERA; against the "head-and-master" provision of the community property system; and against domestic violence—a goal long advocated by the WILPF. Latimer, then, moved easily from racial justice to gender justice through the vehicle of an all-women's peace organization committed to human rights.[88]

In the 1960s, a new all-female group formed to protest the accelerating nuclear arms race, Women Strike for Peace. Founded in 1961 by white middle-class women, WSP advocated international disarmament and opposed atmospheric nuclear testing.[89] Historian Andrea Estepa observes that the women in WSP "claimed a particular moral authority on issues of war and peace because, they argued, as women and as mothers, they had special responsibility for nurturing and protecting life."[90] Formed primarily by mothers in their thirties and forties, it soon began to attract younger women such as Casey Hayden (about whom we will learn more in the next chapter), who was working with the youth branch of the YWCA in the South when she met members of WSP. The women made a lasting impression on her, Hayden said later: "In its simplicity and Quaker-like speaking from the heart, this group was much like SNCC or the Y. It was also devoted to direct action, speaking truth to power."[91] The group that began out of concern about the dangers of nuclear fallout took on a new cause as the war in Vietnam geared up in the mid-1960s. Members began "draft coun-seling" (helping men who wanted to avoid active service in Vietnam find ways to do so) as well as staging public protests against the United States' escalating involvement in Southeast Asia.

WSP activities led some women directly into feminist activity, particularly into the women's liberation movement, which tended to attract student radi-cals. At the second women's liberation conference, held in Illinois, the New Or-leans Women's Liberation group wrote, "About ten of us have been function-ing as Women Strike for Peace pickets and draft counseling. Whenever we got together and weren't talking about action plans, we talked about how dreadful men are. . . . What a few of us would like to see our group turn into is an action group—completely women; that is more or less drop out of activities with men unless acting as a women's unit.—And women's liberation as just a part of the meetings." This is consistent with similar draft resistance groups in the North, which spun off women's liberation organizations as well.[92]

Meanwhile, in Washington, D.C., another group of young feminists, includ-ing Shulamith Firestone and Peggy Dobbins of the New York Radical Women, began to push WSP and other peace advocates toward a more clearly articu-lated feminist position. Following the antiwar demonstration known as the Jeannette Rankin Brigade in 1968, they held their own march to Arlington Cemetery to symbolically bury a dummy representing "Traditional Woman-hood." Sue Munaker, who, like Peggy Dobbins, had spent the past year in New Orleans, made the connection between peace activism and feminism explicit in "A Call for Women's Liberation," published in 1968: "Out of the frustration of try-ing to find our place in the anti-draft movement, we have come to realize that our total lives have been spent defining ourselves in relation to men."[93] Many other women who founded the first independent feminist groups in New Or-leans were also antiwar activists.

White and black women activists of the 1950s generation can best be described as politically liberal. That is, they sought to remove artificial barriers to equal-ity in the law, economy, finance, and other areas of life, but they did not cri-tique capitalism itself. They sought to gain acceptance of the idea that males and females were more similar in abilities than conventional wisdom taught, and they wanted to destroy socially constructed barriers to realizing one's full potential as a human being. Their presentation of themselves as matrons of respectability should not cloak the fact that these ideas were daring, even bra-zen, in the conservative South of the mid-twentieth century. Though politically liberal, feminists who challenged the South's traditional patriarchal culture seemed radical at the time.

This chapter has highlighted the proto-feminist organizations in Louisiana that had the strongest impact on the independent feminist organizations that developed in the 1960s and 1970s. Not only did these organizations produce the greatest number of self-identified feminist women, they also provided monetary support. The next chapter examines the role of religion in producing feminists, although it is important to note that the two were not mutually exclusive. In other words, many of the women who came to feminism through the LWV, for example, may also have been active in United Methodist Women. Religion, and especially a feminist spirituality, were larger factors in the development of feminist consciousness in the South than they were elsewhere, showing us yet again how taking the northern model of feminists—who were exclusively secular—as the standard blinds us to the richness of feminism and the multiple ways in which it manifested itself in different regions of the country.

"In the Eyes of God"

Religion and Louisiana's Second Wave, 1950–1985

For several years, Fran Martinez Bussie served as president of the board of ERA United, a statewide umbrella organization working for ratification of the Equal Rights Amendment. Born in New Orleans and raised Catholic, Fran Bussie converted to Methodism as an adult. In her capacity as president of ERA United, she frequently gave public talks designed to build a broad base of political support for the ERA, which would, if ratified, render unconstitutional all laws effecting gender discrimination against men as well as women. Her speeches typically argued for women's equality by referencing religious authority as well as the Bible. Before an audience at a YWCA in Shreveport, Louisiana, for example, she pointed out that "the 1976 General Conference of the United Methodist Church said, 'The Gospel makes it clear that Jesus regarded women and men as being of equal worth.'" To a devout Christian like Fran Bussie, there could be no higher authority than Jesus's words in the Gospel. To bolster her argument, Bussie also referenced other major Christian and Jewish denominations that supported equality for women, among them the General Assembly of the Presbyterian Church, which had issued a statement saying, "God made both men and women equal in his sight; hence any discrimination on the basis of sex which assumes an inherent inferior-superior relationship is contrary to the will of God." Even the Catholic Church had come out against sexism: "Vatican II's official teaching states, 'every type of discrimination based on sex is to be overcome and eradicated as contrary to God's intent,'" Fran Bussie told her audiences in Baton Rouge, New Orleans, and elsewhere in Louisiana. "People who claim that these laws [that discriminate against women] are based on the

Bible are either unaware of the unjust principle upon which so many of our laws are based, or are reading a different bible than I am. As a Christian I am appalled by laws that give so much power to, and literally deify, the husband. The only real solution I see to the various and unsurmountable problems that most women must at one time or the other face is the ratification of the Equal Rights Amendment."[1] Fran Bussie illustrated that for Louisiana feminists, and probably for many women like her throughout the South, gender equality was consistent with Christian principles. Indeed, devout women like Bussie came to feminism because, not in spite of, their faith commitment.

Religion and feminism have had a fraught and complicated relationship in the United States. The first-wave women's rights movement of the nineteenth century had been extremely anticlerical because Western religions were male dominated and therefore espoused a patriarchal interpretation of the Old and the New Testaments. Elizabeth Cady Stanton, the intellectual giant of nineteenth-century women's rights and coauthor of *The Woman's Bible* (1895), concluded that the fight for equality could never be won as long as it had to be waged among "men who accept the theological view of women as the author of sin, cursed of God, and all that nonsense."[2] Because she saw religion as a source of women's oppression, in her multivolume (and multi-authored) *History of Woman Suffrage*, Stanton slighted its role as a force that motivated many feminists of her era.[3]

Likewise, feminists in the twentieth century argued that male authorities had co-opted religion and used it to serve their purposes. Men, in their view, had twisted the original radical egalitarianism of the founders (Hebrew prophets, Jesus, or Muhammad), replaced it with patriarchy, and then proceeded to oppress women, contrary to the founders' original intent. Among Christians, the Pauline epistles have been the most contentious, since Christian denominations that sought to exclude women from decision-making roles repeatedly cited Paul's dictum that women must be silent in the churches and subservient to men. Those verses, plus several hundred years of male construction of Holy Writ, led to the commonly held belief that woman's subordination was divinely ordained. Feminists, however, rejected that interpretation and sexist theology in general. In many cases, they also rejected their faith traditions, but among Louisiana feminists I interviewed, even those who had decommitted often noted that their religious upbringing had had a profound effect on their social conscience.

Despite male control, several Christian denominations as well as Reform Judaism nurtured subcultures that encouraged egalitarian ideals. As the editors of the *Encyclopedia of Women and Religion in North America* note, "Social justice traditions within Catholicism, Judaism, and Protestantism paved the way" to feminism.[4] Some Catholic sisters and priests as well as Protestant and Jewish clerics declared that working to achieve economic, racial, and gender justice was a mandate of the sacred texts. Feminism, in other words, offered a critique of hierarchy and oppression that fit squarely within the social justice and egalitarian ethos of Western faith traditions.

Furthermore, feminist spirituality, while not denying the place of tradition, authority, and reason, foregrounds the individual's own experience in this world as a vehicle toward spirituality. These experiences may range from ecstasy (a passionate and authentic experience of the Divine) to good works. Prominent Catholic feminists Rosemary Radford Ruether, Maria Riley, and Margaret Ellen Traxler, for example, connected the development of their feminist consciousness to involvement in the civil rights movement. Those elements are not mutually exclusive: lived experiences hone a consciousness acquired from study of the Scriptures.[5] Furthermore, feminist spirituality aims to transform this world "so that it more nearly resembles the ideal other world that is our model," as feminist theologian Carol Ochs put it.[6]

Religious motivation for feminism was probably more pronounced in the South than elsewhere in the United States, both because religion holds enormous sway in the Bible Belt and also because few other institutions promoted social justice. To give one example of this phenomenon, Anne Braden, an Episcopalian who advocated civil rights long before most whites had ever considered the idea, described her childhood church in Alabama as "the most far-reachingly decent influence in my walled-in childhood—and probably the most radical in my life."[7] Additionally, the women profiled in *Deep in Our Hearts: Nine White Women in the Freedom Movement* almost universally note the importance of their faith traditions in encouraging their social justice activism.[8] And the University of Virginia's Project on Lived Theology contains the religious testaments of many southerners such as Jane Stembridge, daughter of a white Baptist preacher, who joined the sit-in movement in Greensboro, North Carolina.[9] Stembridge participated in the SNCC meeting at Waveland, Mississippi, where, as we will see in the next chapter, the grassroots women's movement emerged from the black freedom movement.[10] Historian Susan Hartmann, in her discussion of Church Women United, an organization of black and white progressive southern churchwomen, argues convincingly that "the feminist convictions of religious women grew in part from their historical experience in the churches."[11] Just as theology provided the grounding philosophy for Martin Luther King Jr. and the members of the Southern Christian Leadership Conference, progressive religious denominations offered spiritual, psychological, ideological, and material support to activists in the women's movement as well.

Religiously devout feminists worked within their churches and synagogues to expand women's leadership opportunities and give them more decision-making power. When women tried to bring about equality, faith communities often pushed back, sometimes vehemently and categorically, other times patiently and with moderation. But as feminists continued to press for change in the twentieth century, one Western faith tradition after another began to admit women to greater roles within the church hierarchy and even to ordination. At times women gained very little when they sought to increase their power within the institution, as happened in the Roman Catholic Church. Yet the battle within their churches helped to politicize many women and to push them into open support of secular or independent feminist groups dedicated to women's emancipation and power sharing throughout society.

Independent feminist organizations were staunchly secular, in part because they included women from a variety of Christian and Jewish faith traditions, and because as liberals they respected differences. A person's religious convictions, liberals believed, were private, not public, matters. Politically active feminists tended to put their faith in the authority of the law rather than of the Divine, and therefore they expended energy in legal and political fights in the secular arena rather than in the religious one. As a result, faith was seldom a matter for discussion or public disclosure. To find it, a historian must go digging.

Because churches and synagogues were such dominant institutions in the social life of almost everyone brought up in the postwar South, that digging reveals, not surprisingly, that religious training led some women to embrace feminism. In addition to imparting a commitment to social justice, churches, Jewish temples, and their campus organizations also provided material benefits to activists, such as meeting places. In later chapters we will see how religious convictions motivated others not normally associated with the independent feminist movement to support some feminist goals, including antirape and antiviolence efforts and even abortion rights. This chapter examines how faith traditions encouraged self-identified feminists to work toward ending not just racism and sexism but classism and heterosexism, too.

There is a fairly stark religious divide in Louisiana between Protestant north and Catholic south, with Jews concentrated in New Orleans. The parishes east of the Mississippi above Lake Pontchartrain (called the Florida Parishes because they were once part of Spanish Florida) were heavily Protestant, due to a great deal of Anglo settlement before and after the American Revolution, but Italian immigration in the late nineteenth century infused a good bit of Catholic influence there as well. Italians, like Cajuns, also fanned out into southern Louisiana, which, thanks to the French and Spanish colonizers, has traditionally been predominately Catholic but not uniformly so. Since the Louisiana Purchase, at least, there have always been a sprinkling of Protestant churches among the many Catholic ones, and as New Orleans grew, so did both its Protestant and Jewish populations. At the time of the Civil War, New Orleans had the largest Jewish population of any southern city. The floodtide of immigration in the late nineteenth century included Jews from western Europe as well as many Catholics from southern and eastern Europe. By the early 1900s, most towns in Louisiana of any size had a few Jewish families, most likely merchants who opened retail stores on the main street, and at least one Jewish temple. New Orleans had several temples representing different branches of Judaism (Reform, Orthodox, and Conservative).[12]

Louisiana is among the most churched of all states. Catholics have always been the largest single denomination, and that remained true in the 1970s as well. With more than one million adherents, Catholics constituted 47 percent of the churchgoing population in 1971, while 50 percent of Louisiana's churchgoers attended Protestant churches. Of the Protestants, Southern Baptists, with close to half a million members, claimed the largest flock; Methodism was second with a bit over one hundred thousand, and Episcopalian a distant third with about thirty thousand. Other Protestant denominations were far behind those in numbers, and Jews constituted about 2 percent of the population. About 80 percent of African Americans were Protestant in 1971, a majority of them Baptist.[13]

Among Louisiana feminists for whom religion was an important factor in their moral development, a few denominations stood out: Methodist, Episcopal, Unitarian Universalist, Lutheran, Catholic, and Reform Judaism. Interestingly, very few Louisiana feminists were attracted to any of the New Age religions that are associated with feminism elsewhere. Voodoo, an Afro-Caribbean religion that has a reputation of being female dominated, gained a few adherents in later years, but feminists expressed interest in it only after the heyday of the second wave. It was not a religious belief system that brought anyone to feminism. Established mainstream religions, particularly those that have national or international structures and a tradition of women's missionary work, did that.

Methodism

Methodists were overrepresented among second-wave feminists in Louisiana and arguably in the South, at least partly because southern Methodist women had a long history of progressive activism through their national, regional, and local churchwomen's organizations. There were activists for women's rights among the women of the Methodist Episcopal Church, South (MECS), which had broken away from the Methodist Episcopal Church (MEC) before the Civil War, and also among the African American and Anglo southern women who were members of the MEC. African American historian Bettye Collier-Thomas characterizes the Methodist women's organizations in the nineteenth and twentieth centuries as "the leading liberal religious organization[s]" among white women.[14]

A strong missionary tradition among Methodist women helps account for their unusual leadership roles. Since the nineteenth century, Methodist women had developed and supported missionary work both in the United States and abroad. In the southern United States, they established missions for African Americans, immigrants, Indians, and those for whom English was a foreign language. In Louisiana, this included people of French ancestry known as Cajuns (a shortened form of "Acadian"), who spoke a French dialect. Women spent a good deal of time and effort raising money, which by itself was a form of organizational training, to support those missions. Even more importantly, they insisted on maintaining control of that money; thus, though the institutional church remained male dominated, women's divisions within Methodism were female controlled.[15]

Methodist women were extraordinarily active in the reform movement at the turn of the twentieth century known as the Social Gospel. Based on the ideas of theologian Walter Rauschenbusch, among others, the Social Gospel emphasized improving conditions in this world rather than concentrating solely on preparing one's soul for salvation in the hereafter. The movement gripped every major Protestant denomination in existence at the time, but in the former slave states, Methodist women were the most active participants. Their desire to improve the material circumstances of the poor and oppressed propelled Social Gospelers into political action. Thus, Methodist women in the South became politically involved as part of their divinely inspired mission. To increase women's ability to influence the political process, Caroline Merrick and her fellow Methodists worked (unsuccessfully) to get Louisiana to ratify the Nineteenth Amendment in the early part of the twentieth century.[16]

Well before women of other white Protestant denominations, Methodist women came to believe that racism was a sin that needed to be eradicated. Encouraged in the effort by African American women, white women developed a systematic program for interracialism within the Methodist Episcopal Church, South, in 1920, led by Carrie Parks Johnson of the Women's Missionary Council.[17]

Southern Methodist women also worked against lynching in a systematic and organized way. They joined Jessie Daniel Ames when in the 1930s she founded the Atlanta-based Association of Southern Women for the Prevention of Lynching (ASWPL) to try to bring an end to this inhumane practice of extrale-gal mob murder that was almost uniformly carried out by whites against blacks in the South. In 1941, Ames reported that forty thousand of the organization's forty-three thousand members were Methodist.[18]

The interracial actions of white southern Methodist women, while impres-sive and laudable, and far beyond what any other white-dominated religious groups were doing at the time, appear magnanimous to us in the retelling, but we should not lose sight of the fact that it was black women who brought white women to interracialism in the first place. Lugenia Burns Hope and the National Association of Colored Women urged Methodist women to undertake antiracist efforts and in dialogue with white Methodist minister Will Alexander, assisted in the formation of the racially integrated Commission on Interracial Cooperation (CIC) in 1919 (of which Jessie Daniel Ames was a member).[19] Black Methodist women, notes historian Mary Frederickson in her study of southern Methodists from 1880 to 1940, profoundly shaped the actions of white Meth-odists, although too often white women were either blind to the guidance they received from black women, or they disguised it. White churchwomen described themselves as "helping" and "teaching" black women, and black women often went along with the ruse. Women of color were careful to make their needs known to white women in a nonthreatening manner, but it was a symbiotic relationship, Frederickson notes, in which "white churchwomen came to rely on their counterparts in the black church for help in developing reform agendas and in carrying out interracial programs, and black women came to rely on white churchwomen for needed resources to be used in their own communities."[20]

Not only did black women help to drive Methodist interracialism, often without credit, but black Methodist churches advanced gender equality within the denomination sooner than did white ones. The African Methodist Epis-copal Zion Church (AMEZ) ordained women as deacons in the 1890s, and the African Methodist Episcopal Church extended ordination rights to women in 1948. Due to a shortage of trained male preachers, women in the Christian Methodist Episcopal church led congregations and had used the title "rever-end" since 1870, long before the church officially granted them ordination rights in 1954.[21] Thus, in the area of gender equality, black churches were more advanced than white ones.

Southern Methodist women both white and black worked to overcome the limitations of Jim Crow not just through their own churches but also through the YWCA, as discussed in the previous chapter.[22] Interracial activities, because they were a form of protest against established authority and white male patri-archy, became the forerunners of feminism.

The Social Gospel tradition reasserted itself in the 1950s and 1960s and led many Methodists into radical activism. Many southern white women came directly from campus ministries into movements for civil rights, anti-imperialism, and women's rights. Historian and second-wave feminist Sara Evans asserts that "the Methodist Student Movement (MSM) . . . [of the 1950s] represented a revitalization of the Methodist tradition of social action and concern." "In the late 1950s, throughout the south," Evans notes, "the MSM harbored the most radical groups on most campuses." The MSM's journal (*motive* magazine) was published in Nashville, yet another site of southern protests against injustice. In March 1969, *motive* published an issue about the women's liberation movement that inspired many readers to join the movement themselves.[23]

Methodist women, then, were disproportionately represented among feminists of faith because they had absorbed a strong tradition of Christian egalitarianism and compassion for those who were powerless and oppressed. Louisiana native Ollie Tucker Osborne, the daughter of a Methodist minister, was one of many Methodists in Louisiana who carried her social conscience into feminist activism. Born in Ruston, in northern Louisiana in 1911, she married and moved to New York City, and graduated from New York University in 1932. She spent the next twenty years working in business, public relations, and advertising in New York before moving back to Lafayette, in south-central Louisiana, in the 1950s.[24] She revived the LWV chapter in Lafayette, and using those connections as well as the YWCA, she spearheaded a campaign to support ratification of the ERA and established the Acadiana Women's Political Caucus, an affiliate of the Louisiana Women's Political Caucus. ("Acadiana" is the unofficial name for a heavily Cajun region of southwest Louisiana.) In 1975, Osborne organized the first conference on Louisiana women, held on the ULL and jointly sponsored by the university, the Louisiana State Bureau on the Status of Women, and many other "leading statewide organizations of women," including the AAUW and the LWV.[25]

Osborne, raised by a Methodist preacher, undoubtedly felt a duty to God and to her Methodist heritage when she devoted her free time to advancing women's equality. But she also received the stamp of approval from her institutional church. Under the leadership of Theressa Hoover, the first African American to head the Women's Division of the Board of Global Ministries, the United Methodist Church began expressing strong support for the women's liberation movement in 1970.[26] The Board of Church and Society of the United Methodist Church came out in support of the ERA in 1972 and prepared a pamphlet, *The Church, Religion, and the Equal Rights Amendment*, proclaiming that equality of men and women is biblical. The board based the justification on the creation story in Genesis ("male and female he created them": Genesis 1:27–28), on the actions of female heroines and prophets in the Bible (Deborah, Miriam, Queen Esther, Anna, and Lydia), and on Jesus's equal treatment of women: "The Gospel makes clear that Jesus regarded women, men and children equally. In contrast to the contemporary male-centered society, Jesus related to women with respect and sensitivity, as individual persons.... We urge all United Methodists to work through the appropriate structures and channels toward ratification of the Amendment by their respective states."[27] Fran Bussie, whose speech opened this chapter, took this to heart.

In addition to Fran Bussie, Evelyn Cloutman, and Ollie Osborne, another Louisiana Methodist emboldened by her faith was Dorothy Mae Taylor, the first African American woman elected to the Louisiana state legislature (in 1971). "To be honest," Taylor said later, "I was somewhat afraid after I won the election because I knew that I would be the only Black woman out of 105 overwhelmingly male, overwhelmingly white legislators. So I prayed and prayed ... and the answer to my fear came to me in church on Sunday morning when the choir began to sing, 'If Jesus goes with me I'll go anywhere.' It was then that I knew that God had a plan and purpose for my life."[28] After five years in the Louisiana legislature, Taylor joined the New Orleans City Council, where she soon became the first African American woman to serve as its president. A lifelong member of Mount Zion United Methodist Church in New Orleans, she never stopped working within her church. She credited her faith with giving her the courage to face many hurdles, a great deal of criticism, and a storm of controversy when in 1991 she sponsored an ordinance to integrate the Mardi Gras krewes. Taylor said that to have served eight years as an elected official "and not made a difference in the lives of others, especially the oppressed, would be sinful." Because "God calls on man and woman to address the needs of His children," she said, she "took on the big boys of ... racism, segregation, discrimination."[29] Taylor, about whom we will learn more in chapter 8, was one of the firmest supporters of the ERA in the Louisiana legislature.

Though this is not a term she would have used to describe herself, Dorothy Mae Taylor embodies Alice Walker's definition of a womanist, a black woman who exhibited a "holy boldness," an assertive spirit that came from her religious devotion and the support of her faith community. Not all womanists were Methodist, but a good number were. Sociologist Cheryl Townsend Gilkes interviewed African American women for her project on community workers and soon realized that "the religious experience was such a taken-for-granted aspect of their lives that the women usually did not mention it." When she asked them specifically about their religious life, they looked at her in a way that said, "You have to ask?" "what country are you from," or "Did your mother raise a fool?"[30] For many feminists of color in Louisiana, too, their faith was a given. Because these women considered it unnecessary to enunciate, it is easy for historians to miss the significance of religion as a motivation for black women's public activism.

Episcopalians

Some Louisiana feminists found spiritual solace in the Episcopal Church, the American version of the Church of England. Although the denomination was predominately white, two of the first women ordained as priests in the Episcopal Church of America were women of color: Pauli Murray, originally from Virginia, and Barbara Harris, from Philadelphia. Despite their class privilege (or perhaps because of it), Episcopalians tended to be social moderates. Wealth allowed them to contribute to causes quietly and, in their view, respectably, behind the scenes. At the turn of the twentieth century, they had supported settlement houses in ethnic neighborhoods around the country where physical and medical conditions were horrible. Indeed, a significant number of the first settlement-house workers were Episcopalians, including Ellen Gates Starr of Hull House in Chicago and Mary Simkhovitch in New York. Twenty-nine settlement houses established before 1910 were begun by Episcopalians, including Kingsley House, founded in 1896 in New Orleans by Trinity Episcopal Church. Some settlement houses openly challenged the prevailing views about the poor and minorities. Kingsley House, for example, opened the first integrated swimming pool in the city of New Orleans in 1957.[31]

Well-educated people are often drawn to the Episcopal Church because it encourages debate and rational inquiry, allows disagreement on social issues, values an intellectual understanding of the Divine, and concedes that the Scriptures do not contain the answers to everything. Though some of its members may be willing to conduct social experiments that challenge the status quo, the church's lack of dogmatism also means that conservative members are quite comfortable within its halls. Historian Joanna Gillespie characterizes southern Episcopalians well, describing them as "known for their avoidance of absolutisms" but "occup[ying] a relatively liberal position in terms of morality and social activism among Protestants."[32]

The Episcopal Church's unwillingness to take principled stands on major social issues sometimes nagged its practitioners. Jonathan Daniels, an Episcopal seminarian killed in Selma, Alabama, during a voting rights drive there, castigated his church: "Liberalism [for Episcopalians] seems to mean not hating—and not doing anything to rock the boat."[33] The church encouraged individuals to follow their conscience, using the Scriptures and the teachings in the Book of Common Prayer as their guide, but did not issue policy statements for its members. This left room for social and racial experimentation, even audaciousness, on the part of some congregants.[34]

Most Episcopalian women, typically married to well-placed men, did not publicly advocate feminism. The exceptions to that rule tended to be members of church parishes affiliated with universities. Feminist Episcopalians in Louisiana included Emily Hubbard, a member of the LWV and a delegate to the International Women's Year conference, and Janet Pounds, both members of St. Alban's Episcopal Chapel at Louisiana State University (LSU) in Baton Rouge. Pounds attended LSU as an undergrad and for her master's degree in chemistry and went on to work for the petrochemical industry in southern Louisiana. St. Alban's, she reported, was "very liberal." Janet Pounds, who lobbied for Louisiana's ratification of the ERA in the 1970s, carried with her for years an article originally published in *Catholic World* titled "Jesus Was a Feminist." The author of that article was Leonard Swidler, an editor of the *Journal of Ecumenical Studies* and a faculty member at Temple University. In it he argues that Jesus "promoted the dignity and equality of women in the midst of a very male-dominated society: Jesus was a feminist, and a very radical one. Can his followers attempt to be anything less—*de imitation Christi*?"[35] Pounds, an active Episcopalian, drew on this article frequently when giving speeches in churches or when answering objections from religious conservatives that women should stay home and be quiet.[36]

Probably the most famous Episcopalian to hail from Louisiana was Kim Gandy, a participant in the anti–domestic violence movement and the crusade to abolish head and master. While still in law school, she cofounded the Jefferson Chapter of NOW in 1975 and served as state NOW president from 1978 to 1981. After she earned her law degree in 1978, she advocated for women in her practice. Extremely smart and capable, she was eventually tapped by the national NOW. She served as NOW's national secretary (now called vice president for membership) from 1987 to 1991 and as national president from 2001 to 2009. Following her tenure at NOW, she held leadership positions at the Feminist Majority Foundation and then became president and CEO of the National Network to End Domestic Violence (NNEDV).[37]

Kim Gandy met other progressives, male and female, through the Chapel of the Holy Spirit, the Episcopal Church in New Orleans affiliated with Tulane University. A tiny A-frame building, Holy Spirit sits a few short steps away from the Tulane campus across Broadway Street. Gandy had been raised Presbyterian and joined the Methodist Wesley Foundation in college. For a time, she attended a Methodist church in New Orleans but joined Holy Spirit because its pastor, Prim Smith, had run against the conservative incumbent John Hainkel for his House seat in 1975. Hainkel headed the committee that kept stopping the

ERA, and Gandy admired the man who had challenged him (and lost). Hainkel's opposition to the ERA angered Kim Gandy mightily, and she was heartbroken that Smith had lost. When she bought a house in New Orleans, she made sure it was in Hainkel's district so she would be able to run against him, which she did, four years later, in 1979. She lost, too, even though the district Hainkel represented included Loyola and Tulane Universities and was home to many liberal intellectuals. Gandy's house was near the chapel, and she enjoyed the people there. She recalled, "It was a politically minded social justice church. I liked all that, and the messages. It fit my view of the world."[38]

One of those like-minded persons whom Gandy met at the Chapel of the Holy Spirit was Corinne Freeman, who eventually married the priest who served that congregation after Prim Smith, William Hazzard Barnwell. Like many feminists, Corinne Freeman Barnwell had a deep faith commitment and wide-ranging national and global influences. The grandchild of Presbyterian missionaries to China, daughter of a noted surgeon (father) and a professional therapist (mother), Corinne lived in Philadelphia and then in California before she headed south to assist with Freedom Summer 1964 in Mississippi. In 1965, Corinne settled in New Orleans, as did her sister Margery, who married David Billings, the pastor at St. Mark's Methodist Church.[39] That same year the headlines announced President Johnson's surge in Vietnam, when he sent to that unpopular war 500,000 soldiers. "We were conducting anti-war meetings and activities," many led by Mike Duffy, a former Catholic brother, who held meetings in a Catholic parish house uptown. (Note again the importance of safe religious spaces in nurturing rebellion against the status quo.) "It was very stressful," Corinne remembered. "Many people were fired from their jobs or had their phones tapped." Freeman joined a CR group in 1967, married attorney Ben Smith (a marriage that ended in divorce in 1973), got an MSW from the Tulane School of Social Work, and devoted the rest of her volunteer and occupational life to helping others. She was on the founding board of Planned Parenthood when it began in Louisiana in 1981 (Louisiana was the fiftieth state in the union to get a Planned Parenthood clinic).[40] Barnwell is typical of Louisiana feminists in that she was well educated, married, an activist in progressive causes, and a member of a liberal mainstream religion. Her experiences outside the South contributed to her ability to think outside local conventional norms, to her unwillingness to accept the hierarchical system of oppression she encountered when she moved to the South, and to her belief that a better system of social relations was attainable.

The Episcopal Chapel of the Holy Spirit, where Kim Gandy and Corinne Barnwell met, was feminist-friendly and could even be considered a nursery of Louisiana feminism. Another such church was St. Mark's Methodist on the edge of the French Quarter.

St. Mark's Community Center—Social Justice Incubator

There are few better examples of a faith community supporting progressive change in Louisiana than St. Mark's Community Center. St. Mark's has been a liberal seedbed from its founding as a settlement house in a poor New Orleans neighborhood in 1909. Owned and run continuously by the Women's Division of the General Board of Global Ministries of the United Methodist Church in Louisiana from 1909 to 2005, the women never relinquished control of the center to a male board (as often happened with other religious settlement houses, such as Kingsley House). Following Hurricane Katrina in 2005, it was reorganized as the Rampart Street Community Center, but it is still located in the same building erected in 1923 on the corner of North Rampart and Governor Nicholls Street at the edge of the French Quarter and is still supported in part by the United Methodist Women. Also on the property is St. Mark's United Methodist Church, a separate entity led by male pastors until the 1970s, when the first women pastors began to serve.[41]

St. Mark's was ahead of the curve in many ways. It provided services equally and without discrimination to blacks as well as whites in the surrounding New Orleans neighborhoods before that was legal and played a major role in the Save Our Schools movement during the New Orleans integration crisis of 1960. The pastor of the church at the time, Andy Foreman, broke the white boycott of William Frantz Elementary by keeping his daughter in school with Ruby Bridges, despite the very real danger that such a stand presented to both himself and his family. David Billings, the first person to hold both the pastorate of the church and the directorate of the center (from 1977 to 1981) says that St. Mark's saw itself as an incubator for social justice. It gave space to and supported community-oriented groups that were so controversial no one else would consider granting them the use of their facilities.[42] When feminists were first looking for places to hold public meeting, St. Mark's welcomed them. It hosted International Women's Day (March 8) events, CR sessions, and NOW meetings.[43]

In addition to its early support of feminist activities, St. Mark's was far ahead of others in embracing homosexuals. It was one of only two churches in New Orleans (the other being the Unitarian) that offered to host memorial services for twenty-nine people who died in the worst arson fire in New Orleans history, June 24, 1973, at The Up Stairs Lounge.[44] Located on the second floor of a building at the corner of Chartres and Iberville Streets in the French Quarter, The Up Stairs was a well-known gay hangout. It also housed a gay congregation, the Metropolitan Community Church, in the back room, where gay men, sometimes with their families, could openly worship without fear of condemnation. (Troy Perry founded the Metropolitan Community Church in 1968 in

Los Angeles. The New Orleans branch, established in 1970, was one of several in the United States at the time.) On this Sunday evening, about sixty people, including mothers of some of the men, gathered to celebrate the fourth anniversary of the Stonewall riots. Two hustlers who disrupted the church service were thrown out, and at least one (perhaps both) came back with Molotov cocktails and gas cans and set fire to the place. Burglar bars trapped people inside. The pastor of the church, Bill Larson, along with twenty-eight other men and one woman, died in the fire. Police investigators determined that the arsonists had saturated the stairs with an incendiary liquid that created a "wall of fire" when the patrons opened the door. Some people escaped out the back door by hopping over rooftops to safety. The main suspect committed suicide and was never charged. Some of the charred bodies were still hanging out the window, in full view of spectators, the next day. Others were fused in a heap on the floor. The city's response to the tragedy reveals the limits of New Orleans's reputation for tolerance of homosexuals. Though he vigorously denied the rumors, Archbishop Hannan reportedly instructed his clergy not to hold Catholic funeral services for any of the victims nor allow them burial in Catholic cemeteries. In the days after the fire, neither he nor any city official issued a statement of regret over the tragedy, although a few weeks later, in a gesture of support, Mayor Moon Landrieu appointed gay and lesbian representatives to the Human Relations Committee, which advised the mayor.[45]

It was liberal Protestant denominations that reached out to the scorned and outcast, in this case to a group of people regarded as sinners by the church, as mentally ill by the psychiatric profession, and as criminals under the law. Rev. Evelyn Barrett offered the mourners use of her Unitarian Church, but it was too small and was far from the French Quarter. In yet another first, St. Mark's at the time was pastored by Rev. Edward Kennedy, the first black minister ever appointed to a white congregation in Louisiana. With the full backing of Finis Crutchfield, the Methodist bishop of Louisiana, Rev. Kennedy offered the use of his sanctuary. Bishop Crutchfield not only attended the service, held one week after the fire, but he also encouraged other Methodist ministers and congregants to do likewise. Presiding over an audience of about three hundred people, Troy Perry, the founder of the Metropolitan Community Church, officiated, with Kennedy's assistance. No other Protestant clergy offered similar support to the families, partners, and friends of the fire's victims.[46]

St. Mark's stepped up its outreach to the gay and lesbian community in the years to come. It donated space to the Head Clinic (a clinic in the French Quarter that offered free services to people in need) and the gay VD clinic. It also opened its doors to the New Orleans chapter of the Daughters of Bilitis, a lesbian social and political organization founded in California in the mid-1950s.[47]

In keeping with its tradition of embracing all Christians regardless of their sexual orientation, St. Mark's Church became the first reconciling congregation in Louisiana in 2012.[48] The reconciling movement is "a program which provides UMC congregations with a method of publicly declaring themselves open to gay and lesbian membership." Though at the time that it declared itself a reconciling congregation its pastor was a man, David Billings, this stance was the logical outgrowth of the influence of women inspired by the Social Gospel. Long before the 1960s, the women of St. Mark's supported those who defied societal norms.[49]

Unitarian Universalist

The Unitarian Universalist Church was probably the most left-leaning of any Christian denomination. The Universalist Church had been cofounded in colonial New England in 1780 by one of the United States' first true feminists, Judith Sargeant Murray, who married the first Universalist minister. The Universalists were the first American denomination to ordain women, in 1838. The Unitarians waited until after the Civil War (1871), although this was still a century earlier than the mainstream Christian denominations. Confined mostly to New England in the nineteenth century, both denominations expanded outside their original geographic origins in the twentieth century but remained overwhelmingly white. The merger of these two denominations in 1961 created a liberal congregation that rejected much Christian orthodoxy while encouraging thoughtful critique of biblical texts, independent thinking, and moral justice. Unitarians and Universalists generally had progressive social views and favored the expansion of civil rights for women as well as minorities.[50]

Unitarians tended to be forward thinkers and progressive public activists. Elizabeth Wisner, the leader of the Tulane School of Social Work, was Unitarian. Katherine (Kit) Baker Senter, born in New Orleans in 1926 (Newcomb, 1947), a champion of poor women's rights to birth control and the black freedom movement, was Unitarian, as was Roberta Madden, cofounder of the first NOW chapter in Baton Rouge and an activist with Common Cause. Cathy Cade, one of the founders of the feminist movement in New Orleans, also credits the Unitarians with helping her acquire a passion for social justice.[51]

The pastor of First Unitarian Church in New Orleans in the 1970s, Rev. Albert D'Orlando, and his wife, Catherine Cohen, an obstetrician/gynecologist, were in the forefront of progressive causes in the city. D'Orlando arrived in New Orleans to pastor the church in 1950 and led it to become the first church in the city to racially integrate. As a result of his antiracism and other outspoken liberal ideas, D'Orlando became a target of the anti-Communist witch hunt led by

the House Un-American Activities Committee (HUAC) in 1958. The Unitarian
Church backed him 100 percent and donated money to assist the integration
of Tulane and several public schools. D'Orlando and his wife both supported
the ERA and other feminist causes because they understood the Bible to mean
that all people, regardless of the circumstances of their birth, were equal in the
eyes of God.[52]

Like St. Mark's, the Unitarian Church was gay-friendly and reached out to
the families of the victims of the Up Stairs Lounge arson fire. First Unitarian
was the church where Susan LosCalzo, a lesbian feminist active in antiwar and
gay rights efforts, established a gay and lesbian group in the 1970s. LosCalzo
also worked on a feminist newspaper in New Orleans, *Distaff*, edited and produced by another feminist who found a comfortable home in the Unitarian Universalist Church, Mary Gehman, a native of the North whose broad-minded
outlook came from multiple international connections.[53]

Mary Gehman had grown up in Philadelphia in a Mennonite community
and spent her JYA in Germany, where she began to appreciate the way people in
other countries viewed the United States. Whereas she had been taught, in the
midst of the Cold War, that the United States was the savior of the free world,
she learned that others viewed the United States as an arrogant bully that
forcefully threw its weight around without respectfully consulting the objects
of its "help." This epiphany caused her to think critically about the United
States' history of oppression of ethnic minorities, particularly people of color,
something that Europeans were quick to point out. When she came back to
the United States, she joined the antiwar, civil rights, and other protest movements in New York City. Gehman participated in the radical feminist protest
of the Miss America Pageant in Atlantic City in 1968. She relocated to New Orleans in 1972, lived for a time in a women's collective with her baby (whom she
raised by herself, since her husband had abandoned her), and took a job with
the Department of Welfare. There she met and befriended Donna Swanson, an
African American coworker, with whom she produced, off and on, the longest-
running feminist newspaper in the Deep South, *Distaff*. Gehman had worked
briefly at the *States-Item* in New Orleans and was disappointed at the way
women were treated as reporters and in the news itself. "No one was covering
the movement," she said, so she decided to start a newspaper that would. The
idea began in 1971, the brainchild of a group of women assisting Barbara Scott
in her campaign for the state legislature. As Gehman described it, "we wanted
a place for women's issues to be reported on and discussed, issues like reproductive rights, abortion, sexual identity, equal pay for equal work, race effects
on women, and property rights within marriage. We focused on these things
because the male-controlled media either ignored or sensationalized them. We

also wanted a place for women artists, writers, poets and essayists to publish their work, and a newspaper that endorsed and actively supported women candidates for political office."[54] *Distaff* was always short-staffed and never made money because businesses were afraid to associate themselves with feminism and would not buy ads. Most of the advertising came from progressive religious groups like the Unitarian Universalists or from other feminist organizations. *Distaff* limped along for a few years only because of the financial assistance of Donna Swanson's husband, who bankrolled the operation until it finally closed shop for good in 1982. Though it was hardly radical, a feminist newspaper in 1970s New Orleans was still a daring venture, and it is unsurprising that the Unitarian Universalist Church supported it.[55]

Lutherans and the Walther League

Lutheranism profoundly influenced at least two New Orleans feminists, Sue Laporte and Marguerite Redwine. As young women, both had been members of the Walther League, the youth ministry of the Lutheran Church—Missouri Synod, one of the more conservative branches of the Lutheran Church. At its 1968 convention, the Walther League, swept up in the zeitgeist and embracing the spirit of "participatory democracy," reorganized itself into a "youth-led ministry of caring."[56] Adult "consultants," who, as determined by the teenage leaders, were willing to trust young people's decision-making ability, assisted the group, but the teenagers decided what specific "Christlike" issues they would take up and where. Under their leadership, the Walther League became quite radical. Headquartered in Chicago, it employed six full-time staffers in the 1970s—including Sue Laporte—and mobilized thousands of eager, principled volunteers. Seeing themselves as caring "followers of Jesus Christ," they worked in various social-justice causes across North America. This was the responsibility of members of a faith community, they argued: "There is no question of whether or not we as the church should confront issues plaguing the world today, even controversial ones. In fact, if we try to take a neutral position, we will perpetuate the conditions that exist now, simply by our inaction." The Youth Organizing Manual that Laporte and the other staffers authored called on Lutheran youth to "Analyze everything! Think! Argue! Use this book to get your friends together, to plunge into God's world and to begin a new life."[57]

Laporte's parents and grandparents had set examples of standing up against injustice by opposing racial segregation. Laporte was born in New Orleans's Ninth Ward, a working-class neighborhood, and grew up in the Gentilly area of the city. Her father was French Catholic, her mother Lutheran. Her maternal grandfather was a Lutheran minister, and her mother worked as the administrator of Redeemer Lutheran Church in the Ninth Ward, a German church in an integrated neighborhood. Her grandmother was the office assistant to the pastor, George Herbek, for many years.[58] Sue attended a Lutheran parochial school through the seventh grade, but her mother removed her from the school, against the church and the pastor's urging, when it refused to integrate. Even as an elementary school child, she, along with her best friend, took a stand and refused to sit in the white section of the segregated bus. She took her seat next to black women on the bus, despite being attacked by the other white children. Her faith commitment, along with the example set by her parents, gave her the courage of her convictions.

Laporte's activism on behalf of the poor and oppressed continued through her high school years. She attended public high schools in New Orleans. As a senior, she joined the national Walther's League's "Hunger Chain" and organized a thirty-mile "Hike for the Hungry" in New Orleans (1969). She reported that the Hike for the Hungry was "before such things as pledge walks were common, and it was perhaps one of the first activities of this sort, if not the first, ever held locally." (Liberal Democrat and later mayor of New Orleans Moon Landrieu, a Catholic, was one of her sponsors.) Laporte left New Orleans to attend Valparaiso University in northwestern Indiana, about an hour's drive from Chicago. "Valpo" was a liberal Lutheran university founded originally in 1859. A hot spot of youth activism, Valparaiso encouraged students to engage in civil disobedience if they believed it consonant with Jesus's mission and work. While Laporte was at Valparaiso, the Walther League hired her to organize Lutheran youth in the Deep South (Louisiana, Alabama, Mississippi, and Florida) around social issues such as eliminating racism, ending war, and addressing world hunger. She attended UNO during this two-year commitment (1970–72). Because the Walther League paid her a mere $150.00 per month, she qualified for and received food stamps. This gave her an appreciation of how hard it is to be poor, which was a deliberate strategy on the part of the Walther League.[59]

The training for the regional youth staffers was eye opening for this bright, young southern woman, as it involved traveling from one coast to another. Laporte recalled, "We conducted a summer youth gathering at the Red Hook Indian Reservation in South Dakota, and we went to New York City for one of the Lutheran Church in America youth gatherings at Madison Square Garden. By the time I returned to New Orleans, I was full of spirit for bringing news of the Social Gospel to the Lutheran young people of this region." To live out this spiritual commitment, Laporte became involved in the Peace Action Center, an organization of the Episcopal Chapel of the Holy Spirit that opposed the war in Vietnam. She also started the Racial Justice Youth Council, which sought to teach young people about racial injustice. "It was my job with the Walther League to be involved in the left-leaning movements of the day, and I was," she explained. "During this time, I met the many radical groups and individuals in New Orleans who were advocating social change. And I met, and became involved with, Sandy Karp," another radical feminist lesbian.[60]

The elders within the Missouri Synod were increasingly uncomfortable with the leftward drift of the Walther League. At its 1971 convention, the Missouri Synod began discussing a resolution designed to unseat the youth leadership and bring the league under the control of church elders. In the end, that is what happened, but for a few short years, the league was run by idealistic young people who thought that their actions could bring about lasting changes for the better, particularly changes that would help disadvantaged minorities.[61]

Meanwhile, the efforts of the Racial Justice Youth Council (RJYC) that Laporte had started in New Orleans Lutheran churches bore little fruit. While black people eagerly attended, whites refused. After a massive effort to get the word out in both white and black Lutheran congregations in New Orleans, the RJYC's "Dip-In" at Audubon Park Pool drew 450 people, 98 percent of them black. The only whites who showed up were ministers and their families of the RJYC. This was only one of many attempts by the RJYC to get white Lutherans in the same room as blacks, but as Laporte said in her official report in November 1972, "all failed."[62] She found this experience profoundly discouraging.

With young people increasingly losing their grip on leadership roles in the Walther League, Laporte left her paying position but continued as an advisor for another year while attending UNO. "Looking for 'real work' I took a job with State Civil Service as a Driver's License Examiner, and then as a 'welfare worker,' the state Office of Family Services," Laporte recounted. "Sandy Karp [her partner] got an opportunity to go to France for a year on an exchange program through her doctoral advisor at Tulane, so we went to live in Strasbourg, France, during the year 1974–75. I attended the classes for strangers (*etrangers*) at the Université de Strasbourg, and we managed to find the local radical feminist movement in that city while there. That's how I ended up giving a speech there on International Women's Day in 1975. When we returned to NOLA, I applied to, was accepted at, and even managed to secure some scholarship money to continue my undergraduate work at Newcomb College of Tulane University."[63]

Upon their return to New Orleans, Sue Laporte and Sandy Karp joined Mary Gehman in running The Clothesline, a clothing exchange designed to help poor women acquire professional clothing. An attempt to function outside the capitalist system, much like the Salvation Army or Goodwill, the clothing exchange operated without cash and used coupons instead. The idea was that those who had more should share with those who had less—a Judeo-Christian concept.

It did not succeed, partly because nobody made any money (although Sandy drew a small salary), and the women all needed to get paying jobs. It was an idealistic and ethical vision that did not work in the end, but while it lasted, Laporte believed that they "made a real difference in the lives of people [they] touched."

Laporte graduated magna cum laude from Newcomb College in December 1976, with a degree in linguistics. During this time, she helped to found the Women's Center on Jackson Avenue, a woman's space that appealed to many radical feminists and women coming to terms with their homosexuality. She recalled,

> After finishing my degree at Newcomb, I went to work for the City of New Orleans, then led by its first African American Mayor, Ernest "Dutch" Morial. I was still under the illusion that working for the City was closer to working for the common good, but I was mistaken. I had grown discouraged with the conservatism of the Missouri Synod church, and did not find that to be any place for me as a lesbian feminist. I had grown and the church had stayed the same. I had had the "coming out" talk with my parents after Sandy and I separated, and that ushered in a prolonged period of little contact with my family.[64]

Meanwhile, in the 1970s she also worked with the feminist newspaper *Distaff* and other feminist initiatives in New Orleans, such as Sisters Helping Sisters (an abortion referral service) and NOW. She joined members of NOW when they lobbied for ratification of the ERA at the state legislature. In the late 1970s, she developed Terpsichore, the Women's Music Collective, which brought women artists of Olivia Records to New Orleans and sold their recordings, and in 1980, she was one of the organizers of the Take Back the Night March in New Orleans. Lutheranism, then, exposed Laporte to global issues, and her experience at a liberal college in the North gave her a new perspective on her birthplace.[65] Those experiences also shaped her life and career paths. She explained,

> I eventually chose to put my education and talents to a different use than climbing the civil service ladder, and applied for, was accepted to, and attended Loyola University School of Law. I started in the night school program while I was still working for the Fire Department, changed to the day school, worked my way along with clerkships at legal firms, and graduated cum laude in May 1989. I had the privilege of clerking for Chief Justice Pascal F. Calogero Jr., of the Louisiana Supreme Court, the year after I graduated. And although I investigated positions with various legal services agencies, the tug of paying off law school debt dictated that I look elsewhere for job opportunities in a law firm. My

opportunities for activism led me to work as the chairperson and chief organizer of Celebration, the statewide Louisiana lesbian and gay conference, for several years after graduation. Later I was recruited to serve as the chairperson of the Forum for Equality, and I did so from 2001 to 2002. I'm presently on the board of that organization.[66]

Opposing heterosexism was consistent with the other radical Christian egalitarian values Laporte had imbibed from her experience in the Walther League.

Marguerite Redwine, another member of the Walther League as a young woman, grew up in Baton Rouge, raised primarily by her mother, a nurse, and her mother's family after her father was killed in World War II. Even though her mother was Catholic, her grandfather raised her as Lutheran. Summer youth camps and the Walther League taught her to how to express her faith through deeds, a lesson she never forgot. After graduating from LSU and earning a master's in education (guidance counseling) from Loyola University in New Orleans (1971), she had several lucrative professional options (she worked at Proctor and Gamble for a while, making very good money). But she ultimately chose service work. "I wanted to work in ways that put my faith into action," she explained. "I wanted to help others in society and in the community." She switched to the Episcopal Church in the 1990s because her children had gone to Trinity Episcopal School, and she was impressed with the people she met there. She served on the Trinity vestry and helped it start a counseling service that charged on a sliding scale, thus enabling people to receive help who could not otherwise afford it. As associate director of the YWCA in the 1970s, she and the executive director, Carmen Donaldson, launched a number of new programs, including rape crisis services and an anti–domestic violence program.[67] We will learn more about both of these initiatives in chapter 4, but suffice it to say here that, after a period of resistance to what Redwine and Donaldson proposed, many other religious women got behind these programs, including Catholics.

Catholicism

Feminism arose within the Roman Catholic Church around the time of the Second Vatican Council (Vatican II, 1962–65), which historian Mary J. Henold describes as "an inspiring but overtly sexist event." The call for new, more powerful, roles for women in the church came from Catholic women themselves. In other words, feminism originated within the faith and was not imposed from the outside. Letters and editorials with a distinctly feminist tone began appearing in Catholic publications in 1963.[68] Mary Daly, a laywoman with a doctorate in religion who had attended Vatican II as an unofficial observer, published the first book-length critique of the church's history of misogyny in *The Church and the Second Sex*, in 1968 (which almost got her fired from her job at Catholic Boston College). A pioneer in feminist theology, Daly ultimately "rejected Christianity as irredeemably oppressive" and stopped writing as a theologian after her book *Beyond God the Father: Toward a Philosophy of Women's Liberation* in 1973.[69] Other influential feminist theologians have continued to publish, hopeful of transformative changes within the Catholic Church. Among them is Rosemary Radford Ruether.

Ruether began writing powerful critiques of patriarchy in the 1960s that helped to establish Euro-American feminist theology. A Roman Catholic Church historian, theologian, and ecofeminist, she saw all oppressions as interlinked: plunder of the environment and exploitation of workers, women, and minorities were all the result of male privilege and the construction of the male body as powerful and strong and the female body as passive and weak. Her work was profoundly influential among educated Catholic women in the 1960s and 1970s, although not all were as radical as she. Daly and Ruether can be considered the founding mothers of feminist theology in the United States, but many more would follow.[70]

Catholic feminists sought to transform their church from within and used techniques such as letter writing, organizational meetings, and dialogues with the hierarchs. Because they typically did not take to public protests, it was easy for outsiders to overlook the ways in which many of the faithful had begun agitating for change. Catholic feminism, in fact, had been percolating for decades within religious orders of nuns and sisters, who knew what it was like to be exploited by sexism. "Their lives were circumscribed by an ancient patriarchal hierarchy in which they had no representation. Men passed judgment on their choice of work, their living quarters, their salaries, their political activity, their public statements, and what clothes they put on in the morning. Perhaps no other set of American women more intimately understood the complexities and humiliations of patriarchy," historian Mary Jo Henold has written.[71]

One of those feminist nuns in Louisiana was Sister Fara Impastato, who taught theology at Loyola University for twenty-eight years. Born in New Orleans in 1920 of immigrant parents and educated in Catholic schools, she demonstrated an independent streak at an early age: She rejected an offer of a scholarship to St. Mary's Dominican College because she had decided to "enter a convent," the Eucharistic Missionaries of St. Dominic, at the age of nineteen.[72] She chose the religious life for spiritual reasons, certainly, but also because she had a desire to "not be dominated, and to have some solitude and some autonomy." Those are qualities conducive to feminism, and over time Sister

Fara followed the spirit of the age and joined many other Catholic sisters in criticizing the church's patriarchalism.[73]

After teaching in rural Louisiana for several years, Impastato returned to school and graduated magna cum laude from Loyola in 1949 with a BA in education and history. In 1952, she earned a PhD in Catholic theology from St. Mary's School of Sacred Theology at Notre Dame and joined the faculty at Loyola in 1966 as an assistant professor of religious studies.[74] She founded the Sisters Council of the Archdiocese of New Orleans in 1967 and affiliated it with the National Assembly of Women Religious (NAWR), a group that advocated women's empowerment within the church and in society at large. She was also an active member of the Leadership Conference of Women Religious, a liberal organization that challenged the hierarchs' teachings about women. Sisters, she wrote in 1971, wanted to serve "but not servilely." Along with many other women religious in New Orleans and across the United States, she called for the church to open leadership roles and the priesthood to women.[75]

Autonomy was not easy for any woman to achieve in the 1950s, but it was even more elusive for Catholic women, who were taught to marry young and produce as many children as God intended. Entering the religious life, as Sister Fara indicated, presented one alternative. Sisters were independent professionals who built and ran their own institutions (schools, hospitals) and rejected marriage, motherhood, and modern beauty standards in order to live and work in communities of women. Louisiana Catholic women educated in sex-segregated Catholic schools found the nuns to be inspiring role models for independent womanhood. Corinne "Lindy" Boggs, born in 1916, who would become the first woman from Louisiana elected to the House of Representatives, went to a convent school at age nine. She recalled, "I learned there that women did everything. The nuns were principals, directors of hospitals, presidents of colleges. It didn't occur to me that women couldn't do anything they wanted."[76] Janet Mary Riley, an attorney born in 1915, attended Ursuline College, the sister school of Loyola University in New Orleans. Riley, who in the 1970s would lead the fight against the husband's control of community property in Louisiana (covered in chapter 9), credited the Ursuline sisters with helping her to develop a feminist consciousness.[77] Nuns at Ursuline College, she remembered, instilled in their students the idea

that the state exists to serve the individual by using its God-given authority to create an environment in which he is assured those freedoms necessary to work out his salvation, for instance, freedom of speech and of religion, freedom from oppressive inequalities enforced by law, the freedom of fair trials, and freedom from unreasonable police searches. We were taught that, important as it is to support the form of government permitting freedom, it is personally more important to form a right conscience, including a social consciousness, an awareness of the problems of people outside our circles, and to aid in attaining a better society. Such an understanding of the function of government, and the development of a social consciousness, are necessary attributes of a lawyer.[78]

Nuns were inspirational for Vaughan Burdin Baker, too. Born in 1937, Baker graduated from the Academy of the Sacred Heart in Grand Coteau in St. Landry Parish in 1954. Grand Coteau was a bucolic little town of about one thousand people in a predominately French Catholic area not far from Lafayette, where Baker grew up. The Religious of the Sacred Heart, an international French order that founded schools along the waterways in early Louisiana, operated the academy. The nuns were formidable and highly exacting and had close ties to the nearby Jesuit seminary. Indeed, Baker described them as "the female version of Jesuits." The Jesuits, among the most progressive and intellectual of all religious orders, supplied professors to teach religion classes at Grand Coteau, courses that Baker found enormously mind-expanding.[79]

The sisters modeled unbending righteousness, in Baker's view. For example, for a time there was a small girls' college associated with Grand Coteau. The mother superior, Reverend Mother O. Lapeyre, announced in 1953 that she was going to admit black students, despite the resistance of some of the alumnae. "I highly respected her strong moral stand," Baker recalled. Unfortunately, the women's college closed the next year due to financial difficulties. Another time, the mother superior shocked the board by hiring Elizabeth Bentley, who was associated with the Communist Party, to teach political science at the college. These principled positions stuck with Baker forever: "I was immersed in a Catholic tradition of defiance against wrong."[80]

After she married, Baker moved to Plaquemines Parish to teach school in 1960–61, the same year that the infamous New Orleans school integration crisis occurred when four black first-graders were selected to begin integrating two formerly all-white elementary schools. The photos of little Ruby Bridges being escorted by U.S. marshals through screaming mobs of white women and men who threatened her and her family as she entered William Frantz Public School horrified Baker. With Reverend Mother Lapeyre's words and actions on behalf of racial integration fresh in her memory, Baker was indignant at the behavior of her fellow white Louisianans. She was even more horrified when the principle of the school where she taught gave students days off to travel to New Orleans and join the insult-hurling crowds. She hated, too, that Plaquemines Parish's boss, Leander Perez, the leader of the Greater New Orleans White Citizens Council, was the chief instigator of the mob's actions. These events sickened her and raised her sense of moral outrage at injustice, something that she would carry over into the fight for women's rights.[81]

Jesuit clerics and an order of French nuns who opened her mind to intellectual exploration of religious beliefs, a woman in command who stuck to her principles despite the displeasure of the school's financial backers —these experiences gave Baker a much more expansive view of the world than many of her contemporaries in local public schools. She went on to become a historian on the faculty of ULL, where she started a women's archive, wrote some of the first histories of Louisiana women, and developed and taught the university's first courses (perhaps the first in the state) in women's history in the mid-1970s. Cleary the nuns had been powerful female role models for her.

Another Louisiana feminist influenced by nuns was Lorna Bourg, born in 1942 in Crowley, Louisiana, in the center of Cajun Country. Bourg attended a Catholic school in Baton Rouge run by the Sisters of St. Joseph. The sisters introduced her to the concept of otherness through their attention to the condition of people in other cultures. During Lent, the students saved their pennies to give to foreign missions. "It was very exciting to feel like you were doing good work somewhere in the world," she said later. It gave her a sense of global economic justice and fairness to others that she never forgot. She attended Saint Mary's Dominican College in New Orleans and majored in philosophy and theology, then earned a master's degree in psychology from ULL. The 1960s civil rights, antipoverty, and women's movements, all of which she participated in, greatly influenced her. She joined the same order of nuns who had taught her so well, but the regulations and cloistering proved to be a bad fit for her personality. After twenty-four months, she decided that a nun's life was not for her; rather than spending so much time on her knees praying, she wanted to be an activist. In 1969, she founded the Southern Mutual Help Association, an organization dedicated to assisting laborers in rural southern Louisiana. In 1977, she served as a delegate to the International Women's Year Conferences in Baton Rouge and in Houston, where she helped to craft plank 22 in the national platform, which concerned services for rural women.[82]

Women-run schools, churches, and convents, then, gave Catholic women experience in leadership. As a result, women religious were often in the forefront of demands for women's equality both within the church and in society at large. Beginning in the 1950s, nuns, in dialogue with the Vatican, began asking for reforms that would allow them to "do more to make themselves relevant in the world." The "new nuns" began writing feminist articles in the Catholic press in 1963 as the Second Vatican Council convened in Rome. The reformist, modernizing spirit of Vatican II gave hope to many Catholics that the governing hierarchy would move in the same direction as the mainline Protestant

and Reform Jewish congregations to advance women's rights within the institution. To their great disappointment, however, Catholic clerics rejected calls
for women's ordination and power sharing within the church. Nonetheless, sisters and other Catholic women interpreted council documents as supportive
of feminism. Additionally, Vatican II encouraged the new nuns to shed their
habits, wear street clothes, leave their convents, and engage the social issues of
the day. Subsequently, nuns became involved with civil rights, the peace movement, and the movements for liberation in Latin America and elsewhere in the
third world.[83]

In 1970, more than thirty diocesan sisters' councils organized the NAWR to
promote social justice and to communicate the concerns of rank-and-file sisters to their official leadership and Rome. The NAWR organized CR sessions
among women religious and began to battle for women's right to participate
in the sacramental life of the church. In 1971, the Leadership Conference of
Women Religious (LCWR), an organization of superiors, endorsed the ERA, and
the NAWR soon followed suit.[84] Likewise, women religious in Louisiana lent
their support to ERA United, an umbrella organization dedicated to getting the
Louisiana legislature to ratify the Equal Rights Amendment (more about that
in chapter 8).

Contrary to popular perception, NOW was not hostile to spiritual women.
Quite the opposite: it welcomed women of faith and sought to encourage them
to challenge patriarchal control of their denominations.[85] In Louisiana, Sister
Joelle Maurer and Sister Mary Theodosia Laufer were members of the first NOW
chapter in Baton Rouge, founded in 1971; both also worked full time on the Lit-
urgy Commission of the Catholic Diocese of Baton Rouge, positions typically
reserved for priests. In February 1972, they presented a program about how "the
Lord's prophets" (i.e., men) had "put across" the idea that "God created women
for lesser roles." Presumably they, like many other Catholic women religious at
the time, made the case that the exclusively male prophets and princes of the
church had distorted the word of God.[86]

Louisiana Catholics who believed in a greater role for women within the religion continued to argue their case.[87] Many sisters from Louisiana attended the
Women's Ordination Conference in Detroit in November 1975. Most of the male
clergy who wrote for the New Orleans archdiocesan newspaper, the *Clarion
Herald*, said not only that ordination of women to the priesthood was right but
also that it was only a matter of time (a rather short time, in their view) before
it came to pass. Unfortunately, those hopes were dashed when, shortly after the
Detroit conference, the National Conference of Bishops once again affirmed the
proscription against women's ordination, and in 1977 the Vatican issued a declaration against it.[88]

Religious orders also sent delegates to represent them at the International Women's Year conferences in Baton Rouge and Houston in 1977, where they backed most planks in the National Plan of Action. The resolution in support of lesbian rights passed without amendment, and every member of the Louisiana delegation—including Catholic sisters—voted in favor of it.[89]

Another Catholic woman who had taken vows of poverty, chastity, and obedience and who dedicated herself to women's equality was Janet Mary Riley, an attorney and the first female professor on the law faculty at Loyola University in New Orleans. Riley was a member of a pontifical secular institute, the Society of Our Lady of the Way.[90] Unlike women religious, who advertised their membership in an order by wearing habits, secular institutes encouraged "the law of discretion," whereby members kept their vows secret if making membership in the society known would hinder their apostolate.

Her dedication to this group helps explain Riley's life of service to others. Among other things, she spearheaded the campaign to reform the head-and-master provision of the Louisiana Civil Code. Since 1808, the civil code had designated the husband the head and master (also sometimes referred to as "lord and master"), which meant he had the right to control, manage, and alienate the community property without his wife's consent.[91] As a *feme sole*, the reform of the matrimonial regimes system, to which she devoted many uncompensated hours and years of her life, did not affect her personally. But she was bothered by the larger moral issue of inequality and the plight of some married women subjected to onerous heads and masters in the 1970s. She regarded the rewriting of the archaic head-and-master provisions of the state's community property regime as her religious and moral responsibility, her duty to God. Her decision to live singly and devote herself to an apostolic mission through her career as a law school professor gave her the inspiration as well as the time to study, to think, and to work for reform because she was not constantly being pulled into a domestic realm by the demands of a husband and children.[92]

Janet Riley was never one to publically oppose her church's position on women's ordination. However, she did quote the passages from Vatican II often used by feminists to justify a greater role for women in the church and society. And after winning passage of the matrimonial regimes reform, she defended the change by quoting Pope John Paul II, who said in 1980 "as part of his year-long series of talks on the theology of marriage and the body, that husbands and wives must treat one another as equals in a mutual, two-sided, sharing, personal relationship." The biblical references to man as "master" of his wife, the pope said, were "dictated by the social marginalization of woman in the conditions of those times." In other words, the oft-cited verse in Genesis where God tells the woman to submit to her husband as her master must be understood as a product of the historical circumstances of the day rather than as "a natural law for all ages." That an unmarried woman (citing an unmarried pope) theorized marriage equality is perhaps puzzling, but as we have learned, freedom from marriage gave Riley and many other unmarried women like her the necessary time to work toward creating a legal framework for equality within marriage, an institution that she herself had forsaken.[93]

Judaism

Not all southern feminists of faith were Christian, of course. Some were ethnically Jewish. Even if they no longer practiced their faith traditions, Jews' cultural commitment to ending oppression affected their worldview in a variety of ways. A central tenet of Judaism is *tikkun olam*, "to repair the world," or to leave it a better place than it was before one's life, and to many Jews in Louisiana, this meant ending sexism as well as racism. Judaism, like Christianity, has more than one branch (Conservative, Orthodox, Reform), and even within those groups there were multiple opinions about women's rights. Orthodox Jews generally did not support gender equality, but most Louisiana (and most southern) Jews are Reform, and Reform Jews have typically been in the forefront of both civil rights and women's rights. To give examples of two forward-thinking social reformers introduced in the previous chapter, Betty Wisdom and her aunt Rosa Keller both acknowledged the positive influence of Reform Judaism in their lives. Rosa's husband was Jewish, and Betty's father was one-fourth Jewish. "He brought us up to be extremely proud of that," Betty said in a 1995 interview. As a result of that religious heritage, she continued, "neither of my parents were haters." Her parents found the attitude of white supremacists "repugnant." Jewish women or women with ties to Judaism (as in Wisdom's case) were overrepresented among white women in the black freedom movement and in the women's movement.[94]

While Rosa Keller and Betty Wisdom were most associated with reform movements that predated feminism, numerous Jewish women in Louisiana joined or assisted the independent feminist movement. Among them were Karen Davis, Sue Munaker (a northerner who spent about a year in New Orleans), Sandy Karp, Evi Seidman, Felicia Kahn, Flo Schornstein, and Dorothy "Dottie" Zellner. Zellner, born in the North, was a "red diaper" baby (a child of Old Left radicals) who learned from her immigrant parents a working-class Jewish radicalism.[95] In 1960, Zellner joined the Congress of Racial Equality (CORE) and assisted with the sit-in movement in New Orleans. Zellner reported that she found the rabbis quite conservative. When she approached Rabbi Jules Feibelman at the largest synagogue in New Orleans, Temple Sinai, and asked for public support for the black freedom struggle from the Jewish community, "he sputtered that the Jewish community was already insecure and couldn't support an action as controversial as a sit-in and then ordered [her] out of his office."[96] Liberal or radical Jewish activism in Louisiana was far more likely to come from Jewish women, and in particular the National Council of Jewish Women (NCJW), than it was from rabbis.[97]

Founded in Chicago in 1893, the NCJW was a Jewish effort akin to the Social Gospel movement. Jewish women in New Orleans, which had by far the largest Jewish population of any Louisiana city, formed a local branch of NCJW in 1897. Jewish women in other Louisiana cities eventually followed suit, if or when their temple populations became large enough. In Shreveport, a commercial center on the Red River in northwest Louisiana, the women organized an NCJW chapter in 1919, but the women of Temple Sinai in Lake Charles did not do so until 1948. Because of the small size of the congregation of Temple Sinai, Lake Charles's NCJW chapter was always rather small, and it folded in 1966. This was probably more common than the New Orleans experience, where the NCJW reported 1,400 members in 1975; its vigorous chapter supplied more than one national NCJW president over its history.[98]

Nationally, the NCJW adopted a liberal agenda that local chapters followed. As a body, the NCJW, which in 1970 claimed 110,000 members across the United States, opposed nuclear weapons, McCarthyism (the anti-Communist witch hunt that had targeted more than a few Jews), and the Vietnam War. The national board advocated civil rights for all Americans and supported workplace rights and economic justice issues. Though the NCJW had traditionally opposed the ERA because it threatened protective legislation for women, it changed its position in 1970 and endorsed the amendment at its national convention. The New Orleans chapter supported the national agenda, but at the state level, its members were most active in lobbying for the ERA, state support for day care for working mothers, and reproductive choice for all women. The New Orleans chapter, like the national board, was actively pro-choice. In the early 1970s, it was the largest donor to Louisiana's Clergy Counseling Service (the subject of chapter 5), which counseled women with problem pregnancies and explained the options available to them, including abortion. As will be discussed in chapter 6, it was a major supporter of the first rape crisis service in New Orleans.[99]

Members of the NCJW were archetypical Louisiana feminists. Generally well-placed and fashionably dressed, they came to feminism from a religious commitment to social justice. They were broad-minded and well educated and took pains to increase their knowledge about women's rights at home and around the world. NCJW members read and reported at chapter meetings about the status of women in other countries. This global outlook was common among feminists in Louisiana, although for those who were not churched, broadmindedness and a transnational perspective came from influences that we will explore further in later chapters. Also common among Louisiana feminism was anti-imperialism, and the NCJW was on record as endorsing anticolonialism. In addition to raising money for Israel, local chapters often solicited funds in support of freedom movements around the world.[100]

Felicia Kahn, a graduate of Newcomb and in the 1960s a board member of the Greater New Orleans Council of Jewish Women, exemplifies a Jewish feminist. Like many other Louisiana feminists, Kahn's political involvement began in the LWV. Starting in the 1950s, she served on the board of the New Orleans chapter on and off for twenty years or more. Her lifelong commitment to serve her community continued through the civil rights years, when she worked in voter registration and voter education projects and in the movement to keep the public schools open after they integrated. These activities earned her a reputation as a person who could win the support of both whites and blacks. As a result, she became the first white person on the board of the (black) Dryades Street YMCA when it integrated in 1970.[101] Always very political, she held a number of positions in the state Democratic Party, the IWO, and the New Orleans chapter of the National Women's Political Caucus, which she helped to found in 1972. When the New Orleans NCJW voted to send women to the Louisiana Constitutional Convention of 1973 to ensure that it gave sufficient attention to protecting human rights, especially women's rights, Felicia Kahn was one of the women who attended. She was also an organizer of the Louisiana International Women's Year Conference held in Baton Rouge and a delegate to the Houston conference.[102]

Felicia Kahn's sister-in-law, Flo Schornstein, another graduate of Newcomb College, well represents the confluence between devotion to a faith tradition and civic activism. Schornstein has served as president of the New Orleans NCJW, president of the Southern District of NCJW, a national NCJW board member, and an honorary vice president. As was the case with many other women who supported feminism in the 1970s, it was not her sole cause. She attacked oppression and abuse on many fronts and even serves as a role model for "ecofeminism," a respect for the environment that many feminists have embraced. A short list of her civic involvement includes service to the board of the Jewish Community Center, the New Orleans Urban League, the City of New Orleans Human Relations Committee, the Dryades Street YMCA, and the Women's Division of the Jewish Welfare Fund. Her paying jobs include executive director of the Touro Infirmary Foundation and director of the City of New Orleans Department of Parks and Parkways in the 1970s and 1980s. She is most proud of forming the public-private partnership, Parkway Partners, which works with volunteers to improve and maintain the city's parks, neutral grounds, and urban forests.[103]

Jews such as Dottie Zellner and Sandy Karp who joined the autonomous women's movement in New Orleans were more likely to come from working-class backgrounds than were members of NCJW. Yet even these radicals, who espoused some version of socialism, were upwardly mobile and well educated. Perhaps they were no longer practicing Jews, but they had taken from their Jewish heritage a strong commitment to freeing all humans from systems of oppression, a principle they continued to act on all their lives.

Those faith traditions that had their roots in Europe—Presbyterianism, Episcopalianism, Catholicism, Unitarianism, Judaism, and Methodism—were most likely to produce feminist critiques of church and of society. These religions encouraged broad-mindedness, tolerance of differences, education, and rational inquiry. They also had deeply rooted traditions of service ministries and of both home and foreign missions, which tended to produce a global outlook.

The Christian denominations least likely to produce political feminists or to produce a feminist critique of religious leadership, dogma, and structure were those that were more parochial in membership and in outlook, such as Southern Baptists. The exceptions to this are the African American Baptist churches, of which Rupert Richardson and George Ethel Warren were both members. Both women were prominent leaders and considered themselves feminists, but Warren, at least, was unhappy that her denomination restricted the role of women. She stopped attending her church, Tulane Avenue Memorial Baptist Church in New Orleans, because it did not allow women in the pulpit. When she died in 1996, her wake was held in that church, but her daughters arranged for a different congregation, Christian Unity Baptist Church, to host the funeral. Rupert Richardson joined Shiloh Baptist Church in Baton Rouge at least in part because it had two women as associate pastors.[104]

Alternative Religions

Conservatives in the United States denounced feminists for being anti-God, antifaith, and antifamily. While a few feminists fit that description, most were put off by the patriarchal nature of traditional institutions, including the family, and sought to create more female-centered ones. Many feminists of the second wave drifted away from the religion of their upbringing because they despised male control of the faith, and some founded or joined entirely new belief systems based loosely on pre-Christian European goddess religions. For example, Starhawk, born of Jewish lineage, helped establish modern Wicca, which emphasized female leadership and female deities, in Los Angeles. Very few Louisiana women became Wiccans, and those who did were not politically active feminists. Barbara Melançon Trahan and her partner, Tahnya Giordano, opened Mystic Moon, a feminist and Wiccan bookstore in New Orleans in the 1980s.[105] It was a meeting place for the small number of women interested in Wicca.

Not all female-dominated traditions are Wiccan or European in origin, however, as Luisha Teish, a native of New Orleans, makes clear in *Jambalaya: The Natural Woman's Book of Personal Charms and Practical Rituals*. Teish researched this book because she wanted "to reclaim women's knowledge and power" by rejecting the patriarchal religions and returning to a more nature-centered "WomanSpirit movement." Teish, who did not participate in the Louisiana feminist movement, "shows how the Caribbean and West African traditions she grew up with in New Orleans provided access to a worldview devoid of patriarchal dualisms."[106] She along with many other women in search of spiritual roots helped to revive interest in woman-centered traditions that had been suppressed and forgotten by most. One such tradition is voodoo. No politically active feminist in Louisiana in the 1970s was motivated by or even involved with voodoo, but it is such an endless source of fascination and curiosity today that it was important to address the question of whether voodoo had any place in the modern women's rights movement in Louisiana history.

The Catholic Church and secular authorities had forced voodoo underground in the nineteenth century, fearing its power among African Americans. Since the 1970s, however, a virtual cult has emerged around the figure of Marie Laveau, the legendary voodoo queen of the nineteenth century. Laveau is the subject of three recent book-length studies by scholars Carolyn Morrow Long, Martha Ward, and Ina Fandrich. Contrary to earlier, racist and sexist interpretations that denounced Laveau as a prostitute, a snake handler, a devil worshiper, a cannibal, a witch, or a sorcerer, these authors portray her as the well-respected priestess of a legitimate religion that, due to its fluid and place-based nature, allowed female practitioners a great deal of autonomy. One of those authors, Martha Ward, is a feminist and a professor of anthropology at UNO who established the Women's Studies program there in the 1980s. Unlike male-dominated religions characterized by rigorous dogma and rigid hierarchies, voodoo, she says, is a fluid and spontaneous practice devoted to caring for the marginal and the dispossessed.[107] Ward has begun learning its practice, but she is also a regular churchgoer, a member of Grace United Methodist Church in New Orleans. While there are voodoo priestesses in New Orleans today, nearly all—perhaps all—come from outside the city.[108]

In Louisiana—and presumably throughout much of the south—New Age religions had relatively shallow roots and were typically short-lived. Traditional Western religious beliefs provided the moral framework that led women to feminism. Southern women from the liberal faith traditions turned their religious convictions into activism as they sought remedies for injustices against all women, not just women of their own religion, class, or ethnic background. Two of the most important of those, Mary King and Casey Hayden, wrote an influential manifesto that generated CR sessions nationwide. Their story interweaves Louisiana with other states in the Deep South, particularly Texas and Mississippi, with international intellectual currents, religious influences, and the impact of African Americans. New Orleans sat at the confluence of all those influences, and it is there that some of the first stirrings of grassroots feminism emerged. How and why that happened in the mid-1960s is the subject of the next chapter.

CHAPTER 3

"Their Courage Inspired Me"

Black and White Gulf Coast Women and

Grassroots Feminism, 1960–1968

In the days before the Internet and cell phones, ideas circulated among social movement activists via mimeographed position papers and newsletters as well as by travel to meetings.[1] Conferences served a dual purpose: the exchange of information and rest. Movement leaders looked for safe spaces where they could convene in seclusion and peace, far from the stress, frustration, and hidden dangers that activism wrought. Among their favorite spots were churches and church-affiliated retreat centers, especially those associated with the YM or YWCA or with the Methodist Church. The gathering that ignited the women's liberation (WL) movement occurred when SNCC, seeking to put some space between its staffers and volunteers and the outside world, chose the Gulfside Methodist Assembly grounds in Waveland, Mississippi, for its November 1964 retreat. Out of this meeting would emerge a grassroots WL movement in the United States.

Several white women from Louisiana attended "the Waveland meeting," as it is usually called, including Cathy Cade and Kathryn "Kathy" Barrett. The Louisiana women were deeply affected by what transpired there and left the retreat energized and emboldened by a position paper, "Women in the Movement," written by two SNCC staffers, Mary King and Sandra "Casey" Hayden. This paper, which has since become somewhat famous, critiqued the treatment of women in SNCC by the organizations' male leaders. For Kathy Barrett, a paid organizer for the Southern Student Organizing Committee (SSOC), the ideas in the paper instantly clicked. She brought a copy back to New Orleans with her, "eager to pursue the issue of women's role in society and in the movement." She called a meeting of female activists from many organizations operating in the city, including the SSOC, the Southern Conference Education Fund (SCEF), Students for a Democratic Society (SDS), SNCC, and CORE, and shared the memo with those who assembled. As it had for Barrett, the paper sparked emotion and excitement among the women, who wanted to continue meeting together—without men—to discuss it. The meetings of these women in New Orleans may well have been the first CR sessions anywhere in the country. It is no accident that the memo and the WL groups that developed around it were the product of a three-day retreat at an African American refuge on the Mississippi Gulf Coast.[2]

To southern historians, "place"—which someone has defined as geography with feeling—matters. Place matters for this book in its foregrounding of the South in the national narrative of the women's movement, and it matters for this chapter in elevating the role of New Orleans and the nearby Mississippi Gulf Coast in that movement. The 1964 SNCC retreat brought together white and black southerners who had experiences and understandings of oppression and injustice unique to this region. The confluence produced a pivotal document of the modern women's movement, and once again, religion—particularly Methodism—was critical to the mixture.

The Mississippi Gulf Coast had served as a summer escape for white New Orleans residents fleeing fetid drinking water and disease-producing swamps ever since a railroad connected the city with the seashore in 1869. But while Bay St. Louis, Pass Christian, and nearby Waveland had become fashionable sites for summer homes of superrich white elites, Gulfside was a modest and affordable retreat center for African Americans, the only one of its kind on the Gulf Coast. It was the brainchild of the gifted and indefatigable Robert E. Jones, the first black bishop of the Methodist Church.[3]

Robert Jones, born in Greensboro, North Carolina, moved to New Orleans following his graduation from Gammon Theological Seminary in Atlanta in 1897 and soon became well known in the city for social justice leadership on behalf of his race. "He was instrumental in the formation of the city's first Colored YMCA" and in "every big race movement in New Orleans," according to the NAACP's *Crisis* magazine. Committed to increasing racial understanding and mitigating white prejudice and hostility, Jones was confident that the Methodist Episcopal Church (which, it will be remembered, had both white and black divisions) could be "a forum for racial understanding and a venue where the best of both races could come to understand each other better." A retreat center on the Gulf Coast could facilitate this process, Jones believed. As bishop, Jones presided over black Methodists in a district spanning West Texas, Louisiana, and Mississippi. From his headquarters in New Orleans, he frequently traveled to Bay St. Louis for his job and to visit his wife's family. While en route, he scouted a possible location for a beach resort for African Americans. When he learned that a crumbling old mansion near Waveland, owned by the Deblieux family, was for sale, he knew he had found just the right spot. Jones raised the money for the down payment, cultivated relationships with local white bankers and civic leaders, and acquired the loans and the property, which he subsequently donated to the Gulfside Association. To purchase the property without arousing the suspicion or ire of local whites, Jones, who was mixed race, hid his African American heritage. He was frequently mistaken for white, and he "passed" when it served his people and his mission to do so. There was no better time when strategic passing was called for than this, Jones believed, for he was hopeful that this land would serve not just as a resort for African Americans seeking a relaxing vacation by the seashore but that it would also be a safe haven where progressive people could gather, without fear, and map a better future for black America.[4]

The Gulfside Chautauqua and Camp Meeting Grounds opened in 1927. For the next few decades, it more than fulfilled Jones's dream of serving as a sanctuary from racism. It proved invaluable to the black freedom movement. For example, Constance Baker Motley developed her strategy for desegregating the University of Mississippi in retreat at Gulfside, and Thurgood Marshall met there with NAACP lawyers. It also organized freedom schools and thereby became the logical choice for SNCC's strategy meeting in 1964. Kathy Barrett, like many Louisiana women involved in jump-starting the grassroots feminist movement, attended that meeting because she had a network of acquaintances in civil rights circles. Furthermore, Waveland was but a short fifty-five-mile train ride from her home in New Orleans. Revolutionary ideas moved across that railroad line along with her.[5]

Barrett was primed to do something with King and Hayden's position paper. Born in Baton Rouge to Catholic parents, she had moved to New Orleans in 1963 to attend Loyola University. Uncomfortable with the all-white student body's racism and conservatism, however, she dropped out in 1964 to become a full-time campus traveler for the SSOC, a white organization dedicated to combating racism among whites. The SSOC maintained close contacts with SNCC and CORE in Mississippi and Louisiana, and Barrett knew many of the activists in those organizations. Some of the women in their circle had already begun questioning the role of women in the movement, Barrett remembers, which is why the memo struck such a chord with her. When she returned from Gulfside, she called those women together to discuss the gendered nature of power. The group included several native Louisianans, a few Tulane students, and a couple of northern white women who had come south to work with SNCC in Freedom

Summer 1964. Activist experiences had given them an understanding of oppression that the average white Louisiana woman lacked.[6]

The same can be said of one of the paper's authors, Sandra "Sandy" Cason, from little Victoria, Texas, for whom YWCA and civil rights experiences were formative. Cason had attended the University of Texas at Austin, where she worked for the student Y and became involved in interracial activities in the 1950s. Finding her classes at the university boring and unfulfilling, she chose to live off campus in a racially integrated one-of-a-kind Christian Faith-and-Life Community (CFLC), where she and the other sixty or so male and female members (living in sex-segregated dormitories) became part of the new Christian left. The students pored over the writings of theologians who had inspired the Social Gospel half a century earlier and also works that were new or newly rediscovered, among them the writings of Danish religious philosopher Søren Kierkegaard (1813–55), widely regarded as the founder of Christian existentialism.[7] Existentialism has no agreed-upon definition, but it typically refers to the quest for a life of meaning. For some, this is a mystical or spiritual search; for others, it may be entirely cognitive. For most people, it is both.[8] This blend of Social Gospel and Christian existentialist theology led Casey Hayden and others in the Christian left to the belief, as her biographer puts it, that "being Christian meant recognizing that all humans—white and non-white—were equal in God's eyes and accepting responsibility for helping the disadvantaged."[9]

The leadership philosophy of W. Jack Lewis, CFLC's founder and a Presbyterian minister, also had an impact on Hayden and the grassroots feminist movement that she helped to ignite. As someone who believed in religious leadership of the laity, Lewis encouraged community students to intensive study and had the students read and discuss the activist German theologians Dietrich Bonhoeffer and Reinhold Niebuhr.[10] He also encouraged them to dedicate themselves to aiding "the starving, the sick, the estranged, the oppressed, and the imprisoned." Casey Hayden said that the CFLC provided a powerful model of a "beloved community," stating, "I experienced the creation of empowering community, and within it an image of myself, in terms of which I then lived. Later, I understood the movement on this model. Our image of ourselves in the southern Freedom Movement was that of the Beloved Community, created by the activity, the experience, of nonviolent direct action against injustice."[11] The "beloved community" idea flowed through religious groups such as the CFLC and the YWCA—where "living-room dialogues" and the like approximated similar attempts at understanding—into the freedom movement, particularly SNCC, and into the new WL movement, where, in CR groups, women arrived at a political understanding of oppression within a supportive community of other women.

The grassroots feminist movement that she helped inspire also bore the mark of Casey Hayden's interest in the writings of French philosopher Albert Camus. Algerian-born Camus had been active in the resistance to French colonialism in his native land and had originally seen the Communist Party as the best hope for colonial independence. However, he turned against Communism after learning of the brutality of the Stalinist purges and was expelled from the party in 1937. He moved to France, where he befriended Jean-Paul Sartre and Simone de Beauvoir for a time, although they eventually had an intellectual falling-out. Camus devoted himself to the cause of international human rights, personally demonstrating his conviction "that humans give meaning to their lives through action against injustice." In *The Rebel: An Essay on Man in Revolt* (1951), he honored the role of the countercultural rebel on a search for justice. Casey Cason found inspiration in Camus' "insistence that such action was even more meaningful when undertaken without expectation of success, since this acknowledged that action derived its moral value from resisting oppression rather than from eliminating the injustice." Camus and Bonhoeffer taught the students that "the way to be human was to refuse to be complicit" with evil.[12] This, in addition to her experience of racism in Texas, moved Casey Hayden to commit herself to ending oppression of any kind.

The YWCA was key to Casey's mental and activist growth, as it was for many other southern feminists. After graduating from the University of Texas in 1959, Cason (not yet Hayden) moved to Harlem to continue interracial work with the YWCA. When the sit-in movement spread across the South, she returned to Austin to participate in those direct actions along with her African American friends from the CFLC. Recruited by Constance Curry to attend the National Student Association's (NSA) Southern Student Human Relations conference in Minneapolis, she gave a talk that pricked the moral conscience of her audience and drew the attention of the man who would become her husband, Tom Hayden. As the two became closer, she familiarized Hayden with the writings of Camus. The intellectual exchange forever changed Tom Hayden's vision and life's mission.[13]

Upon her return to the University of Texas in 1960, Casey Cason met Ella Baker, cofounder of SNCC, who encouraged her to continue antiracist work on several fronts. Hayden, like King, credited Baker with helping them understand the principles of radical democratic organizing. Though hardly radical, Cason's efforts to desegregate the university and local facilities that refused to serve blacks brought her national acclaim, including an article in the *New York Times* and a personal letter from Eleanor Roosevelt. In 1961, she moved to New York to be closer to Tom Hayden. They soon married in a ceremony in Austin at the Christian Faith-and-Life-Community. The two fellow activists shared ideas and organizational ties. Casey served on the national executive committee of SDS and together with Tom attended an SDS meeting at the end of December 1961, in Port Huron, Michigan. Though Hayden never gave her credit, Casey not only typed but helped to draft SDS's most famous work, the Port Huron Statement. It reflects a variety of influences, including works of Karl Marx, C. Wright Mills, and John Dewey, but it also reflects the expression of Christian existentialism that Casey learned at CFLC in Texas.[14]

The Port Huron meeting also resulted in an impromptu proto-feminist CR session that helped to shape Casey Hayden's emerging gender consciousness and would greatly influence the position paper that circulated at the Waveland meeting. On New Year's Eve 1961, she and the other women conferees, troubled at the men's tendency to dismiss the women's viewpoints and refusal to allow them to make decisions within the group, met to discuss their concerns. The men did not take this critique of their behavior lightly and treated the women hostilely thereafter. Indeed, the tension over this issue destroyed Casey's marriage to Tom Hayden. (They separated in 1963 and divorced in 1965.)[15] This first discussion of the gendered nature of power, wherein the women considered how the personal became political, was the taproot of a nascent WL movement. Though the meeting was in the North, its primary intellectual influence came from southern liberals steeped in existentialist Christian theology.

After she and Tom Hayden split, Casey moved to Atlanta in 1963 to take a job assisting James Foreman, SNCC's executive secretary, in fund-raising and recruiting volunteers. Because she had been trained by the YWCA to organize and administer programs, and because she had contact with the kind of students who were likely to support SNCC, she was a perfect fit for the job. While in Atlanta, she met and befriended Mary King, who also worked for SNCC. Mary, the product of six generations of Virginia ministers, shared Casey's interest in the writings of Camus and the works of European feminists. King's father, a Methodist minister, had trained at Union Theological Seminary under the liberal religious philosophers Paul Tillich (1886–1965) and Reinhold Niebuhr. From her father, King gained a lifelong commitment to social justice causes.[16]

The Second Sex and *The Golden Notebook*

In addition to liberal theologians, King, Hayden, and some Louisiana feminists of the early to mid-1960s took intellectual inspiration from Simone de Beauvoir and Doris Lessing. Mary King wrote, "Casey [Hayden] and I had an insatiable appetite for these two authors [Lessing and Beauvoir] and especially for Beauvoir's global perspective." Betty Friedan's *The Feminine Mystique*, on the other hand, "seemed irrelevant and marginal to us. . . . It was amazing to us that black

women in the United States were not cited once. Our own civil rights movement was not mentioned, even though it was then roiling the structures of the
South." But their copy of Beauvoir's influential *The Second Sex* "was underlined,
creased, marked up, and finally coverless from [their] study of it." Likewise, one
Louisiana feminist said that Beauvoir and Lessing were more important to her
than Betty Friedan because *The Feminine Mystique* "didn't resemble [their] lives
because it didn't account for the lives of working women, southern women, or
black women."[17]

Beauvoir's *The Second* Sex was published in 1955, Lessing's *The Golden Note-*
book in 1962, and Betty Friedan's treatise on domesticity, *The Feminine Mystique*,
in 1963. While Friedan's book, a best seller, deserves credit for raising the consciousness of a portion of the well-placed, affluent white women of the nation,
it did not spark a grassroots feminist movement. Friedan did not call for any
collective action on the part of unfulfilled and discontented women suffering
from the malaise produced by the idealized "feminine mystique." It was southern women, borrowing the techniques of "participatory democracy" that they
learned in SNCC and based on the principles of Christian existentialism, who
did that.

Lessing and Beauvoir resonated with southern women because those two
authors drew on the experience of military occupation—of their homeland or
of colonized others—as they developed sympathy for the oppressed. Doris Lessing (1919–2013), born in Iran to British parents, was a daughter of the colonizers. She grew up in Rhodesia (today Zimbabwe) and went to school in Salzburg,
Germany, before ending up in a small London flat, divorced with a young child.
There she hosted a steady stream of scholars and leftist intellectuals in a kind
of working-class salon. She had sexual relationships with many of the men,
among them Nelson Algren, an American best known as the author of *The Man*
with the Golden Arm. (Algren, to whom we will return in a moment, also had an
intense and long-lasting love affair with Simone de Beauvoir.) One of her admir-
ers described Lessing's semiautobiographical novel *The Golden Notebook* (1962)
as "the single most important work of feminist fiction in this century."[18] Often
cited as the first feminist novel, it broke new ground in exploring issues that
women in the United States were not used to critically evaluating—marriage,
motherhood, and female friendships—or even to discussing, such as sexual
freedom and fulfillment. The novel's protagonist, Anna Wulf (widely regarded
as Lessing's alter ego), was promiscuous, and many of her paramours were married men. Lessing allowed her protagonist the kind of sexual autonomy that
had long been common among male heroes but had been largely untouched
by women writing about women. Lessing's exploration of the erotic drew the
readership of young women on both sides of the Atlantic. Her theme of mean-

ingful work and women's search for wholeness was equally as thrilling for this generation of young women.[19]

In her later years, Lessing denounced European feminists and said it was "stupid" to see *The Golden Notebook* as a feminist novel. She was simply writing about her own experiences, she insisted, and was amazed that people found a woman's voice so shocking. In a 1982 interview with Terry Gross on NPR/WHYY's *Fresh Air*, Lessing connected the second-wave feminist movement with intellectual trends emanating from the European left in the decades that preceded it when she claimed that her friends and comrades had been discussing in the 1940s and 1950s the ideas she wrote about in *The Golden Notebook*. The women who called themselves the "second wave" only thought they had discovered those ideas, but she and her friends "had been discussing them for years." She also insisted that her mother had been a feminist, and that she had brought her daughter up with feminist ideas. In other words, the feminist movement was not new at all. She was arguing, however, that its origins were in the European (secular) left, not in the American South.[20]

Meanwhile, Beauvoir's controversial book, *The Second Sex*, a long, rambling, difficult work published in France in 1949, had also created a sensation. Blanche Knopf, wife of the publisher Alfred A. Knopf, knowing that existentialism was all the rage among American college students at the time, picked up a copy while in France and pushed her husband to publish an English translation. Unhappy that Knopf wanted to condense it, Beauvoir refused to work with translator H. M. Parshley, and as a result, the English-language version that appeared in the United States in 1953 contained a number of mistranslations and omissions.[21] On both sides of the Atlantic, critics denounced both its author and her arguments.

Beauvoir sought to deflect the hostility she encountered on a daily basis by claiming that Jean-Paul Sartre, her philosophical partner and lifelong companion, was the true source of the revolutionary ideas in *The Second Sex*. She downplayed her creative intelligence, claiming repeatedly that she, unlike Sartre, was not a real philosopher. But private papers and letters released after Beauvoir's death in 1986 make clear that theories about women's oppression expressed in *The Second Sex* were Beauvoir's and that she developed the idea of woman as "other" at least partly due to her association with Americans. During her fifteen-year long-distance love affair with Algren, Beauvoir visited and toured the United States frequently, once stopping in New Orleans. (The sultry heat did not agree with her, and she never went back.) Having lived under German occupation twice in her life, Beauvoir sympathized with subjugated people such as African Americans in the United States. Her curiosity was aroused by the systematic, intense racism she witnessed on her travels, and she acquired a copy

of *An American Dilemma* (1944), the massive and influential study of race relations compiled by Swedish economist Gunnar Myrdal. The volume included an
appendix written by his wife, Alva Myrdal, titled "A Parallel to the Negro Problem." *The American Dilemma* inspired Beauvoir to write a comparable book
about women because she found that "Myrdal point[ed] to many very interest-
ing analogies between Negroes' and women's status."[22] Thus there is yet another
important female-to-female transmission of ideas: Alva Myrdal first compared
women and blacks. Beauvoir picked up on that idea and universalized it, fil-
tering it through her own experiences with defeat, conquest, oppression, and
powerlessness.

Richard Wright's novels *Native Son* and *Black Boy* also had a profound effect
on Beauvoir. She knew Wright, a native of Mississippi, and his white wife, Ellen,
through Algren, who introduced them. The Wrights eventually moved to France
and became part of Beauvoir's intellectual circle. Their experiences as an interracial couple encouraged Beauvoir to see how white men had relegated both
black men and all women into a position of otherness. Beauvoir cites both
Wright and the Myrdals in *The Second Sex*.[23]

Thus the concept of otherness that permeated *The Second Sex* came in part
from Beauvoir's philosophy education, her connection to French thinkers
including Camus and Sartre, and her experiences with racism in the American
South. The last explains why the book resonated among southern white women
working in the black freedom movement in Louisiana, Mississippi, Georgia,
Texas, and elsewhere in the Deep South: they could relate to it because it was
about them. The transnational movement of ideas had come full circle without
any of the participants really knowing it, literally flowing through the bodies of
Americans such as Algren and Wright, Lessing and Beauvoir, from the United
States, across the Atlantic, and back to the United States again, much enriched
by its intellectual journey.

Beauvoir's powerful concepts informed many leaders of the WL movement
besides King and Hayden. Kathie Sarachild, who also worked in the SNCC
Mississippi Freedom Summer Project, cited *The Second Sex* as the source of
her radical feminist views. In 1975, she wrote that Beauvoir was "the French
woman who exposed male supremacy for this era and gave us our feminism."
Ti-Grace Atkinson, Roxanne Dunbar, and Shulamith Firestone also credited
her. Indeed, Firestone dedicated *The Dialectic of Sex* to her feminist hero, and
Betty Friedan (*The Feminine Mystique*) and Kate Millett (*Sexual Politics*) relied
heavily on *The Second Sex*. But for all of Beauvoir's brilliant insights, her book
stopped short of advocating action. That first call for women to come together
and analyze their oppression came from the King-Hayden memo; the models
for that action were native to the South: Ella Baker and the black female freedom fighters in SNCC.[24]

The memo was the result of escalating tensions between whites and blacks within SNCC. Among other things, black workers were upset about the Democratic Party's failure to seat the Mississippi Freedom Democratic Party at the 1964 convention and were considering ousting all white workers. In fact, that would happen shortly. King and Hayden, who had dedicated their social activism to the cause of civil rights, found this prospect devastating. They were particularly upset that black women would, in their view, turn against them because they had long had deep respect for the "competent young black women" who worked to register voters in some of the most intractably white supremacist states from Louisiana to Virginia. Ordinary southern black women, as well as more famous African American women with whom they had worked, like Ella Baker, Diane Nash, and Ruby Doris Smith Robinson, had been their role models. Women, Mary King wrote, "were the backbone of organizing all over the south."[25] King and Hayden hoped that the position paper would help heal the rift between blacks and whites. In sisterhood, they thought, they might again find solidarity across the color line.[26] They circulated the memo anonymously, afraid that it would cause mockery (which it did). Though the goal was to reach out to black women, with a few exceptions, most black women in SNCC responded with "indifference or antagonism."[27] Some black women had always felt empowered, at least in part because they contributed economically to the family's household income. They did not appreciate the white women's complaints about "their men's" treatment of white women in the movement.[28] They had bigger fish to fry and continued organizing their communities.

In 1965, King and Hayden circulated a longer memo to forty-four other women activists in progressive organizations with whom they had worked, hoping to generate a conversation. They did not envision that it would touch off a movement that would soon be known as "women's liberation." They titled this one "Sex and Caste," in part because the terms "gender" and "sexism" were not in wide currency yet, and in part because they were familiar with the Hindu caste system, a type of social structure into which one was born and from which a person could not escape. In yet another example of the transnational movement of ideas ending up in an influential southern manifesto, the "caste" analogy occurred to King and Hayden because people who had worked with Gandhi in the independence movement in India had trained civil rights workers. Simone de Beauvoir also used the term "caste" in *The Second Sex*. Hayden biographer Harold Smith describes the differences between this memo, much longer than the first, and the original: "It differed from their previous memo in being written solely for women, in critiquing women's subordinate position throughout society rather than in just one organization, in insisting that personal relationships were political, and in attempting to create a women's network to address women's issues." This time they signed their names.[29]

Black women ignored this memo, much as they did the first one, but it had tremendous appeal among young white women activists. "'Sex and Caste' was a watershed in women's history," writes Harold Smith, "in part because it challenged the widespread assumptions that female subordination was the 'natural order of things' and that personal relationships were not politically significant."[30] The authors concluded that "the problems between men and women" and the difficulty women experienced in functioning in society as equal human beings were "among the most basic that people face," and raised the possibility of a women's movement to address these concerns.[31] That last part distinguishes the King-Hayden manifesto from both *The Second Sex* and Betty Friedan's *The Feminine Mystique*, which issued no call for women to unite against their oppressors. When *Liberation* magazine, published by the tiny War Resisters League, printed the memo in April 1966, the results were explosive. As Mary King interpreted the phenomenon, "With widening distribution and study, it was often employed as a kickoff for consciousness-raising groups in what would become a grass-roots women's movement across the country."[32] That memo, in the words of Clayborne Carson, a historian of the civil rights movement, became "an opening salvo of the feminist movement of the 1960s."[33]

Though King and Hayden would no longer work for SNCC, the women's movement that they helped to ignite (but did not join) benefited a great deal from the crossover of personnel with SNCC. Feminism borrowed from SNCC and from Martin Luther King's Southern Christian Leadership Council the tactic of nonviolence, which was important to the WL movement as it was to the black movement because, as Mohandas Gandhi insisted, nonviolent civil protest can be undertaken by people of any abilities. It does not require strength and is therefore inherently democratic. Old people, women, and children can engage in nonviolent protest. Radical democratic organizing techniques, participatory democracy, direct action (putting one's body on the line), and attempts at sisterhood across class and ethnic lines were all strategies that originated in SNCC. Such endeavors were not always successful, but in the name of gender solidarity, white women tried hard to bridge historic, yawning gaps between women caused by racial and class differences.

The Personal Is Political

One of the people who joined Kathy Barrett's CR group was Dorothy "Dottie" Zellner, a Jewish woman married to Bob Zellner, a white Methodist SNCC fieldworker. The couple had two small children, but they did not share child care or parenting responsibilities equally. Dottie received the memo while she and Bob were living in New Orleans, where they regrouped with others following the intense, stressful, and dangerous voting rights drives in Mississippi and rural Louisiana. Zellner reported later that she was skeptical about the idea of woman's oppression at first and had to be dragged "kicking and screaming" to the first "rap session" in New Orleans. She believed that the focus on women distracted from the mission of civil rights, and she did not (yet) understand that women suffered from institutional and systemic oppression. Movement people did not talk about personal matters such as who diapered the babies or arranged for child care while parents worked on getting African Americans registered to vote. There were more important problems to grapple with than these, Zellner argued. Disputes about the division of labor in one's household and decision-making power in one's personal relationships had no place in these discussions, she believed. Indeed, it was a result of Zellner's argument about this very question with Carol Hanisch, a friend and fellow civil rights worker living in Gainesville, that Hanisch wrote the famous memo "The Personal Is Political," which became the slogan of the new movement.[34]

The women in New Orleans and Gainesville, in other words, groping for a way to articulate their angst about the existing order, coined a phrase to describe what Betty Friedan had called "the problem that has no name." Far from being a personal sense of dissatisfaction with one's life, a neurosis, or differences in body mass and strength, "the problem" was gender discrimination created by social norms. It was both intensely personal and necessarily political, for it involved a restructuring of thought, cultural values, and laws to resolve. Reading "Sex and Caste," women all over the country eagerly discussed the personal issues the memo raised. In these CR sessions, women began to see that gender inequality permeated their households, marriages, and jobs as well as the institutions to which they belonged (and often dearly loved) such as universities, churches, and male-run activist organizations such as SNCC and SDS. When they realized that their experiences were not unique to them (a "click" moment), they began to understand the political nature of women's second-class status. In CR groups, women sought an understanding of shared circumstances within a "beloved community" of other women. They discussed each other's personal circumstances and debated the mimeographed papers emanating from similar circles around the country. Louisiana feminists produced some of their own position papers, as well.[35]

The WL wing of the feminist movement emerged from CR groups in New Orleans. Like the black freedom movement from which it sprang, WL emphasized a radical participatory democracy (meaning no one person was ever the leader) and direct action techniques. For the most part, the women's liberationists were younger than the women described in the previous two chapters who came to feminism from church work and single-sex organizations like the

LWV. For the most part, their brand of feminism remained separate and apart from the more mainstream feminist organizations like NOW, although, as we will learn in chapter 7, the New Orleans women also cooperated on a number of initiatives.[36]

Community Education

Through civil rights work, early women's liberationists found one another in New Orleans, and more people found these young feminists through a "free university" course that Kathy Barrett and her friends Cathy Cade and Peggy Dobbins, both students at Tulane, developed in 1966. (Dobbins and Barrett knew each other through the SSOC.) Locating anything they could about women's history and sociology, the young women developed the first extracurricular women's studies class in the South and one of the first in the nation. The class, which met for a time in Barrett's living room, drew on earlier models of community education projects in twentieth-century America.[37] Originating with the Old Left in the early 1900s, extracurricular education was based on the idea that the academies served the interests of the ruling class and did not address or even acknowledge the needs, history, or culture of the poor and dispossessed. In yet another example of a son of the South becoming a prophet of oppositional consciousness, Myles Horton, a radical Christian, founded Highlander Folk School in Tennessee in 1932 for precisely that purpose: to help adults (originally, the local people in Appalachia) value their culture and develop organizational strategies for long-term change. Generations of labor and civil rights activists from around the South learned techniques as well as protest songs at Highlander, including Rosa Parks and Martin Luther King.[38] Less well-known but nearly as important was South Carolina teacher Septima Clark, who made "citizenship education a cornerstone of SCLC's [the Southern Christian Leadership Conference's] mobilization strategy," according to her biographer, Katherine Charron.[39] Likewise, SNCC organizer Bob Moses created "freedom schools" during voting rights campaigns in Mississippi and Louisiana, and Kathy Barrett taught in a CORE-sponsored freedom school in New Orleans in 1965. The SCLC-, SNCC-, and CORE-sponsored schools offered African Americans lessons in civics, the U.S. Constitution, and the legal system in the United States. The teachers—all volunteers, black and white—explained to African Americans, most of whom had never voted, how to navigate the tricky registration process.

Citizenship schools operated on the assumption that people who do not know their rights cannot demand redress, and people who had been deprived of their history (particularly the history of activism) are disempowered by that lack of knowledge.[40] Considered a "major achievement" by scholars as well as participants in the civil rights movement, these schools included a gendered dimension that resulted, ironically, from the fact that the most prestigious—but also the most dangerous—assignments (i.e., voter registration) went to male volunteers, while teaching roles were often relegated to female volunteers.[41] Women working in the southern black freedom struggle, then, were more likely than men to carry the model of radical community education into other liberation movements. Louisiana feminists in Mississippi and Louisiana pioneered in applying the principle to women who were in the process of questioning traditional patriarchal structures, including those that guided educational institutions.

The idea of "free universities" taught by volunteers spread among cultural and political dissidents during the 1960s and 1970s. Whether in Berkeley, California, or what began as the New School in New York City, or among civil rights workers in Louisiana and Mississippi, they shared certain commonalities: they challenged the conformist, uncritical, and right-leaning curricula of the universities; they sought to create an egalitarian setting for learning and teaching; they abandoned academic structure and formality; and they created a casual, intimate atmosphere that stimulated free and open discussion. Dedicated to transforming thought as well as action, they helped like-minded individuals find one another and develop a sense of shared values and purpose.[42]

Though they were eventually joined by some faculty and students from UNO, the original attendees in that first free class were white men and women who knew one another from voting rights drives in Mississippi. Besides Cade and Dobbins, Matt Herron, a photographer for SNCC, and his wife, Jeannine, and SNCC field workers Dottie Zellner and Jeannette King attended. Jeannette King, a social worker from Jackson, Mississippi, was married to Ed King, Methodist chaplain at Tougaloo College, a school for African Americans just outside Jackson. The Kings participated in voting-rights campaigns, SNCC, and the Council of Federated Organizations (COFO), as well as the effort to attain recognition for the Mississippi Freedom Democratic Party at the 1964 Democratic Convention.[43]

Cathy Cade, too, had extensive experience with the methods and tactics of the civil rights movement. In the early 1960s, she attended Spelman College, an all-female historically black college in Atlanta, on an exchange program run by the school where she was enrolled, Carleton College in Minnesota. Carleton, a liberal Congregationalist college, operated exchange programs with HBCUs in the United States. One of her classmates at Carleton who joined the same exchange program was Chude Pam Allen, who became one of the founders of the New York Radical Women. At Spelman, Professor Howard Zinn, a leftist pro–civil rights historian and political activist, influenced them enormously.

Finding out what life was like for black women in the American South had a profound effect on both Cade and Allen. With Zinn's encouragement, Cade joined the civil rights crusade swirling around her in Georgia: she assisted SNCC's office in Atlanta and was jailed, along with many others, when she participated in the march for civil rights led by Martin Luther King in Albany. Sitting in jail for nine days in Georgia radicalized her and ensured her commitment to opposing "the establishment," as the sixties generation generally referred to authorities in the United States, be they police, politicians, or college administrators. She took this oppositional consciousness with her into graduate school at Tulane, where she became active in SDS and civil rights efforts. She, like Barrett, understood that women had been denied a history and had received little attention from the academy, and that a course incorporating writings by and for women was long overdue. This first women's studies class in New Orleans, like others that would follow, was important both for personal development and as a means of outreach. Eventually, the model was adopted by the New Orleans Public Library in the 1970s when movement participants went to work there.[44]

Some of those who joined the first CR groups in New Orleans in the mid-1960s were not interested in political battles as much as they wanted to explore possibilities for their lives. But Kathy Barrett believed it critical for women to engage in collective action in order to bring about significant societal and institutional change. Barrett said that CR groups were a "good jumping off point," but she found them ultrademocratic and individualistic and not political enough to do any good. "They became almost like self-help groups," she said, and "dissipated energy" instead of organizing for reform. Having worked for years in the SSOC and on civil rights projects, she understood the need for political strategizing. "My heroes tended to be women leading the human/civil rights struggle," she stated. "As organizers and leaders, their courage inspired me. I wanted to learn from and emulate Ella Baker, Virginia Collins, Fannie Lou Hamer, and Anne Braden."[45]

Kathy Barrett, disgusted with the conservatism and racism of her home state, moved away in 1966, but she left behind an institutional legacy: The course that began in her living room among friends became the inspiration for women's studies programs at UNO and at other New Orleans universities (see chapter 6). Unknown to each other, Peggy Dobbins and Kathy Barrett both moved to New York City. Almost miraculously, they ran into each other on the street one day and ended up joining the same CR group. Both got involved in radical women's liberation, but Barrett soon left New York City for the West Coast. Dobbins stayed in the Big Apple, where she was part of the formation of

New York Radical Women. She also cofounded WITCH (Women's International Terrorist Conspiracy from Hell) and helped organize the feminist protest of the Miss America pageant in 1968. Cathy Cade moved to San Francisco after she graduated in 1970, where she came out as a lesbian and continued to be active in a variety of social justice causes. All these women continued their activism in one form or another in places outside Louisiana, but the early formation of their feminist consciousness came from their years in New Orleans, the crossroads and rendezvous point for southerners seeking respite after exhausting voting rights campaigns and after the stressful Waveland retreat in November 1964.[46]

The SNCC conference at Gulfside brought together in one space black and white women and their intertwined activist lives. The position paper that resulted was the product not just of the experiences of these women; it was also the result of their exposure to European Christian existentialists and Simone de Beauvoir. Notably, none of those influences came from the northern United States. Instead, the most important flow of information may have been from South to North and not just in 1964. When Casey Hayden attended SDS in Michigan, or when she and King mailed their position paper to their network of activists, when women like Peggy Dobbins and Kathy Barrett moved from Louisiana to the more famously feminist urban centers of the North, they brought their ideas and strategies of resistance with them. When women from Louisiana attended the first and second women's liberation conferences (both of which, significantly, were held at religious camps), they shared their experiences with the women assembled there. Southern women, in other words, sometimes exported feminist ideas and methods to northern and western women, rather than the other way around. Because these women tended to shun the limelight, their role in the creation of a national grassroots feminist movement is easily overlooked.[47]

Movements by definition do not exist in isolation. The point of conferences was to share ideas and strategies that the attendees could take back home. Mimeographed position papers and self-published booklets served the same purpose. Sometimes, Louisiana women borrowed extensively from what they were reading or hearing about happening in different places, especially as the 1960s wore on and the movement exploded around the country. But even where Louisiana women learned from the example of women elsewhere, their efforts were still local and homegrown. As such, the movement could look very different not only from one state to the next but also from one town to the next. That is certainly true of the antiviolence effort, to which we turn our attention in the next chapter.

CHAPTER 4

"To Empower Women"

The Crusades against Sexual Assault and
Domestic Violence, 1972–1997

Lafayette, a medium-sized city situated along the Vermilion River in southwestern Louisiana, by 1970 had become the urban center of both Cajun culture and the petrochemical industry in that section of the state. Lafayette's population expanded rapidly along with Gulf Coast oil production. Refineries imported business-minded white-collar males from outside the area as engineers, technicians, and managers and hired local men for heavy, often dangerous, blue-collar labor. Many men, natives as well as outsiders, were deeply invested in this industry, which, by extension, had substantial political influence in both Lafayette and Baton Rouge; its enormous weight, unsurprisingly, caused both cities to lean right.[1] In the midst of this conservative hub, news reporter Kathleen Thames wrote a candid series on sexual violence in 1973 for the *Lafayette Daily Advertiser*. She reported on changes around the country that provided rape survivors with better services than what currently existed in Lafayette, decried the shame of sexual assault and the tendency to blame the victim, and characterized the Lafayette parish coroner, Dr. Henry Voorhies, as unsympathetic and uncooperative. Thames cited compelling evidence: "At a public hearing a couple of years ago, for instance, he commented that a particular woman could not have been raped because she was fat and had pimples. He disagrees with statistics which indicate that nationally only two percent of all reported rapes are unfounded," and said that wasn't true in Louisiana. Dr. Voorhies expressed views typical of the "rape culture" of that era, wherein women were viewed as seductresses and men as pawns in their lair. Thames, whom one of her friends described later as "a flaming liberal lesbian," did not allow Voorhies's comments to stand uncorrected. She lauded feminists as the only people trying to reform rape laws and create new ways to think about sexual assault as a crime of power, not of passion. Years later, Lafayette feminists still talked about her hard-hitting reporting with awe.[2]

That a fairly conservative newspaper in a heavily Catholic area of Louisiana headlined the issue of sexual violence indicates that by 1973 a great deal of public discussion already surrounded the topic. People from many different backgrounds, including those who favored few other feminist goals, threw their support behind efforts to reduce violence against women—including forms of assault that occurred behind closed doors and were cloaked in secrecy. Once convinced of the magnitude of the problem, nearly all progressive religious denominations in Louisiana defended the establishment of rape crisis centers and related measures such as police sensitivity training, the creation of battered women's shelters, and the strengthening of rape laws and domestic violence laws to make arrest and conviction of offenders easier. People of faith defended women's right to feel safe inside the home as well as in public, and their right to be treated with dignity when they were victims of a sexual assault, regardless of whether they knew the perpetrator. Conservatives pushed back, arguing that efforts to stem male violence against women violated family privacy. But almost as soon as the services were offered and women began taking advantage of them, rape crisis and battered women's shelters gained powerful support from multiple quarters. By the 1990s, agencies and programs in Louisiana designed to secure women's safety had become professionalized and institutionalized and could claim an impressive degree of success.[3]

History of Rape Awareness/Redefining Rape

Historically, the crime of rape was narrowly defined, with easily recognized perpetrators and victims. In the eyes of the prosecutors and the general public, no crime had occurred unless the victim was virginal and probably white, unless she had been violently assaulted, and only if she could prove that she had fought back. In the United States, furthermore, rape has always been racialized, a legacy of slavery. Slave girls and women had no right to refuse consent and therefore could not technically be raped. Just as wives were expected to submit sexually to their husbands, so, too, were slave women. Because whites saw African-descended women as hypersexualized Jezebels, a black female who "cried rape," in the view of whites, must have seduced her white attacker and then lied about it. In this scenario, the victim was the (presumably falsely accused) man. Conversely, while white men were seldom prosecuted for rape, black men were routinely executed—often extralegally by lynching—on no more evidence than a white woman's testimony.

When white men went unpunished for rape, when women had little political, judicial, or narrative power, rape became surrounded by a great deal of myth. Historical misunderstandings contributed to what feminists called a "rape culture" in which women were blamed for being raped (because they must have asked for it). Because of these common misperceptions about who rapists really were, white women felt dangerously safe when they often were not. They failed to recognize that white men not only raped black women with impunity—indeed, almost as sport—but they also got away with raping white women. Because white women as a rule did not report sexual assaults, including incest or other sexual violence within the domestic circle, few people recognized the prevalence of the crime. The truth, then as now, is that, like all crimes, rape was most likely to occur within the same ethnic group, not across racial lines. But white women did not want to disgrace the men in their families upon whom they depended for economic sustenance and social rank, so they kept mum. Their silence protected the assailant and sustained the myth that rape was something black men did to white women. This myth exonerated white men, the most powerful group in society.[4] Rape, then, was yet another manifestation of patriarchal privilege. White men raped because they could; women were powerless to stop them either in private or in public through the courts. When all law-enforcement authorities, jurors, and judges were men, this was the logical result.[5]

The historiography of the antirape movement traditionally began with the work of white feminists in the twentieth century. As with any new avenue of historical inquiry, however, further research and attention to marginalized groups recovers a much longer and broader history than women in the twentieth century were aware of, keeping in mind that in the 1970s women's history did not yet exist as a field. Historian Estelle B. Freedman traces the history of political critiques of rape in the United States back to the first half of the nineteenth century. Moral crusaders and abolitionists raised the issue in the antebellum period, and first-wave suffragists continued to challenge white men's ability to rape with impunity. Freedman foregrounds the role of African Americans in pushing back against the myths of the black male predator and of the black female as a seductive, duplicitous Jezebel. African American journalists, antilynching crusaders like Ida B. Wells, black women's clubs such as the NACW, and the NAACP "challenged the designation of rape as 'The Negro Crime,' an association that justified lynching as a means of punishing or preventing all interracial sexual relations."[6] In the 1930s, Jesse Daniel Ames and thousands of southern white women (overwhelmingly Methodist) in the Association of Southern Women for the Prevention of Lynching (ASWPL) insisted that white men cease lynching black men in a supposed chivalrous defense of white womanhood. The all-white ASWPL had the support of black club women in the South, too, although concerns about white reprisals against them and the men in their communities forced them to keep a low profile.[7]

Southern blacks attempted to take a stand against the racial injustice in rape prosecutions when Recy Taylor, a young black married mother walking home from church services in Abbeville, Alabama, was abducted and gang-raped by a group of white thugs. Even though Taylor identified her attackers, they were never charged with the crime. Rosa Parks, working for the NAACP, investigated the crime; the Alabama NAACP publicized it; and Taylor, her husband, and the black community where they lived refused to remain silent. The black response to Taylor's rape, author Danielle McGuire argues, became a catalyst for the civil rights movement that began in Montgomery, Alabama, a few years later. However, it did not galvanize a nationwide movement against rape.[8]

Most women of the World War II generation who had been assaulted or otherwise coerced into sex remained reluctant to tell their friends and families, much less report the crime to skeptical authorities or go public with it, as Recy Taylor and her outraged husband had done. Because of the shame and stigma surrounding rape (indeed, sexual issues of any kind were considered inappropriate topics of polite conversation in the conservative postwar era), if sexual assault was ever discussed at all, it was in private, embarrassed, anguished, whispered conversations. When so few people in their circle of friends or family talked about it, most white women assumed rape was something that happened to black women, not to them.

In CR sessions around the country in the 1960s, the silence around sexual assault was broken. As white women shared their experiences, they began to understand that sexual violence and coercion were the result of patriarchy, a vestige of the days when the law supposed a wife to be a man's property, when society assumed that "boys will be boys." They deconstructed the myth that blamed rape on women's provocative dress or behavior. White women began to understand something that black women had always known: their "behavior" could consist of little more than acting and dressing as social norms dictated that they should. Women came to recognize that they were not at fault for what had happened to them and that they should not feel shame or guilt. Rape was a political problem and therefore a matter of public policy. In other words, "the personal was political." For many white women, awareness that sexual aggression was a by-product of male dominance was their "click" moment that led them to support a feminist agenda. They got angry.[9]

Though the first modern feminist theory of rape had been published in 1948, it was not until a discernible women's liberation movement was well under way that the issue received public attention, and then it came primarily from radicals.[10] In 1970, Kate Millett identified rape as a "weapon of the patriarchy" in *Sexual Politics*. In 1971, Susan Griffin, a Berkeley activist, published an exposé in the radical press about sexual assault, and the New York Radical Feminists held the first "speak-out" on rape.[11] With a goal of bursting through the shame and stigma associated with sexual violence, and also to debunk myths about rape and show that it could happen to anyone, even nice girls, speak-outs featured women sharing their stories. Speak-outs were a vehicle for empowerment, a way for women who had been assaulted to show that they were resilient survivors rather than pitiable victims. Such forums were also a form of political activism in that they served as an organizing and recruiting tool for those seeking to change an unresponsive and unsupportive legal system.

The antirape movement spread like wildfire. NOW took a position against rape at its national conference for the first time in 1971, and in 1973 created its Rape Crisis Task Force primarily for the purpose of advocating changes in rape statutes. Susan Brownmiller's 1975 book, *Against Our Will*, which defined rape as a crime of power rather than passion, Freedman says, "alerted the public to the nascent feminist anti-rape movement." Brownmiller's book was a best seller and forever shifted the paradigm for understanding sexual assault.[12] National attention helped galvanize local initiatives. In the North and the West, as the preceding examples show, the initiative came from radical white women—the only ones daring enough to broach the subject in public. But in Louisiana, and perhaps throughout the South, while radical women played an important role in the creation of counterinstitutions, the antirape crusade came from many quarters, including from universities. In New Orleans, it began in 1973 with the formation of a dedicated Human Relations Committee (HRC) Task Force, buttressed by research conducted by two male professors at UNO and a male student at Tulane.[13]

At the time, of course, the subject was so new, virtually no academic research on sexual assault, or of media coverage of it, existed. The study done by Daniel J. Abbott and James M. Calonico, two UNO professors, which analyzed the New Orleans's newspapers' rape coverage, showed another way in which racism operated in the city. Their findings, perhaps unsurprisingly, were published in an alternative New Orleans newspaper, the *Vieux Carré Courier*—bought in 1973 by Philip Carter, son of well-known liberal journalist Hodding Carter. By comparing the *New Orleans Times-Picayune*'s coverage of rapes in the early 1970s to reports of rapes in the New Orleans Police Department's files, they were able to document "serious distortions of reality." The *Times-Picayune*, they concluded, was much more likely to sensationalize rapes of white women by black men, while rapes of black women barely received mention. The afternoon competitor paper, the *New Orleans States-Item*, was no better. The professors correctly pointed out that nearly all rapes were intraracial (they occurred within racial groups), yet the media created a hysterical fear among white people of black rapists while ignoring the rapes of black women, which routinely went unpunished. The *States-Item* sponsored an all-white group, Women against Crime, to defend women against this supposed threat to their safety, ignoring the fact that women were more likely to be living with the man who might hurt them than they were to encounter a predator on the street.[14]

Another male, this time a student in June Twinam's class at the Tulane School of Social Work in 1973, Robert Maddox, conducted additional research on rape in New Orleans. Maddox interned with the New Orleans Human Relations Committee, a volunteer citizens group founded in 1969 to advise the city about race relations, so he was particularly interested in the racial dimensions of the rape issue.[15] His study confirmed that race not only determined the media's reporting of rape; it also determined how the police and other law enforcement treated female survivors. He revealed the horrible treatment complainants suffered at the hands of the all-white New Orleans Police Department (NOPD). The woman was taken to police headquarters, where two male police officers, who believed that "at least half of all rape complaints were unfounded," delivered a barrage of questions designed to "break down" an alleged victim whom they believed to be lying. Police were much more likely to be suspicious of a woman of color, especially if her attacker was white, but regardless of her race or ethnic background, they kept her in the interrogation room for hours. Police officers had received no training, and there was no "mechanism for controlling the quality of the interviewing," Maddox reported. This harrowing experience would have been nearly unbearable for any woman, but it was even more traumatic for a woman of color. Maddox noted that "blacks in the ghettoes and slums of urban areas distrust[ed] and dislike[d] the police" and thus were much less likely to report crimes of all types. It was reasonable to assume, then, that the underreporting of rapes among African-descended women was far higher than among whites, particularly if the perpetrator was white.[16]

Maddox's report called for an overhaul of the procedures for handling rape cases. The Orleans parish coroner, Dr. Frank Minyard, medically examined the victim, although the exam might not take place until the next day when the office opened for regular business hours. The coroner made a police report but offered no treatment. Minyard told the victim to see her regular physician if she had concerns about pregnancy or venereal disease but gave her no referral for psychological counseling. At no point in the process of reporting a sexual assault did a woman see another female face.[17] Public testimony from a woman using the pseudonym "Madelyn" confirmed Maddox's findings.

At a speak-out against rape in New Orleans, Madelyn described the attack and the callousness of the police. After a neighbor forced himself into her home and raped her, she escaped and fled to her grandmother's house nearby. Her grandmother called the police, who arrived quickly and put her into the police car. The male officers made her lie on the floor after they spotted the perpetrator in his car and pursued him in a high-speed chase. She was terrified, and they offered no comfort. Madelyn recalled, "I was all messy; I was sick; I had these bite wounds on the vagina; I felt filthy; I was panicked, felt like an animal in this police car going down the highway 100 miles an hour." After they caught the man, they took her back to the crime scene—her own house. Even though her parents were there to offer comfort, they "shoved [her] in a room alone." She stated, "They wouldn't let anybody talk to me, nobody touch me. I was in a room with about nine policemen and they were throwing one question at me after another. They asked, 'Did he have an orgasm? Did he try to beat me? Did he threaten my life? Did I enjoy it? Were we lovers?' These questions were asked over and over again" for hours. Finally, they took her to the hospital for the coroner's examination, where she waited alone for another hour before the examination, which confirmed the rape. Then she was required to give another statement. "After I gave that statement they said I would have to give the statement over and over again," Madelyn testified. "I was questioned so much I couldn't even think. I got really sick afterwards."[18]

This woman, like many sexual-assault survivors, exhibited symptoms of posttraumatic stress, an ongoing trauma exacerbated by society's rape culture. Madelyn explained the shame of dealing with people who thought that she deserved to be assaulted: "They figure nice women don't get raped, just bad women. Or women who are prostitutes." Her family, including her husband and children, took it well and helped her, but "the outsiders were terrible. [Her family] had to sell the house. The rapist's family lived right by [them]," and they taunted her children, saying they were going to rape them, too, and that they would kill them. The neighbors sympathized more with the man who had been convicted and sentenced to jail than they did with his victim. The grand jury of twelve men was no better. They asked her questions such as "Did you like it when he touched you?" Her treatment at the hands of police and the lack of empathetic care and counseling available to her was standard practice in the 1960s and early 1970s. Yet testimonies like hers also challenged pervasive rape myths and helped to create a new feminist understanding of rape as an act of power in which the victim was blameless.[19]

The Reform Movement Begins

New Orleans

In the wake of the publicity surrounding rape generated by the UNO professors and Robert Maddox's research, June Twinam, the assistant director of the Regional Health Authority, a social worker, and Maddox's instructor at the Tulane School of Social Work, convinced the HRC to create a special rape task force. Twinam put together a group that cut "across economic and racial lines" and, in her view, was unlike any previous organized effort among women in New Orleans. Task force members represented the Ladies Auxiliary of the Chamber of Commerce, the New Orleans Women's Center (representing lesbian radical feminists), the YWCA, the Junior League, NOW, and universities in the city. The task force advertised its weekly meetings and held them at City Hall so that the public could attend.[20]

Mary Capps, a radical feminist with a PhD in sociology from Tulane University, headed up a subcommittee of the task force that would make recommendations for services. Radical feminists, also often referred to as the "women's liberation" wing of the 1960s and 1970s feminist movement, eschewed most existing institutions because they were hierarchical and controlled by men. Much as the black power movement sought to create separate institutions and communities as a means of empowering African Americans, radical feminists sought to build institutions run by women. They wanted all-woman spaces where they could develop autonomy and not have to depend on men economically or otherwise. Rejecting patriarchy and centralized decision making (as well as partisan politics), they envisioned new creations that, ideally, would ensure participatory democracy and complete equality. "Radicals believed that alternative institutions would not only satisfy needs unmet by the current system," opines historian Alice Echols, "but could, by dramatizing the failures of the system, radicalize those not served by the system."[21] Distrustful of professionals who operated within a criminal justice system that had not only failed to support survivors of sexual assault but had even revictimized them, radical feminists created a variety of counterinstitutions around women's unmet needs, including abortion referral networks (called Sisters Helping Sisters in New Orleans), health clinics, and rape crisis centers. Independent rape crisis centers, says historian Estelle Freedman, "became a cornerstone" of the antirape movement.[22]

Like many other leaders in the women's liberation movement in the South, Mary Capps first developed a consciousness of oppression and of "othering" from witnessing racism. Born in Joplin, Missouri, in 1940, Capps moved to Jefferson Parish (a suburb of New Orleans) during World War II. Her parents, being from a midwestern state, had a perspective on race that differed from that of the whites among whom they now lived; they challenged the prevailing norms of white supremacy and encouraged their children to do the same. From her parents, she became aware of the injustice of white privilege and felt called to end that privilege where she could. In high school, Capps participated in a citywide integrated committee of Girl Scouts that resulted in the desegregation of the statewide Girl Scouts conferences, a move that incited her classmates to call her a "nigger-lover." Capps learned early that doing the right thing could make one extremely unpopular.

By the time she graduated from East Jefferson High School in 1958, she had already developed strong antiestablishment and anticlassist values. Her experience at Newcomb College as a scholarship student reinforced those values. Most of the other Newcomb students had graduated from private high schools, and Capps sensed the classism that emanated from some of them. Though her parents were middle class, they were not from an old, wealthy Louisiana family with an established pedigree or a lot of money to make up for it, the kinds of families that most of the girls at Newcomb came from. This reinforced her empathy with oppressed working-class people who worked hard but could never quite measure up to middle-class standards of respectability.

Like many Louisiana feminists, Mary Capps spent time in other countries, which helped her develop a critique of the hierarchies of oppression that co-existed in the South. During her junior year abroad (JYA) in 1960–61, Capps studied at the University of Nottingham. As it happened, this was the same year of the infamous New Orleans school integration crisis. The photos of Ruby Bridges being escorted by U.S. marshals through screaming mobs of white people made front-page news not just in the United States but internationally. Images of the white racists' contorted, hate-filled faces, along with reports of the unprintable racial epithets that members of the crowd hurled at a tidily dressed little black girl with a white bow in her hair, embarrassed the city and the nation. Living in England while this happened, Capps was ashamed to be from New Orleans. This experience made a lifelong impression on her. Being abroad gave her a vantage point that overrode parochialism and local mores.

Capps had already begun developing a strong sense of gender discrimination even before she graduated from Newcomb with honors in 1962. When she applied for graduate school at Tulane in sociology, one of her Newcomb professors informed her that the Department of Sociology was going to offer her a good scholarship. However, when her acceptance letter came, no scholarship offer was included. The dean of the graduate school at Tulane, she discovered, had moved her name below all the male applicants accepted by the department, which was legal in the years before Title IX of the Civil Rights Act. Capps's indignation and outrage helped her turn the situation to her benefit: she accepted three assistantships on the condition she did not have to do the work, since the scholarship could not be recovered. The school agreed. She also received a National Institute of Mental Health (NIMH) fellowship, which funded the remainder of her time in New Orleans. In graduate school, she met and befriended fellow women's movement activists Virginia Peyton, Cathy Cade, and Peggy Powell Dobbins.

Capps wrote her dissertation on a Great Society program, Total Community Action, which had the first interracial board in New Orleans, and she earned a PhD in 1970. While finishing her doctoral work, she took a job as an assistant professor at the University of Guelph in Ontario, Canada, in 1967 and helped found the Guelph Women's Center. While at Guelph, she developed pioneering courses on the ideology of white supremacy, the ideology of male supremacy, and the sociology of knowledge. Following her graduation, she took a post-doctoral fellowship granted by the Canada Council to research and document the 1926 general strike in England and Wales. With her partner, Virginia Peyton, she moved to London. As part of her research, Capps and members of the London Women's Film Collective filmed interviews with women from coal-mining families who had participated in the 1926 general strike. This research expanded her knowledge of and sympathy for the working class.

In England, Capps and Peyton joined the London Women's Liberation group and met Selma James and her husband, C. L. R. James. Selma James and Maria-rosa Dalla Costa (of Padua, Italy) were in the process of writing *The Power of Women and the Subversion of the Community*, a book that greatly influenced Capps's thinking. In 1971, Capps and Peyton traveled to Denmark to investigate women's activism, and they connected with the Danish women's movement, which included women from all walks of life—housewives, students, blue-collar and pink-collar workers, academics, prostitutes, and porn stars as well as executives. For the first time, they also met lesbian feminists.

Capps's exposure to various models of radicalism in Europe informed her belief that services provided to victims of sexual assault should be independent from male-dominated institutions such as the police force and hospitals. She investigated other services around the United States and recommended fol-lowing the model of the program in Washington, D.C., which had been started by radical women in 1972. The Washington women had published a widely dis-seminated pamphlet, *How to Start a Rape Crisis Center*, "hoping that their expe-riences and insights might prove useful to fellow activists elsewhere." Also, the D.C. rape crisis center's policy "was to take a neutral stance on whether women should report rape; the collective simply provided victims with information on what was likely to result. They neither encouraged nor discouraged reporting" so as to avoid "expos[ing] a victim to even more pain and suffering." Capps recommended this model of an autonomous "third party reporting center" where the victim was neither required to identify herself or to report the crime, but could give details of the rape and a description of her attacker if she chose to. Minyard, the Orleans parish coroner, also thought the autonomous center a good idea because it would encourage the victim to come forward and provide information that would assist the police in locating and prosecuting offenders. Capps told June Twinam that she wanted to be the director of the new independent service, and Twinam agreed to back her. "June was definitely an ally to me," Capps said. "In certain ways June's respectability 'covered' the more radical work that we were doing through the RCC."[23]

Capps was well aware of the racial dimensions of the crime and understood that the rape crisis center needed to serve the needs of women in the African American community. She was impressed with the YWCA's "One Imperative to End Racism" and with the local YW's programs and services for women and girls in the black community. That there were African American women on the board of directors and among the staff also convinced her that the YW, as an all-woman organization with its own building and resources, was the best possible home for the new service.[24]

The HRC accepted the task force's recommendation and requested that the New Orleans YWCA (a United Way agency) operate the project. The YWCA's director, Carmen Donaldson, who had a master's degree in social work, had recently hired Marguerite Redwine (introduced in chapter 2) to develop programs that would address the needs of women and their families. The two women agreed that a rape crisis service fit the YWCA's mission, and they convinced the board of directors, "consisting of strong black and white community leaders," to agree. Redwine hired Mary Capps, part time at first, to set up the service, do community outreach, and recruit volunteers. Capps did research to help train the volunteers, and the YWCA opened the rape crisis hotline on Mardi Gras Day in 1974. More than thirty volunteers, some of whom were members of the National Association of Social Workers, handled the phone calls along with Capps, the only paid staffer.[25]

Pressure from radical feminists, from the city's special task force, and from media publicity forced changes in official procedures. Volunteers at the rape crisis hotline now sent women to Charity Hospital for treatment and to Pontchartrain Mental Health Clinic (a state-supported institution) for psychological counseling. Survivors were no longer required to give their names or to report the crime to the police in order to receive care. If the only thing they wanted was a sympathetic ear, they got that as well.[26] The coroner's office, *Distaff* reported in 1974, "once scandalous in its treatment of rape victims, has initiated many reforms in the last year. There are part time rape escorts to accompany victims from the police station to the Coroner." African American counselor and city attorney Bernette Johnson talked them through the pelvic exam, and afterward she explained the court procedures, thus demystifying a stressful, embarrassing, and frightening process.[27]

Under intense pressure, the Orleans Parish district attorney's office also began to institute reforms. In August 1974, District Attorney Harry Connick hired two special rape investigators, Ruth Ann Carter, a graduate of Stanford University in California, and an African American, Rose Marie Eady, a graduate of Dillard University. Neither were police officers at the time, and they had to go through the regular police academy training, after which they received further training in forensic investigative techniques with special emphasis on the handling of rape complaints and the treatment of survivors of sexual assault. The effort was designed to provide a close working relationship with the NOPD and the Orleans Parish coroner's office in rape cases. The partnership would, they hoped, encourage more women to come forward by boosting the prosecution rates. "I believe," Connick said, "that rape victims will be more responsive to women than to men investigators. This should unquestionably lead to greater prosecutive efficiency and to more assistance to the victims of this horrible crime."[28] Women were pleased because "traditionally the NOPD ha[d] been one of the chief culprits in the intimidation and harassment of rape victims."[29]

In the mid-1970s, money from government agencies began to flow toward rape crisis centers. In 1975, the New Orleans YWCA on Jefferson Davis Parkway at the intersection of Jefferson and Tulane Avenue received a grant from the Comprehensive Employment and Training Act (CETA, part of President Johnson's antipoverty program). This money was used to hire Donna Myhre, who took over from Mary Capps as director, and two additional staff persons. Myhre had a master's degree in psychology and a background in civil rights work in Mississippi. She had chaired the Tombigbee County's Human Relations Council (which brought her under the surveillance of the state sovereignty commission) and was a devout Christian. Capps was delighted that Myhre, whom she described as "a strong, righteous woman," took the job she was leaving. Myhre held the position of director of the Rape Crisis Service (RCS) for eight years and during that time strengthened relationships between it and other agencies such as law enforcement. She held sensitivity training sessions for all police officers, although she encountered some resistance. Myhre reported, "Some of them [male officers] just never got it."[30]

Radical feminists stressed female strength and agency and sought to counter the image of women as helpless victims. The self-defense movement would soon arise out of the antirape movement because many advocates, including Donna Myhre, rejected the notion that women were timid and weak and instead believed that they could learn how to overpower attackers. She was therefore unhappy with the NOPD's use of Frederic Storaska's book and film, *How to Say No to a Rapist and Survive*. Storaska's message was that women were no match for the rapist and should not fight back. Donna Myhre cited research indicating that women who resisted frequently got away from their attacker; she believed that self-defense training was key to rape resistance. Capps recalled, "Donna was very committed to this issue. She and others contacted law enforcement, military liaisons, etc., to try to convince them to stop showing Storaska's film. She had meetings with NOPD on this. They seemed to listen but kept using the film." In New Orleans as elsewhere, karate classes and self-defense demonstrations would become part of the package of antiviolence efforts. (Betty Brooks, a driving force behind multiple feminist initiatives in Los Angeles, was a physical education professor who had grown up in Louisiana. She so successfully taught hundreds, perhaps thousands, of southern Californians how to defend themselves against larger attackers that her methods were picked up and used by many other teachers elsewhere.)[31]

Donna Myhre may not have won that immediate battle, but in the long run she and the other women involved in the antirape movement won the war. The radicals could never totally disassociate rape crisis services from existing institutions, but now that they had made the issue a subject of public conversation, it was no longer a source of shame and isolated mental torture, a hidden problem that women were afraid to discuss. Survivors of sexual violence began coming out of the closet; demand for services increased. Once women had greater control over the process and female volunteers assisted along the way, a survivor could expect to be treated with compassion rather than with suspicion, and the process became more humane and less judgmental. The criticism and blame began to shift to the male perpetrator where it properly belonged. Additionally, those involved in antirape efforts—which increasingly included survivors themselves—began replacing the term "victim" with "survivor" in standard parlance. That, too, became part of the process of empowerment.

Historian Maria Bevacqua calls rape "a bridge issue," in that it united people of various ethnic, political, and socioreligious backgrounds. The support of the YWCA, the city's task force, and the New Orleans branch of the National Council of Jewish Women (NCJW) shows that this was true in New Orleans. The NCJW provided significant financial support to the RCS. Believing that preventing rape was far superior to counseling a victim after the fact, the NCJW helped the RCS initiate an education campaign. A 1975 announcement went to the principals of local schools, informing them that an educator was available to speak to schools:

> The Young Women's Christian Association's Rape Crisis Project, in conjunction with the National Council of Jewish Women, is establishing a Speaker's Bureau to carry out a community wide program of rape education. Our community education program is designed to assist women and girls in preventive efforts both as individuals and on a group basis. We will attempt to correct various racial and sexual myths about rape, which is the fastest growing crime of violence in the country. Cultural folklore and misinformation contribute greatly both to the high incidence of rape and the inadequacy of present measures for its prevention and control. We urge you to utilize our new service.[32]

The NCJW's funds allowed Mary Capps and Donna Myhre to do more outreach and to bring in Celeste Newbrough as community relations director.

Newbrough was a New Orleans native from a churchgoing family. Her father was a Baptist missionary, and her mother, Norita Massicot Newbrough, a Unitarian. Norita Newbrough, one of the first women artists in the French Quarter, modeled an employed, high-achieving woman who followed her dream and who fully supported her daughter's feminist efforts. As with many southern feminists, Newbrough's activism began with a commitment to advancing the black freedom movement. While attending LSU in Baton Rouge, Newbrough, a member of the Junior League, used that organization as a platform to sponsor an interracial panel discussion on race. Also while in Baton Rouge, she met Sylvia Roberts and assisted her on the Lorena Weeks case (discussed in chapter 9). Roberts introduced her to the Baton Rouge chapter of NOW. At the time, Newbrough worked for President Lyndon Johnson's antipoverty program, the Office of Economic Opportunity. When she joined NOW, she encountered resistance from the black men in the office, who had been on her side as long as she fought against Jim Crow and for integration. They saw her "conversion" to feminism as an attack on them personally and on the civil rights movement generally. They stopped speaking to her. Hurt and puzzled by their hostility, like many other women of the New Left, Newbrough found this ostracism a "click" moment; she soon joined a CR group in Baton Rouge. After graduating from LSU with a degree in English in 1967, she moved back to New Orleans and enrolled in graduate school in sociology at Tulane. She, her mother, and several female faculty members at Loyola University (next door to Tulane) helped to found the first NOW chapter in the city in 1971. (Loyola, a Jesuit institution, had a very leftist Human Relations Institute.) When Newbrough's mother, a life-long resident of New Orleans, died shortly afterward, Rev. Albert D'Orlando, pastor of the First Unitarian Church, presided at the funeral.[33] Not long after her mother's death, Newbrough, an out lesbian, left NOW and went to work for the RCC.

Radical lesbians were extremely important to the antirape and antibattery movements, as well as to the abortion-rights effort in New Orleans (discussed in chapter 5). Mary Capps had become aware of her attraction to women in college; Donna Myhre, the mother of six children, had only recently left heterosexual relationships. In addition to Capps, Myhre, and Newbrough, two of the clinical social workers at the Pontchartrain Mental Health Center, Nikki Hufford (later Alexander) and Betty Spencer, were lesbian. Nikki Alexander explained why she got involved in rape crisis:

> I was in the personal process of coming out as a lesbian myself. Some of the counseling work was just part of my assignment at my place of work. My interest in the work grew stronger from there as I personally met more feminists, most of whom happened to be lesbians. I could see that the work was political for many of my lesbian friends, but it was much more personal for me. I was just drawn to it and knew that it was necessary to help empower the women who had been raped or molested so that they would no longer view themselves as victims. And to aid them in appropriately placing their anger on their abusers, not on themselves. I wanted to help women and children who had been traumatized move through that trauma and come out a more powerful person on the other side. Maybe with some knowledge that there were others who had been through her/his journey to help them feel stronger and less vulnerable and alone.[34]

Women-identified women like Nikki Alexander and Mary Capps were attracted to the work at least in part because they cared deeply about other women.

Alexander and Betty Spencer came up with the idea of forming a support group open to any survivor, not just their patients, in search of emotional support and talk therapy. Alexander reported that she started the Peer Support Group in 1977 after she had been counseling rape victim/survivors for about three years, and "many of them expressed a desire to talk to other rape victims." She explained, "For a long time it was a fantasy I had, of a place where rape victims could drop in to talk, whenever they wanted to." She and Spencer began holding weekly meetings at the YW for anyone who had been raped, including those who had suffered incest as children. The Tuesday-night Peer Support Group meetings, which averaged six to eight women of all hues, functioned as CR sessions, a unique service among rape crisis centers at the time. The women found sharing their stories therapeutic, and they created for themselves a more permanent support network by forming lasting friendships in the group. Some found it even more life changing to channel their anger into action. One was Sue Willow Schroeder (also lesbian), who became a cofacilitator of the Tuesday-night meetings and an RCC volunteer before founding two organizations (discussed later) that galvanized many other victim-survivors into action.[35]

The irony of having such a high percentage of lesbians involved in the antiviolence movement is that they were less likely than straight women to suffer battering by men, although they could certainly be harassed on the street or raped, a danger faced by all women, and they could be battered by female partners. Why, then, were they drawn to this crusade? Mary Capps said that lesbians got involved because the threat of violence affected all women. It was an issue that crossed race and class lines. She also noted that "being lesbian frees up a lot of energy because you're not spending time trying to please men." In other words, lesbians had the freedom to help other women who were more dependent on men, emotionally, legally, and financially. There was also the principle of the matter. Clay Latimer said, "It was about the solidarity of sisterhood. We thought we would all protect each other." Some found the work appealing because they were most comfortable in all-female settings. Self-help groups created a nurturing environment where survivors could make friends and find nonthreatening companionship.[36]

The originators of the rape crisis services were white, but they understood the need to reach across racial boundaries. In New Orleans, Mary Capps explained, "it was RCS policy and practice to be racially inclusive in volunteer recruitment and training, advocacy, publicity, public education and services. I brought my knowledge and analysis (sociologist, feminist, antiracist) to the job so the RCS had a sociocultural, historical and political component in our work. For example, in trainings and in public speaking we spoke about the stereotype of black males as rapists of white women. We also talked about racial differences in reporting and sentencing. We held public events at locations where women of different races and classes would be comfortable, such as public libraries and neighborhood community centers." Likewise, Donna Myhre, who had a background in civil rights work, was sensitive to black women's concerns and insisted that one of her two staffers be African American (Cheryl Clark filled that spot). Also, Genevieve Short, a social worker and YWCA board member, was both a volunteer leader and a volunteer counselor from the beginning at RCS. African American women in the rest of the country did not always have good experiences within the white-dominated antirape movements, but the research done by sociologist and head of women's studies at UNO, Janelle White, who worked in antiviolence services in the Crescent City and thus could speak from her own experience, found little evidence of racial tensions there. White interviewed four black women in New Orleans's antiviolence agencies for her dissertation, "Our Silence Will Not Protect Us: Black Women Confronting Sexual and Domestic Violence." While she documented persistent cultural differences between whites and blacks, she spoke highly of Mary Capps and the other women she worked with, noting that they were very progressive and were doing "great things" on race. Her research supports the thesis that southern white liberals who had been involved in antiracist movements may have been better at working with black women than northern white women were, because the latter had far less contact with people of color.[37]

In Louisiana at least, black women did not object to the way rape crisis advocates offered services. Women of all racial backgrounds called the hotline, served as volunteers, and joined the grassroots organizations that arose from those efforts to provide services to female victims of sexual violence.[38]

Elsewhere in Louisiana

In cities around Louisiana, mainstream women's organizations took up the cause. In Lafayette, outrage about the public comments made by the coroner, Henry Voorhies, spurred women to create the Mayor's Commission on the Needs of Women in 1974 or 1975. (In addition to the comments quoted in the newspaper at the beginning of the chapter, the women were aghast that Voorhies had stated publicly that rape required a woman's willingness to allow penetration, or else it would not happen.) The members of the mayor's commission created a coalition of women's groups to sponsor a public hearing on rape at the Lafayette Public Library in 1978. The other sponsoring organizations were the local chapters of NOW; the LWV; the AAUW; Onyx, an African American women's group; and Les Amis, another local women's organization.[39]

The event was not without controversy. Sarah Brabant, one of the organizers—a member of the local NOW chapter and the Lafayette Mayor's Commission on the Needs of Women—said they took a lot of flak for sponsoring the hearing because they "were not supposed to be talking about things like this in public!" Attorney Sylvia Roberts, the moderator, explained to the two hundred or so attendees that this was indeed a unique event for Lafayette, and it was no wonder people were shocked: "We have not had women talking about their experiences. This is one of the taboos of society: women do not talk in public. And so, in the whole country, there have been very few of these." The hearing included interviews with rape survivors, counselors, and medical professionals. One woman told her story of being assaulted and impregnated by an eighteen-year-old when she was eleven. The woman, twenty-five years old when she participated in this speak-out, said the man was indicted but never went to trial because her dad talked her out of going forward. Rape survivors also described insensitive treatment at the hands of the coroner or of police investigating the crime. Coroner Voorhies implied that they really wanted to be raped, or that they had intercourse with a boyfriend, or that they put themselves in a risky situation and it was thus their fault they had been attacked. Panelists pointed out that rough handling by male authorities deterred women from reporting the crime.[40]

The public hearing established the need for a woman-run rape crisis center, and the Lafayette Mayor's Commission on the Needs of Women took this as its special project. Sarah Brabant, a professor of social anthropology at ULL and a NOW member in addition to being a founder of the mayor's commission, investigated the two existing rape crisis services in the state and decided on a third alternative. The one in New Orleans, in her view, was too antimale, and the one in Baton Rouge was under the authority of the district attorney's office. District Attorney Ossie Davis instructed the director to stop providing services to anyone who refused to report the attack. "When the director of the center was fired for objecting, and the entire staff and volunteer corps resigned in solidarity with her, the paid workers were replaced with criminal justice professionals and new volunteers were recruited."[41] This was exactly the type of co-optation by the state that Brabant, like Mary Capps in New Orleans, sought to avoid.

Brabant decided to establish a rape crisis service in Lafayette that was independent of the police and served the needs of the woman but was not antimale. She saw the survivor of sexual assault as a patient who needed medical care, so the commission got Charity Hospital to agree to host the RCS because the women could receive treatment there and would not be required to report the crime. Brabant encouraged men to get involved as escorts, believing that it was best for victims/survivors to learn to trust men again. The men were vetted and entirely sympathetic to the plight of the women, and they were glad to help. Gender diversity was complemented by racial diversity. As with the Lafayette women's commission, both black and white women sat on the board of the RCS.[42]

In Louisiana, then, there were at least three different models of rape crisis services. Because these services were so new and grassroots, diversity in delivery of services and management of centers was the norm. To increase collaborative learning and cooperation among them, leaders of these services established the Stop Rape Crisis Center in Baton Rouge as a central clearinghouse.[43] Though these new services represented great leaps forward from the humiliating, dismissive treatment a woman who reported sexual assault received before 1973, their efforts were, in many ways, palliative. As director of the YW's Rape Crisis Service in New Orleans, Donna Myhre spent a great deal of time talking to community groups as well as to officials, and she noticed that the provision of services to rape survivors was less controversial than "stopping men from

doing what they wanted to do."[44] Most grassroots organizers of rape crisis services like Mary Capps, Donna Myhre, and Sarah Brabant sought to stop sexual
assault by changing cultural norms and putting perpetrators of sexual assault
behind bars. That goal, however, would require more effective prosecution,
which would in turn require changes to Louisiana's antiquated rape laws.

Reform of Rape Laws

Louisiana's rape statutes were outmoded; as a result, women seldom reported
sexual violence in part because they knew the perpetrator was unlikely to be
prosecuted or, if so, unlikely to be convicted. The New Orleans YWCA issued a
report showing that in 1974, out of almost four hundred reported rapes in
Greater New Orleans, only twenty-nine people were convicted. The YWCA's
board of directors announced that it would support reforms in the law because
"the statistics clearly indicate[d] the great difficulty of investigating and con-
victing rapists." The board "urge[d] support of the [proposed] rape bills."
Women from all over the state joined the Louisiana District Attorney's Association to lobby for a variety of reforms designed to change this broken system.[45]

This process was under way all over the nation, and it came from district
attorneys as well as feminists and their allies, as Maria Bevacqua has demonstrated in her history of rape awareness. "The reforms most frequently sought
were redefining rape, graduating (or 'staircasing') offenses, easing extreme
evidentiary burdens (including corroboration and resistance requirements),
limiting the admissibility of evidence of the victim's sexual history (rape shield),
repealing mandatory instruction from judges to juries, and removing the spousal exemption." In 1975, the American Bar Association called for a revision of
the corroboration requirements and penalties and advised replacing all references to victims of rape as "female" with gender-neutral language. At about
the same time, the Louisiana legislature tasked its advisory body, the Louisiana
State Law Institute, with removing all gendered language in Louisiana's laws.
This mandate alone required changes in the sexual-assault statutes, but the
antiviolence advocates, of course, wanted far more.[46]

Louisiana women from many different backgrounds supported strengthening the rape laws in order to make them more effective. The New Orleans
branch of the NCJW organized a coalition of many women's groups to help get
reform bills passed by the legislature. (*Distaff* was a member of the coalition
and regularly reported on the pending bills.) The NCJW urged citizens to write
their legislators in support of the proposed changes, and its board drafted a letter to Louisiana legislators indicating their position in no uncertain terms: "The
1400 members of the greater New Orleans Section NCJW are working to reform
the rape laws in Louisiana."[47] The current law had only two categories of rape:

simple and aggravated. "Simple rape" was limited to instances when the victim
was incapable of understanding the act; was tricked, drunk, or drugged; or was
a child. The other option was "aggravated rape," which carried the death penalty.
In this category, the "female" was required to "resist to the utmost" or be under
the age of twelve. Representative Billy Tauzin, the author of the bill to create a
middle category, pointed out that the current statute required a woman to put
her life on the line before it could be prosecuted, the only crime in the state
where that was true. He spoke for many others who believed it unreasonable to
expect the victim of a violent crime to be able to prove that she had "resisted to
the utmost."[48] Furthermore, because the penalty was death, prosecutors were
reluctant to bring charges and juries reluctant to convict. A more moderate
punishment would ensure a higher percentage of convictions. Tauzin's bill
would make homosexual rape a crime, which it had not been previously, and
proposed a new category, "forcible rape," a middle ground between simple and
aggravated rape. Supporters hoped that forcible rape, because it was punishable by one to twenty years, would bring more convictions.[49]

The other major reform advocated by the NCJW was a "rape shield" law. Rape
shield laws "restricted defense lawyers' ability to dredge up a victim's sexual history in order to portray her as a tramp who 'asked for it.'"[50] Putting the victim
on trial was a holdover from the days when it was commonly believed that a
sexually active woman could not be raped, because (the thinking was) if she
had consented once, she would consent again. This had always disadvantaged
victims who were not in a position to refuse a man's advances, at least not without severe consequences—slaves, servants, employees, wives, and prostitutes.
Now that women had access to birth control and the sexual revolution was well
under way, it was even more inappropriate to require chastity of the plaintiff.
The NCJW's opinion was that "prior sexual history is irrelevant in determining
whether or not an actual rape occurred." The board encouraged members to
undertake a letter-writing campaign to their legislators.[51]

Thanks to support from many different quarters, feminists won the battle to
revise rape laws. Both proposed bills passed: Tauzin's bill to create the category
of "forcible rape," and the rape shield law. The latter prohibited the use of the
victim's prior sexual conduct and "reputation for morality" as evidence in the
case. The point of this law was to encourage a victim to report rape "without
fear of being put on trial herself."[52]

Cultural transformation typically lags behind legal changes. When rape laws
came up for discussion, men in southern legislatures behaved quite badly. They
snickered and made humiliating jokes within earshot of the women. In 1977,
female legislators in Georgia sponsored a bill to reform the rape laws in that
state. When the bill reached the floor of the house, Cathey Steinberg recalled, "I
never saw a group be so obnoxious in my entire life." The representatives "made

jokes, they whistled, they hooted, they made comments like, 'she deserves what she gets,' and they laughed and they chuckled. They hooted and *tabled* the bill."[53]

Likewise, the Louisiana legislature functioned as an "old boys' club," where locker-room humor was the norm on sexual issues. When Baton Rouge feminist Holley G. Haymaker went to lobby for the ERA in 1972, Representative Shady Wall from Ouachita Parish, a large man dressed in a white linen suit, put his arm around her and said, "Honey, you wouldn't want to be using the restroom with a dirty old man like me, now, would you?"[54] In 1980, there were only 3 women—Diana Bajoie, Mary Landrieu, and Margaret Lowenthal—in a body of 144 that comprised the Louisiana legislature, and though their presence made a huge difference to women's rights advocates, there were too few of them to change the good-ole-boy nature of that body.[55] Diana Bajoie, who was in her thirties, had first entered the house in 1976 and moved to the senate in 1980. Mary Landrieu, daughter of Moon Landrieu, mayor of New Orleans, entered the house in 1980 at the age of twenty-three. In addition to being young and female, those two women had the added disadvantage of representing New Orleans, a city a world apart from the rest of the state, little understood by the more conservative members of the legislature and little respected. Bajoie also suffered from incessant ridicule because she was African American, while Mary Landrieu's added handicap among these older men was her good looks. "I was beautiful and had a great figure and that made it hard for me to be taken seriously. It was a very unwelcoming place for women; there's no two ways about it," Landrieu recalled. When she was sworn in, she received wolf whistles. The third woman, Representative Margaret Lowenthal from Lake Charles, was a bit older than the other two, but not by much. Everyone else was a white man in his fifties, sixties, or seventies. "It was a club that men ran, men belonged to, and where men made the rules," Landrieu recalled in an interview after she left the United States Senate in 2015. "It was clear they never contemplated admitting women to membership, clear that they didn't expect women to last long or to take leadership roles." But Landrieu was determined to act as an advocate for women because so few other people did.[56]

Even in the legislative chambers, women's issues, particularly if they involved sexual matters, were greeted with ribaldry and derision from men. Bajoie recounted that when a bill to make marital rape (or spousal rape) a crime came up, "the men saw it as a joke" and belittled it on the floor. The bill was tabled, which killed it. "I took the mike and told them I didn't think that was funny," she recalled. "It was not a laughing matter, and it was a sensitive issue for many women." This was enough to get legislators to take it off the table and discuss it again. That, Bajoie believed, "was one of the critical moments, and a turning point for women. It was no longer expedient to laugh about issues involving women on the floor of the legislature. After that, men began to get on board."[57]

Baton Rouge attorney Ayn Stehr, a lobbyist for antiviolence efforts, joined with other anti–domestic violence advocates, telephoned the men, and shamed them into bringing it back up. The spousal rape bill eventually passed, although compared to many other states, Louisiana's law was more lax. It said that husbands and cohabitors could not be charged for rape of spouses unless there was a court order of separation or a court order prohibiting physical or sexual abuse. It removed the exemption from the two more-serious types of rape but not simple rape. That took another decade, with women's rights advocates pushing for it the entire time.[58]

Women working on behalf of antiviolence efforts persuaded the Louisiana legislature to allocate money for both rape crisis services and the new battered women's shelters. Controversy about who would control those subsidies and about the effect that state funding might have on what had begun as a grassroots movement swirled almost immediately. Like many other radicals around the nation, Mary Capps and Donna Myhre feared the consequences of accepting money from the male-controlled state. They believed that the state could and would become "co-optive," meaning that it would undermine the grassroots women's efforts by absorbing the movement's leaders, issues, and goals. Radicals tended to distrust existing organizational structures, seeing them as patriarchal and controlling. The New Orleans rape crisis women were also suspicious of anyone who cooperated with state agencies or institutions, believing they were copping out. After the NIMH began to fund rape projects, it held conferences on rape, too. But at such a conference in Atlanta in May 1977, Capps and Myhre complained that "no effort had been made to assure participation by rape crisis centers." Capps and Myhre, then, saw themselves as waging an uphill battle against the co-optive state.[59]

Capps and Myhre expressed a concern common among grassroots organizers, generally young women who were nonprofessionals. At the time, of course, there were no professional "rape counselors," since no such field of study had ever before existed. The radical women had been the first to ally with victims against hostile and suspicious criminal-justice authorities and were among the first to raise public awareness about sexual assault. They created the new services, and their fear was that the woman-centered approach they had pioneered—which encouraged the victim to assume control of her case—would be lost when professionals who had never been part of the feminist movement got involved.

To the radicals, professionalization undermined their goal of transforming society. With outside money, Capps averred, "came re-definition of rape and batterment—from political terrorist acts against women to social problems and finally to individual problem." Social-service bureaucracies accepted and cooperated with established authority, promoted professionalism and individual counseling, required hierarchies, and set up escalating dependency on funding sources. This was problematic because conservative governments, radicals feared, would use funding as a means of leverage and would attack the programs by lesbian-baiting and "incitement to violence against women."[60]

Most people involved in the antirape movement, however, such as the YWCA's Marguerite Redwine, had no problem with using state money and resources. They wanted to work with established institutions that investigated and prosecuted sexual assault but also reform them by injecting a new feminist consciousness into procedures, making them more sympathetic to and protective of the victim and willing to punish the offender. Furthermore, even though rape crisis services today take money from established authorities, they still emphasize "restoring to the victim a sense of control over her own life."[61]

Capps and the other radicals involved in the antirape movement encouraged victim-survivors to take action through public events to demand institutional changes within state institutions such as the police, the DA's office, and medical units. Political action could be therapeutic and empowering. One survivor, Sue Schroeder, formed two organizations, Women against Violence against Women (WAVAW) and All Rape and Incest Survivors Emerge (ARISE), out of the Tuesday-night Peer Support Group. The two organizations included black and white survivors along with women from the feminist-activist community. As radicals were wont to do, they used (nonviolent) direct-action techniques to raise awareness of gender-based violence and male authorities' disregard for the same. They sponsored speak-outs against rape in which women read their stories of attacks; organized a court watch group for rape trials; and held at least one demonstration in front of city hall to "call attention to the inaction of city officials to the rising crime rate in the city." Another way to publicize this issue was to stage a Take Back the Night March.[62] Similar marches, in which women walked "through dangerous neighborhoods to signify their strength in numbers and their refusal to limit their mobility," had been occurring in the United States and internationally since the mid-1970s. Both NOW and radical women promoted these demonstrations of solidarity among women. The Louisiana Coalition against Domestic Violence (LCADV), an organization of shelter directors, sponsored a Take Back the Night march in Baton Rouge every year in conjunction with its annual meeting.[63]

Take Back the Night events brought women of different backgrounds together in one locale to challenge male control of public spaces. New Orleans's organizers were Liz Simon, Donna Myhre, Mary Capps, Sandy Karp, Sue Laporte, Lynette Jerry, Barbara Trahan, and Judith Cormier, all lesbians, but not all out of the closet. The leaders did not want the demonstration limited to a small group of radical feminists, nor did they want it limited to white women. To emphasize the point that violence could happen to any woman at any time, they wanted it to be a broad-based community event. To that end, they publicized some meetings in advance, solicited and received donations from multiple individuals and groups (including two Catholic organizations, Our Lady of Holy Cross Church and the Sisters Council to the Archdiocese of New Orleans), and recruited black and white women, heterosexual as well as lesbian, to help organize and advertise the event. Judith Cormier, a Cajun from Church Point, Louisiana, who had recently left her husband and come out as a lesbian, recalled that the women spent countless hours in advance planning meetings and on the phone. They wanted women to "experience the feeling of strength and power to act in their own behalf with the goal of making the streets of [the] city safe both day and night." Men were allowed to show support by lining the march route with candles and flashlights, but they were not permitted to participate in the march itself. Staging a wholly woman-led and woman-defined march demonstrated that women were punching back against fear and intimidation.[64]

The day before the march at the end of January 1980, Sandy Karp called a press conference to inform reporters of the goals of the march. She explained that threats of or fear of violence curtailed women's freedom of movement and announced, "The coalition is putting the community on notice 'that these conditions are intolerable.'" Another goal was to establish a clearinghouse of information and referrals to agencies that could help female victims who did not know where to turn following an attack. She presented a report to city officials outlining what the city and others could do to combat violence against women.[65]

Marchers gathered on a Saturday night at St. Mark's Community Center. When the sun set, about seven hundred women proceeded through the French Quarter for a rally and speaker presentations at Washington Square, between Frenchman Street and Elysian Fields in the Marigny. Area women spoke out about their experiences as victims of violence before the keynote speaker, feminist writer and artist Kate Millet, took the stage. The newspaper coverage focused on Millet's speech:

> [She] told the angry crowd of women that they were being deprived enjoyment of the nighttime world primarily because of the prevalence of the crime of rape. "The night is for delight, joy, fun, laughter ... but that's also the world we've been forbidden from for so long. It has been taken from us. You don't go out at night because of the fear of being raped, beaten, dismembered or killed. In order to enjoy life, you have to risk it. But we're not going to put up with it anymore," stated Ms. Millet to the roars, cheers and applause of the crowd.[66]

Her talk was followed by a statement of demands and intentions of the marchers (the same one presented by Sandy Karp at city hall the day before), a reading by march organizer Kathy Kendall, and a self-defense demonstration.

The organizers hoped that a permanent umbrella organization might emerge from the cooperative network they had forged to produce the Take Back the Night march. However, that possibility crumbled almost immediately when the group became suspicious that a woman who went by the name of Yvette, who had attended many of the public meetings but was otherwise unknown to them, appeared to be a mole or a saboteur. Because some radical women, especially those involved with the Women's Center, had been surveilled by the FBI's COINTEL program, they were extremely wary and suspicious. They never found conclusive proof, but "Yvette's" behavior frightened many of the lesbian organizers, especially those with children. In the 1970s, homosexuality was still an enormous liability; a mole could do serious damage to them personally and professionally if she outed them. The mothers were afraid that the courts would take their children away from them. As Cormier said, "It was sad, because we were no danger to the community." Their methods of bringing about change were always peaceful, designed to get attention and publicity that would help eliminate the rape culture and male control of the streets. They might have been ideologically radical, but they were not violent revolutionaries. Ironically and sadly, their desire to promote a shared goal of ending male violence against women was undermined by another woman, and the coalition fell apart.[67]

A more permanent advocacy group formed in 1982 in Baton Rouge, the nonprofit Louisiana Foundation against Sexual Assault (LAFASA). Its goal was to coordinate and push forward efforts toward "eliminating sexual violence through education, program support, and social change. Membership includes sexual assault centers, allied organizations and supportive individuals." Today LAFASA "advocates to policymakers on the behalf of individual survivors, communities and stakeholders in order to affect social justice and a comprehensive approach to preventing social violence and providing services to survivors of sexual violence at the local, state and federal levels." Female-run organizations like this, which inevitably became bureaucratic as they systematized operations, nonetheless represent a significant advance over those alternatives that existed before 1970, all of which (the coroner's office, police, hospitals, and district attorneys) were male-dominated.[68]

The antirape movement in New Orleans drew support from the city, from faith-based organizations, and from radical feminists. Within a few years, the movement had spread all over the state, and women from many backgrounds—well-educated women and those with little more than a high school diploma, heterosexual women and lesbians, white women and women of color (especially through the YWCA), well-placed women and those of limited means—came together to help change the culture surrounding women's bodies. Defining the ways in which sexual assault restricted and sometimes destroyed women's abilities to function as coequal citizens of the polity is one of feminism's great successes.

Battered Women's Movement and Anti–domestic Violence Reforms

Like sexual violence, domestic battery was another hidden, shameful problem for which no services existed in 1970. Beating his wife was considered a husband's prerogative, and society saw no reason to stop him. "Laura," whose alcoholic husband both beat and raped her on a regular basis, broke the silence about her ordeal at a speak-out in New Orleans in 1977. She revealed that she or her children had called the police on more than one occasion, only to be told that the police would not intervene in "domestic disturbances." When they did respond, the police said that it was Joe's house and that they "should try to work it out." The police would not even write up a complaint, Laura explained. One officer finally told her that she would get a faster response from the police if, when she called, she lied and said that someone was breaking into her house. "I began to realize that I really had no one on my side if not even the police would help me," she said. She finally fled with her children, in fear of her life, and stayed in one room of a relative's house while Joe remained in the family home. She and her children lived in a cramped environment where the children slept on the floor. Joe harassed her constantly, riding up and down in front of the house at all hours. Even though Laura obtained a legal separation, the judge said that he could not order Joe out of the house. Horrified by tales like this, Louisiana feminists, like their sisters across the country, vowed to change the system that favored men over women.[69]

Unlike previous explanations that depicted domestic violence as an individual psychological problem of both the batterer and the victim (who supposedly "wanted to be battered"—the myth of masochism), 1970s feminists analyzed this problem as resulting from gender inequality. The structural problem of male dominance in the home and in society allowed men to batter with impunity and prevented or discouraged women from escaping violent situations. Suzanne Pharr, a radical lesbian who lived in New Orleans in the late sixties and early seventies and who subsequently became active in the antiviolence movement, observes, "Male violence is fed by their sense of their right to dominate and control and their sense of superiority over a group of people who, because of gender, they consider inferior to them."[70] To try to correct the problem, feminists and their allies established safe spaces for women seeking refuge from their batterers (a short-term solution that, they hoped, would break the cycle of dependence). In 1979, three freestanding shelters offering temporary housing for women and children fleeing domestic violence opened in Louisiana. For a longer-term remedy that would allow victim/survivors to fashion independent lives for themselves, feminists and their allies turned to law enforcement and the criminal-justice system as the main solution to the problem.

Like the antirape movement, the antibattery movement began as a grassroots effort among women who had no training except their own direct or indirect experiences with domestic violence. Before feminists made an issue of what they initially called "wife beating," there was virtually no attention paid to it. Marriage counselors and social workers referred to it as "family maladjustment" and blamed both parties equally. Women in violent relationships, they said, wanted to be abused. Police, if called during an altercation, as Laura illustrated, did not intervene, considering it a domestic dispute and not a crime. The rebirth of feminism in the 1970s changed all that. The shelter movement began not in the United States but in England when Erin Pizzey joined with other women to establish a shelter for battered women, Chiswick Women's Aid, in London in 1971 and sparked a movement around the country. Pizzey, whose husband was a journalist, supplied the newspapers with a steady stream of horrible accounts of women beaten by their husbands and published a book, *Scream Quietly or the Neighbors Will Hear*, that helped raise awareness of the problem.[71] Pizzey, along with other British activists and the National Women's Aid Federation, pressured Parliament into passing a law giving broader protection to battered women in 1976.[72]

Pizzey inspired American feminists, too. As in the antirape movement, the first phase of the movement was grassroots; it originated among women who identified themselves as "formerly battered" and their feminist allies. In Minnesota, they set up a hotline for battered women in 1972 that evolved into a shelter in 1974; in 1973 in Pennsylvania, Nancy Kirk-Gormley, a woman who had fled her husband after ten years of beatings, established the first NOW Task Force on battered women, which evolved into a more permanent organization within a year. Also in 1973, the first freestanding physical shelter for abused women and children in the United States opened in Phoenix, Arizona. In 1975, national NOW formed a task force to examine the issue, and Del Martin, one of the task force coordinators, helped to spark a nationwide movement by publishing *Battered Wives* in 1976. (Martin is best known for founding the first lesbian organization in the nation, the Daughters of Bilitis, in the 1950s, of which there was one chapter in New Orleans.) In addition to founding shelters, participants in the movement to stop violence against women sought to raise awareness of the issue through public education and to influence legislation and public policy.[73]

New Orleans feminists quickly detected the need for battered women's services, too. Clay Latimer, working then as an administrative assistant to YWCA director Carmen Donaldson, discovered that when she gave talks around the state about how the head-and-master law privileged husbands and discriminated against wives, women would approach her afterward, shy, nervous, and ashamed, and begin to tell her about abuse in their homes. Because there were no institutions to handle such situations, Latimer sent them to the rape counselors at the Y.[74] Thus YWCA telephone counselors began to learn about the widespread problem of domestic violence, too. Likewise, Nikki Alexander found that women suffering emotional or physical abuse in their intimate relationships came to the meetings of the Peer Support Group she held every Tuesday at the Y. She and the other rape crisis counselors began to analyze domestic abuse in much the same way that they understood rape: it occurred because women lacked control of resources that would allow them to leave their batterers. It occurred because men held inordinate power in society, against which women were powerless. It occurred because women had no place to go. They needed a safe haven to escape abusive relationships and begin to break the cycle of dependency.

The women at the YW wanted to provide that service, but sheltering victims required space and money. Governor Edwards told the YWCA directors that he would help secure Title XX (Social Security) funds if the Y could come up with a $12,000 match. Board member Bonnie Conway (Mrs. William B. Conway) secured a grant in that amount from the United Thank Offering of the Episcopal Church. With these funds, the YW board hired Jan Logan, who had a master's degree in counseling, as director of the new program in 1977.[75] The money only went as far as paying Logan, who supervised a dedicated hotline for those in crisis (and trained the volunteers); it was not enough to provide residential services. Since there was no profit to be made and the corporate world was therefore uninterested, funding for the New Orleans YWCA Battered Women's Program had to come from government grants, nonprofits, individual donations, and religious organizations. This service, which offered individual and group counseling and referrals, was the only one in Louisiana and was one of the few in the South. Jan Logan noted in 1978 that the program had received an overwhelming response: "In less than six months, we have served 500 women and their children."[76] Congresswoman Lindy Boggs praised the New Orleans Y program for its community support, noting that it had "brought together a host of local public agencies and private, non-profit groups to work cooperatively on the problem. The Y consortium include[d] representatives from the police, the municipal courts, the city council, social service agencies, local universities,

women's groups, religious organizations [including the NCJW], the CETA and
Title XX Federal Programs, and volunteers."[77] The Y's counseling and referral
service continued to operate until Hurricane Katrina in 2005.

Anti–domestic violence (anti-DV) educators and crusaders like Jan Logan
found it difficult to convince the general public that domestic violence even
existed, because it had seldom been prosecuted. Raising awareness of the issue
was therefore a top priority, and the International Women's Year (IWY) conferences in 1977 helped to do so. By featuring workshops on domestic violence,
IWY conferences made it a women's issue and part of the feminist agenda. The
Louisiana Women's Conference's session on battered women featured Betty
Spencer as chair. Spencer, the social worker who counseled rape survivors
at the Pontchartrain Mental Health Center, was on the faculty of the Tulane
School of Social Work and was a member of the New Orleans Feminist Therapist Collective. The session's panelists included Virginia Ellis, former director of
the Baton Rouge Rape Crisis Center, and Donna Myhre of the New Orleans RCS.
These three women had become self-taught counselors of women traumatized
by sexual assault. Because the problem was seldom discussed and the public
had no idea how widespread battering was, the panelists at the IWY conference
session marshaled data to buttress their case. Domestic violence calls in Baton
Rouge, a city of about 285,000, totaled about 2,000 annually. In New Orleans,
police received over 200 calls per month; and in the much smaller city of Lafayette, police received 1,632 calls in 1976.[78]

One of the reasons people were reluctant to believe the enormity of the problem was because they thought that a battered woman could easily exit the situation. The most frequently asked question was, "Why do women stay?" Spencer
explained that in addition to having few resources and no place to go, women
felt ashamed, or they feared the insensitivity of police and courts. As one survivor reported about her previous experience with abuse, "no one in the community seem[ed] to care." Women at the IWY conference in Baton Rouge resolved
to change that situation. They passed a resolution recommending that "federal
and state funds be provided to establish transitional housing, child care, peer
counseling, career training, legal consultation and legal representation and
Rape Crisis Centers."[79]

Clay Latimer, one of the delegates to the Baton Rouge conference, asked
for and received funding from the IWY committee for a public forum on battered women, partly to publicize the services offered at the Y in 1977. Jan Logan
organized the panel, which included Betty Spencer and Millie Charles, an
African American social worker and head of Southern University–New Orleans's Department of Social Welfare. Congresswoman Corinne "Lindy" Boggs, to
whom we will turn in a moment, was the featured speaker.[80]

The IWY conferences in Louisiana and in other states increased public understanding and mobilized resources for women trapped in battering relationships. The national convention, held in Houston, not only passed a resolution urging action against domestic violence but also awarded grants to new programs, including one at the YWCA in Baton Rouge. By the end of 1978, with the help of local, state, and federal funding, more than three hundred shelters for battered women had opened around the country.[81]

Catholics and the Antiviolence Movement

Once feminists began publicizing the widespread but unspoken and largely hidden problem of intimate partner abuse, Catholic women from many quarters rallied to support the cause. In 1977, the National Assembly of Women Religious (NAWR), meeting in New Orleans, passed a resolution "promoting and encouraging the establishment of shelters and self-help programs for battered women." The NAWR was known for its advocacy of women's empowerment within the church and in society at large. But even the Catholic Daughters of America (CDA), a conservative group of laywomen that mobilized against the ERA, went on record in support of crisis centers for abused women and their children, and the CDA provided financial support to one in Washington, D.C., called The House of Ruth.[82] The House of Ruth recruited Representative Corinne "Lindy" Boggs, a Catholic Daughter, to serve on its board.

Lindy Boggs became the first woman to represent Louisiana in the House when in 1972 she was elected to fill the seat of her husband, Hale Boggs, after he was killed in an airplane crash. A direct descendant of Louisiana's first governor, William C. C. Claiborne, a Newcomb graduate, and a quintessentially gracious southern lady, Lindy Boggs supported the ERA and distinguished herself in Congress as an early advocate for abused women and children. Boggs credited the founder of the House of Ruth, Dr. Veronica Maz, for sparking her concern about family violence. It had begun as a shelter for destitute and homeless women (the "bag ladies" who huddle over grates in the daytime and sleep in abandoned cars on the streets at night, Boggs explained), but as soon as it opened, many of the women who knocked on its door were fleeing violent relationships. "My experience at the House of Ruth led me to gather information on this issue and to bring it to the Congresswomen's caucus for research and eventually legislative action," Boggs recalled. Boggs became chair of the House's "crisis intervention task force," which collected data from all fifty states about domestic battery and child abuse.[83]

Working from that data, Boggs and Congresswoman Barbara Mikulski (D-Md.) cosponsored the Domestic Violence and Treatment Act and introduced it into Congress several times beginning in the 1977–78 session. Among

other things, the bill would have provided grants of $50,000, funneled through
the states, to programs that demonstrated "broad community support," such
as the YW's program in New Orleans. In a press conference designed to drum
up political support for the struggling bill, Boggs maintained that the problem
of battered women and children was "a tragic one of frightening proportions"
and could not be ignored. "Domestic violence has been a hidden problem," she
informed her listeners, "such as rape and child abuse were at one time. Like
these problems, spouse assault is grossly under-reported. I am hopeful that our
bill and the discussion which it will produce will help everyone understand the
enormity of the problem and will act as a catalyst to bring together the various
programs, organizations and laws that can be helpful in offering early relief and
long range solutions."[84]

Thinking it a noncontroversial measure, she was shocked when it encountered opposition from conservatives. She said that debates about the act "occasionally met with snickers and misguided political sniping," but the lobbying
campaign was far more serious than she acknowledged. Conservative Republican senators Orrin Hatch of Utah and S. I. Hayakawa of California circulated a
letter to their colleagues stating that such "legislation represents one giant step
by the federal social service bureaucracy into family matters which are properly, more effectively and democratically represented by the states and local
communities."[85] Providing money for shelters, Boggs quickly found out, generated heated debate.

Conservative Opposition

Anti-DV activists supported shelters as a way to break the cycle of violence,
because, as Mary Capps has said, shelters changed "the context in which battering occur[red], in that women are no longer trapped in violent situations
and men can no longer assume that women are available victims. Adequate
shelter space removes one of the major supports for batterment: women's cap-
tivity in a vulnerable situation."[86] Shelters, by providing a safe space for her and
her children, empowered a woman to make the decision to leave the man who
was battering her.

But while grassroots antiviolence activists supported the idea of shelters,
others regarded this remedy that put space and walls between a woman and
her intimate male partner as intrusive and antifamily. Conservatives contended
that women were safest in the home with male protection, so when women left
the home for a shelter, their reaction was to charge that shelters were lesbian
operations where predatory women recruited other women into their "homosexual lifestyles" as lovers. The aforementioned Suzanne Pharr has analyzed
this tendency to "lesbian bait" in *Homophobia: A Weapon of Sexism*: "When a

male abuser calls a woman a lesbian, he is not so much labeling her a woman who loves women as he is warning her that by resisting him, she is choosing to be outside society's protection from male institutions and therefore from wide-ranging, unspecified, ever-present violence. When she seeks assistance from woman friends or a battered women's shelter, he recognizes the power in woman bonding and fears loss of her servitude and loyalty; the potential loss of his control." Conservatives believed that women should be dependent on men. A woman-identified woman was perceived as a threat to the nuclear family precisely because she had moved outside dependence on men. Since no straight woman in the 1970s wished to be called a lesbian, and even queer women avoided being outed because of the potential harm to themselves and to their loved ones, homophobia buttressed male control of women.[87]

The "New Right" (so called to distinguish it from the anti-Communist-focused "old right"), a coalition that included fundamentalist Protestants, anti-abortion Catholic activists, and Orthodox Jews, opposed programs against domestic violence because they associated them with feminism, which in turn they associated with an attack on "motherhood, the family and Christian values." The Moral Majority, with an evangelical Protestant base, organized a campaign of untruths against Boggs's Domestic Violence and Treatment Act, saying that it offered "one more chance for bureaucrats to cozy up" to "radical feminists" and asserting that "battered women's shelters [made] women promise to divorce their husbands in order to enter the shelters." Archconservative Sen. Gordon Humphrey (R.-NH) declared that the government had no business intruding in family disputes and suggested that the shelters were "opposed to traditional families."[88] In Louisiana, Darryl White in Baton Rouge, a former city court judge affiliated with the Family Forum, and Sandy McDade in Shreveport, affiliated with Phyllis Schlafly's Eagle Forum, actively lobbied against funding and shelter efforts and opposed all measures to give to nonfamily members rights that had traditionally belonged to the family.[89]

Though Louisiana's senators were not among the New Right (they are better classified among the Blue Dog Democrats), they were no help to Lindy Boggs when she sought votes for passage of the Domestic Violence and Treatment Act. Russell Long was absent when the vote was taken, and Senator J. Bennett Johnson voted "no" because of what he said were his objections to federal intrusion into state matters. While the outlook for passage of the bill in 1980 appeared bleak, Lindy Boggs said, "We're not going to let them [recalcitrant senators] off the hook. The hopes of the people in the shelters have been raised too much to let them down now."[90] Boggs pointed out that bill had the cosponsorship of 104 members of Congress, and—to counter those opponents who argued that it was unbiblical—that it had earned the endorsements of the American Baptist Women, the American Jewish Congress, the Episcopal Church, the Lutheran Council of the United States, and the archbishop of New Orleans. The United Church of Christ in New Orleans also wrote a letter of support, saying, "As a Christian community, we endorse this Bill in the interest of justice, equity and family survival." Once again, liberal Protestant denominations, Reform Jews, and broad-minded Catholics supported the effort to end violence against women, while conservative Protestants argued that domestic matters were the responsibility of the head of household, regardless of his behavior. Boggs continued to lead on this issue, not just in Washington but also in her hometown of New Orleans.[91]

Crescent House

Urged on by Representative Lindy Boggs, Catholic women in New Orleans established a shelter modeled on the House of Ruth. Barbara Songy, head of the thirteen-thousand-strong Catholic Daughters in Louisiana, reported that Lindy Boggs had come to her, one Catholic Daughter to another, saying that she wanted "to help all the battered women who were sleeping in cars with their children."[92] Boggs reported it slightly differently, giving credit to the women on the ground, saying, "The Catholic Daughters of America have invited Dr. Maz to come help them start a House of Ruth in Louisiana." That shelter, Crescent House, the first of its kind in the state, opened its doors in 1979 as a result of assistance provided by the Diocese of New Orleans and the Louisiana Women's Bureau.[93]

The head of the Louisiana Bureau on the Status of Women, Pat Evans, was also Roman Catholic and had attended Catholic schools in New Orleans. Her political instincts told her that Archbishop Philip M. Hannan's endorsement would abet efforts to secure state funding for battered women's programs. She also understood the importance of data in convincing lawmakers to support any new program, so she commissioned a study that reported "alarming statistics" on the frequency of family violence crimes in Louisiana.[94] Then she took her case to the Catholic Church. In addition to its political and cultural influence in Louisiana, the church ran the largest charitable organization in the state, Associated Catholic Charities (ACC), which had a good track record of responsible fiscal management. She arranged for the archbishop and Barbara Songy of the Catholic Daughters to meet with Governor Edwards to convince him to find money for the program. When Archbishop Hannan was called away at the last minute, another Catholic legislator and friend of the governor, Senator Nat Kiefer, whose mother was a Catholic Daughter, filled in for the archbishop. To the delight of all in the room, Edwards agreed to allocate start-up funds in the budget of the Department of Health and Human Services. Archbishop Hannan promised to donate a house that the archdiocese had recently renovated as a home for troubled youth, and asked Sister Anthony Barczykowski, head of ACC, to administer the program. Through a network of Catholics in government and the generosity of the archbishop, Crescent House opened in September 1979, a short walk away from the office of Associated Catholic Charities.[95]

The board of Crescent House included Congresswoman Lindy Boggs, and Barbara Songy served as its first president. Songy was a British woman who had married a Navy veteran and lived the rest of her life in Metairie, a suburb of New Orleans. Metairie was a "white flight" community, one of the places where whites opposed to school integration had moved in the 1960s. It was the district that elected a former Grand Wizard of the Ku Klux Klan, David Duke, to represent it in the state legislature in the 1990s. Yet, somewhat surprisingly at first glance, Songy, head of the state chapter of the anti-ERA Catholic Daughters of America, supported the first free-standing shelter for survivors of domestic abuse in Louisiana.

Given conservative opposition to anti-DV efforts, some feminists had reservations about the anti-ERA Catholic Daughters operating a shelter for abused women. Feminists were concerned that Catholics' motive may have been to reconstitute patriarchal marriages and encourage women to go back to their abusive partners. But Jace Schinderman, the first director of Crescent House, reported, "While running Crescent House for seven years never once did I get a scintilla of pressure to return a woman to her spouse. The ERA had nothing to do with saving women's lives and getting them out of dangerous situations. We were trying to protect them and their kids and help them rebuild their lives. It resonated as an issue at a basic level of justice beyond feminism. It was beyond ideology."[96] Schinderman, a young Jewish Newcomb graduate (NC '73) with a degree in English, had worked for the YWCA program for a year under Nancy Aronson, her friend and coreligionist, before moving to Crescent House. As with rape crisis services, women of all political and religious backgrounds came together to provide a previously nonexistent service.[97]

Pat Evans knew that the shelter program would need a steady supply of money, and she calculated that since many Louisiana legislators were Catholic, having the backing of the archbishop improved the chances of successfully wrangling appropriations from the legislature. The start-up funds Edwards had allocated provided money for renovating and opening Crescent House but nothing beyond that. The first two programs—one run by ACC and the other by the YWCA—limped along on Title XX funding and donations from private charities and individuals until Evans persuaded Governor Edwards to set aside $2,000,000 to support services for battered women. Evans and Kiefer also persuaded the legislature to pass a bill in 1979 creating a shelter program, and in

1983 she along with other anti-DV activists succeeded in getting a marriage license tax passed to provide consistent funding for the program.[98] Within a short period, the anti-DV movement had shifted public opinion enough to garner, in Louisiana alone, millions of dollars for programs. Now backed by the state, shelters opened around Louisiana, some in rural regions because women living in remote areas insisted on it.[99]

Using Title XX funds, Baton Rouge began a shelter program in 1979 that also had the support of local charities and the city. Ayn Stehr, the director of the shelter in Baton Rouge for many years, says that the Catholic Daughters provided a great deal of assistance there, too. They volunteered every day, preparing meals, doing clerical work, transporting the women, and so forth. They were "very self-sacrificing and never proselytized." Nor did they ever condemn the women for leaving their husbands. They sympathized with the victims/survivors and wanted to preserve their dignity. "We were all on the same page about that," Stehr said. To avoid conflict, Stehr and other pro-choice staffers simply did not discuss abortion or reproductive rights with their eager—though conservative—volunteers.[100]

Calcasieu Women's Shelter

Lake Charles lies about four hours west of New Orleans on Interstate 10. An inland port city and the parish seat, its population of about seventy thousand in 1979 included substantial numbers of Catholics. But much like New Orleans, Calcasieu Parish had an ethno-religious mix of people that included large numbers of Methodists and Baptists and a healthy sprinkling of Jews. Evelyn Cloutman, the Methodist social worker introduced in chapter 1, assembled supporters of a women's shelter from many all white liberal denominations. The founding board included Rabbi Sherman Stein of Temple Sinai in Lake Charles and a Methodist preacher, Rev. L. A. "Tony" Richardson. Among the Catholic representatives were Bernardine Proctor, Cloutman's friend in the LWV (introduced in chapter 1); Lloyd Barras (president of the board when it incorporated), a teacher in Catholic schools, charter member of Our Lady Queen of Heaven Catholic Church, member of the LWV, the Lake Charles's Mayor's Commission for Women, St. Patrick Hospital Auxiliary, and a Catholic Daughter; and Sister Mary Jeanette, a Sister of Charity serving as a representative of St. Patrick Hospital. Sister Jeanette convinced St. Patrick's to donate the old Olivetan Benedictine Monastery at Chennault Airpark as the first shelter space.[101]

These men and women, along with representatives of law enforcement, raised money and readied the building to open in 1981. Funds also came from the Louisiana legislature, thanks to the assistance of the southwestern Louisiana delegation, which included the first female legislator to represent this area, Margaret Lowenthal.[102] Male legislators were also supportive of the efforts, as were men on the women's shelter board. "Rabbi Stein and [Methodist pastor] Reverend Richardson were pro-feminist men who understood that this was a women's issue in which women should take the lead, but that the women also needed the help and support of the men," who were in a better position to gar-ner and deliver resources, shelter director Ann Polak recalled later. The men did not try to usurp the women, Polak remembered, something that shelter direc-tors (all of whom were women) greatly appreciated.[103]

Because battered women's shelters were a new phenomenon and there were no best-practices standards yet, the first board of the Calcasieu Women's Shel-ter kept its location secret and did not advertise its services out of fear that stalkers would come after the women who sought housing there. The shelter, therefore, depended heavily on donations (and volunteers) from area churches. By the early 1980s, however, the board was willing to broaden its outreach, and to that end, it hired Ann Polak, a feminist and liberal Catholic with strong ties to the community, as executive director in 1986. Polak's experience with the LWV and the AAUW gave her a reputation as a pro-woman advocate. These were the characteristics that the board sought, and under her leadership the program raised enough money to move the shelter from an industrial park on the out-skirts of the city to a permanent location in a residential neighborhood within easy reach of anyone living inside the city limits in 1992. In 1999, a new wing dedicated to schooling resident children at the shelter opened. The shelter's official history lauded the interfaith efforts and Cloutman's role in particular: "For the past twenty-six years Evelyn Cloutman has remained a supporter and volunteer of the shelter. The Jewish community has always been of great sup-port and St. Patrick Hospital and the Sisters of Charity of the Incarnate Word have supported the shelter financially and allowed their employees time off to serve as Board members."[104] Wherever there were well-established (white) churches and synagogues, there was backing for feminist measures designed to stop violence against women.

Black churches, however, were not part of the first wave of support. African American scholars who study the antiviolence movement, such as Janelle White, have documented many reasons why African Americans were less likely to support it, among them the stigma that came from the historic stereotyping and racist images of black men and women's sexuality described at the begin-ning of this chapter.[105] Barbara Cahee, an African American woman who has worked in the rape crisis center in Lake Charles for thirty-five years, agrees with those scholars and says that there is far more shame associated with inter-personal violence in the black community. "There are already so many negative images of African Americans that they don't want to add to those stereotypes. They want to focus on the positives." Cahee, a faithful Baptist, also reports that many black women are religiously devout, and their churches are very patriarchal. The women believe that if abuse is occurring, they should "pray about it." Cahee finds that frustrating, especially when it comes to sexual abuse: "They still refuse to turn in the men for sexual abuse, be it incest or rape." Although black women nationwide are less likely to report sexual assault than are white women, the opposite is true in Louisiana; however, black women are less likely to follow through with prosecution and are less likely to return for services, such as counseling. While women in black churches eventually began to volunteer and donate supplies that African American women might need (such as ethnic hair products), "black churches have never supported the sexual assault program," Cahee said, rather indignantly. "They help the anti-DV program [now, in 2015], but not sexual assault. They pretend it doesn't exist in the black community." As a professional and long-term counselor trained to assist women of all hues who call for help after a sexual trauma, Cahee finds this outrageous: "How can we help our daughters if we don't acknowledge the fact that incest and rape exist in our community?"[106]

While clergy and houses of worship often provided resources that helped shelters get started in Louisiana, survivors of domestic abuse quickly became involved as well. Survivors knew that channeling their emotions and energy into creating solutions to the widespread problems of domestic violence could be healing and empowering. Many formerly battered women founded or directed shelters. One was Ayn Stehr, who became director of the Baton Rouge shelter following her recovery from a near-fatal single incident of intimate partner violence. In 1979, Stehr was divorced with a young child when a man she was dating entered her home and shot her several times after she tried to break up with him. He left her for dead and went to his office and shot and killed himself. The doctors told her it was a miracle she lived. It was a difficult road back to health, but the experience was transformative: "I felt spared for a reason," she said. "I felt like I had been called to do this." A native of Alexandria, Louisiana, Stehr had always considered herself a feminist. Like many Louisiana second-wavers, she had been a social worker, but after becoming director of the Baton Rouge shelter in 1982, she went to Southern University Law School and obtained her law degree in 1992. She thus is one of those Louisiana feminists who learned the law so that they could more effectively work to protect women. She devoted significant time and energy to strengthening state laws against domestic abuse.[107]

Legal Remedies at the State Level

Second-wave feminists frequently turned to the state to redress inequalities such as unequal pay and exclusion from educational and occupational opportunities. The antiviolence movement, too, looked to the state to address the problem of intimate partner abuse. The 1979 Louisiana law sponsored by Nat Kiefer was extremely weak and did not make domestic violence a crime. There was still no way to prosecute abusers or keep them from harassing their targets until women in the legislature authored and drove through—against strong opposition—the Domestic Abuse Assistance Act in 1982. Attorney and Louisiana NOW president Kim Gandy wrote this "spouse out of the house" bill. Mary Landrieu and Diana Bajoie worked with sympathetic men in the house to get it passed. Assisting them was Maurice Durbin (a woman), the first paid lobbyist for women's issues in Louisiana. Durbin proudly reported, "The Domestic Abuse Assistance Act allows a judge to issue protective orders in cases of family violence, including allowing the abused spouse and children the use of the family home and to receive support when necessary. This was a tremendous step in a state that still maintains a very macho image of the husband."[108] Ayn Stehr said that the Louisiana Sheriff's Association opposed the bill because its members did not want to make a written report every time they went on a domestic violence call (which indicates that they felt overwhelmed by the number of calls they received), and the Clerks of Court Association opposed it because the law said that clerks of court had to give women temporary assistance until they got a lawyer. But the women persisted, and the law passed. This achievement not only protected women but also "sent the message that such abuse was not socially sanctioned."[109] During the battle for its passage, one state representative questioned the need for such programs, repeating the old myth that "many battered women want to be abused."[110] Such ideas die hard and only with consistent pressure from pro-woman advocates.

Sylvia Roberts, Kim Gandy, Ayn Stehr, and other female attorneys, sometimes with the help of the (mostly male) District Attorneys Association—a powerful lobbying group in Baton Rouge—worked hard, often against considerable opposition, to make batterers accountable and the crime punishable. They assisted female legislators in pushing for greater protections for survivors of domestic violence and for making it easier for district attorneys to prosecute repeat offenders. Margaret Lowenthal authored a bill designed to prevent retaliation or harassment by spouses who were under court orders to stay away from their homes. Announcing the bill, Lowenthal said, "There is nothing to protect the victim at this time from harassment. People are not being protected when their emotions are the highest."[111] The bill took two years to pass and even then referred only to final or permanent court orders, not temporary restraining orders (TROs). Connie Willems, another activist attorney working to increase penalties for batterers, reported that it ran into difficulties because conservative men in the legislature thought it unfair to men who might need to go home to get clothes or other essentials.[112]

Legal Remedies at the Federal Level

Lindy Boggs's efforts at the national level resulted in increased awareness of the problems women faced in domestic violence situations and paved the way for more-comprehensive legislation enacted a decade later. She secured support for selected family violence programs through the Law Enforcement Assistance Administration (LEAA) in the 1970s, but that program was completely defunded in 1980. Four years later, with the support of conservatives and President Ronald Reagan, Congress passed a watered-down version of the bill she had originally sponsored with Barbara Mikulski. Under the umbrella of the Child Abuse and Prevention Treatment Act (which conservatives supported), it authorized the Department of Health and Human Services to establish a shelter and services program and appropriated about $7 million (a fraction of the sum originally requested) to fund them.[113] That program continues today.

In 1994, after four years of debate, a more-comprehensive bill, the Violence against Women Act (VAWA), passed Congress. Among other things, VAWA provided money (lots of it, $1.62 billion, almost a sixfold increase over what it had been) for both rape crisis services and battered women's shelters. Historian Fred Strebeigh properly gives credit for VAWA's passage to Senator Joe Biden, its sponsor; to Biden staffer and attorney Victoria Nourse; to Sally Goldfarb of the NOW Legal Defense and Education Fund; and to Pat Reuss of the Women's Equity Action League (WEAL). But Boggs's antiviolence initiatives during the previous decade and a half established domestic violence as worthy of national concern and showed that funding shelters and prevention efforts could make an enormous impact. Though Biden's bill had greater reach and included civil rights provisions (later struck down by the Supreme Court), it owed a great deal to Boggs's earlier efforts. VAWA was "a broadly popular piece of legislation, supported by half the Senate, dozens of Congress members, and scores of grassroots women's organizations from coast to coast."[114] It was not universally popular, however. VAWA remains controversial with conservatives unhappy about what they consider the overreach of federal power and the fact that the money goes to provide services for undocumented immigrants, same-sex couples, and Native American women.[115]

Diversity and Disagreement in the Anti-DV Movement

All movements for social change are fractious; there is never unanimous agreement about solutions to the problems they seek to address. Some in the national anti–domestic violence movement have, since the early years, voiced concerns about solutions arrived at by the original advocates. For example, the early reformers focused on separation-based remedies because they believed that women should not remain in violent relationships. But such solutions are problematic and do not always work. They may not deter the batterer, who only redoubles the violence when he returns, and as all research shows, the most dangerous time for a woman in an abusive relationship is when she attempts to leave it (as Ayn Stehr's story illustrates). Critics say that increasing police power may actually do more harm than good, because when the abuser gets out of jail, he is often angry and in a vengeful mood and takes it out on the woman. Furthermore, arresting the batterer often removes the woman's primary support system, including child support. The abuser cannot work or pay child support if he is in jail. A woman sometimes simply wants her partner to be a good husband and father, and she remains hopeful that counseling will change his behavior.[116] Knowing that the violence and threats to her safety may in fact be the most acute after a period of separation, the abused woman does not always want a separation-based remedy. Ayn Stehr, however, believes that going back to the way things used to be would be far worse. "It's not a simple problem, and there are no simple solutions," she says. "It's complicated, and we are constantly revising our approach as we learn and as we include more voices in the discussion."[117]

Mandatory arrest policies cause difficulties, too. In the early years, advocates believed that arresting the perpetrator would not only stop the immediate threat to the victim's safety and give her time to get help, but it would also deter repeat offenders. Louisiana anti-DV activists learned, however, that untrained officers tended to arrest both parties, especially if the woman had defended herself. There was no mandatory law enforcement training, so the police did not know how to do "predominant aggressor analysis" to decide who to arrest. In that case, they arrested both people, even though the woman might have slapped or scratched only in self-defense and not as part of an overall pattern to control her partner.[118]

In the mid-1980s, Ayn Stehr and Jan Logan worked with the LCADV and the Louisiana Sheriff's Association to craft legislation that allowed law enforcement officers a more flexible response when they received a domestic violence call. Police were not required to arrest anyone, but they could make an arrest without a warrant if they believed that the victim was in imminent danger; they did not have to see the violence but could make a determination based on a victim's statement only. They had to inform the victim of protective orders and about criminal proceedings that would result; provide transportation to a place of safety; and help her get medical attention. Later revisions increased penalties for violation of restraining orders and expanded the law to include dating violence.[119] In 1997, Stehr also helped to shepherd through the legislature a law that created the Louisiana Protective Order Registry and required the use of uniform order forms by all Louisiana courts in domestic, dating, and family violence cases.[120] Now officers consider arrest history, whether there is an order of protection in effect, and other factors, and if they believe there is probable cause that someone has been abused (including dating partners), they are required to arrest.[121]

Proper training is also important, and law schools typically do not provide that. Only Tulane University Law School today offers training in domestic violence law. "It's a continuous process," Ayn Stehr noted, because new lawyers and judges are not necessarily familiar with the dynamics of intimate partner abuse and need help understanding both the law and the psycho-sociological factors that figure into a victim's decision making. Stehr has tried to address these deficiencies by providing much of the training herself, working independently as a consultant and trainer after the LSU Law Center cut its Family Law/Family Violence Clinic program.[122]

Disagreement has also arisen within the movement over "one size fits all" policy models. Women who appear at shelters are often of a lower socioeconomic class, but abuse can happen at any income level; the difference is that women with more money and education have resources to help them escape in ways that poorer women do not. Abused women can be of any ethnic group; they might be immigrants who are particularly vulnerable, gay, straight, bisexual, or transgendered, and they have a variety of personalities (they are not all meek). They have different goals, aspirations, and priorities, too. Approaches to domestic violence have changed at the micro level as providers recognized these differences.[123]

Race complicated matters, too, just as it did in the antirape movement. Most DV shelter directors were white, but most of the clients in Louisiana shelters were black, and there was, of course, a historic animosity and mistrust between black and white women. While many shelter directors were sensitive to this and worked hard—as Mary Capps had—to ensure that their white staffers and volunteers understood the special circumstances of black women's lives, a cultural divide still existed. Yolanda Perrilloux, an African American who worked at the Baton Rouge center in the 1980s as a training coordinator, said that the white women often did not understand that the black women coming into the program had few resources and were not always in a position to leave their batterer. Women of color also were reluctant to share their information with white counselors, fearful that it might be used against them, for example, to take their children away from them. Frequently the black clients, for reasons of self-preservation, lied to the white women. The white women resented that deceit and wrote reports saying that the client was "not being honest." The white women also complained about the many children the black women had, about their lack of education, and so forth. Sometimes they portrayed the black women as mentally ill. In other words, they were not respectful, and the black women knew this, which only caused the distrust to worsen.[124]

Perrilloux said that in her shelter, religious differences could also come between white staff and clients of color. Black women were often very religious, and some unchurched white counselors told them not to rely on God or Jesus but to take charge through restraining orders and the like. Black women resented what they considered an attack on their faith. "They relied on God and Christ," Perrilloux said, in a way that white women did not, in part because African American women had little else they could depend on. On the other hand, Perrilloux said she understood the white women's position, because in her Baptist church, the preacher had told her that she must go back to her abusive husband and try to work it out. She knew that wasn't right and paid no attention to his advice. Barbara Cahee, mentioned earlier, also reported this phenomenon.[125]

Perrilloux described the training program that Barbara Davidson and Pam Jenkins, in conjunction with staffers like Perrilloux, developed at the Baton Rouge shelter as forward-thinking on race, perhaps even ahead of its time. Others apparently thought likewise, because the curriculum became a model for the state. The curriculum was based on the feminist philosophy that women were not at fault for their situation. They did not need long-term care because there was nothing wrong with them, and nothing they had done had caused their predicament. The training included modules focusing on differences in race, class, and sexuality between shelter directors and staff and the women in the shelter. The LCADV, made up of shelter directors across the state, developed standards that encouraged shelters to put minority women and formerly battered women on their boards and on staff and to offer training modules on race such as those developed at the Baton Rouge shelter. Perrilloux was also on the first "Women of Color" task force put together by LCADV. Such a willingness to listen to victims and learn from them is a basic tenet of feminist values.[126]

In addition to racial differences, sexual orientation sometimes became an issue. Gay women and men across the country challenged the presumption that batterers were always male. They pointed out that people in same-sex relationships could also be abused and that at least some shelters did not recognize this fact. In New Orleans, this did not appear to be a significant issue, perhaps because of the presence of its sizable lesbian community. Crescent House made it clear from the start that it served the needs of anyone who had been abused by an "intimate partner," regardless of her sexual orientation. Whatever the disagreements, Louisiana feminists recognized that constructive debate and disagreement are a pathway to creating societal change, and they have worked to make the movement aware of differences.

The gains made by the antiviolence movement were quite striking, in retrospect. Kentucky antiviolence activist Carol E. Jordan, director of the Institute for Policy Studies on Violence against Women at the University of Kentucky, has said, accurately, that "the first two decades of the domestic violence and anti-rape movements resulted in more legal reforms for women than the previous three centuries combined."[127] The antirape and the antibattery movements drew skeptics and doubters at first, but after feminists' massive education campaign in the 1970s, people of diverse religious backgrounds came to support both movements. Though some male political conservatives continued to oppose it, antiviolence initiatives unified women across a spectrum of viewpoints, both feminist and antifeminist, even as they competed with one another for funding and sometimes squabbled about the treatment of the women who sought their help. Formerly battered women and (mostly) secular feminists had first raised awareness about domestic violence and changed the paradigm for understanding it as a crime that necessitated state intervention, but religiously devout activists, even those who might have classified themselves as political conservatives, joined forces with female attorneys, district attorneys, lesbian feminists, and social workers to build political support for the antibattery movement. This movement shattered the 1950s complacency about the home as a haven and the family as a source of emotional comfort and sustenance. Feminists and formerly battered women had shown that it could be hell, not just for women but for children, too, if it remained a sacrosanct space that men controlled.[128]

Unlike rape and battery, the movement to ensure access to safe, legal abortions was far more polarizing. While repeal of restrictive abortion laws had the support of women and of clergy in the liberal faith traditions—by and large the same religious denominations with histories of progressive women's activism that we learned about in chapter 2—women and clergy in the Catholic Church and in conservative Protestant denominations denounced abortion as sinful. On this issue, the subject of the next chapter, which seemed to pit one human life against another, women could not come to a meeting of the minds.

Radical women at the New Orleans Women's Center, 1973. Sue Laporte holding pencil in mouth, Judy Shaw, Lynn Miller on floor next to her (hand to chin), Mary Capps in chair to back, Sandy Karp in rocking chair; Melanie Owens on floor next to Sandy. *Photo by Pat Denton. Pat Denton Collection (14-007), Newcomb Archives and Vorhoff Library Special Collections, Newcomb College Institute, Tulane University.*

Chapter leaders of the League of Women Voters, 1980. The LWV was one of several proto-feminist organizations that familiarized women with the legislative process and schooled them in lobbying techniques. Front row, left to right: Marilyn Barfield, Baton Rouge; Sue Oppliger, Shreveport; Willie Mount, Lake Charles (later to become the first woman mayor of Lake Charles and the first woman elected to the state senate from her district. Second row: Hilda McQuarter, New Orleans League education chair; Nancy Harrison, vice president, New Orleans League; Joan Houghton of Baton Rouge, state legislative chair. *Ollie T. Osborne Papers, Collection 93, University Archives and Acadiana Manuscripts Collection, Edith Garland Dupré Library, University of Louisiana at Lafayette.*

Woman Creates poster. Celeste Newbrough, Virginia Peyton, Mei-Kwang Lu, Leslie Canaan, daughter of Andrea Canaan. *Photo by Ann Wakefield. Newcomb Archives and Vorhoff Library Special Collections, Newcomb College Institute, Tulane University.*

In 1980, New Orleans feminists organized a "Take Back the Night March" to challenge male control of public spaces and to publicize the fact that the streets were not safe for women at night. This photo was taken after a news conference at city hall in which Sandy Karp read a prepared statement explaining that fear of violence curtailed women's freedom of movement and thus their opportunities. Sue Schroeder holding her son David, Sandy Karp (kneeling, left), Judith Cormier standing behind Sandy, Lynette Jerry holding Jennifer Myhre (child), Donna Myhre (at right of Sandy), Eddy Marshman (kneeling, right). *Photo by Gerri Geer. Gerri Geer Collection (08-002), Newcomb Archives and Vorhoff Library Special Collections, Newcomb College Institute, Tulane University.*

The Take Back the Night organizers held multiple meetings to develop a plan of action, train volunteers, and encourage feminist solidarity. Left to right: Eddy Marshman, Donna Myhre, Jennifer Myhre, Mary Capps. *Photo by Gerri Geer. Gerri Geer Collection (08-002), Newcomb Archives and Vorhoff Library Special Collections, Newcomb College Institute, Tulane University.*

Dorothy Mae Taylor with a schoolboy, ca. 1980. In 1971, Taylor became the first African American woman elected to the Louisiana legislature, and while there, she backed most measures sought by feminists, including the Equal Rights Amendment. In 1986, she became the first to win election to the New Orleans city council. *Pat Denton Collection (14-007), Newcomb Archives and Vorhoff Library Special Collections, Newcomb College Institute, Tulane University.*

Louadrian Reed, president and state chair of the Louisiana Women's Political Caucus, presenting an award to Representative Corinne "Lindy" Boggs at the LWPC state convention, ca. 1981. Lindy Boggs was the first woman to represent Louisiana in the House of Representatives. The LWPC commended Boggs for her "continuing support of women through legislative achievement in domestic violence prevention, women's business enterprise and economic and educational equity." According to *Louisiana Weekly*, the LWPC "was moved to present this award to Boggs for her part in introducing (in coalition with three senators and members of the Congresswomen's Caucus) the Economic Equity Act, a package of bills seeking to equalize treatment of women in the areas of income and inheritance taxes, pensions, insurance coverage, and job opportunities." *Photo by Pat Denton. Pat Denton Collection (14-007), Newcomb Archives and Vorhoff Library Special Collections, Newcomb College Institute, Tulane University.*

Sidney Barthelemy and Lindy Boggs, seated at table, Louisiana Women's Political Caucus convention. Barthelemy, a Creole who had once studied for the priesthood, was a longtime supporter of the Equal Rights Amendment in the Louisiana legislature. He was mayor of New Orleans from 1986 to 1994. Boggs coauthored a federal bill to assist victims of domestic violence and was a featured speaker at the Louisiana Women's Conference held in conjunction with the International Women's Year in 1977. *Photo by Pat Denton. Pat Denton Collection (14-007), Newcomb Archives and Vorhoff Library Special Collections, Newcomb College Institute, Tulane University.*

At the Louisiana Women's Political Caucus convention, held in New Orleans, Representative Mary Landrieu, a newly minted member of the Louisiana house, presented Bland Cox Bruns with a commendation recognizing her as the first New Orleans woman elected to the Louisiana legislature in 1950. Bruns, a founding member of the Independent Women's Organization and an honorary member of the Louisiana Women's Political Caucus, served in the house for two terms and was active in Save Our Schools. Bruns was part of the cohort of older women who paved the way for politically active feminists such as Mary Landrieu in the 1980s. *Photo by Pat Denton. Pat Denton Collection (14-007), Newcomb Archives and Vorhoff Library Special Collections, Newcomb College Institute, Tulane University.*

ERA: A New Day Jazz Funeral and Celebration parade, July 3, 1982, in New Orleans. Rosa Keller on the left, Carolyn Kolb in the back holding one side of the banner, Pherabe Kolb, her daughter, holding the other side. The event, organized by Louisiana Women's Political Caucus chair Pat Denton, was a show of support from women of differing ages, races, classes, and political persuasions as they marched together in support of gender equality. *Photo by Judy Cooper. Pat Denton Collection (14-007), Newcomb Archives and Vorhoff Library Special Collections, Newcomb College Institute, Tulane University.*

ERA: A New Day Jazz Funeral and Celebration, 1982. "Generic Feminist Organization" singers at the mike in Jackson Square, where the parade ended. Left to Right: Nikki Alexander (front row), Virginia Peyton (dark hair, back row), Dru Moody (white hair, back row), unidentified woman holding sheet music (front row), Sue Laporte holding guitar, Lynette Jerry (far right) sing a song written by Sue Laporte. The Louisiana Women's Political Caucus organized the jazz funeral to publicly express disappointment at the failure of state legislatures to ratify the ERA. Louisiana Women's Political Caucus Report, Autumn 1983. *Photo by Judy Cooper. Pat Denton Collection (14-007), Newcomb Archives and Vorhoff Library Special Collections, Newcomb College Institute, Tulane University.*

Pat Denton, chair of the Louisiana Women's Political Caucus, speaking to the crowd in Jackson Square at ERA: A New Day Jazz Funeral and Celebration, 1982. The purpose of the event was to publicly express disappointment at the failure of state legislatures to ratify the Equal Rights Amendment and to celebrate commitment to future passage (as yet unfulfilled). Denton noted that those present at the event "truly" represented the American people—"not just the white, two-parent, two-child family," a not-too-subtle dig at the ERA's opponents. *Photo by Judy Cooper. Pat Denton Collection (14-007), Newcomb Archives and Vorhoff Library Special Collections, Newcomb College Institute, Tulane University.*

Vaughan Burdin Baker, pictured in 1979. In 1977, Baker established the Women in Louisiana Archival Collection, the first of its kind in the state, and a research division focusing on women at the Center for Louisiana Studies at University of Southwestern Louisiana (now the University of Louisiana at Lafayette). Among the most valuable of the papers she collected are those of Ollie T. Osborne, who was involved in a variety of feminist causes in the 1970s, and who edited the booklet that accompanied the International Women's Year conference in Baton Rouge in 1977. The women's division was eventually subsumed within the larger Archives and Manuscripts Collection at Dupré Library, which is where Baker also deposited her own papers. *Photo in the possession of Vaughan Baker Simpson.*

Official International Women's Year photo of Fran
Bussie, a Methodist who represented the AFL-CIO at the
IWY conferences in Baton Rouge and in Houston. Like
nearly everyone in the delegation from Louisiana, she
supported the National Plan of Action adopted at the
Houston convention in 1977, even though some of its
planks (notably, the one in support of lesbian rights)
were controversial. *Ollie T. Osborne Papers, Collection 93,
University Archives and Acadiana Manuscripts Collection,
Edith Garland Dupré Library, University of Louisiana at
Lafayette.*

Official photo of Sibal Suarez Taylor, program chair
for the International Women's Year conference held in
Baton Rouge in 1977, the preconference where delegates
were elected to the meeting in Houston. *Ollie T. Osborne
Papers, Collection 93, University Archives and Acadiana
Manuscripts Collection, Edith Garland Dupré Library,
University of Louisiana at Lafayette.*

Clay Latimer, Martha Wren Gaines, and Ollie Osborne at the annual state convention of the National Organization for Women, Baton Rouge, 1976. Gaines, born in 1937, was southern regional director of NOW. Women of all ages, socioeconomic groups, and political backgrounds worked together in Louisiana NOW. Latimer was elected state coordinator at this convention. *Ollie T. Osborne Papers, Collection 93, University Archives and Acadiana Manuscripts Collection, Edith Garland Dupré Library, University of Louisiana at Lafayette.*

ott-hóma ta-yé-ha il-locóca
Indian Women's Meeting

the firſt
LOUIŚIANA CONFERENCE
for
NATIVE AMERICAN
WOMEN

Louisiana Conference for Native American Women, sponsored by the Louisiana Bureau for Women and held at the Coushatta Indian Reservation Community Center, Elton, Louisiana, November 1977. Native American women speakers on the program included women from the local Coushatta tribe as well as from other American Indian tribes. *Ollie T. Osborne Papers, Collection 93, University Archives and Acadiana Manuscripts Collection, Edith Garland Dupré Library, University of Louisiana at Lafayette.*

Women of different races and classes joined the March on Washington in support of an extension for ratification of the Equal Rights Amendment in 1978. Ida Martinez, left, holding AFL-CIO flag; Sibal Suarez Taylor, standing right; Fran Bussie, kneeling left; Roberta Madden, kneeling center; and Ruth Lincecum Hebert, kneeling right. *Janet Allured Collection, Newcomb Archives and Vorhoff Library Special Collections, Newcomb College Institute, Tulane University.*

Roberta Madden, Great Women's Reunion, ca. 1999. Robbie Madden and Sylvia Roberts cofounded the NOW chapter in Baton Rouge and chaired workshops at the International Women's Year conference in Baton Rouge. Madden served on the board of ERA United, an umbrella organization dedicated to generating support for ratification of the Equal Rights Amendment, and was a founding member of the Baton Rouge Commission on the Needs of Women and a board member of the Louisiana Women's Political Caucus. *Pat Denton Collection (14-007), Newcomb Archives and Vorhoff Library Special Collections, Newcomb College Institute, Tulane University.*

Maurice Durbin, lobbyist; Annabelle Walker, New Orleans National Organization for Women president; and Ida Martinez, AFL-CIO and NOW member, Great Women's Reunion, ca. 1999. Durbin lobbied for feminist legislation, especially antiviolence reform. *Pat Denton Collection (14-007), Newcomb Archives and Vorhoff Library Special Collections, Newcomb College Institute, Tulane University.*

Fran and Victor Bussie, pictured with Valerie Harper (middle), at the annual AFL-CIO convention, ca. 1978. Bussie brought in Harper, a famous TV actress, along with actor Alan Alda, as speakers, to raise the profile of the event and to urge ratification of the Equal Rights Amendment. Both actors had been outspoken in their support for ERA. *Janet Allured Collection, Newcomb Archives and Vorhoff Library Special Collections, Newcomb College Institute, Tulane University.*

Rupert Richardson's International Women's Year photograph, 1977. She worked for the state assisting the Department of Health and Hospitals in addition to serving as a national, regional, and state officer of the NAACP and Women in Politics. *Ollie T. Osborne Papers, Collection 93, University Archives and Acadiana Manuscripts Collection, Edith Garland Dupré Library, University of Louisiana at Lafayette.*

Sylvia Roberts at the International Women's Year conference in Baton Rouge. She along with Clay Latimer and Janet Mary Riley were panelists at the IWY session titled "Women and the Law." Roberts practiced law for sixty years in Baton Rouge. She successfully argued the case of *Weeks v. Southern Bell* in 1969. Thereafter, in addition to her law practice, she devoted considerable energy to programs designed to prevent intimate-partner violence, particularly teen dating violence. *Ollie T. Osborne Papers, Collection 93, University Archives and Acadiana Manuscripts Collection, Edith Garland Dupré Library, University of Louisiana at Lafayette.*

Left to right: Sister Clara Borque; Mindy Milam, chair of the Jefferson Parish National Organization for Women; Pat Denton of the Louisiana Women's Political Caucus (wearing shirt reading "Southern Feminist"); Geraldine Ferraro; and state representative Mary Landrieu, during Ferraro's 1984 run for the vice presidency on the Democratic ticket with Walter Mondale. *Private Collection.*

CHAPTER 5

"Murder or Mercy?"

Expanding Access to Abortion and Birth
Control in Louisiana, 1960–1974

In 1971, two twenty-something New Orleans women discussed their illegal abortions with *New Orleans States-Item* reporters Patsy Sims and Joan Kent. "Anne," a Catholic and a nurse, had been pregnant twice. The first time, she went to a home for unwed mothers and gave the baby up for adoption, an experience so traumatic she vowed never to do it again. The second time, she got an illegal abortion, which she found far less emotionally wrenching than giving away a baby that she had given birth to. Terminating the pregnancy, she reported, "didn't affect me emotionally, physically, psychologically or in any other way—it didn't even affect me financially." Anne's procedure cost her only thirty dollars, so it is likely that it was the work of a midwife or other paraprofessional who surreptitiously provided illegal abortions in Louisiana before the 1973 Supreme Court decision in *Roe v. Wade* made abortion legal throughout the United States. Though Anne did not describe her provider, the other woman, "Beth," a student, identified hers as a licensed physician in town. It was expensive—five hundred dollars—but Beth said he did it in his office and gave her antibiotics and pain medication. The doctor also told her to call him if she had any problems. Though she had no complications, and so little discomfort she did not even need to take the pain pill, she was grateful that he had agreed to provide not just the abortion but also the follow-up care, should she need it. Because the procedure was against the law, "he could have said, 'You don't know me anymore.'" She had the abortion on a Friday and was back in school on Monday. "Practically all of my friends" knew, Beth said, and she also reported that she knew at least four other women who had had abortions, though none, apparently, had gone to the same physician as she. Clearly, many practitioners offered this service to women who demanded it, and knowledge about how to obtain underground abortions was the subject of many discreet conversations among sexually active women. The experience in New Orleans was similar to almost every city in the United States at the time.[1]

Though his identity cannot be ascertained for certain, the physician who performed Beth's abortion may have been Dr. Horace Hale Harvey III, who had set up an unlawful but thriving abortion practice in New Orleans in 1969. Beth's account certainly fits the description of Harvey. Though he revealed nothing about his own practice, Harvey was quoted in the *States-Item* expressing concern that some medical professionals took advantage of women seeking abortions in Louisiana: "Doctors tell girls they are pregnant when they aren't and then charge outrageous prices ($500) for abortions." Or they gave the woman "pills" to cause miscarriages. "They don't work but the doctor takes the girl's money" anyway. Harvey had established the Community Sex Information and Education Service, "a private, non-profit organization formed by a group of local physicians, social scientists, psychologists, counselors, sex educators, and lawyers who [were] concerned about sexual problems in their communities," in 1970. Though it may indeed have provided counseling and education about reproduction and sex, it probably also included abortion referrals.[2]

H. Hale Harvey III was from a well-established family that held significant property in the New Orleans area.[3] Harvey's father, Horace Hale II, was Catholic, but his mother was Protestant, and in those days, the church required children in a "mixed" marriage to be raised Catholic. Despite his Catholic training and the church's long-standing teaching that abortion was murder, Harvey believed he had an ethical responsibility to assist women seeking to terminate pregnancies. An intellectual, Harvey had begun a PhD program in philosophy at Tulane, which he interrupted to attend LSU medical school in New Orleans to learn more about medical ethics. He completed both degrees, and in his dissertation, he referred to abortion as an epidemic that presented physicians with a moral dilemma.[4]

By all accounts, Harvey sought to provide women a safe and professional alternative to unscrupulous scoundrels. His reputation was good enough that the Clergy Counseling Service on Abortion (CCS) in New York sent women to him for the procedure. Then in 1971, when New York changed its abortion laws to allow pregnancy termination for any reason in the first trimester, Harvey, in an agreement with the CCS, moved to New York City and opened the first free-standing clinic in the nation to provide legal abortions. He was one of many male doctors in Louisiana who were "moral pioneers," physicians of conscience who took a pro-woman approach toward the practice of abortion.[5]

Anne and Beth's stories come from a six-part series on abortion in Louisiana (with a focus on New Orleans) called "Murder or Mercy?" that *New Orleans States-Item* reporters Patsy Sims, Joan Kent, and Bettye Anding researched and wrote in 1971. The importance of female reporters covering issues of concern to women, even if their stories remained confined to the women's section of the paper, is worth noting. Sims, Kent, and Anding interviewed local doctors, psychiatrists, clergy, state legislators, and women in the New Orleans area who had undergone abortions. The series won a Press Club Award for best newspaper series of the year, so it was well worth the effort, but that the paper was willing to allow three reporters to spend time investigating this subject indicates that abortion was getting a lot of attention in the early 1970s. Even doctors, the reporters noted, "seeing the handwriting on the wall, are willing to speak out on this until-now hush-hush subject."[6]

The reports made clear that men and women who sought to provide Louisiana women with safe abortions before *Roe v. Wade* engaged in daily, often public, acts of civil disobedience, techniques they had learned from the civil rights movement. They established referral services and a network of abortion providers whom they had personally investigated, sometimes at their own peril, for safety and considerate treatment of their patients. Thus the campaign to remove anti-abortion statutes drew upon the techniques used by the southern black freedom movement. Like that struggle, too, the reproductive rights movement drew sustenance from the ethical concerns of a wide array of religiously devout people, including men, who believed that they had a responsibility to put their faith into action in the temporal world.

The crusade to liberalize abortion laws had broad support among liberal faith traditions. Non-Orthodox Jewish sects have long supported reproductive freedom for all women (not just for Jewish women), including abortion, and women in the National Council of Jewish Women began working on behalf of the legalization of abortion in the 1960s. Liberal Protestant denominations, too, believed that empathizing with and providing emotional support to women faced with a crisis pregnancy was a moral imperative. The compassionate response, liberals reasoned, was to treat women as moral free agents, capable of making the decision that was right for them at that time. They trusted that a woman, in most cases, chose abortion not for selfish reasons but because she had concerns about her family, either her immediate one or the family of the world. In other words, women who sought to limit their fertility brought to bear on their decision a relational dynamic that elevated the lives of existing humans, particularly their own children and families, and the health of the global ecology. Environmentalism, new to the 1960s, intersected with the desire for human population control. Thus, the restoration of a woman's right to reproductive control was part of the ecofeminist movement that grew out of feminism. This was as true in Louisiana as it was elsewhere in the United States.

Criminalization and Decriminalization of Abortion

In order to understand what motivated those men and women, a brief history of how and why birth control and abortion had both been criminalized in the mid- to late nineteenth century is in order. Historically, abortion had not been criminal as long as it was performed before "quickening"—the point in the pregnancy when the mother first feels life. In the mid-nineteenth century, by all accounts, the incidence of abortion began to increase. Because aseptic techniques had not yet been developed, it could also be exceedingly dangerous for the mother. Evangelical Protestants, distressed about the growing rate of abortion even among married women, and the American Medical Association, concerned about paraprofessionals performing the operation under unsafe conditions, pressured the federal government to enact the Comstock Law in 1873. Named for Anthony Comstock, an antivice crusader, the law made the interstate transportation of both abortion and birth control devices and information illegal. Comstock himself became a special inspector to the post office whose job was to inspect the mail for any "pornographic" materials, which included birth control or abortion information. The once-thriving mail-order business in contraceptive "shields" (condoms or diaphragms), pessaries (primitive IUDs), pills, and advertisements for practitioners quickly went underground.[7]

Following the federal example, states passed "mini Comstock Acts" of their own. The laws varied somewhat from state to state, but as a general rule by the end of the nineteenth century it was illegal everywhere in the United States to sell birth control or abortion devices or to assist anyone in procuring an abortion for any reason except to save the life of the mother. A doctor could prescribe birth control for "therapeutic" reasons, but unless the patient was from a family of some means, he was unlikely to do so because of the risk. Some doctors, when faced with a patient in distress, discretely slipped her the name of someone in the area who specialized in the procedure. This might be a doctor, a midwife, a former nurse, or a paraprofessional.[8]

Beginning in the 1950s, states began to liberalize their abortion laws to allow therapeutic abortions to preserve not only the mother's life but also her health, which might include her psychological as well as physical health. However, fearing prosecution, hospitals in the United States set up multiple hurdles for women to clear before they could secure even a therapeutic abortion. Many women—determined to make their own decisions about their bodies and their future—circumvented these obstacles by traveling to other countries; if they lived in the South, this usually meant Puerto Rico, Cuba or Mexico. Such a costly trip required a woman to come up with the money not just for the abortion but also for travel expenses. Unless she had her own stash of cash, this money was probably scraped together by friends and family members, who obviously supported her decision. All these people became part of the underground dynamic for change.[9]

In the 1960s Louisiana had two statutes regulating abortion that contradicted each other. The Criminal Code prohibited all abortions, with a penalty of imprisonment at hard labor for one to ten years. The second statute, the Medical Practices Act, said that abortions could be performed by a licensed physician with the consultation and approval of another licensed physician. However, in reality, only when a procedure resulted in the woman's illness or death was the provider likely to be prosecuted, and then the highest crime for which he or she could be charged—if the woman died—was manslaughter, not felony murder.[10] One Mrs. Ethel Bowden, a fifty-five-year-old midwife who operated a "confinement house" in Shreveport, was charged with manslaughter after a woman was found dead in the house as the result of an abortion. The paper reported that this was the second abortion-related death in Shreveport within the past week (another woman had also been charged with criminal manslaughter in the previous death).[11] Louisiana's criminal act was normally applied to nonphysicians and doctors who did not follow the procedure set out in the medical practice act.[12]

Criminalization created a rampant black market industry in abortifacients (mixtures and drugs taken orally or in the form of douches) and in procedures performed by physicians or by paraprofessionals who specialized in abortion services. One woman born in 1922 remembered that during the Great Depression, "there were abortionists on every corner" in New Orleans. She guessed that there were many abortion providers in the Crescent City because it had a large number of prostitutes, and prostitutes "needed abortions." (She probably underestimated the number of "nice" girls who also sought abortions.) Since physicians in Louisiana caught providing abortions could have their medical licenses revoked, most gynecologists eschewed it. One researcher, sociologist Nanette J. Davis, has argued that the fear of being prosecuted meant that "criminal abortionists were often medical rejects—physicians afflicted with alcoholism, drug addiction, mental illness, senility, and loss of licensure from other crimes—who were able to develop a successful practice in a profitable, albeit illegal, field." Others, however, disagree with that conclusion and contend that regular MDs provided most abortions before *Roe v. Wade*. In the 1950s, Alfred Kinsey claimed that "nearly 90% of the operative abortions . . . performed today are being performed by physicians, most of whom are not recognized as abortionists." A Boston doctor estimated that he and one other physician performed 90 percent of the illegal abortions in that city. Studies of abortion doctors in several U.S. cities, Rickie Solinger has determined, show that they "worked for decades doing hundreds of abortions a year, with very few complications and little contact with the law." In Louisiana, while paraprofessionals certainly provided abortions, so too did regular physicians and doctors in training. Reporters Sims, Kent, and Anding interviewed five doctors selected at random for the series on abortion that ran in the *New Orleans States-Item*. Perhaps because they were concerned about protecting their reputations and licenses, none of those physicians would go on record saying that he favored abortion on demand or that it should be a woman's right, but all five said they knew where to send women who sought abortions. Through whispered conversations or on pieces of paper slipped to them by their personal physicians, women—who surely knew that a self-induced abortion was far more dangerous than one provided by someone with knowledge and experience—learned to whom they could turn. In their own courageous act of civil disobedience, they defied the law, took charge of their reproductive lives, and got themselves to a physician.[13]

The urban legend among poor women in the New Orleans environs was that residents at Charity Hospital (where most interns and residents at LSU's medical school took their training) provided abortion services during their off hours and told the women to present the next day or two complaining of a miscarriage, which would be followed by (and officially reported as) a dilation and curettage (D&C). Or they told the women to attempt a self-abortion and, once having started the process, to present at Charity's emergency room in the middle of the night, where the resident on duty would perform a D&C, no questions asked.[14]

Other New Orleans hospitals publically disavowed that they engaged in such covert techniques. Doctors at Ochsner Hospital and Baptist Hospital in New Orleans said that they strictly complied with the Medical Practice Act, which required the "consultation of two or more doctors other than the woman's own obstetrician." The head of Ochsner's obstetrics and gynecology department, John C. Weed, insisted, "Abortions are done here for two reasons only: danger to the life or health of the mother because she has a chronic disease, or severe emotional distress. These patients are suicidal, not just disturbed. In these cases we seek psychiatric consultation." When pressed, he felt it necessary to say that Louisiana hospitals did not perform abortions "simply to accommodate the patient." The hospital committee, he averred, prevented such a thing, or so he said for the record. It is likely that there was little concern about the practice at Charity because the women who went there were disproportionately poor and black. It is not a stretch to think that the community cared far less about abortions procured by people widely regarded as an underclass than they did about pregnancy terminations by white middle- or upper-class women.[15]

Criminalization, in fact, created a class divide: a woman of means might be able to get a doctor to prescribe a hospital abortion, or she could travel abroad to get one. John Montjoy, a lawyer who received his JD from Tulane, in 1969 argued that the system was discriminatory "against the indigent and the Negro," who "must either resort to a low priced unskilled abortionist, self-abortion, or bear an unwanted, often illegitimate child." The *New Orleans States-Item* reported flatly that to procure an abortion, "when you get down to it, it's not who you are, but who you know." Dr. Genevieve Arneson, medical director of West Jefferson Mental Health Center, counseled women who had had abortions and those who had borne babies they did not want. In her experience, she observed, "If you have enough money, it is no problem to get an abortion. I have seen brochures telling about package deals for abortions in foreign countries where it is legal. For about $1500, you get transportation, hotel and a hospital abortion. If wealthy women have the freedom to make their own decision, why shouldn't all women?" Lower-class women did not have that luxury, and they turned to a paraprofessional or else self-aborted, often suffering severe infection and sometimes death as a result.[16]

Louisiana's poor sought abortions from neighborhood practitioners who may have been trained as licensed practical nurses or just as nurse's aides. The fee could range from fifty to seventy-five dollars, a lot for a black woman who, if working as a domestic, might make only ten dollars per day. If severe complications arose, she might go to one of the state's public hospitals, which provided emergency medical care for the indigent. If the hospitals would not help them, women might go to a midwife or a "drugstore physician" who operated in low-income neighborhoods. Women who sought permanent fertility control— typically after they had had several children already and considered their families complete—begged their doctors for a hysterectomy. If they went to Charity Hospital, the resident on duty likely honored their wishes. Women with few other resources turned to sterilization, in other words, as the only surefire method of birth control.[17]

But young women like Beth, especially if they were still students who had not yet married and borne the children they wanted, may have taken their chances with an illegal abortion. Though it was kept out of the news at the time (almost surely to protect the family and the reputation of the school), a student at Newcomb College, Tulane's private and expensive coordinate school for women, died from an abortion in 1963. June Emily Wall, a freshman from nearby Harvey, Louisiana, died at the hands of a previously convicted eighty-four-year-old New Orleans abortionist, Ann Corinne Sharp. Wall's death from a botched abortion was passed down through the lore of the school, rumored but never confirmed, until the details were uncovered by an undergraduate in Tulane professor Karissa Haugeberg's class on reproductive rights in the fall of 2014.[18]

Ann Sharp was one of many abortion providers prosecuted in Louisiana in the years after World War II. Sentences varied widely. Electra Courville, alias Mrs. Electa Dore, age forty-five, an abortion provider in little New Iberia, situated in a majority-Catholic area of central Louisiana's bayou country, received a sentence of three years at hard labor in the Louisiana State Penitentiary in January 1954. However, she remained free pending appeal, and the outcome of her case is unknown.[19] Others paid a fine or spent a short time in prison and typically went right back into practice.[20]

It is impossible to estimate how many illegal procedures occurred annually before 1973, in Louisiana or elsewhere, or to know how many women died. Because it was against the law, medical practitioners and hospitals had every incentive to disguise the practice. No one wanted documentation that might lead to an embarrassing and possibly career-ending arrest, trial, and conviction. The *New Orleans States-Item*'s series quoted a health-care provider as saying that well-established physicians gave women what they wanted but "they [didn't] call it an abortion. They call[ed] it a dilation and curettage (D&C)." Charts recorded women presenting with hemorrhages, blighted ova, premature separation of the placenta, or other such ills, any one of which might reasonably have been treated with a D&C. Everyone acknowledged that deaths due to abortion were also disguised to avoid risk of prosecution. In Louisiana during 1968–69, six abortion deaths were reported to the State Department of Health. But these figures were "the tip of the iceberg," according to the head of that department, Dr. Andrew Hedmeg. "Abortion deaths are generally reported in other terminology," he acknowledged.[21] The commander of the NOPD homicide division, Captain Anthony Polito, pointed out that obtaining "the real facts" about abortions that resulted in the woman's illness or death was practically impossible "since the Louisiana Criminal Code prohibit[ed] the procedure for any reason and fear of the law [was] a factor in concealment." The homicide division of the NOPD had five abortion cases in 1969 and made two arrests. During 1970, three cases were reported and another two arrests made. Captain Polito emphasized that these statistics were "positively not a true picture of abortion in New Orleans because," he asserted, "most are not reported to us. We don't hear about the abortions that go all right. Those brought to our attention are the ones in which the woman has had an abortion under the most unsanitary conditions and as a result severe complications set in" and "the girl" goes to the doctor or hospital. Clearly, women sought to control their reproductive lives, regardless of the risk to their health, and not just unmarried women who found themselves pregnant without possibility of a marriage, as an increasing number of investigative studies throughout the country showed.[22] Sex researcher Alfred Kinsey reported as far back as 1953 that 22 percent of *married* women had had at least one abortion by the time they turned forty-five, and that the average number for each woman was not one abortion but two. The public perception that women who terminated pregnancies were prostitutes, "degenerates," or "tramps" was inaccurate.[23] Despite, or perhaps because of, the dangers associated with criminalization, a network of trusted counselors and providers—some professional, some paraprofessional, some feminists, some clergy—developed to help women find the best care possible.

National Demands for Change

By the 1950s, illegal abortion had become a public health problem too big to ignore. Hospitals in major U.S. cities had entire wards dedicated to caring for women who came in dying from botched abortions. Doctors assigned to their care were required by law to demand that the sick woman tell them who had performed the procedure so that the police could arrest him or her. Many shied away from treating the patient because the attending physicians often became suspects themselves; they did not care to be interrogated by the police and have their practice called into question, perhaps amid a blaze of publicity. That they were unable to assist dying women was bad medicine and contrary to the Hippocratic oath.

Timidly at first, voices arose from virtually every geographic area of the United States calling for reform of antiquated laws. Planned Parenthood Federation of America had never advocated abortion (Margaret Sanger had denounced it as an abomination), but in 1955 the newly hired medical director, Dr. Mary Calderone, organized a conference called "Abortion in the United States." When the proceedings were published in 1958, they showed that while illegal abortion was widespread, thanks to antibiotics (which had only recently become commercially available), it was no longer dangerous. If it had been criminalized in the nineteenth century because of the danger to the woman, that reason no longer existed. Abortion, if performed under aseptic conditions, by the 1960s was ten times safer for women than childbirth.[24] Alan Guttmacher, the new director of Planned Parenthood, asked the organization to call not just for reform but for outright repeal of restrictive laws. He was astounded when the Planned Parenthood board responded in the affirmative.[25]

Besides Planned Parenthood, another major impetus for liberalization of abortion laws came from the conservative American Law Institute (ALI). This organization of judges, lawyers, and law professors drafted and promulgated a widely respected model penal code (in all fields) for states to consider enacting. In 1962, the ALI recommended that states revise their abortion statutes to permit "therapeutic" abortions under a wider array of circumstances. However, the ALI, an organization of male professionals, was primarily concerned with protecting doctors from prosecution for performing an abortion that they judged medically necessary or in the patient's best interest. Twelve states quickly enacted the model law. Though Louisiana was not among them, seven were former slave states.[26] The ALI did not make a feminist argument that women had the right to control their own fertility. By its own admission, this was a "cautious" call for expanded access to legal abortion.

Across the country, momentum for change built. In the mid-1960s, the Society for Humane Abortion opened an office in San Francisco, and scholars and lawyers in New York City formed the Association for the Study of Abortion (ASA). After years of internal and sometimes acrimonious debate, the ACLU issued a statement in 1967 calling abortion a "civil right" and saying that physicians had the right to do them without threat of criminal sanctions. Doctors, worried about liabilities, helped guide the American Medical Association (AMA) to call for greater access to abortions for most women. In 1970, the AMA issued a policy statement stating that "abortion is a medical procedure and should be performed only by a duly licensed physician and surgeon," and that the physician should be guided "by the laws of the community" but also by "good medical practice," still a rather restrained foray into untested waters.[27]

Not just in the United States but all over the Western world, as medical practices improved and as limiting fertility became a desirable goal for couples seeking upward social mobility, countries began to loosen or entirely repeal restrictive abortion laws. Scandinavian countries had allowed abortion for thirty years by the time health-care professionals in the United States even began discussing it. Japan's 1948 law permitted it under a limited set of circumstances, and in 1967, Great Britain made it legal in most cases.[28] Women of means could afford to travel to those countries and secure a safe abortion in a hospital. Louisiana women seeking abortions were more likely to go to Puerto Rico or Mexico simply because they were closer and therefore less costly. Abortion was not legal in either place, but it was ubiquitous and the law was unenforced.

Publicity surrounding two major health catastrophes for pregnant women caused a discernible shift in public opinion in favor of decriminalizing abortion. In the early 1960s, many women in Europe took the prescription medication Thalidomide for headaches or pregnancy-induced nausea and subsequently gave birth to severely deformed babies with stunted, flipper-like, or missing arms or legs. Though the Food and Drug Administration had not approved Thalidomide's use in this country, some women received it by mistake. One was Sherri Finkbine, a Phoenix mother of four, well known as the host of the children's television show *Romper Room*. Even though her doctor recommended an abortion, the hospital would not agree to it. Finkbine called the local newspaper to advise women of the dangers of Thalidomide just before she and her husband boarded a plane for Sweden, where she received her abortion. When she returned, she told her story to *Redbook*. She said that the Swedish doctors had told her that "baby" was not the best term for the severely deformed lump she had been carrying. Though she did not refer to her religion in the interview, Finkbine held to the Reform Jewish view that until it has an existence separate from the mother and breathes on its own, a fetus is a "growth," a part of her body. Even though she received hate mail and death threats from those who believed differently, Finkbine, the married mother of four, was neither antichild nor antifamily. In her view, conserving her time and energy and her family's resources for the health and safety of her four existing children was morally acceptable, even desirable. According to a Gallup poll, 52 percent of Americans approved of what she had done.[29]

The second major health issue in the early 1960s was a rubella (German measles) epidemic. If a woman was infected early in her pregnancy, rubella was likely to cause severe fetal deformities, fetal demise, or short, sometimes horrendous lives for the child. The rubella epidemic garnered enormous publicity, and young state legislators, more inclined toward reform than the previous generation, began introducing bills that incorporated significant elements of the ALI's Model Penal Code's provisions for relaxing abortion restrictions.[30]

As a result of these high-profile cases, support for decriminalizing abortion increased sharply among people from a wide range of ethnic and religious backgrounds in the early 1970s. In June 1972, 64 percent of Americans indicated that they agreed with the statement: "The decision to have an abortion should be made solely by a woman and her physician." This Gallup poll found less support in the South, but nonetheless a majority of southerners (53 percent) agreed with the statement, while 40 percent did not.[31]

That Gallup poll does not break down responses by race, but other evidence shows that African American women supported reproductive rights just as much and perhaps more than did white women. The debates surrounding family planning among African American activists in the 1960s have been well documented.[32] Black men expressed concern that white people sought, through birth control and abortion legalization, the destruction of the black race (a genocide argument). Even Jessie Jackson opposed abortion rights in the 1970s, but he changed his mind in the 1980s. From the beginning of the debate, women of color expressed conflicting opinions about the ethics and need for

abortion law reform, but some pushed back against the reactionary position
of African American men. Frances Beal, head of the Black Women's Liberation
Committee of SNCC, wrote in 1969: "Black women have the right and responsibility to determine when it is in the interest of the [black freedom] struggle
to have children or not to have them and this right must not be relinquished."[33]
Shirley Chisholm, who had supported abortion reform while a New York assem-
blywoman and who became the first African American woman in Congress,
"dismissed the genocide argument when asked to discuss her views on abortion
and birth control":

> To label family planning and legal abortion programs "genocide" is male rhetoric,
> for male ears. It falls flat to female listeners and to thoughtful male ones. Women
> know, and so do many men, that two or three children who are wanted, prepared
> for, reared amid love and stability, and educated to the limit of their ability will
> mean more for the future of the Black and brown races from which they come
> than any number of neglected, hungry, ill-housed and ill-clothed youngsters.[34]

As early as 1968, poor black women organized in the National Welfare Rights
Organization advocated reproductive freedom. They insisted that states could
not make welfare benefits conditional on enforced use of birth control or, even
worse, sterilization and fought those tendencies. But they also adhered to a
feminist belief that every woman, regardless of her income level, had a right
to choose for herself how many children to bear and raise, and they therefore
called for increased access to both contraception and abortion for women of
limited means.[35]

Though lack of documentation prevents definitive statements regarding
black Louisiana women's opinions about abortion and birth control, it is clear
that they sought the procedure. After abortion became legal in 1973 and the
Delta Women's Clinic opened on St. Charles Avenue in New Orleans, Susan
Jane Allen, who worked there, noted, "Black women were very supportive of
our efforts. We had so many great women who worked there, including graduates of Xavier Prep [a black Catholic prep school], and others who had gone off
to the Seven Sisters and came back with degrees in social work or psychology
but couldn't get jobs in the city. They were half of our counseling staff. The other
half were white, and also graduates of great schools. They were typically New
Orleans natives who had gone off to school and came back home."[36] In recent
years, black women in Louisiana as elsewhere have joined a movement for
"reproductive justice," represented by the organization Sister Song. Branches of
the organization exist in Louisiana, but they work closely with Planned Parenthood, which has always had white directors in the Bayou State.[37]

Louisiana, unlike many other southern states, has no documented history of forced sterilization. This is probably due to the influence of the Catholic Church, which opposed such procedures. Charges of involuntary sterilization of clients were leveled against an innovative program begun by Dr. Joseph Diehl Beasley, but such charges have never been proven and, given the goals of the Louisiana Family Health Foundation (FHF), were highly unlikely. Because it gives us a glimpse of the class nature of reproductive practices in Louisiana at the time the program was launched in the 1960s, its history is worth exploring.

Social Justice and Reproductive Rights in Louisiana

The FHF was the first statewide family planning program for poor people in the United States. Its founder, Dr. Joseph Beasley, brought with him to Louisiana impressive credentials. A private physician in Atlanta in the 1950s before joining Tulane's faculty, where he was a professor in the medical school, he was former chair of Harvard's Department of Population Sciences and of Planned Parenthood-World Population. Like many in the 1960s, he had become fascinated with the idea of a "population bomb," or the possibility of the explosion of the human population, and wanted to find a responsible way to avert the coming disaster. He chose Louisiana as his "laboratory" because it resembled a developing country: the state ranked at the bottom by almost every measure of quality of life—illiteracy, illegitimacy, and infant mortality. His goal was to design a program that would help women in the third world control how many children they bore and, by lowering fertility rates, raise their standard of living. Cultural anthropologist and UNO professor Martha Ward, who chronicled the life and death of this groundbreaking program, argues that the FHF had an extraordinary influence on the development of family planning programs everywhere.[38]

At the time when the FHF began in 1964, birth control was outlawed in Louisiana, partly because of the influence of the Roman Catholic Church. As a result, Louisiana had a shockingly high number of unwanted children and babies born to single mothers, and a correspondingly high rate of infant mortality and child abuse, particularly among the poor. Virtually all poor women delivered their babies in the state-operated public hospital system, usually without any prenatal care. Seeking to mitigate those ills and provide basic preventive health care to poor women, Dr. Beasley worked out an arrangement with the Catholic Church. He got the church behind him by pointing out the lack of hospital births, the high number of maternal deaths in childbirth, and the high rates of infant mortality. He agreed that the FHF would provide birth control only to married women and would not offer abortions or abortion referrals. (It did not begin supplying birth control to unmarried adolescents until 1972, and then to very few.) He promised that no patient would be persuaded to use any birth control method contrary to the church's teaching, and indeed the rhythm method was among the seven forms of contraception explained to clients at the clinic. Also as part of the deal, Planned Parenthood agreed not to enter Louisiana. The governor, John McKeithen, backed the program once he knew that the Catholic Church would not oppose it, so long as no state funds were used. To assist Beasley in offering services while avoiding a legislative battle and publicity that might result, the governor convinced the attorney general to "reinterpret" Louisiana's restrictive birth control law in 1965, the year that the first of 144 FHF clinics in Louisiana opened in Lincoln Parish (a rural parish in the northern part of the state).[39]

Funded by the federal government and prestigious private charities such as the Ford, the Rockefeller, and the Kellogg Foundations, the program, as Beasley put it, sought to offer "hope to many who suffered unnecessarily: women in poor health, whose infants were most likely to die; teenagers, many unmarried, whose children were born retarded or premature; and battered or neglected children, whose mothers lacked emotional strength and community support." To the founders of the FHF, "the lack of personal freedom to choose indicated society's lack of commitment to all its children." This was an expansive ethical vision that excluded a selfish desire to reproduce oneself and included a desire to ensure quality of life for all children.[40]

Unusual for 1965, Beasley and his colleagues insisted that the staff and clientele be racially integrated. Prohibited by the governor and the Catholic Church from advertising, Beasley pioneered a system of neighborhood outreach whereby workers went door to door to visit potential patients. For the few years that it operated (from 1965 to 1974), the Louisiana FHF gave thousands of poor women the first preventive health services they had ever received. Grateful black women, Ward reports, "had come to believe that they and their children were receiving excellent health care for the first time."[41]

Despite spectacular growth and enormous demand, black nationalists charged Beasley with genocidal intent, and accusations of involuntary sterilizations and embezzlement forced the operation to close in 1974. Convicted of fiscal mismanagement, Dr. Joseph Diehl Beasley served two years in federal prison for misusing government funds. Beasley has always maintained his innocence, and the charges of involuntary sterilization were unfounded. Federal guidelines were vague, and Beasley as well as the federal government maintained lax supervision of associates who ran programs.[42] Martha Ward defends Beasley and FHF, saying, "Not one single charge of patient maltreatment was leveled at the program." Nor was there any coercion of patients, all of whom were treated with dignity and respect—a critical strategy, as far as Beasley was concerned. Furthermore, the program left a lasting legacy, Ward notes, in that "the medical services offered . . . still serve as a model in the United States. Many key administrators in family planning or maternal health care systems around the world were trained in Louisiana."[43] The real problem was that other medical professionals felt as though Beasley was creating a system of "socialized medicine" that impinged upon their client base (even though they had never served poor women well, if at all). Competitors to this program, which included doctors in private practice, targeted it and Beasley. "If I had it to do over again," Beasley reflected as he was about to enter federal prison in Florida, "instead of making Family Health a non-profit philanthropic group, I would organize it as a private for-profit endeavor. In this society, people understand private for profit organizations," but, he said, they are suspicious of nonprofits. It is sad but true that (as one reviewer of Ward's book put it) there were enormously powerful "forces operating against free choice in health care for those most in need of it."[44] After serving his two-year sentence in a federal prison in Florida, Beasley went into private practice as a pediatrician (his specialty) in Amityville, New York.[45]

Though the attempt to provide free birth control failed in Louisiana, Beasley and the foundations that supported him represented growing public support for women's reproductive rights. Indeed, even though Beasley and the FHF were gone, the program was not. The Louisiana Department of Health and Hospitals took over his clinics, changed the name of the program to Louisiana Family Planning, and continued to offer reproductive health services, described by someone who worked there as "a wonderful resource in each parish for women who could not afford private doctors for family planning. At that time, any girl who was of child bearing ability could access the LFP clinics without parental consent."[46]

Beasley represented many of his generation who were concerned about the strain that an exploding human population, if unchecked, placed on the earth's resources. This apprehension had been growing since the 1940s, but the 1968 publication of best-selling *The Population Bomb*, by Stanford University professor Paul Ehrlich and his wife, Anne Ehrlich (who was uncredited), created near-hysteria about this issue.[47] In 1969, Congress created, at President Nixon's request, the Commission on Population Growth and the American Future, chaired by John D. Rockefeller III and on which Joe Beasley served.[48] At the grassroots level, chapters of Zero Population Growth (ZPG) sprang up. Louisiana's chapter, formed in 1970, met monthly in New Orleans at the First Unitarian Church, pastored by Rev. Albert D'Orlando. President John H. Bertel wrote to the *New Orleans Times-Picayune* that a world crisis would emerge if the current rate of population growth continued. "Imagine trying to feed twice the population of the world today, a very dismal prospect considering millions of people are starving and malnourished right now." The Louisiana Chapter of ZPG, he said, "is trying to educate and encourage people to voluntarily limit their family size." The group supported free and easy access to both birth control and abortion.[49]

Calls for significant changes to Louisiana's abortion codes included the voices of attorneys. In 1969, John Montjoy, quoted earlier, wrote a piece in the *Tulane Law Review* urging modification of Louisiana's laws. Louisiana had one of the lowest rates of therapeutic abortions in the nation, Montjoy determined, because "the medical profession ha[d] been excessively reluctant to risk either criminal prosecution or social stigma." The result was that women went elsewhere for legal abortions, self-aborted, turned to criminal practitioners, or bore a child "for which they [were] unable to provide." Montjoy asserted, "A reform of Louisiana's abortion laws presents no significant threat to the major civil law concepts which have existed for so long in this state." Citing polling data that documented majority support among Louisianans for the American Law Institute model, Montjoy urged revision of Louisiana law to make abortions more widely available and physicians less wary of prosecution.[50]

Half a century earlier, Margaret Sanger, the founder of Planned Parenthood, had called for the end to all laws that criminalized birth control by saying that no woman could call herself free if she could not control her fertility. That argument resurfaced in the 1960s, as feminists made the case for repeal of abortion restrictions using the same line of reasoning that they used to combat sexual assault and domestic violence, which was simply that women had a right to bodily autonomy. Sandy Karp, a member of the Louisiana Citizens for Abortion Law Reform, rejected the traditional view of women, as she put it, as "breeders or as property." Modern society should begin to see women as adults with moral free agency that extended to their right to voluntary motherhood. Unlike the more cautious calls for reform issued by the male-dominated professional associations that preceded them, feminists demanded repeal of all laws limiting women's ability to obtain an abortion "on demand." "The question is not whether there will be abortions but whether they will be legal or illegal, safe or unsafe," Karp told the *New Orleans Times-Picayune*.[51] Karp was one of the founders of Sisters Helping Sisters, an abortion counseling and referral service that advertised in the alternative newspaper the *Vieux Carré Courier* and in *Distaff*.

Setting up an abortion referral network and vetting the providers to whom they referred women was one form of direct action, something that people take to when the political system fails them. An even bolder form cropped up in other cities around the country when feminists began taking control of the process of providing abortions. In Chicago, a grassroots network of feminists (who, to disguise their identity from the police, called themselves "Jane") taught women how to perform abortions safely, in their own homes, using a new vacuum aspirator, a simple device that women could make themselves. Some Jane members also learned how to perform abortions using the D&C instruments, which allowed them to bypass the highly problematic male paraprofessionals to whom they had formerly referred patients. By its own records, Jane performed more than eleven thousand procedures between 1969 and 1973. Though there is no evidence that women in Louisiana provided a similar service, elsewhere in the country, many other women did.[52] Should abortion again become unavailable in the United States, there is every reason to believe that similar self-help networks would spring up to fill the unmet need.

Clandestine abortion was the real "problem that had no name." This was the unspeakable truth of women's lives. Like rape and domestic battery, it was a shameful secret. Borrowing a technique first begun by Frenchwomen, including Simone de Beauvoir, U.S. feminists brought abortion "out of the closet" by publicly announcing that they had obtained unlawful procedures and calling for repeal of state statutes criminalizing abortion except in very rare circumstances. Just as they had removed the stigma from rape by telling their stories, they did the same with abortion. In reality, this was another type of direct action, and it came in a variety of forms. In the first issue of *Ms.* magazine (Spring 1972), for example, fifty-three women, including Jacqueline Michot Ceballos from Louisiana, signed their names underneath a petition proclaiming, "We have had abortions." The inspiration for this was the public attestation by 343 prominent Frenchwomen that they had undergone abortions. "This *act de révolte*," the *Ms.* petition declared, "dramatized their individual determination to take their lives and liberation into their own hands. It also showed their willingness to stand with and to speak for their less well-known sisters, who were forced to suffer unwanted pregnancies or illegal abortions in silence." *Ms.* magazine encouraged the "millions of other American women" who sought repeal of laws restricting reproductive freedom to divulge their own experiences of illegal abortion, too. Such publicity, by indicating how common the practice was, worked to shift public opinion.[53]

As women began telling their stories about illegal abortion, they exposed the lengths to which women were willing to go to obtain one. Not only did women risk death from sepsis, but the conditions they endured in order to acquire a back-alley abortion could be horrific. Clandestine procedures often took place in a hotel room, with the woman blindfolded, without sanitary surroundings, procedures, or instruments. Paraprofessionals were notorious for taking advantage of women who came to them for help. Sometimes the man demanded sex as part of the payment, since he was doing her a great favor and because he figured she was probably a loose woman anyway. New Orleans reporter Bettye Anding quoted a local woman who found a doctor to perform an abortion but who insisted that she "go to bed" with him and pay him five hundred dollars first. She refused, but many other desperate women did not.[54]

As evidence of the shady nature of black market abortion services accumulated, support for repeal of existing abortion statutes (rather than reform) gathered strength. In 1967, NOW adopted a "bill of rights" that included "the right of women to control their own reproductive lives by removing from penal codes the laws limiting access to contraceptive information and devices and laws governing abortion."[55] In 1968, both the ACLU and the American College of Obstetricians and Gynecologists endorsed far more extensive access to abortion than either of their earlier more cautious statements.[56] In 1969, advocates for repealing abortion laws held what they billed as the First National Conference on Abortion Laws in Chicago. Betty Friedan, representing NOW, was there. So, too, was Lawrence "Larry" Lader, a New York journalist whose investigation into the history of abortion practices convinced him that laws prohibiting abortion were unjust, unpopular, and unenforceable. When he said as much in an article in the *New York Times Magazine* in 1965, he was inundated with calls and letters from women all over the country desperate for referrals to the doctors he had written about.[57] Out of the Chicago conference came a new organization, the National Association for Repeal of Abortion Laws (NARAL, now NARAL Pro-Choice America). NARAL was the first organization to call for outright repeal, not just reform, of abortion statutes, and the first to couch its argument on the rights of women, rather than for the protection of doctors.[58]

Even though abortion was an age-old method of fertility control, and abortion providers operated almost openly everywhere, religious denominations paid little attention until the pill came on the market in 1960 and feminists began to demand repeal of Comstock laws. Virtually all Protestant denominations had dropped their objections to birth control in the 1930s (a result of the Great Depression), and by the 1960s, even the most conservative Protestant denominations considered therapeutic abortion ethical.[59] Only the Roman Catholic Church continued to condemn artificial birth control and abortion in all circumstances. In 1968, Pope Paul VI issued an unanticipated encyclical, *Humanae Vitae*, which declared both contrary to the moral order. It created a storm of controversy among Catholics, clergy and laity alike. By the time of its release, a majority of Catholics in the United States supported the use of artificial birth control (as they have continued to do as of this writing), and they objected immediately. The next day, eighty-seven Roman Catholic theologians published a dissenting statement in the *New York Times*, saying that married couples should be trusted to make their own decisions about artificial contraception. Lay Catholics, outraged at the papal pronouncement, demonstrated at the November meeting of the National Conference of Catholic Bishops in 1968. To calm the controversy, the conference issued a statement saying that the decision to use artificial contraception was a matter of individual conscience, although it condemned abortion and opposed liberalization of abortion laws.[60] Yet even on the issue of abortion, not all lay Catholics agreed with the hierarchy's decision. A 1972 Gallup poll showed that substantial majorities in all categories, including Catholics, favored leaving the decision up to a woman and her doctor. There is significant evidence that many who visibly and vocally opposed abortion, even those who picketed outside abortion clinics after 1973, sought the clinics' services for themselves or their daughters when they believed it necessary to their welfare. In other words, what they said about abortion in public could be entirely different from what they practiced in private.[61]

Baptists maintained that individuals were capable of making rational and ethical decisions about their reproductive lives. The American Baptist Convention issued a statement in 1968 saying that abortion should be left up to the woman in the first trimester, and Southern Baptists called for making therapeutic abortion available in a wider variety of circumstances. The *New Orleans States-Item* quoted Grady C. Cothen, president of the SBC-affiliated New Orleans Baptist Theological Seminary, saying in 1971 that "since Baptists believe in the priesthood of each believer, it is requisite for the individual to decide these issues for himself [*sic*]."[62]

Soon a wide range of churches, in addition to rabbinical organizations and the NCJW, supported NARAL and its goal of repealing anti-abortion restrictions. These included the United Methodist Church, Episcopal Churchwomen, Church Women United, the Unitarian Universalist Association, the United Church of Christ, the United Presbyterian Church, the YWCA, the National Association of Social Workers, the American Friends Service Committee, NOW, and the NWPC.[63]

The Clergy Counseling Service on Abortion/Problem Pregnancy

Beginning in New York City, members of liberal Protestant and Jewish denominations organized to actively assist women seeking abortions. Because they counseled women in their congregations who came to them with problem pregnancies, clergy were well aware that abortion providers operated openly in just about every city in America. Police raids, although highly publicized, were fairly rare. In 1967, the Reverend Howard Moody, pastor of Judson Memorial Church on Washington Square in New York City, brought together nearby clergy to learn about the procedure and to discuss their options. After seeking legal advice, twenty-one local ministers and rabbis founded the Clergy Consultation Service on Abortion (CCS).[64] Moody's colleague at the church, Arlene Carmen, posing as a pregnant woman, visited physicians who offered abortion services. She "assessed their concern for women, their skill, and their willingness to charge a reasonable fee. Without Arlene Carmen, there would have been no Clergy Consultation Service." Within a few years, more than two thousand clergy were involved in the national CCS all over the United States, including Louisiana.[65]

Like most other movements in this period, the CCS took inspiration from the civil rights movement. Arlene Carmen and Howard Moody discuss the social, medical, ethical, and spiritual inspiration for the founding of the CCS in their first-person account, *Abortion Counseling and Social Change: From Illegal Act to Medical Practice*. They recruited for their first meeting clergy who had been active in civil rights battles in New York as well as in the South. They explain, "It was to those clergy whose liberal attitudes and commitments had been clearly established that we turned for help in developing the original nucleus of the Clergy Consultation Service on Abortion." To CCS chronicler Justin Wolff, the connection between civil rights and abortion rights was clear. Not only was "the clergy referral movement rooted in a long tradition of Protestant activism," but "the civil rights movement and the abortion rights movement shared the same sense of fighting for a higher morality." That higher morality, in the latter case, was rectifying injustices done to women seeking bodily autonomy.[66]

Moody's new organization decided to alert the media so that women would know about the service it offered. The CCS gave its story to the religion editor of the *New York Times*, and on May 22, 1967, the paper carried a front-page story about the CCS. Surprisingly, this news did not generate any backlash, not even a statement from the diocese, which indicates that the public was used to stories of illegal abortions and was rather indifferent about the entire saga. Within months, 1,500 ministers and rabbis, including many college chaplains advising students (a high-risk population), had signed up for CCS training. Using the shield of the confidentiality of pastoral counseling, clergy provided women with contact information for abortion providers outside the country, either in Mexico (where it was illegal but the law was not enforced) or overseas in one of the countries where abortion was legal in most circumstances. They also helped find funds for the woman's travel and took no money themselves for their services, lest they be accused of personally profiting.[67]

Many CCS members were campus ministers in the South, even in highly conservative states. For example, Rev. J. Claude Evans, the head chaplain at

Southern Methodist University in Dallas and father of historian Sara Evans, established the CCS in Texas. Before *Roe v. Wade* overturned Texas's strict law, the Texas CCS referred about six thousand women for abortions in states where it was legal. Just as would be true after legalization, the woman's religion made no difference in her choice of abortion. Sarah Weddington, the attorney who challenged Texas's statutes in federal court, correctly observed that "if twenty percent of a community's population was Methodist, then twenty percent of the women seen by Clergy Consultation were Methodist."[68]

Louisiana had a CCS, too, though it called itself "the Louisiana Clergy Consultation Service on *Problem Pregnancies*" rather than "on *Abortion*," because "problem pregnancy" was a less explosive term. As Rev. Howard Moody explained it, the title had been a source of discussion among the clergy who began the CCS in New York: "I knew that the word abortion could not be used in public. . . . It was simply verboten. And I said, 'I think we ought to redeem that word so that it could be spoken publicly.'"[69] He prevailed among the New York clergy, but clearly the Louisiana clerics adopted a less confrontational approach. They began a chapter of the CCS in the New Orleans area in the summer of 1970 and soon expanded to other Louisiana cities. Most of the members were campus ministers associated with the Methodist, Episcopalian, Presbyterian, Lutheran, Jewish, and Unitarian Churches. In New Orleans, these included Roy B. Nash, Methodist campus minister, and Rabbi Hillel Fine, campus rabbi, both at Tulane, and Don Rogers, Baptist campus minister at UNO. Elsewhere in the state, William M. Finnin of the United Campus Ministry advised women at LSU, and Rev. Brady Forman, of the Wesley Foundation (the Methodist student organization), counseled women at Southeastern Louisiana University in Hammond.[70]

Many clergy involved in the CCS had formed personal connections with one another during their years of civil rights activism when they had marched and even gone to jail together.[71] One was Rev. Albert D'Orlando of First Unitarian Universalist Church in New Orleans, whose wife, R. Catherine Cohen, was an OB-GYN. Both had been leaders in the black freedom movement in New Orleans. Because any white person who supported integration in the South was presumed to be a Communist, D'Orlando was investigated by the HUAC. The reward for this progressive activism was a plot to bomb the church and the parsonage where D'Orlando and his wife lived in 1965. Fortunately, the prospective bombers were too drunk to carry it out, the plot failed, and no one was hurt, but everyone involved became even more sensitive to the danger that could befall those who challenged the status quo in Louisiana.[72]

The New Orleans CCS advertised in several French Quarter newspapers, in campus newspapers, and on college bulletin boards. Ads explained the service this way: "Clergy Consultation Service on Problem Pregnancies makes available in Louisiana without charge counseling and personal help in decision-making and/or referral for problem pregnancies." The CCS reported in 1971 that it was getting about ten calls a week from women throughout the South wanting abortion referrals, which is not a particularly large number, but then there were three other referral services operating in New Orleans at the same time: the Women's Medical Assistance, run by Marle Rossi; the Community Sex Information and Education Service, run by Douglas R. "Sandy" Mackintosh; and the New Orleans Women's Center's group, Sisters Helping Sisters.[73] Furthermore, the local CCS was not the only one available. According to Florence Andre, counselor at Newcomb College, CCS services from outside the area "flooded" college campuses with literature. It is conceivable that students preferred to call the more distant ones because they feared that word might get back to their families if they went to a local counselor. Andre reported that "since her arrival at Newcomb little more than a year [earlier], she ha[d] heard of at least a dozen girls who ha[d] had abortions." Obviously, there was tremendous demand for abortion services.[74]

The Louisiana CCS statement of purpose followed the model of the original New York CCS and put the personhood of the woman ahead of any potential personhood of the fetus. It opened by declaring that the members of the service believed that abortion laws in Louisiana were not just immoral but that they were also "depersonalizing," and that the procedure should be decriminalized. But until that happened, the CCS encouraged women to come to this "free counseling service"—the organization's refusal to take any money was an important ethical component of the process. To convey that its concern was indeed for the women it counseled, and that it was not functioning as a recruiting service for any abortion practitioner, the CCS counseled women "not only before, but during and after the birthing process." Using the slogan of "Each Child Loved!", the CCS argued (surely accurately) that "adequate information and counseling [was] not generally available in the south about problem pregnancies." The members of the clergy service hoped "to provide more professional and competent counseling and personal support to the increasing numbers of people, young and otherwise, who [found] themselves about to become parents when they [did] not desire this usually happy event." Members of CCS offered compassionate counseling, legal advice, and sometimes financial assistance as well as referrals.[75]

The CCS in Louisiana emphasized that it was not pushing abortion as the solution to problem pregnancies. Rev. Robert John Dodwell, pastor of St. Anna's Episcopal Church on Esplanade Avenue in New Orleans, told Bettye Anding, "We try to help women experiencing unwanted pregnancies to come to a rea-

sonably mature decision about how to deal with their problem. At some agencies in town, you walk in and they don't say anything but 'do you want an abortion referral?' I think people should be told about the alternatives to abortion.
And the other agencies don't tell them. They also sometimes refer them to less
reputable abortionists."[76] His explanation indicates that finding abortion referrals in New Orleans was not difficult, yet CCS counselors underwent orientation and ongoing training to ensure compliance with the following guidelines:

> Women will be counseled on their options: 1) get married; 2) have the child and
> remain single; 3) place it for adoption; 4) abortion. If the client chooses an abor-
> tion, we provide information about competent medical help only outside the
> jurisdiction of the State of Louisiana. Also, no client is seen without a written
> statement from a physician asserting to proper examinations and duration of
> the pregnancy.[77]

Generally, the Louisiana CCS took positions on the conservative side. One
member, Rabbi Victor Hoffman, head of the Conservative Congregation of New
Orleans, averred that, on the one hand, "there is solidly grounded Rabbinic
interpretation that abortion is allowed in cases of rape." However, he noted,
"there is no permission in Jewish law for abortion of a fetus thought to be defec-
tive since we cannot really know. But the same abortion might be permitted on
grounds of severe mental anguish to the mother. Ephemeral pain, capricious-
ness, social or economic inconvenience are most certainly never grounds for
abortion in the view of Judaism."[78] Thus Louisiana clerics appeared to be more
cautious in their approach to abortion reform than were New Yorkers, perhaps
because liberal clergy in the previous decade had been targeted by hate groups
opposed to integration and equality for African Americans.

The CCS records deposited in New Orleans do not reveal to whom the clergy-
men referred clients wanting an abortion, nor do the records reveal what the
CCS's relationship with the medical establishment might have been. Its policy
was to refer women only to out-of-state physicians, where there would be less
chance of detection by local law enforcement. "To make referrals within the
State not only compromises the moral and legal status of the counselor, but the
client's and entire association's as well," said the Louisiana CCS's policy statement. This makes collecting data about where its clients went difficult, but it
was likely to New York City's CCS-sponsored clinic run by Hale Harvey.[79]

Among the most daring of those seeking to overturn Louisiana's abortion
laws was Dr. Sidney C. Knight, a physician practicing in the suburb of Metairie,
who considered performing abortions an act of civil disobedience (a conscious
decision to challenge an unjust law). First charged with criminal abortion
in 1964, he was prosecuted three more times thereafter and had his medical

license suspended for a time. Benjamin E. Smith of the Louisiana Civil Liberties Union represented him, but not for free. Knight reported spending as much as $80,000 for his defense, a fortune in those days. He argued for decriminalization on moral grounds. "The Louisiana law is the most oppressive in the land. It doesn't stop abortions: it murders our young women. I have a 17-year-old daughter. If she desired an abortion, the matter should be up to her." Making a feminist argument, he asserted, "A woman should have the fundamental right to decide when and if she should bear a child. Her body, especially her reproductive system, belongs to her and not to the state." He understood that his defiance of the law would not budge legislators, and, just like minorities agitating for civil rights, reproductive rights advocates would need to turn to the courts. "I feel we've kept our law as long as we have because the legislators are afraid of the religious minority which is against it," Knight said. "Therefore, it's like the integration laws in southern states that would never have passed the legislatures. It took the Supreme Court to change those just as it will to change the abortion law."[80] Knight was only one of many "physicians of conscience," as historian Carole Joffe calls them, in Louisiana before the Supreme Court's decision in *Roe v. Wade*. Historians Joffe and Leslie Reagan, while not ruling out other motives, argue that the main reason physicians defied the law was their experience in hospitals with women who had had illegal abortions. Tired of watching women die or come near death and sympathizing with women in pitiable circumstances, they acted out of a conviction that women had the right to control their own reproduction.[81]

Exposure of the dangers associated with criminal abortion, along with the concurrent Thalidomide scare and rubella epidemic, raised awareness about the need for reform or repeal of what Howard Moody called "heartless and inequitable law[s]" restricting abortion. Religious denominations, feminist organizations and individuals, and now major professional groups issued policy statements in support of reform. As a result, "between 1967 and 1971, seventeen states decriminalized abortion, reflecting a change in public opinion: 15 percent of Americans favored legal abortions in 1968, and by 1972, 64 percent did."[82] California passed the most liberal abortion law in the nation in 1967, signed by Republican governor Ronald Reagan. New York State legislators, under intense pressure from feminists and from the ccs, passed a law that allowed abortion on demand through twenty-four weeks of pregnancy, and, unlike other states that had reformed their penal codes, New York did not have a residency requirement. As a result, it became the destination for most abortion referrals. Marle Rossi of New Orleans's Women's Medical Assistance sent an average of ten women a week to New York and could have sent "an unlimited number if they just had the money."[83]

On July 1, 1970, the day New York's new law went into effect, the nation's first and busiest legal abortion clinic opened its doors. Its director and chief provider, as we learned earlier, was Horace Hale Harvey III, who had pioneered the model of the freestanding abortion clinic not tied to any other institution. After consulting with Dr. Sidney Knight and doing extensive research on the subject, he had discovered that Europeans were using a new technique, the vacuum aspirator, instead of the more dangerous D&C. Because it was not yet available in the United States, Harvey read everything he could get his hands on and had some scholarly articles translated into English so that he could order a vacuum aspirator machine built for his use. Vacuum aspiration was an exceedingly safe and simple two-minute procedure. Because there was no scraping of the uterus with sharp instruments as there was with a D&C, there was no need for expensive hospitalization. Harvey was convinced that abortions could now easily be performed in doctor's offices or in independent clinics.[84] Determined to prove his point, he opened his practice in 1969 in a suite of rooms in the Claiborne Towers apartments, which he rented for that reason.[85]

Barbara Yarnell Elizabeth Pyle, a student at Newcomb, met Harvey while he was working on his PhD at Tulane. Harvey, impressed with the young, energetic Pyle, asked her to make trips to Europe to learn more about how Europeans handled both sex education and abortion. She spent her JYA in 1969 at Kings College in England and "hitchhiked around Europe and learned a lot about [U.S.] culture and other cultures." In a London medical supply store, she bought a European version of the vacuum aspirator and brought it back for him.[86]

Harvey became well known for his concern for the patients and for charging fees on a sliding scale. "Women raved about Harvey," Pyle told historian Joshua Wolff.[87] "He did not overcharge!" said one of his clients, Sandy Stimpson, who flew down from Detroit to obtain an abortion from him. Stimpson was impressed that he personally asked each woman if she wanted to go through with it before he proceeded. He also trained female volunteers to offer counseling sessions, wherein they would explain the procedure and educate clients on how to prevent pregnancy in the future.[88] The CCS knew him to be a compassionate doctor who was more concerned about helping the women than he was about profit. Due to Harvey's "disdain for money," his empathy for the women, and the convenience of a nonstop flight from New York to New Orleans, the CCS in New York began referring many patients to him.[89]

Because of this long-standing relationship, then, before the new law legalizing abortion in New York had even taken effect, Dr. Harvey asked Howard Moody if the CCS would like for him to open a center. Twenty-three-year-old Barbara Pyle moved to New York to attend graduate school at NYU, which surrounds Judson Memorial, Moody's church, and helped establish and administer the clinic. Harvey owned the place and was technically the "medical director" (soon to become an important point), but for the first year, nearly all referrals came from the CCS. By all accounts, it was a smashing success, with lines of women waiting outside the door every day.[90] Besides abortion, Harvey also provided the same kind of referral and educational services that he had offered in New Orleans. Barbara Pyle described the hotline as "a telephone service staffed by volunteers who answered callers' questions about birth control, sexually transmitted diseases, abortion, and pregnancy."[91] The aim was to provide comprehensive sex education and thereby arm women with knowledge that would enable them to determine their futures.

After ensuring that women now had access to safe, legal abortion, Moody's CCS chapter disbanded. Other CCS chapters in states where it continued to be illegal (including in Louisiana) began to refer women to New York rather than to the less reputable and more expensive places in Latin America. Though Moody continued to send patients to Harvey's clinic (commonly called Women's Services), their relationship became strained. When New York state increased its licensing requirements in January 1971, it investigated Women's Services and discovered that not only was Hale Harvey not licensed to practice medicine in New York, but he may not have been licensed to practice anywhere. Accused of performing illegal abortions in New Orleans, he had surrendered his medical license to the Louisiana State Medical Board. The national CCS was apparently unaware of this, and Harvey had considered it unimportant because he was technically the "medical director," a paraprofessional. In any case, the state of New York would not allow him to continue to practice, so he left the clinic in the hands of his associate, Dr. Bernard Nathanson, and, with a suitcase full of one-hundred-dollar bills, left the United States, bought land on the Isle of Wight off the coast of England, married, and raised a family. A man who had worked his way through college, paying his own tuition (since his father was a gambler and the family never had much money), Harvey invested wisely and never worked again. A self-described eccentric, he has never given an interview about his experiences as a pioneer in the abortion wars.[92]

Oklahoma-born Barbara Pyle also left the clinic and spent most of the rest of her life as a producer of environmental films. "Her mission," declares her official biography, "is to make critical global issues understandable and accessible to the widest possible audience." After earning a master's degree in philosophy and logic at NYU, she joined Turner Broadcasting System in 1980, where she pioneered environmental programming. The most famous of her creations is *Captain Planet and the Planeteers*, an animated action-adventure series designed to educate children about humans' destruction of the environment. Like many who supported abortion rights, she was concerned not only for women but also for the global ecosystem. "Our planet will not be saved by any one big decision," she said, "but by many individual choices—choices by people like you and me. Television has an important responsibility to provide us with the information necessary to enable us to make these choices." In 1992, the Newcomb Alumnae Association named her Outstanding Alumna of the Year.[93]

Legal Challenges and *Roe v. Wade*

While Hale Harvey conducted his lucrative practice in New York City, back in Louisiana, others challenged the state's anti-abortion statutes in court.[94] Sidney Knight considered filing a federal suit against Louisiana's law, but another Louisiana physician, Dr. Isadore A. Rosen, also represented by Ben Smith, beat him to it. Rosen charged that the law was unconstitutionally vague, but the three-judge federal panel presided over by Judge Robert Ainsworth, a Roman Catholic, ruled against him in a split decision. Writing for a two-to-one majority, Judge Ainsworth opined that state law protected the fetus. Judge Fred Cassibry, on the other hand, "a feisty New Orleans Democratic politician before President Johnson elevated him to the bench," disputed the notion that the state believed life began at conception because the woman seeking the abortion was not prosecuted.[95] There matters lay, in legal limbo, until the U.S. Supreme Court ruled, not on the Louisiana case, but on two others that originated in Texas and Georgia, *Roe v. Wade* and *Doe v. Bolton*.

From two Deep South states came the litigation that ultimately overturned most restrictive abortion laws in the nation. Interestingly, it originated not with physicians but with the people. The first and most famous, *Roe v. Wade*, emanated from community women in Austin and students at the University of Texas (UT), who had begun to publish information about birth control and abortion in the *Rag*, an alternative newspaper sold on campus as well as around town. When the UT Board of Regents banned the *Rag* from campus, the paper's staff contacted local civil rights attorney David Richards (husband of Ann Richards, who became governor of Texas in 1991), who sued the university on First Amendment grounds and won.[96] As a result of the newspaper's success, the activists found themselves fielding calls at all hours from women seeking abortion referrals. Fearing they might be prosecuted under Texas's strict anti-abortion law, they sought advice from a fellow CR group member, twenty-four-year-old Sarah Weddington, a recent graduate of UT law school.[97]

Like many other southern feminists, Weddington was the product of a Methodist upbringing. Her father was a Methodist preacher; she had been a leader in the Methodist Youth Fellowship; and her undergraduate degree was from a small Methodist liberal arts school in Abilene, Texas. After graduating from law school, she could not get a job because no law firm hired women lawyers. Like many other female law-school graduates of her generation (Sandra Day O'Connor, another Texan, among them), she was told by law firms that they would hire her as a legal secretary but not as a lawyer. Also like many other female attorneys insulted in that manner, she turned down those patronizing offers and instead freelanced a bit on her own. With extra time on her hands, she began researching the history of abortion law for her friends running the pregnancy counseling service.

Inspired by the success of David Richards's victory against UT, Weddington and her friends began to consider the federal court system as a route for justice.[98] Though Weddington felt she did not have the necessary experience to file suit in federal court, she was the only licensed attorney who would represent them for free, and "they felt strongly that a woman lawyer should do the case."[99] To assist her in the research, Weddington brought in her former classmate Linda Coffee, then living in Dallas. Coffee located a pregnant plaintiff, Norma McCorvey, listed as Jane Roe to protect her privacy. McCorvey was an unmarried, pregnant twenty-one-year-old who had already borne two children and had relinquished custody of both. The defendant, Henry Wade, was the Dallas district attorney who defended Texas's law prohibiting all abortions not necessary to save a pregnant woman's life. In a major victory for feminists, Coffee and Weddington persuaded the U.S. Supreme Court to strike down not just Texas's restrictions but all state restrictions on abortion during the first trimester of pregnancy.[100] *Roe v. Wade* illustrates how some of the most important lawsuits—those with national implications—that overturned traditional gender arrangements were the result of daring actions taken by southern women.[101]

The Supreme Court simultaneously heard arguments in *Doe v. Bolton*, a challenge to Georgia's law. Unlike *Roe*, which had only one plaintiff, there were twenty-four plaintiffs in *Doe*, including doctors, nurses, social workers, and members of the clergy. "The lead plaintiff, 'Mary Doe,' whose real name was Sandra Bensing, was a 22-year-old married woman with three children and a history of mental illness. Pregnant again, she had sought permission for an abortion, but was turned down because she was found not to meet any of the criteria." The Supreme Court handed down decisions in both cases on January 22, 1973. Siding with the majority opinion written by Justice Henry Blackmun was William J. Brennan Jr., a liberal and the only Catholic on the court. He, like most Catholics at the time, supported expanding women's reproductive rights. Likewise, Justice Lewis Powell, a Virginian just appointed to the court by Republican president Richard Nixon, "pushed Blackmun to extend until later in the pregnancy the time period during which women's abortion decisions received constitutional protection." (Nixon publicly opposed abortion rights but did not impose a "litmus test" on his appointees.)[102]

Within a year of the *Roe* decision, six abortion facilities opened in New Orleans. That one of them was operated by Dr. Knight, who reopened his Causeway Clinic, is unsurprising. Doctors who had provided abortions illegally before *Roe* continued to provide them afterward. Their courage during the difficult times was invaluable in that "techniques and tools developed by physicians who had practiced illegal abortion were adopted by physicians now doing legal abortions."[103] The facility that outlasted all the others was the Delta Women's Clinic, a proprietary health center located at 1406 St. Charles Avenue, ironically, next door to Hale Harvey's old offices. Martha Margaret "Peggy" Cottle, who had worked with Joe Beasley in the Family Health Foundation, was its director, and Susan Jane Allen, a lesbian feminist and a member of Louisiana NOW as well as NARAL, was the community outreach director from 1974 to 1980. The owners, Allen reported later, were "two guys in Philadelphia who had put up the money. We did not meet with any real opposition, except from the politicians. From the instant we opened, we got referrals from doctors all over the state. We did pre-natal care, Lamaze classes, birth control clinics, and so forth. It was a full-service women's medical facility." Then as now, most women who sought the services offered by this and similar clinics wanted their choice to remain private and were unwilling to make a political statement by working at the clinic. It was "the Socialist Workers Party, which included women of all races and classes," Allen said, who made up the staff and volunteers, at least at first.[104] Socialists, who had already demonstrated bravery in challenging prevailing norms by joining a far-left party, probably felt that they had little to lose by working at the clinic; furthermore, as part of their political ideology, socialists had always supported women's right to control their fertility. The volunteers and staff at the various women's health clinics in New Orleans and the one in Baton Rouge were clearly providing a much-needed service. Even a year after the *Roe* decision, hundreds of Louisiana women still went out of state for abortions, partly because of the hostile climate coming from the Louisiana legislature. After the state's attempts to shut down the clinics and harass women seeking services were struck down as unconstitutional, about fifteen thousand abortions were performed in Louisiana clinics and hospitals every year in the 1970s.[105]

The *Roe* decision created enormous controversy and considerable backlash. The Catholic Church and many conservative Protestant denominations denounced it, and the State of Louisiana targeted abortion providers. The Louisiana legislature passed a variety of laws designed to place impediments before women seeking abortions, including mandatory waiting periods and requirements that only hospitals could provide abortions, not freestanding clinics. With the help of attorney Ben Smith, the clinics got temporary restraining orders that prevented the laws from being implemented while they fought the case in court. Smith defended the providers, and Susan Allen testified on their behalf. When she argued that the state had no "expert witness" because none of the men making these rules had ever given a woman a vacuum aspirator abortion, the state lost every case. Attorney General William "Billy" Guste refused to defend them further, and the Fifth Circuit Court of Appeals sided with the plaintiffs' arguments and threw out the laws.[106]

After legalization, all the disparate groups and individuals who had been protesting restrictive abortion laws for years in Louisiana came above ground and found one another. Drawn together by the threats to the newly acquired right to reproductive freedom, they formed the Committee for Safe Abortion Practices to defend legal abortion. The committee compiled a list of recommendations for guidelines "to insure high standards of medical care" for women seeking abortions. It called for publically funded education of those medical professionals who would be performing abortions; recommended that all hospitals and medical facilities, public and private, provide abortion services as part of maternal health and obstetrical programs; and urged that abortion be covered by health insurance. Members of the organization include the Community Sex Information and Education Service, Sisters Helping Sisters, Tulane Women for Change, New Orleans Women's Center, the Clergy Consultation Service on Problem Pregnancies, the Medical Committee for Human Rights, NOW, the ACLU, the Louisiana Committee for Abortion Reform, ZPG, and a group called Women in Change affiliated with UNO. The committee opposed any attempts by the state legislature to restrict access to abortion, and was largely successful during that decade.[107]

In other words, the same groups that had supported the legalization of abortion now worked to ensure women's continued access to the procedure. The YWCA continued to provide referrals for "pregnancy counseling." The rape crisis training handbook and educational outreach explained that their volunteers were "in touch with all available resources for terminating pregnancy, including the Delta Women's Clinic," should a woman become pregnant as a result of rape. Likewise, the Louisiana CCS continued its work. It "explore[d] all alternatives with the pregnant woman, help[ed] her make practical arrangements, and [gave] her support whatever her decision."[108]

Given the implacable opposition of the Catholic Church and its enormous firepower, and given the high visibility of Planned Parenthood as an abortion provider (although 95 percent of its services do not involve abortion), it is not surprising that Louisiana was the last state to establish a Planned Parenthood organization, in 1984. Terry Bartlett, the founding executive director, recruited women to the first board, and once again, liberal religious denominations played key roles. Among the founding members was Corinne Barnwell, a social worker, a member of Trinity Episcopal Church in New Orleans, and wife of an Episcopal priest. Board meetings were held at Trinity, and the second president was Laura Williams, a lifelong member of Trinity. Board members included Martha Ward, professor at UNO and author of the study on Joe Beasley's Family Health Foundation; civic leaders; men and women who were leaders of churches and synagogues; and members of the public health community.[109]

Planned Parenthood, a nonprofit founded and run largely by women, has a much better track record as an abortion provider than do some of the proprietary clinics. One of the male doctors at Delta Women's Clinic, hired from out of state by the proprietors, sexually harassed female staffers and volunteers, and perhaps clients as well. The staff alleged that he stole drugs and equipment for use in his private practice, too. Though the offending physician was eventually fired, nurse Darlene Olivo quit anyway because she believed that the women were not receiving compassionate care there. Nonprofits and female medical practitioners generally provided more responsible and empathetic treatment than what Darlene Olivo witnessed in the early years at the Delta Women's Clinic.[110]

The history of pre-*Roe* abortion practices indicates that even in this extremely conservative and heavily Catholic Deep South state, support for repeal of abortion laws grew rapidly, not just among feminists but among male religious leaders and health care providers, too. Pro-feminist men acted as counselors and abortion providers or as their defenders partly because of their concern for women. If the record of women in Louisiana and in Austin, Texas, is any guide, southern women sought abortions at approximately the same rate as women in the rest of the country. The South was a place where local acts of rebellion sometimes became nationally significant, as the experience of the Austin women showed.

Epilogue

In the years since *Roe v. Wade*, women have come to expect that abortion on demand, at least in the first trimester, will be available to them. However, since the emergence of the Republicans as the dominant party in Louisiana and the rise of the New Right in the 1980s, lawmakers and regulators (which includes agencies such as the Louisiana State Board of Health Examiners) have increasingly been creating obstacles for women and clinics. Women seeking an abortion in Louisiana in 2015 must receive state-directed counseling, undergo a twenty-four-hour waiting period, and be subjected to an ultrasound; minors

must obtain parental consent. While those requirements increase the cost of
an abortion and delay the procedure (thus pushing it further along into the
pregnancy, which no one wants), they are not insurmountable. However, the
state is also trying to shutter abortion clinics. One abortion provider described
the last few years as a "constant period of harassment and intimidation," and
not just for her facility. Ever since Republican governor Bobby Jindal replaced
Democrat Kathleen Blanco in 2008, abortion providers have operated under
the assumption that inspectors from the Department of Health and Hospitals
"are intent on closing clinic doors, rather than collaborating with facilities to
ensure compliance and safety." (Both Jindal and Blanco are Catholic, but Jindal
converted from his native Hindu religion, against the wishes of his parents, as
a teenager.) Regulators forced many to close for trivial reasons such as paper-
work inconsistencies (not because of deaths, sepsis, or lawsuits), while hospitals that amputated the wrong leg during surgery continued to operate just as
before. In 2008, the state had seven licensed providers. In 2016, it had just five,
and the existence of those is imperiled.[111]

In the 2014 legislative session, several antichoice bills passed the Louisiana
legislature: the human incubator bill (HB1274), which could force a pregnant
woman onto life support against her and her family's wishes if she is brain dead;
a bill authored by state representative Katrina Jackson (D-Monroe), which
required hospital admitting privileges within thirty miles of a clinic (modeled
on Texas's law that shut down nearly all its abortion clinics); and HB 1262, which
requires women be given information about psychological impacts after abortions and sex trafficking. When all bills passed through committee and both
houses with almost no opposition, Choice Louisiana declared it a "terrible day
for Louisiana's women." Amy Irvin, of the New Orleans Abortion Fund, declared,
"Once again the Louisiana legislature has let down their constituents. Our representatives in Baton Rouge have chosen to limit women's ability to defend
their families and make the best decisions for their health."[112] The regulations
are being challenged in court, but the federal courts have demonstrated incon-
sistency in their rulings on these and similar laws in other states.[113]

The history of abortion practices in Louisiana informs our current debates
in multiple ways. Women will find ways to get abortions if they want them, and
they and their allies will challenge laws that prevent them from doing so. Historically, women not only used political lobbying and legal challenges to restrictive laws, but they also took to direct actions such as forming their own referral
networks. In keeping with that tradition, a new grassroots movement is afoot
that plans to make medical equipment that allows women to safely self-abort
in their own homes widely available.

Placing hurdles in front of women who wanted abortions, as we have seen, only drove it underground and privileged women with greater resources. The poor, as always, were the most adversely affected, and will be again if the laws are allowed to stand. While women of all races and classes sought abortions even when they were illegal and dangerous, it was primarily college students, women with college degrees, and clergy associated with colleges and universities who organized a kind of underground railroad to assist those women. Universities played critical roles in this change-seeking movement as they did in many others. It is to them that we now turn our attention.

CHAPTER 6

"Cherchez Les Femmes?"

Universities and the Movement, 1965–1990

When Vaughan Burdin Baker attended the rural, tree-shaded campus of the Academy of the Sacred Heart in St. Landry Parish in the 1950s, women's history as a field did not exist. But at this girls' high school in the heart of Cajun country, the students learned women's history of a Catholic sort when they studied female saints. Baker found those venerated lives, as well as those of the nuns who taught her, inspirational. "They gave me courage," she said, "and powerful female role models." Single-sex education was common in Catholic schools and could be important to developing girls' self-esteem, character, and leadership skills. Once she completed her education at Newcomb (another single-sex institution) in 1959 and joined the faculty at ULL, Baker wanted to find a way to give the female students at that co-ed public university a similar empowering academic experience. She became one of several university professors in this state—typically married, heterosexual white women—who founded women's studies courses, archives, and programs. These programs are the academic arm of second-wave feminism and can be considered one of its successes, for they transformed the male-dominated curricula and inspired female students to achieve beyond traditional limitations.[1]

Universities played much the same role as did liberal religious denominations in fostering feminist activism. They provided safe spaces and a community of people interested in exploring new ideas. There like-minded women found one another and formed networks that pushed forward a reform agenda. For some women in the 1960s and 1970s, not only did the university campus provide the necessary preconditions; it also became the focus of their activism.[2] They sought to end gender discrimination against female employees and to end male bias in the curriculum by establishing women's studies courses. They brought to the academy fresh intellectual perspectives, innovative scholarly methodologies, and new forms of pedagogy as well as people whose backgrounds and life experiences were vastly different from traditional academics.[3] ULL literature and gender studies professor Mary Ann Wilson explained its importance by saying, "Women's studies sensitizes women and men to the dynamics of sexual politics, gender relationships, and so forth. Most students have never thought critically about these things in their lives. But it is an uphill battle in south Louisiana."[4]

Vaughan Baker represents those feminists who were active both inside and outside Louisiana institutions of higher education. Baker attended Newcomb College (NC '59), where, in her words, the faculty "encouraged students to follow their dreams, whatever those might be." But dreams may still be limited by practicality, and Baker, like most Newcomb grads, married and began having children in her twenties. With small children at home, teaching seemed like the best career, but she was not happy as a secondary school teacher and did not like the restrictions that motherhood placed on her life. Betty Friedan's book therefore resonated with her and caused her to rethink her choices. After moving back to Lafayette in 1965, she was encouraged by the head of the ULL history department at the time, Amos Simpson, to enter graduate school there, which she did in 1967. (In 1980, Baker married Amos Simpson.) The female faculty profoundly influenced her, especially Judith Gentry—a founding member of the Southern Association of Women Historians (SAWH)—Jean Boudreaux, Sarah Brabant, and Doris Bentley. These women formed an advisory committee in June 1976 that produced annual reports documenting disparities in pay and promotion between male and female faculty. They drew Baker into their circle, though she was still a graduate student. Boudreaux secured a humanities grant that paid for a series of public programs on women. Using those funds, the women on the committee, along with Vaughan Baker, went out into the community to give talks about women's rights and the ERA. These talks "opened up networks and conversations that I otherwise would not have had," she reported later. In other words, the academy broadened her circle of friends and brought her into contact with a community of activists.[5]

In 1973, Amos Simpson and Glenn Conrad, the head archivist at the ULL library, founded the Center for Louisiana Studies when the state historical journal (*Louisiana History*) relocated there from LSU. Baker worked part time at the center, and Conrad supported her idea for creating a women's archive collection as part of the center's manuscript division. University president Ray Authement also backed it and gave her seed money and a small salary. Baker wrote and received grants to raise $20,000 from the Louisiana Endowment for the Humanities for a traveling exhibit. (The panels for that exhibit still hang in the

ULL Department of History.)[6] The role of these three men demonstrates that supportive pro-feminist men in positions of power could be enormously helpful to the success of women's efforts.[7]

Meanwhile, Glenn Conrad left his position as head archivist to run the Center for Louisiana Studies (a unit of ULL), and the new archivist at the university library, according to Baker, did not see the value in collecting women's archival materials. "I knew that the Center at Newcomb had the resources to take over what ULL no longer seemed interested in doing or supporting," she said, so she visited her alma mater, where she met with the faculty and administrators and discussed cooperative efforts to build support for women's archives there. Though ULL did not keep it, Baker can be credited with initiating the idea of a Louisiana archive dedicated to collecting papers and oral histories from women in the Gulf South. ULL's was one of several models (along with those of Smith College and Radcliffe's Schlesinger Library) that Beth Willinger followed when creating the Center for Research on Women at Newcomb.[8]

Along with Judith Gentry, Baker began offering the first courses in women's history at ULL (and perhaps the first in the state) in the mid-1970s.[9] Though, as noted in an earlier chapter, women's studies courses were offered at the "free university" in New Orleans, Baker was apparently unaware of those and drew her inspiration from within the profession. At a conference of the Organization of American Historians, she heard Gerda Lerner and Anne Scott, widely considered the founding mothers of the field of women's history in the United States, discuss the importance of women's history. Inspired, Baker went home and immediately designed a course. She used Lerner's and Scott's books along with many primary sources because so little secondary work was available.[10] A European historian fluent in French, Baker researched French colonial Louisiana women's history, and her article, published a few years later, "Cherchez Les Femmes? Some Glimpses of Women in Early Eighteenth-Century Louisiana," was one of the few pieces of Louisiana women's history in existence at the time. "Cherchez Les Femmes" translates as "look for the women." Baker chose this phrase as a play on the French phrase "cherchez la femme," which means, in effect, that if a crime has been committed, it was probably done by a woman. She explained, "I changed it to 'les femmes' meaning 'search or research for the forgotten women in Louisiana history,' but also to turn around a negative connotation of the term, and use it positively."[11]

Judith Gentry, Jean Boudreau, Sarah Brabant, and Doris Bentley were instrumental in bringing about positive changes in the city of Lafayette as well as in the university itself. They joined with women in the community, those who represented the traditional women's groups, to establish the Mayor's Commission on the Needs of Women in 1976. The impetus for the creation of the commission was the publicity surrounding the coroner's egregious statements about rape victims, discussed in chapter 4. Margaret Gimbrede of the AAUW and of the Acadiana Chapter of the LWV approached Sarah Brabant about establishing a civic women's commission. Brabant in turn approached Jesse Taylor, director of community development at the city; Taylor had worked in voting rights for African Americans, and was the first African American woman to hold a position of that kind at the city. They also invited Doris Bentley, head of the Department of Secretarial Science at ULL, and Isabelle Gant, a leader in the African American community. (Gant was married to Rev. William Gant, a prominent civil rights leader.) These five women had a great deal of respect for one another as professionals. Several had worked together on a joint internship program between the city and the university; the black women knew one another through civil rights activity; and the ERA activity tied the white women together. Brabant considers them all feminist, even though the black women may not have called themselves that. The Lafayette women were assisted by an African American woman from Shreveport who had been instrumental in forming the Shreveport commission and by Pat Evans, director of the Louisiana Bureau on the Status of Women. Evans encouraged all towns and cities in the state to establish these councils to advise mayors on issues of concern to women.[12]

Brabant, as a social anthropologist, had always supported coalition building. She knew that this steering committee of white and black women could be a powerful force. Lafayette mayor Kenny Bowen, a Democrat, supported the formation of the commission. As a way of ensuring their continued existence, he insisted that they obtain a charter from the city council and not be simply a body appointed by the mayor. Having so many African American women on the founding commission was important, Brabant says, because "the white men did not know how to deal with black and white women coming in together" before them; it was a powerful image, and it scared them. "They were floored when we went into the city council meeting," she recalled. Maybe they were intimidated by the unusual alliance of professional women, but certainly the backing of the mayor also helped to convince the men on the city council to grant the women's commission a charter. Among those who joined the commission in the first few years was Methodist feminist Ollie Osborne, whose vehicle for feminism was primarily the LWV, and Vaughan Baker.[13]

Perhaps because of that charter, the Lafayette commission was more enduring and probably more effective than other similar mayor's advisory boards around the state. The Lafayette body, it will be remembered, sponsored the public hearing on rape and helped birth the Rape Crisis Center. It also established a family violence shelter at the Salvation Army (later, Faith House); collaborated with others to create Acadiana Legal Services for the poor; provided job training for displaced homemakers; and maintained a talent bank, which kept records of local women's skills so that the commission could recommend qualified women for government appointments.[14]

Mayor Kenny Bowen unfailingly supported the women's commission and praised its efforts, but he lost the next election to a Republican, who removed all progressively minded women and replaced them with conservative Republicans. The group became less cutting edge, according to both Brabant and Baker. Though it continued the talent bank, it turned its attention primarily to encouraging the establishment of affordable and regulated day-care facilities.[15]

Lafayette's experience was typical of Louisiana, where feminist activity tended to occur in cities with at least one university (New Orleans, Baton Rouge, Lafayette, Lake Charles, Shreveport, and Houma). Feminism was not a rural phenomenon; it was decisively urban, and universities were critical to sustaining the movement. Universities provided the right mix of personnel and the intellectual climate to stimulate the growth of what Richard Florida has called "the creative class," people who think about and then implement progressive changes. Feminist values emphasized diversity and openness to different kinds of people and ideas and thus were consistent with the values ascribed to the "creative class." This class values intellectual capital and coheres around a set of skills and ideas rather than the traditional distinctions based on a person's wealth. Another characteristic of the creative class is the high percentage of gay and lesbian people in its ranks, which was certainly true in New Orleans during this period. Independence of thought and tolerance of differences are themselves attractive assets, and cities that nurture and harbor people with those values grow and thrive. Institutions of higher learning, especially those with strong liberal arts curricula, contribute to that phenomenon enormously.[16]

A university's influence is sometimes indirect, in that it fuels curiosity and a desire for knowledge beyond what is presented in the traditional curricula. Universities provided the space, the networks, and the intellectual and human resources that supported activism, but it was female students and faculty who pressed for the creation of courses on women's history and for women's centers with funding.

New Orleans

New Orleans saw more student activism than did other cities in Louisiana, partly because New Orleans schools drew a more diverse mix of people, many from outside the state. In New Orleans, black and white students participated in a variety of sixties causes, of which feminism was just one.[17] Students at the HBCUs joined civil rights protests, and Tulane students participated in SDS and led protests against the Vietnam War both on campus and throughout the city.

By the mid-1960s, Tulane was a large, prestigious, racially integrated research university that attracted high-caliber students and faculty from all over the world. Though it was private and therefore beyond the financial reach of the average student, it offered scholarships to high achievers who could not afford the tuition. When Tulane students picketed draft offices, women were as visible as men, and many women who joined the women's liberation movement in New Orleans had been involved in the draft resistance movement, Women Strike for Peace, or the Women's International League for Peace and Freedom.[18]

A college education offered a universalizing experience that proved extremely significant in helping women contextualize their world and see it from the view of outsiders. Newcomb's JYA tradition profoundly influenced many young women who later identified as feminists. Those who went overseas during the years of the civil rights movement got an education in how American racism looked to others, and it wasn't good. Judy Cooper, a Newcomb grad raised in the South, discovered that Europeans had a much different view of American racial tensions than she and other white southerners did. "That was a wake-up call for me," she said. "I tried using all the old saws I had been taught by my family to defend white supremacy, but I realized it was indefensible. I changed my mind very quickly."[19] Mary Capps had a similar experience while at the University of Nottingham during the New Orleans school integration crisis in 1960. Capps, Cooper, Barbara Pyle, Susan Tucker (Newcomb grad, feminist, and archivist at Newcomb College Institute), and many other young women had their eyes opened and their minds expanded when they saw and heard what others thought of their home country and state. Experiences abroad gave these women a vantage point that overrode parochialism and local mores.

Universities, like the YWCA, also provided protected spaces, both personally and intellectually. Title IX of the Civil Rights Act prohibited discrimination on the basis of race and gender by universities, and—though many dragged their feet and had to be sued before making any real effort—they gradually began to diversify both their student bodies and their faculty. Women faculty and students sought to develop curricula that focused on women's lives. In most cases, such initiatives came from the students, who were part of a nationwide drive to revamp curricula to make them more meaningful. At UNO, Loyola, and Newcomb, however, women's studies curricula and women's centers were initiated by faculty who came from outside the local area and were attuned to the international movement for gender justice.

Women at Historically Black Colleges and Universities

The universities discussed in the preceding section were all historically white and did not racially integrate until the 1950s or 1960s. HBCUs in Louisiana, on the other hand, did not establish women's centers. Black women activists were more likely to embrace political organizations such as the Black Organization for Leadership Development (BOLD) and the Southern Organization for Unified Leadership (SOUL), in historically black neighborhoods of New Orleans, that promised to deliver real political clout than they were to commit to feminist initiatives.[20]

However, faculty and students, particularly those at Southern University in Baton Rouge (SUBR), lent their support to the women's movement at certain critical moments. For example, they helped organize the two statewide women's conferences held in Baton Rouge, the first in 1976, funded by a CETA grant, and the second in 1977 in connection with IWY. The IWY conferences received funding from the federal government and as such were required to represent all ethnic groups within the state. Organizers tapped the traditional sources of leadership talent: educators, YWCA board members, LWV members, and those who were active in civil rights or political organizing. Clarence M. Collier, who was black, cochaired the 1977 conference in Baton Rouge, along with Shirley Marvin, who was white and had a long political pedigree. Collier was a lifelong member of the Louisiana Association of Educators, past president of the YWCA in Baton Rouge, and vice president of student and community services at SUBR. These women were among the 130,000 who met in every state and territory in preparation for the huge national convention that would meet in Houston, Texas, in 1977. "Members of minority groups ended up attending in proportions greater than their percentage in the general population," concludes historian Ruth Rosen.[21]

Though all socioeconomic levels were represented (special grants provided funding for less affluent women), middle-class and well-educated women tended to be the speakers and leaders. At the Baton Rouge conference, workshops featured speakers such as Earline C. Williams, assistant dean of the College of Education at SUBR and a member of the YWCA in Baton Rouge; Ruth Bradford, a retired professor at Grambling State University; Jewel L. Prestage, chair of the Department of Political Science at SUBR and president of the National Conference of Black Political Scientists; and African American legislators Senator Sidney Berthelemy and Representative Diana Bajoie.

Many African American educators were elected to represent Louisiana at the National Women's Conference held in Houston. Among them were Corinne Maybuce, active on many boards and a Democratic Party leader in her hometown of Baton Rouge; Mildred Reese, an educator and YWCA board member in New Orleans, among other things; Helen Barron, dean of women, SUBR, who served on the boards of the YWCA and Women in Politics; and Shirley C. Temple, a retired teacher from Kentwood, Louisiana (Tangipahoa Parish), who was also active on several boards as well as with the CME Church Missionary Society.[22] They joined two thousand other delegates at what was probably the most diverse gathering of women yet in the second wave. Together they adopted the National Plan of Action, a twenty-six-plank agenda designed to guide the federal government's policies toward women. The plan put ratification of the ERA at its center but also included support for reproductive, lesbian, and minority rights. Though many delegates later recalled their interconnectedness and bonding during the Baton Rouge and Houston events with fondness, the connections among these busy professional women were mostly temporary. African American women, especially those with education, had multiple commitments—to home, family, careers, community, institutions, and numerous service organizations. Being pulled in so many different directions made it difficult to sustain friendships and networks forged with white feminists at ad hoc women's conferences.[23]

Newcomb College

H. Sophie Newcomb Memorial College in New Orleans evolved into the most woman-centered and woman-focused institution in the state. Founded in 1886, it gained a reputation as one of the best schools for white women in the South. It began when Josephine Louise Le Monnier Newcomb donated $100,000 as the initial gift (the first of many) at the behest of Tulane University president William Preston Johnston. Tulane, located in uptown New Orleans, was a private nonsectarian school reserved for white men, and Johnston had developed a plan to establish a "coordinate" college offering a curriculum that would be attractive to southern families looking for a good—but appropriate—education for their daughters. For two years he sought a donor and finally found "Mrs. Newcomb," as she was always called, a wealthy New York widow still mourning the death of her only child, Sophie, sixteen years earlier (in 1870) from diphtheria. Josephine Newcomb had lived many years in New Orleans and had married her husband, Warren, in a ceremony there in 1845. Clearly, she felt some affinity for the city and was thus receptive when President Johnston approached her with his plan for a women's college. Mrs. Newcomb thought that giving the gift of knowledge to succeeding generations was a perfect way to "enshrine her [Sophie's] memory in a manner best fitted to render useful and enduring benefit to humanity."[24] Newcomb became the first degree-granting coordinate college for women in the United States. (Radcliffe was a coordinate college to Harvard but had no degree-granting powers until 1894.)[25] Though it was always a division of Tulane, Newcomb College initially had its own curriculum, faculty, administration, and a separate campus.[26] It gradually began to attract students from all over the South, and eventually elsewhere, because of its fine reputation and affiliation with Tulane.

It is significant, however, that Josephine and Warren Newcomb lived in New York, one of the first states to pass a married women's property act. Upon Warren Newcomb's death in 1866, his family challenged his will and fought to gain control of the estate that Josephine and Sophie had inherited. Mrs. Newcomb successfully defended her (and Sophie's) inheritance and invested the money wisely. The experience taught her the importance of a useful education for women. She thus requested of Tulane's President Johnston that the curriculum for the college be both practical and literary.[27] Mrs. Newcomb subsequently moved to New Orleans to establish legal residence there, hoping to prevent her family from challenging the donation to Tulane. Her relatives did contest the will upon her death in 1901, however, and the college did not receive the final bequest of $3.6 million for another seven years.[28]

The high mortality rate from the Civil War left many widowed or never-married women in need of a respectable way to support themselves. The traditional southern "finishing school" education, wherein girls learned little more than "decorative" arts, was disadvantageous in such an environment. Even the governor of Louisiana, Francis T. Nicholls, sent his daughter Henrietta to Newcomb because, according to her, "Father ... thought if the governor's daughter went to college the other girls might follow her example, so he asked me to give up the idea of coming out [i.e., making her debut in society] and enter Newcomb."[29] Girls needed an education that would equip them with marketable skills, not one designed to win them elite husbands, of which there were fewer and fewer. Given the lopsided gender ratio in the late nineteenth century, a practical education would serve them better. Newcomb filled that gap in several ways, some of which have made the school internationally famous.

Though it took a few years to establish itself, Newcomb eventually offered a rigorous, accredited academic curriculum that provided southern states, many with brand-new public school systems, with a cadre of unusually well-trained primary and secondary school teachers. Many other liberal arts majors went on to attain advanced degrees and become professors at Newcomb. But Newcomb is most famous for developing an innovative enterprise to train southern women as artists and allow them to support themselves (and the program) financially. Working as a collective with its own dedicated buildings, the students learned bookbinding, metalworking (primarily brass and silver made into serving ware or dinnerware), jewelry making, painting, and, most famously, pottery design. Though men threw the pots (since working with the hot and heavy machinery was considered "men's work"), the women designed and painted them. Newcomb pottery has become highly prized and world-famous. From the 1890s until the program ended in 1948, more than one hundred women participating in the program produced over one hundred thousand pieces. Graduates became draftswomen, designers, art teachers, graphic designers, and even city planners. The success of the program brought recognition, awards, and increased enrollment for the school.[30]

In 1918, the school moved to its permanent location on Broadway adjacent to Tulane University. The proximity encouraged the sharing of resources between the two colleges, which had never been completely separate. They gradually began opening their classes to both sexes, and in 1987 the faculties officially merged. Following Hurricane Katrina in 2005, the Tulane administration combined the two undergraduate schools as Newcomb-Tulane College and created the H. Sophie Newcomb Memorial College Institute (NCI). A five-year legal battle to prevent the merger ended in 2011, when the Louisiana Supreme Court refused to hear an appeal of a lower court ruling upholding Tulane's closure of Newcomb College. Mrs. Newcomb's and all subsequent donations, however, have remained separate and under the control of the director of Newcomb College Institute.[31]

Newcomb, then, had a tradition of encouraging self-sufficiency and self-actualization in its female students. Due to state law and at the behest of the donors, those students were originally all white, but in 1963 Tulane integrated as a result of a series of legal challenges.[32] That same year, Newcomb admitted its first African American student, Deidre Dumas Labat (NC '66), a New Orleans native who went on to earn a PhD in biology and become senior vice president for academic affairs at Xavier University of Louisiana, an HBCU.[33] Though in the mid-twentieth century Newcomb somehow got the reputation as a finishing school where prominent southern families sent their daughters to find Tulane men to marry (which may well have been true for some), that notion was mostly a myth, as the life histories of many of the women in this book illustrate. Single-sex education, as Vaughan Baker related, could build women's confidence and speaking skills and even turn them into feminists.

Newcomb had always encouraged rigorous study and practical skills, and the design of the new Women's Center, founded in 1975, continued the tradition of helping women achieve economic independence. When Newcomb associate dean Joseph Cohen proposed the establishment of such a center, he justified it by saying that he regularly counseled adult women seeking "to explore the possibilities of their returning to complete their education and prepare themselves for gainful employment." The goal of the Women's Center was to reach out to adult women whose education had been interrupted or whose careers were sidelined when they married and began having children. Newcomb's center benefited from a fund drive spearheaded and funded largely by alumnae as well as by Newcomb College funds. By 1982, the need for career counseling had largely been recognized, while the interest in the new scholarship on women was gaining momentum among Tulane faculty and students.

As the new director, Beth Willinger sought to promote research and teaching about women and realign the center's mission with that of a research university.[34] With a goal of bringing an academic focus to the Women's Center, she visited Radcliffe's Schlesinger Library in the 1980s, which emboldened her to find a space, separate from the Tulane Special Collections, that would house a new women's archive. The Newcomb Archives began with a small objective: to collect the institutional history of Newcomb, in particular of the pottery and art departments. Gradually it expanded its focus to include the papers of Newcomb alumnae, the history of women's education, and the history of women of the Gulf South. The center changed its name in 1986 to the Newcomb College Center for Research on Women (now Newcomb Archives). Susan Tucker (NC '72) helped to develop the mission of the library and the archives as a centralized repository for women's studies books and periodicals. In 1988, the center hired her as the permanent archivist. In 1989–90, NCCROW became a member of the National Council for Research on Women, "a consortium of independent and campus-based women's centers that focus on feminist research, advocacy and policy."[35] Among the histories that Newcomb Archives has preserved are those of many alumnae, feminists in Louisiana, and other women who became activists or professionals all over the country. In addition to Vaughan Baker, they include Congresswoman Lindy Boggs; Mary Capps; Mildred Fossier (environmentalist, NC '35); Judy Cooper; Felicia Kahn; Flo Schornstein; Susan (Sue) Laporte; Julie Schwam Harris, a contemporary lobbyist for women's rights in Louisiana; Emily Clark (historian, NC '76); and Barbara Pyle (Newcomb Alum of the Year in 1992).

Loyola

Loyola University of the South, fronting St. Charles Avenue and sitting adjacent to Tulane, claims to have established the first academic women's center in the state, though it was less well-integrated into academic life than Newcomb's. Founded in March 1975 at the inspiration of feminist faculty, it operated out of "City College" (the outreach program that offered continuing education credits and night classes to people in the community). The center charged a fee for its classes and seminars but did not require those who attended to enroll at the university. This policy allowed for greater participation by women of all socioeconomic groups, rather than the usual white middle- and upper-class students whom Loyola normally enrolled. Women from all over the state benefited from the daylong workshops, typically held on Saturdays, which offered classes in assertiveness training, public speaking, starting and managing a small busi-

ness, and basic auto maintenance. These one-day seminars frequently functioned as CR sessions. More than one woman took courage and inspiration
from them and struck out on her own as a result. Unlike Newcomb's center,
Loyola's received no institutional funding; it was supported entirely by grants
and by the fees it charged for classes and workshops. The university administration, which disagreed with some of its goals and the views of many of its speakers, generally resented it, and the vice president for academic affairs closed it
and the continuing education division of City College in 1980. In 1987, Sister Fara
Impastato, a feminist theologian who taught the first women's studies course
at Loyola, "Women in Christian Tradition," along with faculty members Nancy
Anderson, Barbara Ewell, Connie Mui, and Carol Mawson, developed the curriculum, submitted a proposal, and secured approval for a women's studies
minor. In 1995, the Women's Center reopened in a permanent space, where it
still resided as of 2016.[36]

The Loyola faculty were generally more liberal than the students. Loyola
was home to several high-profile Jesuit priests who were in the forefront
of movements for change in New Orleans in the postwar period. One with a
national reputation was Father Joseph Fichter, a sociologist with a doctorate
from Harvard, who organized the Catholic Commission on Human Rights
and the Southeastern Regional Interracial Commission, a student group that
began integrating Catholic spaces in New Orleans.[37] Fichter was an ardent supporter of women's rights as well as civil rights.[38] Another was Father Louis J.
Twomey, founder of Loyola's Institute of Industrial Relations (later the Institute of Human Relations) and an active participant in social reform efforts in
the area, especially civil rights and labor union organizing.[39] This institute nurtured and encouraged liberal, perhaps even radical, faculty. After Twomey died
in 1969, he was succeeded eventually by Father Boileau, a founder of the Louisiana Committee for the Humanities (LCH) (now the Louisiana Endowment for
the Humanities).

The New Orleans chapter of NOW grew out of the institute. Gayle Gagliano, a former nun who worked there, and her husband, a former seminarian
who was Boileau's assistant director, secured LCH grants for a seminar series
on women's issues. To show community support, Gagliano got cosponsorship from the YWCA, the Business and Professional Women, the IWO, Church
Women United, the Junior League, the Louisiana League of Good Government, and the local chapters of the LWV. The seminars helped raise awareness
about women's issues, and in August 1970, twelve members decided to establish a local NOW chapter to work on some of the problems that had cropped
up in their dialogues. The institute-sponsored seminars turned into a series
that lasted several years. They served as outreach and recruiting tools for the

women's movement, and when they traveled outside New Orleans, they raised feminist consciousness in less urban areas.[40]

The University of New Orleans

Many professors and students at UNO participated in CR groups and became missionaries for the cause of feminism.[41] UNO, which opened as LSUNO in 1958 on the shore of Lake Pontchartrain in what had once been cypress swampland, was the first public university in the city and the first racially integrated public university in the South. Its women's studies curriculum began very early compared with many other universities in Louisiana. In 1979, when anthropologist Martha Ward offered a course titled Women Cross-Culturally, it filled up immediately, and Ward soon produced a best-selling women's studies textbook. Within a few years, Ward had helped to establish a women's center at UNO, and in 1990 the center hired a full-time faculty member from outside the university as director. By 2005, the women's studies program had grown enough that the university's supervising board approved a major. However, that occurred just as Hurricane Katrina swept ashore, putting the university—and the program— out of commission when Lake Pontchartrain overflowed and drowned large segments of the city under twelve feet of water, including the UNO campus. Between 2008 and 2015, under Louisiana's Republican-dominated governor and legislature, the university was hit with severe cuts to state appropriations. When funding declines, women's studies (or women's and gender studies), which critics believe to be nonessential, is often the first to be cut. Fortunately, the courses continue to be offered and remain popular, even as enrollment has declined precipitously at UNO.[42]

Elsewhere in Louisiana

About fifty miles upriver from New Orleans lies Baton Rouge, Louisiana's second largest city. The state capital continuously since 1879, following an interruption during the Civil War, Baton Rouge was a port city of about 285,000 people in 1970. Some moved there to attend one of its two large universities (the flagship LSU campus and its African American counterpart SUBR), others to work in the many chemical plants and oil refineries located along the rivers and bayous that supplied both their transportation and their waste needs. Situated on the east bank of the Mississippi River, Baton Rouge had once been part of British West Florida; its population was thus more heavily Protestant and teetotaling than the Queen City to the south. Politically quite conservative, LSU was one of the last flagship universities in the United States to offer a women's history course and one of the last to establish a women's studies program (in 1991).

The Baton Rouge women's movement reflected the city's conservatism. Though the Baton Rouge NOW chapter was gay friendly and welcomed people of all sexual orientations, there were few out lesbians in the city and thus few openly gay women in the movement there. Roberta "Robbie" Madden, cofounder (with Sylvia Roberts) and longtime leader of the city's NOW chapter, said, "NOW was considered very radical in Baton Rouge."[43]

Robbie Madden was representative of NOW members in that she and her husband were both connected to LSU. The couple moved from the Midwest when LSU hired David Madden as a member of the English faculty in 1968. Robbie got a job as editor of the LSU Press, and as a result of her connections, nearly all the women involved in the formation of the Baton Rouge chapter of NOW were in some way associated with LSU or with SUBR. They included Maureen Trobec Hewitt, an editor at LSU Press; Mary Metz, a French teacher; and Helen Wheeler, a professor of library science. As the years went on, students got involved as well. Rebecca Wells, a native of Alexandria and now famous as the author of the female-centered *Ya-Ya* books based in Louisiana, was a student at LSU when she joined the NOW chapter there and helped lobby for the ERA. Wells described the college experience as important to helping her "grow out of the southern belle-ness, the culture that formed [her]." The Baton Rouge NOW chapter gradually branched out to include more professionals and crafts-women throughout the 1970s, too, but it was never a very large group.[44]

Black women on the faculty of SUBR provided much of the black feminist leadership in Baton Rouge. Southern, the state's first public college for African Americans, had been founded by the white-supremacist Bourbon legislature in 1879. By 1970, it was the largest black university in the country, and it attracted a talented collection of faculty from all over the nation. Ollie Butler Moore, the dean of women, and Pinkie Gordon Lane were both on the founding board of Baton Rouge NOW. Lane, a native of Philadelphia and a graduate of Spelman College, was a trailblazer in more ways than one. She was the first African American woman to earn a PhD from LSU, was nominated for the Pulitzer Prize in 1979, and became the first black woman to hold the position of Louisiana Poet Laureate (1989–92).[45]

The story was similar around the state. In Lafayette, Ollie Osborne, married to an English professor at ULL, chaired the Evangeline ERA Coalition, established the Acadiana Women's Political Caucus, organized two early Lafayette women's conferences, and chaired the Louisiana International Women's Year committee. Lafayette also had a NOW chapter for a time.[46] In Rapides Parish in central Louisiana, Alexandria, the parish seat, was home to LSU-Alexandria, at that time a two-year feeder college to the flagship LSU campus. Alexandria had no NOW chapter, but women there organized a Rapides Committee for Equal

Rights in 1974. In Monroe, where Northeastern Louisiana University is located, Linda Sievers founded a NOW chapter and championed feminist causes. Nearby in Ruston, home of Louisiana Tech, Trudie Hays led a NOW chapter that at one time had as many as thirty-eight members, "which," she speculated, "was probably the largest chapter per capita in the state." In Houma, home of Nicholls State University, Muriel Arceneaux organized a NOW chapter and a local branch of ERA United. And in Hammond, on the north shore of Lake Pontchartrain, Nadine Henneman formed a CR group and ran a NOW chapter made up largely of women affiliated with Southeastern Louisiana University.[47]

Universities, then, were incubators of social action. Of course, university-educated women represented a small subset of the population in this state, and their visibility in the movement is one reason why feminism was seen as an elite movement. Yet, while universities were important in providing leaders for Louisiana's independent feminist organizations and conferences, they were not the only avenue to feminism. Blue-collar women worked toward equality for women on the job, often through their unions, and many working-class women joined the radical feminist movement, which was younger and overtly class conscious in a way that liberal feminism was not. In other words, feminism in Louisiana sometimes arose from unexpected and untraditional places. The next two chapters examine those other sources of second-wave feminism in the Bayou State. Chapter 8 also interrogates what caused Louisiana women with feminist leanings to come together in coalitions to achieve movement goals.

CHAPTER 7

"We Are All Sisters"

The Politics of Sex and Sexuality, 1965–1985

Roxanne Dunbar was already well known for her work in a variety of left-wing causes when she moved to New Orleans in 1970, bent on teaching southerners how to build a feminist movement. But by the time she arrived, as we have learned, the movement was already well established: there were at least six CR groups operating in the city and NOW had just organized a New Orleans chapter. Dunbar met with a loose organization of radical women called the Women's Liberation Coalition (WLC), whose members included Lynn Miller, Sue Laporte, Sandy Karp, Kathy Hall, Kathy O'Shaunessy (a former nun), Susan LosCalzo, and Phyllis Parun.[1] Dunbar (later Dunbar-Ortiz) formed an organization called the Southern Female Rights Union (SFRU) to spread feminism across the region, but it never amounted to much. The New Orleans feminists described it as a shadow organization that had an office and a few staffers but no memberships.[2] Dunbar's supercilious air and unwillingness to dialogue respectfully with the local activists rubbed them the wrong way. They also disagreed with her focus (which was not on feminism per se) and her advocacy of violence. Her ideologies, coupled with the fact that some of her associates stockpiled weapons, brought her under the watchful eye of the FBI's domestic counterintelligence program (COINTELPRO). Even though the local women did not agree with violence and felt that Dunbar's concentration on liberating Cuba had little to do with them or with feminism, the New Orleans WLC was infiltrated by at least one mole and continually surveilled by local law enforcement.[3]

It is possible that the WLC would have been infiltrated and surveilled even without Dunbar's presence, because COINTELPRO targeted many groups around the country that it considered radical and subversive, including civil rights and antiwar groups. Part of the mole's purpose, besides gathering information and reporting it to the FBI, was to sow seeds of dissent and create suspicion among members that informants were among them.⁴ This certainly happened in New Orleans. The presence of the police parked outside their building night and day increased tensions, but relations with Dunbar had never been good. Her ideological dogmatism proved antagonistic to nearly everyone, and in 1971 she fled the city on the lam from the FBI. There followed months of acrimonious dialogue in the form of letters and position papers back and forth until the New Orleans women decided it wasn't worth the energy and severed ties with her completely.⁵

New Orleans feminists had reason to be suspicious of Dunbar's presence and her tactics. They were not recruited to feminism by her and were unimpressed with the SFRU, which they deigned to join. The grassroots movement was already going strong when Dunbar arrived in New Orleans, yet, in still another example of how southern women's grassroots feminist organizing went unrecognized by outsiders, Dunbar-Ortiz said almost nothing about the locals in her memoir. Maybe the bad blood has something to do with that, but there is another possibility. Although it was never overtly articulated, their clashes, while rooted in ideological and cultural differences, may have been compounded by the fact that Dunbar was straight, and most of the local WLC women identified as lesbian or, as we would say today, sexually fluid.⁶

Dunbar's apartment on Jackson Avenue, located in the Irish Channel, morphed into the first women's center after Lynn Miller took over the lease and turned it into a space where no adult men were allowed.⁷ This became the unofficial headquarters of the WLC. Several CR groups met there, as did action groups that studied the problems of women in prison, rape, male-centered health-care delivery, and lesbianism. The local women also used it as the headquarters for Sisters Helping Sisters, an abortion referral service. Most of the women in the WLC already identified as lesbian or soon would. The WLC was ideologically to the left of NOW, but there were frequent interchanges and cooperation between these two groups, in part because New Orleans NOW was often led by lesbian feminists, too. In 1970, the WLC issued a statement saying that the local feminist groups in the city stood together in their goal of eliminating gender oppression:

> The woman's [sic] rights movement in New Orleans is represented by a broad spectrum of interests. On one hand there is the neo-Marxists who have dedicated themselves to organizing maids and housewives. Another group is concerned with alerting women to their oppression and providing services for those trapped by man made laws. A third group [NOW] is concerned with the repeal

of discriminatory laws and the equalization of opportunity for women in society as it is now constituted. Still another is working to fight the inhuman conditions imposed on black women by a racist society. All of these groups are the women's movement in New Orleans. All of us are sisters and meet with a common understanding of our collective problems. Thus, through this broad based coalition of interests, the women's movement can serve as a model to other groups who are deeply committed to the abolition of all oppression, as are we.[8]

Perhaps this statement was a response to the animosity generated by the intruder, Roxanne Dunbar, and represents a figurative circling of the wagons. In 1970, in Bible Belt Louisiana, it would have been highly unusual for even a group of radical women to issue a political statement that discussed sexual identity. Behind the scenes, though, this was certainly something they grappled with.

Political lesbianism was just emerging, and its newness created controversy within feminist circles in Louisiana, but far less than in the rest of the nation. In New Orleans, which had flourishing gay neighborhoods, bars, and hangouts that both provided a supportive community and served to attract gay women to the city, lesbians were instrumental in cofounding or leading not just the radical organizations but some of the liberal groups in New Orleans, too, including NOW and the National Women's Political Caucus (NWPC). Their presence created less discomfiture among feminists groups in the Crescent City than in the more conservative areas such as Baton Rouge, but even there they were welcomed. For the most part, lesbian feminists worked fairly comfortably alongside heterosexual women in Louisiana. Confounding popular perceptions, this conservative Bible Belt state produced an oppositional culture that allowed straight and woman-identified feminists to join forces against gender injustice.

The movement in New Orleans was heavily lesbian partly because New Orleans itself was such a flamingly different place. The presence of first-rate universities that drew people from all over the world, combined with its long history as a thriving port city, gave it a well-deserved reputation of not just tolerating but encouraging cultural diversity. In fact, its reputation for nonconformism made it a tourist attraction and provided an important source of revenue for the city, which thus had further incentive to protect nonconformists.[9]

New Orleans's Vieux Carré, also known as the French Quarter, harbored a gender-bending and nonconformist bohemian subculture and an antiauthoritarian ethos that supported radical women's groups. The thirteen-by-six-block area bordered by Canal on the west (the "neutral ground" on Canal demarcating the "American" section from the "Creole" French Quarter) and Esplanade on the east constituted the original city of New Orleans. Laid out by the royal engineers of Louis XIV in the 1720s, it retains its original grid pattern today. Street names reminiscent of the city's origins conjure up its continental past: Burgundy, Dauphine, Bourbon, Royal, and Chartres, which run roughly parallel to the Mississippi River, intersect with Iberville, Bienville, St. Louis, St. Peters, and eight more. A walkable area, it has the distinction of being the largest collection of colonial buildings in the United States today. Though its venerated status has pushed up rents and hotel room rates for modern travelers, in the second decade of the twentieth century, it had fallen into disrepair and become a slum. As a result, it attracted immigrants and starving artists, including Sherwood Anderson and Tennessee Williams, whose plays set in New Orleans (*A Streetcar Named Desire*, for one) made him a household name. It was in the French Quarter, where he could experiment without censure, that Williams came out as gay.

Revitalized in the 1930s and afterward by a preservation movement led by women and a few (mostly gay) men who planted themselves in the district to prevent its being razed for "development," the Quarter has never lost its wacky flair or its quirky charm. Home to artists from the staid and stable to the wildly eccentric, it proved inviting to free-spirited people who subverted the status quo. When it was a cheap place to live (akin in many ways to New York City's East Village), it attracted young people in particular, often poor, artistically inclined, and more likely than average to be gay.[10] The antiauthoritarian ethos of the French Quarter seeped into other areas of New Orleans, too, and encouraged young women to challenge standards of ladylike behavior in a way that women in other cities in Louisiana considered unseemly.[11]

The French Quarter had a reputation for tolerating gender-bending, something that it continues to capitalize on as part of the tourist trade. During Mardi Gras—a no-holds-barred weeks-long festival during which the krewes (private exclusive clubs) sponsor lavish costume balls and parades—revelers costume as their opposites. Paupers parade as kings and queens, the wicked feign the sacred, businessmen suit up as jesters, matrons slide into vamp costumes, men wear lavish ball gowns and wigs and fool many into thinking they are women, while women don tuxes and pose as men.

Mardi Gras's cultural impact ripples out beyond the confines of its calendar season, which runs between Twelfth Night and Shrove Tuesday every year. The proximity of a permissive gender-bending culture has fueled experimentation with lifestyles and identities and encouraged rebellion against existing capitalist structures. The antiauthoritarian and antiestablishment ethos visible in the Quarter inspired some women to join the feminist movement as they explored new identities for themselves. With an in-your-face pluralism, so obvious in music, culture, and costume, New Orleans activists felt free to express themselves in a variety of nontraditional ways, including in direct (or "zap") actions, public demonstrations, and radical publications. Women seeking relationships with other women began to find one another, if not in the Quarter, then in the midcity region of New Orleans, but few became politically active.

Costuming and its commercial spin-offs attracted both gays and lesbians in the twentieth century but produced little political activism in the 1970s except for two short-lived groups, the Gay Liberation Front (GLF) and the Gay People's Coalition (GPC), and a longer-lived Daughters of Bilitis (DOB), a lesbian rights organization. No other city in Louisiana had anything approximating a gay rights organization until after 2000, but even in New Orleans, cultural pursuits tended to take precedence over politics. As a result, the first time an openly gay candidate ran for any political office was in 1990, when Larry Bagneris Jr. campaigned for a seat on the New Orleans City Council and lost.[12]

Even in a city storied for its tolerance of libertinism, being queer could still be dangerous and costly. Gay men were occasionally beaten up on the streets, and in the 1960s and early 1970s, they were subjected to a great deal of police harassment. In the view of Clay Latimer, "Women [did] not get in trouble as much because they [were] quieter and not on the streets as much. Women grew up fearing violence so we are more conscious of the dangers" of overexposure. Understanding that coming out could cost them enormously, many lesbian women kept a low profile.[13]

Most New Orleans woman-identified women saw themselves as feminist first and did not make lesbianism a political issue. Celeste Newbrough, who had been appointed to the Human Relations Committee (HRC) by Mayor Landrieu following the Up Stairs Lounge arson fire, told the HRC, "[While I am] in agreement with the Gay People's Coalition, I feel the things that I, as a lesbian, want, can be gained through women's liberation" because "the aims of the Coalition will be of benefit to men." This was partly because the GPC had the goal of stopping police harassment of gay men, who were often arrested in gay bars or in parks, where they may have been cruising for sex. (Like most states, Louisiana had a centuries-old "crime against nature" law that criminalized sex between two individuals of the same gender.)[14] But the majority of lesbians, Newbrough pointed out, "live their lives so that the law doesn't affect us. We wouldn't be picked up in a rest room by the vice squad."[15] They could, however, be discriminated against in a variety of ways because of their gender, which, unlike their sexual orientation, could not be hidden.

Vicki Combs and a few other New Orleans lesbians did, however, form a chapter of the DOB in the late 1960s. New Orleans was one of only two southern cities to have a chapter of the DOB, the other being Tampa, Florida.[16] The New Orleans chapter, headed for many years by Sharon Dauzat, offered safe space for lesbians in an intellectual, political, and non-bar environment. The group also included African American women. In a chapter of thirty to forty members, mostly in their twenties, anywhere from six to ten were African American, and three were of Asian descent. The New Orleans chapter continued into the 1980s, more than twenty years after the national organization had become defunct.[17]

Some lesbians, notably Lynn Miller, worked with men to found a New Orleans chapter of the GLF, modeled on the original GLF that formed in New York City after the Stonewall Riots, in 1971. Miller, however, soon became disgusted with the chauvinism of the men and left to put her energies into the feminist movement full time. The GLF lived only a few months more after her departure and then fell apart. Because the gay rights movement was male-dominated and fractious, politically aware lesbians like Miller tended to join the feminist movement. (Not all lesbians were feminists, and many lesbians in New Orleans showed little interest in the women's movement.) Yet the existence of the GLF was significant, nonetheless, because, Miller said, it "gave previously closeted gay women and men the courage to come out and added a growing number of lesbians to the feminist movement."[18]

Though Barbara Scott did not join the GLF, she had a major impact on the New Orleans women's movement and eventually on the lesbian movement nationally, too. Scott owned a highly successful cabaret in the French Quarter, the Fatted Calf. Married with three sons, Scott began to develop relationships with women in the late 1960s. Her husband soon left her, but only her close acquaintances knew about her new lesbian identity. When she ran for a seat in the state legislature in 1971, she was best known in the Quarter as a friend of historic preservation. In addition to renovating houses (509–511 Burgundy is still known as the Scott House), she was one of a small group of French Quarter citizens who successfully mobilized against the building of an interstate highway along the riverfront that would have destroyed the historic district. Though a bar owner, Scott was allergic to alcohol and could not drink, so her recreational drug of choice was marijuana. She decided to run for a seat in the state legislature in 1972 in part because she abhorred the laws restricting marijuana use as well as those that criminalized her love life. For the most part, Barbara Scott did not agree with the philosophies of the Republican Party, which refused to endorse her, but she decided to run as a Republican because the Democratic incumbent had a lock on the seat in this city dominated by the Democratic Party, and she could not have won in the Democratic primary. Running as a Republican was her only chance at winning the seat in the general election, held in February 1972.[19]

Scott counted among her close friends Darlene Fife, who, with her partner Robert Head, a Baptist preacher, owned and edited an alternative newspaper,

NOLA Express. That paper inspired Scott and the women assisting her campaign to establish *Distaff,* the feminist newspaper, because they believed the male-dominated papers, which often mocked the women's movement, would not give her campaign fair coverage. Given the revolutionary nature of Scott's platform, they were probably correct. Scott called for the elimination of "all laws relative to sexual behavior between consenting adults." She was, therefore, perhaps the first person in Louisiana to publicly call for repealing statutes that disproportionately discriminated against gays and lesbians. Her platform opened by drawing a parallel that resonated with many liberals: "Just as discrimination against blacks should be eliminated, so should discrimination against other less organized groups." Describing herself as "the feminist candidate," she stated categorically that "the State discriminates against women. The medieval civil code which sharply curtails women's control of their finances must be revised. The state must insure equal employment opportunity for women, black and white, and it must require equal salaries for equal work." The platform also called for an end to regressive sales taxes, which disproportionately hurt the poor, and decriminalization of marijuana. This last plank was cast as a means of ending discrimination against "our youth," whose futures could be ruined for a simple drug conviction.[20] These forward-thinking planks went over like a lead balloon in 1972, and this progressive female candidate soon left her husband and the city for good.

Barbara Scott's district, which included nearly half of the quarter, returned (by her reckoning) 42 percent of the vote, though she claims the opposition made sure that the machines were not working properly on election day. Saddened by the defeat and with her marriage on the rocks, she moved to Eureka Springs, Arkansas, where she bought and renovated the New Orleans Hotel and made it into a resort for feminists. Women—straight and lesbian—came from all over the country to what became a sort of female commune in the remote Arkansas hills. The women in her hotel, some of them fleeing battering relationships, helped her raise her sons, Scott says, since her husband paid no child support. She leased the downstairs bar to another lesbian woman and two gay men from New Orleans, one of whom had worked for her at the Fatted Calf. So perhaps ironically, Eureka Springs, which up to this point had been a retreat for Southern Baptists who came to see Gerald L. K. Smith's *The Great Passion Play,* also became an attraction for gay men and lesbians. They purchased crumbling old buildings in the downtown, renovated them, and turned Eureka Springs into a gay mecca. Since jobs in this remote Ozarks town were sometimes hard to find, in what is perhaps the oddest juxtaposition of all, many "put aside their feelings toward Gerald L. K. Smith and ... found work as cast and crew members in *The Great Passion Play,* still one of the area's largest employers."[21]

The hotel, which she sold in 1978, continues its French Quarter theme today, even hosting Mardi Gras celebrations every year. As reporter Frank Perez noted, "Scott's success in Eureka Springs is also credited with helping that resort town become the 'Gay Capital of the Ozarks.'" The city today (2015) has a disproportionately high LGBT population and celebrates that distinction each year with a lively (gay) Pride Celebration and several Diversity Weekends. In 2014, Eureka Springs was the only city in Arkansas to have a registry of domestic partnerships and the only city in that state to provide employee health insurance coverage to domestic partners. "A gay Mecca in Arkansas might not have happened if Barbara Scott had won her House race in 1972. New Orleans's loss was Eureka Springs' gain," Frank Perez opined.[22] Scott represents yet another cutting-edge soul to have hailed from New Orleans. Her platform is now standard fare in many parts of the United States, but at the time, it was considered quite radical, and it is fair to say that it could have come from no other city in Louisiana but New Orleans.

Aside from New Orleans, there were few out lesbians in the Louisiana feminist movement. Heterosexual women founded and led NOW chapters, and at least at first, they tended to focus on bread-and-butter issues. At LSU, for example, Baton Rouge NOW member Mary Metz documented widespread bias against female faculty in salaries, hiring, and promotion. In 1972, Helen Wheeler and Carol Parr filed a class-action complaint of discrimination against LSU with the Equal Employment Opportunity Commission (EEOC) on behalf of all female faculty. When the EEOC investigation backed up the women's claims, LSU settled out of court by offering back pay to female faculty. Though forcing the flagship university to comply with existing law may hardly seem daring in retrospect, this challenge to traditional patriarchal practices pushed the envelope of respectability in that conservative southern state capital. All the women involved, including the cofounder and president of Baton Rouge NOW, Robbie Madden, were heterosexual, middle-class women. They had invested heavily in a career in academia; eliminating barriers to advancement in those careers was thus a major concern to them in a way that it would not have been to less well-placed or less well-educated women in women's liberation groups.[23]

NOW chapters in other areas of the state were also led by straight women. Leesville, near Fort Polk, one of the largest military bases in the South, had a small NOW chapter for a few years.[24] Shreveport, on the Red River near the Arkansas border, had a fairly large and active NOW chapter (about forty or fifty members at its peak), founded in 1973 by Linda Martin, a biochemist. Shreveport was home to the oldest institution of higher education west of the Mississippi River, Centenary College, a prestigious United Methodist liberal arts college founded in 1825.[25] By 1967, Shreveport boasted branches of LSU and

Southern University as well as Barksdale Air Force Base, a substantial military installation. Martin was born in Kentucky and received degrees in chemistry from the University of Louisville and the University of Kansas. When she moved with her husband to Louisiana, she learned about discrimination firsthand. Although the state had numerous chemical plants and petroleum refineries in need of chemists, she could not get a job. One employer told her frankly "that they couldn't hire a woman because the employees' wives would be jealous!!!" After moving to Shreveport, upon her husband's acceptance of a position at LSU-Shreveport (a two-year feeder school to the flagship university in Baton Rouge), she began working as a chemist in the biochemistry department of the LSU School of Medicine. She earned an MBA (1976) and then a doctorate in finance (1979) at Louisiana Tech while living in Shreveport. A couple of years after founding the Shreveport-Bossier NOW chapter, she became president of Louisiana NOW. Many of the women who joined the Shreveport NOW chapter were either social workers, counselors, members of the LWV, and/or of the progressive "downtown" churches: Church of the Holy Cross (Episcopalian); First United Methodist, which had a liberal reputation; or the local Unitarian Universalist congregation. Some of the Shreveport NOW members were wives of servicemen stationed at the base. Martin coordinated ERA coalition efforts in women's rights throughout northern and central Louisiana and gave frequent speeches on behalf of the ERA and on women's issues. Shreveport NOW members also established the first rape crisis hotline in Shreveport—staffed only by NOW volunteers.[26] Straight women in NOW adopted causes that had once been considered radical or that had been championed initially by radicals. But in a short period of time, where there were fairly few feminist activists, various parts of the movement came together under the NOW umbrella.

The organizer of NOW in Houma, Muriel Arceneaux, a southerner, is typical of feminists outside New Orleans in that she was straight, white, middle class, well educated, and a joiner who was a member of several proto-feminist organizations. Alabama-born Arceneaux had a BA in sociology from the Alabama College for Women. A professional white woman, she was a married caseworker in the Alabama Welfare Department before becoming a social worker. After bearing three children, however, she decided to become a schoolteacher because the schedule was better for mothers. Her first "click" moment came when she divorced and received no child support from her ex-husband. Upon moving to Houma, a Cajun town in Bayou Country near the Gulf of Mexico, she married a Cajun man (Arceneaux is a Cajun name) and became a mother again. After divorcing her second husband, she realized how much Louisiana's head-and-master law harmed women. To effect change, she joined the Business and Professional Women's Club. With a few BPW members and other local women she organized the Terrebonne ERA Coalition. She served on the International Women's Year planning committees and went to Houston representing Louisiana. "From 1973 to 1985," she wrote in her autobiography, "serving in various capacities at the local and state level of BPW, I published a bulletin to inform women of political and other issues. . . . I organized workshops to teach women how to work through government processes, to lobby, to assess the effects of legislation, and contributed articles to the media and made speeches on issues affecting women." She earned a master's in education from Nicholls State University and served as a board member of the Houma YWCA from 1979 to 1987, during which time the Y developed a counseling program for battered women and trained police in handling domestic disputes. (Here, then, is another YWCA housing an antiviolence program.) In small towns, where NOW was likely the only independent feminist organization, it took up many different feminist causes.[27]

Nadine Henneman, a former nurse and subsequently a social worker, was also a well-educated, heterosexual white woman who founded a Louisiana NOW chapter. Henneman was a native of Illinois and had attended college in Iowa before moving to Hammond, the home of Southeastern Louisiana University. Her sister and husband were active in voter registration drives in Mississippi, for which the family endured threats and ostracism. Transitioning from civil rights to social work, Henneman later became a therapist and an anti–domestic violence activist. When she died in 2013, her friends and fellow activists mourned her passing. Said Liz Simon, another New Orleans social worker who volunteered in the battered women's movement: "I spent many an hour with Nadine doing workshops to educate police, mental health workers, and the general public about the dynamics and realities of women in battering relationships. She had an inner force, a powerful one, that kept her going despite the physical challenges she faced. She was a real fighter for what she believed in."[28]

The highly publicized "gay-straight" split in the northern centers of feminist activism was not much in evidence in the Bayou State. New Orleans NOW members, straight and queer, saw lesbian politics as less important than legal discrimination against all women. Clay Latimer, who worked with that organization starting in 1972, allowed that most lesbian members of NOW believed that "the ERA and other concerns that applied to ALL women were priorities, and that other topics (such as lesbian rights) could be addressed after we succeeded in the broader areas. I felt that I was discriminated against more often as a woman than as a lesbian (because that wasn't immediately as evident as my gender was), so I wanted to mount that hurdle first." Latimer has always been out but sees herself as a feminist who only happens to be lesbian. "My goal is to help all women regardless of their sexual orientation," she explained.[29]

The New Orleans NOW chapter was mostly heterosexual, although the first president, Celeste Newbrough, was an out lesbian feminist.[30] Another cofounder, Gayle Gagliano, a former nun who worked for the Institute of Human Relations (IHR) at Loyola University, was married to a former priest. The IHR hosted the New Orleans NOW's organizational meeting, and more than one hundred people attended, an amazingly high number. Although generally homophilic, the group shied away from making lesbianism a public political issue. Feminist lesbians expressed a desire early on to raise issues facing woman-identified women and to integrate them into the movement, and while it caused some controversy, never was it explosive. On March 6, 1971, at the International Women's Day Conference, sponsored by NOW, the WLC, and the Women's Marxist Study Group, there was debate over whether the issue of lesbianism should be raised. But the seminars "Female Sexuality" and "Gay Women" were included, and, much to everyone's surprise, drew by far the most interest from the approximately 150 women who attended, indicating the large number of lesbians who were active in the New Orleans movement from the beginning.[31] The first state coordinator of Louisiana NOW, Dianne Clabaugh, was also out, a fact that, in her view, caused little discomfort to the straight NOW women.[32]

Nationally, NOW had difficulties grappling with the lesbian issue as long as Betty Friedan remained its president. Friedan gained notoriety among feminists for complaining about what she called "the lavender menace"—a reference to lesbians in the movement, which she feared would destroy its credibility. She encouraged her local New York chapter to expel all openly lesbian members. However, upon her departure as president in 1970, leaders more sympathetic to the concerns of woman-identified women succeeded her. In 1971 at its national conference, NOW formally acknowledged the legitimacy of lesbian rights as a feminist issue and two years later set up a task force to study the subject and present a more welcoming environment for women who were in the process of coming out.[33]

Many local chapters followed the national organization's lead.[34] It bothered the members of the WLC that the New Orleans NOW lesbians would not come out of the closet. The non-NOW women wanted NOW lesbians to stand together in solidarity with radicals by outing themselves. There was some talk among the radicals of outing the NOW women, but after discussion they agreed not to, understanding that doing so would put the closeted women's careers in jeopardy. The more-radical women were, for the most part, still students living hand-to-mouth. The women of NOW, on the other hand, were generally professional women, and they could easily have lost their jobs if their employers discovered that they were lesbian.[35]

New Orleans NOW leaders Dianne Clabaugh and Clay Latimer came up with a compromise, a program on lesbian rights called "Dyke for a Night." The program, which was open to the public, was presented once in Baton Rouge and a second time in New Orleans in 1974, and everyone who attended was requested to wear a lavender button emblazoned with the word "DYKE." The goal was to destigmatize the term because anyone in the room could be a dyke. It was an in-your-face action that allowed straight women to "join with [their] lesbian sisters in displaying the term dyke to symbolize [their] sympathy for the problems confronting lesbians and [their] support for their efforts to end the legal and social discrimination from which they suffer, and also to symbolize [their] own recognition of the fact that all feminists are dykes within society to the extent that [all women] are oppressed by a patriarchal society." By publicly wearing the lavender DYKE button, which symbolized coming out, lesbian feminists were rejecting "any guilt or shame associated with their sexual orientation and life-style." As part of the justification for the resolution they adopted in support of the program, the women noted what feminists all over the country had experienced, which was that antifeminists used "dyke" as an epithet to discredit the womanhood of homosexual women and to keep straight women in their place: "The term dyke had been applied to all those women who dared to step beyond narrowly defined female stereotypes." The resolution further stated, "Lesbian baiting has been used as a divisionary tactic to create barriers between lesbian and heterosexual women within the movement and to frighten potential feminists away from engaging in actions directed toward ensuring the equality of women." NOW women resolved to refuse to "allow [themselves] to be drawn into a rejection of either lesbian or heterosexual lifestyles, or to be frightened away from [their] lesbian sisters or the issue of homosexual civil rights." Just as gay men reclaimed the word "queer" from their oppressors, lesbian women in Louisiana determined to reclaim the term "dyke" and accept it "as a term of pride."[36]

Evidence of greater acceptance of homosexuality among Louisiana feminists than among activists elsewhere in the nation comes from a variety of places; one instance is the reaction to the lesbian plank adopted as part of the National Plan of Action at the Houston conference in 1977. In the Louisiana delegation, which included women of various political persuasions from all over the state, not a single voice was raised against it. The Louisiana delegation was seated right behind Mississippi's, and the Louisiana women were horrified when the Mississippi women stood up and turned their backs in protest at the reading of the lesbian plank.[37]

Being called a lesbian in the 1960s and 1970s was nearly as bad as being accused of Communist affiliation. But if straight women in the Louisiana feminist movement believed the presence of lesbians to be a liability, they seldom expressed their reservations. Gayle Gagliano, a heterosexual cofounder of the New Orleans NOW chapter, said, "Rather than a controversy, I recall some concern about effective ways to counter the anti-feminists' use of gay bashing as part of their PR campaign against the women's movement. To my knowledge, there was never an effort, or even a subtly expressed wish, that our Louisiana lesbian members keep a low profile, for the 'sake of the cause.'"[38] Pat Denton, who worked with NOW on occasion, concurred: "As for NOW members, I never heard any of the straight women saying they had any problem with the fact there were several lesbians in the chapter. However, since I was an 'out' lesbian, perhaps they never discussed this in my (or other lesbians') presence."[39] In a 1983 interview, Mary Capps asked Lynn Miller (cofounder of both the Women's Center and the Gay Liberation Front) if it was true that NOW did not want lesbian visibility. Perhaps in the early years, Miller responded, but "NOW is very supportive of lesbians politically and has been for years." Indeed, the Lesbian Resolution adopted by the local NOW chapters acknowledged that "the National Organization for Women recognizes lesbianism as a valid lifestyle and respects the right of all women to define and express their sexuality as they choose."

Most lesbians in the Louisiana movement became feminist first, then moved out of heterosexual relationships into lesbianism not as a political statement but because they finally felt free to express themselves. Lynn Miller's personal experiences within both the gay rights and the feminist movements gave her a unique perspective. She commented,

Those who were truly gay (but closeted) came out and stayed out, especially since there was a newly emerging support system. There were some feminists who felt that it was somehow more deeply feminist to be a lesbian and made it a political "choice" which of course does not really work because being gay per se is not a choice. I was ready to expand my political horizons and women like Sandy Karp and Phyllis Parun, terrific organizers, were instrumental to my involvement in the New Orleans women's movement. We encouraged other lesbians to become involved. Once that interaction began, it became a challenging and learning experience for all of us.[40]

It caused conflict, Miller remembered, because

the feminists were trying to define and empower themselves and each other through the bonds of a new sisterhood and the lesbian element was definitely a complicating factor. Lesbians were learning to redefine their relationship with the other women in ways that did not involve sexist undertones. It was a complex mix-up with a lot of consciousness-raising, self-exploration, experimenta-

tion, and expansion of personal and political boundaries. No doubt it was messy
at times, and mistakes were made, but after all there were no precedents. It
was an intense and evolving period and ultimately it was empowering and productive.[41]

Most productive reform movements are indeed intense, as Miller noted,
and interpersonal struggles often compound the emotional intensity. Reform
is hard work and is likely to be extremely stressful; emotional stress, in turn,
may cause damage to participants' personal relationships. Groups often dis-
integrated because of those problems, so it is significant that NOW remained
strong in Louisiana in the 1970s despite any such conflicts.

Crediting lesbians for being a key source of energy and support for feminism
in New Orleans does not, however, deny the importance of the many straight
women who provided leadership, funding, and publicity. Miller, like the other
lesbians in the movement, is quick to credit the heterosexual women and their
work: "Some of the straight women in NOW [in Louisiana] were more dedicated
than the lesbians. We lesbians were in such turmoil we wore ourselves out. We
had so much emotional upheaval and struggles among ourselves. There were
many straight women in NOW who dedicated their lives to ERA."[42]

The radical women in New Orleans cohered around a feminist lesbianism,
but the ones who were native to New Orleans were not separatists. Too many
of them had sons, and children were part of all gatherings, including pickets
and demonstrations. The separatist radicals came from elsewhere and would
not remain in New Orleans for more than a few years. Suzanne Pharr, for example, was born and raised in Georgia and moved to New Orleans in 1969 to
go to school. She and the local women parted ways when she moved to Arkansas in the early 1970s and became part of a lesbian commune in the Ozarks.[43]
Still, the sheer preponderance of lesbians in the radical wing of the movement
made some of the straight women uncomfortable, and a few left because of
it. They did not report, as some have elsewhere, that they had been "pushed"
out. But being in a minority made some of the straight women, especially those
in long-term committed relationships with men, feel out of place. They either
drifted away or moved out of the WLC into NOW, meaning that the radical wing
became almost exclusively lesbian.

Despite their disagreements, there was seldom open rancor between the
two major wings of the movement. They cooperated on major feminist events,
such as commemorating International Women's Day (May 1) and Women's
Rights Day (August 26). Though one side or the other might initiate a new
reform or institution, in nearly all cases, they worked together to ensure its success. This phenomenon of cooperation may have been more widespread than

once believed. In Atlanta, for example, one feminist reported of her communal household of lesbians in the mid-1970s, "Everyone always went to any kind of demonstration."[44]

The major disagreements with the NOW women were not as much over the lavender issue as they were over ideology. The WLC tended to organize and represent more working-class women than did NOW, which remained predominantly middle class. Many members of the WLC were students in 1970 and may have been the first in their families to attend college. Sandy Karp described the women's liberationists as "a diverse group of women who believed that only a radical change could create the equitable access and distribution of resources necessary to ensure a just society. Radically democratic, the movement was composed of socialists, students, freedom-riders, lesbians, housewives, welfare mothers and newly converted social activists. Organizationally, we worked together through a variety of structures—women centers, consciousness raising groups, study groups, social groups, action groups, and social service providers."[45] It is probably no accident that nearly all the radical women in the WLC were also out lesbians. Lesbians and socialists were both scorned in American society, so, having adopted one or the other of those identities, it was easier to also adopt the second. But NOW, being more centrist than radical, sought respectability; NOW women did not want their sexual identity to put respectability out of reach for them.

Central to the ideology of the women's liberationists was a concern for the economic welfare of women of all races. To the radicals, women could never be truly free under a capitalist system. With the assistance of Sandy Karp and Sue Laporte, who at the time were working for the state Aid to Families with Dependent Children (AFDC) office, the WLC developed, printed, and distributed booklets to welfare recipients stating their rights and informing them about state and federal rules and regulations, to help them avoid being removed from the welfare rolls. They set up community meetings and distributed the pamphlets widely.[46] The WLC worked hard to overcome both racial and economic barriers to sisterhood, which often proved impossible to do. More easily accomplished were alliances with their white sisters in NOW.

Thus, despite their differences, love triangles, and personal feuds, Louisiana feminists worked fairly well with one another and made an effort to do so. Mary Capps, a radical who had major ideological disagreements with NOW, said, "As a general rule, we got along. We were not hostile to each other." Lynn Miller seconded this opinion: "NOW was doing its thing and we were doing ours with no ill will between us as far as I know." And Celeste Newbrough, a founder of NOW who eventually left it to join the radical women's movement, affirms those statements: "We all associated with each other and we had a wonderful time."

They saw one another as a family, a community intertwined by the emotional intensity and the headiness of the cause. After every meeting, even if there were arguments and confrontations, there was inevitably a party where differences were put aside.[47]

These efforts toward cooperation were successful enough that Mary Gehman, in an early chronicle of the New Orleans movement's history, concluded that by 1974 the liberal and the radical factions had essentially merged. "In 1971," she states, "the issues between the two organizations [NOW and the WLC] were clear cut. Today when the women's center is poorly organized and NOW is forging ahead in several media oriented projects, the issues are more vague. As one woman attending both NOW and the [women's] center for the first time said recently, 'I'll be darned if I can tell the difference.'"[48] Ideological differences continued throughout the 1970s and 1980s, but for the most part the disagreements were private and the groups moved toward a philosophy of peaceful coexistence. Lynn Miller reminisced in 2008: "Looking back now I realize that in a few short years the women's movement in New Orleans had grown immensely—so many feminists, straight and gay, were working really well together."[49]

By the 1980s, however, the right-wing backlash against feminism and liberal changes of the last few decades had gained enough strength that controversy over "the lesbian issue" caused serious internal division within the Louisiana Women's Political Caucus (LWPC). Pat Denton, president of the LWPC and an out lesbian (which the group did not seem to mind), was unsuccessful in getting the state chapter to add an amendment to the bylaws stating that they "were to work against discrimination based on ageism, sexual orientation and to ensure reproductive freedom." The members repeatedly told her that they were willing to work for these things, but they did not want them inscribed in the bylaws because they "lived in a conservative state" and feared such statements in the bylaws "would destroy the WPC" in Louisiana. Denton was shocked. At the national convention, the NWPC refused to seat the Louisiana delegation because of its refusal to support the bylaws change. Denton resigned, and the LWPC soon folded.[50] The LWPC included women from more conservative areas of the state, who, as a rule, were less tolerant of lesbians than were feminists in New Orleans and Baton Rouge.

Despite risking their careers and the unqualified love of their near and dear ones, in the early 1980s, more and more women and men came out. In 1981, Ishtar, the first lesbian Mardi Gras krewe, made its debut, decades after the first gay male krewes had begun to organize. Increasing visibility brought increasing acceptance. New Orleans, always more permissive than the more puritanical cities in northern Louisiana, was the first city in the state to pass antidiscrimination ordinances. In 1991, the New Orleans City Council made sexual orientation a protected category, and in 1993 the city enacted a domestic partnership ordinance. Five years later, the city council amended the 1991 ordinance to add gender identity as a protected class, and shortly thereafter, Mayor Marc Morial extended domestic partner benefits to city employees. In 1999, the state appeals court struck down Louisiana's long-standing sodomy law, and in 1992, Governor Edwin Edwards, a Democrat, issued an executive order protecting state employees from discrimination on the basis of sexual orientation. Successive governors through Kathleen Blanco, also a Democrat—and the state's first woman governor—continued that executive order, but they expire at the end of each governor's term, and the protection was not extended under Republican governor Bobby Jindal, who took office in 2008.[51] Neither New Orleans nor Louisiana were out in front on efforts to end discrimination against gays and lesbians, but perhaps their quiet approach smoothed the way for acceptance in a state and a region that prized decorum and respectability.

This, then, is one way in which the public face of the movement in Louisiana differed from the more famous centers of feminism, such as Boston, Chicago, and New York, where there was much finger-pointing, venom, and even character assassination. Sandy Karp summarized it nicely when she reminisced that the Louisiana movement nourished "an irresistible sense of warmth and intimacy that can't fail to make a person feel good."

> This attraction was fully in place in the 1970s for the women of the New Orleans women's community. While it pervaded more traditional-focused organizations like NOW, it was especially pervasive among the new group of lesbian-feminists who were central to the emerging autonomous women's movement. We saw ourselves as part of a worldwide historical effort to make women's experience visible and valued so we were intensely hungry to meet, hear about other women's experience. The movement was so small that self-selected feminists attempted to act upon an ethical code that safe-guarded exploitation in the emergent feminist network.[52]

There may be elements of nostalgia in recollections, because at the time, personal and political feuds created a great deal of anger, dissention, and loss of membership. But the activists who stayed saw to it that none of the controversies destroyed the movement as a whole.

The sisterhood and networks formed by the independent movement and the oppositional consciousness shared by all feminists—liberal, radical, straight, and gay—created enough cohesiveness to allow the women to express subidentities within the larger feminist model. Because of a mutual commitment to major goals, the women were able to work together in support of feminist change in the state. In the end, the movement was undermined not so much by internal divisions as by the general rightward swing of state and national politics at the end of the 1970s. Meanwhile, Louisiana feminists worked to build political coalitions among women of a variety of racial, class, and ideological backgrounds. Their efforts, the subject of the next chapter, brought at least a modicum of legislative success at the state level.[53]

CHAPTER 8

"I Wanted More for My Daughters"

The Politics of Race, Gender, and Class in the Fight
for the Equal Rights Amendment, 1972–1985

It was entirely coincidental that Fran Martinez happened to be in the capitol when the ERA was introduced for a floor vote in the Louisiana legislature in the spring of 1972. Martinez was there on a different mission that day; she had gone to talk to legislators about a bill that would assist Louisiana's mentally ill. Also corralling legislators was the man Fran would soon marry, Victor Bussie, who for forty years headed the Louisiana AFL-CIO (1956–97). Fran and Vic Bussie were passionate about working for the good of the people, particularly those who had little money or resources to get lawmakers' attention. As representatives of unions and advocates for the mentally ill, Martinez and Bussie walked the marbled halls of the massive Depression-era capitol on the banks of the Mississippi River on a regular basis when the legislature was in session. On this day, Fran paid little attention to news that the ERA was about to come up for a vote, assuming—like most feminists at the time—that it would whiz through. "Nobody could possibly oppose that, could they?" she asked rhetorically.[1] To her great amazement, she discovered that they could and, even worse, that the leading foe in the House of Representatives was a woman, Louise Johnson, an insurance agent representing a district in Protestant northern Louisiana.

Johnson was one of only two female legislators in 1972, the other being Dorothy Mae Taylor, a representative from New Orleans. But unlike Taylor, who was a friend to women's advancement, Johnson fought to maintain the status quo. Taylor was African American, urbane, and Methodist; Johnson was a white Baptist business owner representing a sparsely populated area of Louisiana near

the Arkansas border. Fran and Victor Bussie, Dorothy Taylor, and Louise Johnson symbolize the antagonistic forces at work in the rise and fall of feminist
politics in the 1970s. These political divisions among women that the battle for
the ERA exposed proved that there was little "sisterhood" across ethnocultural
and class lines and destroyed any chances that the ERA may have had for ratification. Once male legislators saw that the ERA was an issue that even women
could not agree on, the amendment's demise was all but guaranteed.

To Fran Bussie, Dorothy Mae Taylor, and other Louisiana feminists, Louise
Johnson was a traitor to her gender. Though she was herself a highly successful
businesswoman, Johnson defeated a measure that promised to end discrimination against other women whose circumstances were not as cushy as hers.
Appalled, pro-ratificationists countered by mobilizing against her, writing letters to the editor of her local paper rebutting her arguments, and calling for her
constituents to unseat her, which they did: Johnson lost her bid for reelection
and lost again when she ran for a state senate seat. Louisiana feminists' continual challenge and engagement with her antifeminist rhetoric worked to end the
political career of Louise Johnson. However, while Johnson may have lost the
battle, she won the war, for she succeeded in halting the ERA's progress in the
state legislature. It never recovered from the loss of momentum, and Louisiana
became a nonratifying state, one of many in the South.[2]

In southern states, the fight to persuade legislatures to ratify the ERA
absorbed a great deal of liberal feminists' energy for the better part of a decade
(1972 to 1982). Losing that war was a bitter disappointment, and in retrospect
some feminists believed that their time and energy might have been better
spent on issues that would have measurably improved women's (and children's)
quality of life, such as paid family leave or subsidy programs for nurseries and
day care. But hindsight is twenty-twenty, and as we shall see, their efforts were
not entirely for naught. This chapter examines the background and ideologies of the stakeholders and explains the perspectives of both sides, and in so
doing, destroys one long-held stereotype about feminists. Contrary to popular
myth, the supporters of the ERA were more diverse ethnically, socioeconomically, and religiously than were the antiratificationists (the "antis"), in part
because the pro-ERA forces included labor union women. It was ERA opponents,
rather than feminists, who were lily-white. Predictably, religious affiliation
also played a part in determining which side a woman took: antis were more
likely to claim a religious affiliation, and they belonged almost exclusively to
conservative churches that opposed racial integration. Louise Johnson sang in
the choir at First Baptist Church in rural Bernice, Louisiana. Pro-ratificationists,
on the other hand, either had no religious affiliation or attended one of the lib-

eral denominations discussed in chapter 2. Fran and Victor Bussie, for example, were members of First United Methodist in Baton Rouge, one of the most progressive churches in the state.

The ERA has a long and complicated history. Proposed by Alice Paul of the National Woman's Party in 1923 and given at least tacit support by both the Democrats and the Republicans in their platforms until 1980 (when the Republicans withdrew it from theirs for the first time since 1940), the ERA seemed an obvious choice to some and like the snake in the garden of Eden to others. Initially, many progressive women's groups opposed the ERA because it would undo all the earlier legislation they had supported to protect women from unhealthy conditions in the workplace. Most of the famous women's groups, including the LWV, opposed the ERA until the rebirth of the mass women's rights movement. By 1972, activists had come to realize that protective legislation prevented women from advancing on the job. It was better, they came to believe, for safety regulations to apply to all workers, not just to women. Supported by nearly every major women's group in the country, it easily passed Congress in 1972 and went to the states for approval. But conservatives across the nation waved the banner of states' rights and used a variety of fear tactics to defeat its ratification. It is no accident that most of the nonratifying states were in the South, where "states' rights" was code for defiance of the federal government's mandates on both racial and gender equality. One Louisiana group announced a talk by Representative Johnson, for example, with the headline "Equal Rights for Races Brought Forced Bussing. What Will Equal Rights for Women Bring?" thus conflating the two issues and rallying the same people: conservative whites.[3]

The anti-ERA groups in Louisiana, those that Victor Bussie blasted as "selfishly dedicated to the yesterday instead of the tomorrow," included the Young Americans for Freedom; Louisiana Young Republicans; the Women's Auxiliary of the Chamber of Commerce (representing business interests); Catholic parents' groups; the Farm Bureau (Louise Johnson was a Farm Bureau agent); and the Louisiana Catholic Daughters of America (CDA).[4] There were also ad hoc organizations of conservative white women that popped up to defeat the ERA, such as the one Louise Johnson founded, Females Opposed to Equality (FOE). It is worth examining the arguments of the antis because modern audiences have a hard time understanding, just as Fran Bussie did, how anyone could be opposed to equality, and young people today are perplexed about why the worst enemies of the feminist movement, or at least of the ERA, were other women. Who were antifeminists, and why did they present such formidable opposition?

Arguments against the ERA

Few southerners were neutral about the ERA, and its introduction into state legislatures in 1972 brought both sides out swinging. Once Louisiana and other southern states showed that they would oppose the amendment resolutely and successfully, opponents elsewhere took heart. Buttressed by the arguments of North Carolina's U.S. senator Sam Ervin, Phyllis Schlafly recruited white Christian women into a STOP ERA movement.[5] Like Schlafly's organization, ERA opponents in Louisiana were also generally well-placed white women who did not work outside the home for pay. In other words, they were housewives who depended on male support, and they considered their ability to stay home and take care of their children a privilege. "No women in history have ever enjoyed such privileges, luxuries and freedom as American women," opined Melba McIntosh, chair of the Louisiana Farm Bureau Federation Women's Committee. "Yet a tiny minority of dissatisfied, highly vocal women are determined to 'liberate' you, whether you want it or not!" This was the perspective of women whose husbands made enough money that they could afford to stay home. Clearly, the struggles faced by most black and working-class women, who, out of necessity, left their children in the care of others every day while they worked, was not part of the moral worldview of Melba McIntosh.[6]

White conservative homemakers worried that passage of the ERA would change the rules of the game and that they would be ill-prepared to compete. Swallowing wholesale the arguments of Sam Ervin and Phyllis Schlafly, they concluded that passage of the ERA would, as one journalist put it, "free men first." "Our fear is that this could mean that mothers could be forced to go to work and have to support the family" if husbands shirked their traditional obligations as the breadwinner, said Marilyn Thayer, chair of the New Orleans chapter of Louisiana Women Opposed to ERA. Women who worked now "do it by choice," Thayer believed. "This could change that." Having elected early in their lives to become homemakers, these stay-at-home moms did not have the skills or experience to compete in the workplace. At the same time, they did not recognize, or perhaps they refused to admit, that women frequently encountered the problem of being unprepared for the workplace when husbands died unexpectedly or marriages ended through divorce or abandonment. As Anthony Guarisco, one of the Louisiana legislators who supported the ERA, suggested, "If they who don't feel affected by it don't want the ERA, they shouldn't deny it to those who need it—the working women who have to get in the water with the crocodiles." In the view of the antis, however, "liberation" meant an end to the role of "woman" as they understood it, a role they had trained for and committed their lives to.[7]

Conservatives also repurposed arguments from the 1950s, which indicates that, like feminism, the New Right had deep taproots. Antis recycled states' rights arguments developed in their battle against civil rights, contending that the amendment constituted a power grab by the federal government. "The bill promises women nothing," Louise Johnson shouted. "It doesn't do anything except take the powers away from the states and transfer the powers to the federal government."[8]

Opponents also borrowed Cold War rhetoric to paint feminists as Communists (conservatives frequently conflated liberals and Communists). Before founding STOP ERA, Schlafly was best known as an anti-Communist crusader, and she was thus well positioned to use fear of Communist internationalism against feminists. This anxiety intensified when the United Nations designated 1975 as "International Women's Year." Since most of the antis were homemakers with few institutional or organizational ties outside their churches, they were vulnerable to rhetoric that tied the feminist agenda to totalitarianism and one-worldism.[9] Because antis were married to or otherwise tied to capital, they held greater sway in Louisiana's business-dominated legislature than did feminists, who were less likely to be well-placed women.

One issue that resonated with many Americans across the political spectrum, however, and that caused many women to withdraw support from the ERA was the draft, which, in 1972, was still mandatory for men. Even its supporters believed that an equal rights amendment would mean that conscription would apply to women, too. The conflict in Vietnam appeared to be never ending, and with every passing month fewer Americans supported it. The idea that they might have to send their daughters as well as their sons to fight a no-win war in Southeast Asia caused many people to recoil from the ERA. Furthermore, conservatives charged (falsely) that the amendment would prohibit the military from segregating the sexes in living and bathing facilities. "Men, do you want your wives, sisters, and daughters living in barracks with men?" came the panic-stricken cry of women opposed to the ERA. Amendment supporters countered that, while the amendment would indeed require military service of both men and women, mothers could be exempted, and women would most likely serve in support roles, just as they were doing then. (Only 14 percent of men in the army served in combat roles at that time, too.) ERA supporters pointed out that women currently serving in the military voluntarily were under strict quotas, suffered limitations to their advancement, and were not entitled to veterans' benefits for education, medical care, or home loans. The ERA would eliminate those restrictions and ensure equal access to benefits as well as promotions. Conscription ended in the United States in 1974, but the issue remained a flash point because the draft could be reinstituted at any time, and if ERA were part of the constitution, women could expect to be called up.[10]

Antis also opposed many of the other changes associated with the modern women's movement: abortion, premarital sex, easy divorce, wives working outside the home, and equality in marriage. Typically members of conservative religious denominations such as Baptists and Catholics, these women believed that men and women should remain chaste before marriage and faithful within marriage, and that men were the heads of household. Feminism challenged and, in their view, threatened, all their deeply held assumptions as well as their life choices. The personal was political for them, too, just as it was for feminists.[11] Louise Johnson, their champion in the Louisiana legislature, told a constituent, "I am a Baptist who believes in the Bible and an orderly fashion of living." Asserting that only three groups would benefit from the ERA, "homosexuals, prostitutes, and lesbians," Johnson sponsored a resolution that passed 64–25 in the Louisiana House calling for this and other state legislatures to fight ratification of the ERA. "I'm violently opposed to this being equal to men. I appreciate the way you have taken care of us, and I'd like you to continue doing that," she averred. Johnson, who had founded FOE, named Senator Sam Ervin "Father of the Year."[12]

In opposing the ERA, Johnson represented and articulated the views of Louisiana Baptists and many other evangelical denominations, all of which had well-established networks, phone trees, and other resources that allowed them to easily mobilize their members.[13] The one time the amendment came up for a vote on the floor of the legislature, in 1972, church buses filled to capacity dropped off women wearing hats emblazoned with the words "You Can't Fool Mother Nature" and other such slogans. Conservative women packed the galleries and stopped legislators in the hallways to convey the message that, in their mind, ratificationists and other "women's libbers" were masculinized women who really wanted to be men. Their traditional views of gender arrangements went along with their conventional attire. Joan Kent, a reporter who covered the feminist movement for the *New Orleans States-Item*, noted that even without their signs and stickers, it was easy to pick out the antis because they "wore old fashioned clothing," such as pillbox hats and gloves, while the supporters of the ERA wore more modern, fashionable styles that the antis regarded as less feminine.[14]

Opponents' claims reached the level of near-hysteria based on a good bit of misinformation. They asserted that the ERA would require men and women to use the same public restrooms (in reality, it would only require equal availability of restrooms); that it would mandate abortion rights (it would not); that it would destroy the family and bring about an end to traditional gender roles.

Phyllis Schlafly expressed these views in her address to the statewide CDA convention, presided over by Mrs. Barbara Songy (she always used "Mrs.") in 1976. Schlafly denounced the feminist movement, saying, "Their anti-family goals are, first of all, abortion on demand; and secondly, state nurseries for all children, universally available. The rationale for this is that it's unfair for mothers to be expected to take care of their babies; we have to lift this burden from their backs so the women can be out fulfilling themselves in other jobs which, in their viewpoint, are so much more fulfilling than taking care of children."[15] The ERA was unnecessary, she claimed, because ample legislation already existed to protect women from discrimination. This was a reference to the Fourteenth Amendment and the Civil Rights Act of 1964, which, feminists and their supporters continually pointed out, had failed to stop discrimination against women on many fronts.

Catholics and the ERA

While Schlafly was herself a devout Catholic, and the Catholic Daughters were among the most reliable and well-organized opponents of the ERA, their position was not indicative of the mind-set of all Louisiana Catholics. As discussed in chapter 2, there was a strong strain of liberal Catholicism in the 1970s. Orders of sisters supported ERA United, the statewide organization dedicated to pushing the Louisiana legislature toward ratification of the proposed amendment, and lent their philosophical support to the movement by speaking out.[16] Sister Mary Ann Owens, director of the Justice and Peace Commission of the Diocese of Lafayette, noted, "A good deal of Catholic support has come from nuns' organizations for ERA," when she published a lengthy Christian and Catholic defense of the ERA in the *Baton Rouge Sunday Advocate*.[17]

National polling data showed, in fact, that Catholics were more likely than Protestants to support the ERA, and the church took no official position on the amendment, which helps explain the diversity of viewpoints among the faithful.[18] The *Clarion Herald*, the New Orleans archdiocesan newspaper, contained a multiplicity of voices for and against the ERA. In 1974, the paper had a fairly left-leaning editor, Rev. Andrew C. Taormina, who lasted only eleven months before Archbishop Philip M. Hannan asked him to step down following an editorial denouncing the pope's stance against artificial birth control. During Taormina's tenure as editor, however, the *Herald* endorsed the ERA in its May 16, 1974, edition.[19] Perhaps not surprisingly, the next issue contained a sharp rejoinder from the archbishop, who assured readers that the endorsement was the opinion of the editor, not that of the archdiocese or the Catholic Church. Hannan said that he opposed discrimination against women and backed efforts to legally safeguard their rights. Like most Catholics who opposed the ERA, however, he feared that it would reinforce abortion rights.[20]

Catholics who supported the ERA said repeatedly and vociferously that it would have no effect on abortion rights, which had already been decided by the Supreme Court, and they quoted Vatican II and Pope John XXIII's position on gender equality to substantiate their arguments in favor of the ERA. A pamphlet titled *Catholics and the Equal Rights Amendment* that circulated among feminists in Louisiana opened with the words of Pope John XXIII (1958–63), who noted that "since women are becoming more conscious of their dignity, they will not tolerate being treated as mere material instruments, but demand rights befitting a human person both in domestic and in public life."[21] For many Catholics, equal rights for women and support for the ERA were entirely consistent with their religious tradition. Articulating a similar view was the *Clarion Herald*'s Dolores Curran, a laywoman who wrote a regular column, Talks with Parents, for decades, and who heretofore had never voiced an opinion on any of the controversies swirling around her, perhaps fearing that she might get the boot as had the unfortunate editor Taormina. By 1978, Curran had finally had enough and took a stand: "I oppose abortion and support the ERA," she proclaimed, continuing:

> I know hundreds of Catholic women like me—some women religious, others laywomen—who have spoken out and worked actively against abortion and for the ERA in their own dioceses. That's why I was so disappointed at the American bishops' reasons for rejecting a statement supporting the ERA last spring. They repeated their long-held prediction that passage of equal rights for women might give rise to epidemic abortions. Personally I do not want the bishops to issue a statement for or against ERA. I have never viewed it as a moral but a legal issue.... There is another reason I don't want the bishops to make a statement and that is simply a matter of propriety. We need to get our own pew in order first. How can we ask our country to grant equal rights to women when we don't even consider women deaconesses? When no woman has ever had a vote at a bishops' meeting, even on family matters? ... I resent being told that if I support the ERA I also support abortion, particularly by my own bishops.[22]

Those Catholics who backed the ERA did so for any number of reasons. Working-class Catholics endorsed it along with their unions; ethnic minorities such as Spanish-descended or African-descended Louisianans supported it because the women in those families often worked, and they needed fair pay and equal opportunities that the ERA would guarantee.[23] Vic and Fran Bussie had both been raised Catholic, though they found Methodism more to their liking as adults. Half the legislature was Catholic, and a good number of its members voted for the ERA as well. They were the same legislators who supported civil rights for blacks and union rights for workers, and included Manual "Mannie" Fernandez of the League of United Latin American Citizens (LULAC), Anthony Guarisco, quoted earlier, and Representative Sidney Barthelemy, a Creole from New Orleans who had studied for the priesthood.[24]

The day that Fran Bussie stepped into the state house in 1972 to witness Louise Johnson marching around the chamber holding a sign that read "Kill That Snake" was the first and last time the Louisiana legislature voted on the ERA. Johnson's tactics worked. The amendment that had passed the state senate 25–13 died in the house, 32–65. Antiratificationists then sent it to the House Civil Laws and Procedures Committee, a move calculated to ensure that it would never come up for a floor vote again.[25] Undeterred, Louisiana ratificationists were not about to admit defeat. They organized a statewide coalition dubbed ERA United, planned to introduce the ERA again in the 1974 legislative session, and launched an all-out political assault aimed at pushing it through to ratification.

ERA Supporters

The list of eighty organizations that lent their names to ERA United shows a broad-based liberal constituency. In addition to religious organizations discussed earlier, it included many predominantly female organizations, black, white, and integrated: the YWCA, the AAUW, the AAUP, the IWO, the ACLU, the Louisiana League of Good Government, the National Association of Social Workers, the National Woman's Party (which provided office space in Baton Rouge for a time), the Louisiana Welfare Rights Organization, Women in Communication, the Communication Workers of America (CWA), the NAACP, the General Federation of Women's Clubs, and the Council of Black Women. While ERA United liked to say that the endorsing organizations represented twenty thousand Louisianans, very few of those people actually wrote letters to their legislators or personally lobbied them. But when out-of-towners did drive to Baton Rouge to lobby, they used the office of the Louisiana AFL-CIO on Government Street, a short walk from the capitol, as their headquarters. The women had access to the labor organization's telephone and office equipment, and when early morning committee meetings at the capitol required them to stay overnight, they rolled out their sleeping bags and slept on the floor to save the cost of a hotel room.[26]

If politicians voted according to public opinion surveys, the ERA would now be part of the U.S. Constitution. Polls taken in Louisiana showed majority support for the ERA throughout the 1970s. In June 1976, about two thousand Louisiana voters in selected areas (northern Louisiana and Metro New Orleans) were asked "Would you be for or against the Louisiana legislature passing the ERA?" and the vast majority, 60 percent, were in favor; only 25 percent were against; and 15 percent were indifferent. There was slightly less support in northern Louisiana, and slightly more in New Orleans, probably because of the high concentration of universities. The data tracked with national trends. In almost every sample taken in the state, regardless of where or when, there was little difference between black and white or male and female responses. A survey in 1978 of half men and half women, 25 percent of whom were black, showed that a majority in almost every district supported passage of the ERA. The area with the highest favorable rating was south central Louisiana (61 percent in favor), which was heavily Catholic; the lowest was central Louisiana (45 percent in favor), which was predominantly Baptist or other conservative Protestant. Those numbers stayed fairly stable throughout the decade, despite opponents' increasing clamor against the amendment. A *Baton Rouge Morning Advocate* poll in 1979 showed that Louisianans favored passage by a 64–28 margin with 8 percent in the "don't know" category.[27]

However, polls could be soft, and in the end surveys did not matter as much as votes. National pro-ERA forces gave it little chance of winning in the South and sent no money to Louisiana's ERA coalitions.[28] ERA advocates were thus forced to fall back on local resources, and the support of the state AFL-CIO was critical, not just financially but also politically, because feminists had nothing to bargain or trade in return for a legislator's support.

Victor Bussie led the Louisiana AFL-CIO to advance civil rights and gender justice not just in the workplace but in the law, not just for equal pay but for equality as a moral principle.[29] His wife, Frances Martinez Bussie, the community services officer for the state federation, and Bussie's assistant, Sibal Suarez Taylor (later Holt), helped him exercise the organization's political muscle for the benefit of working women.[30] Like many female labor leaders, Sibal Taylor and Fran Bussie came from working-class backgrounds and had only high school diplomas, at least during the years of their activism. (Many years later, Sibal Taylor Holt acquired a degree in English Literature from Louisiana State University.) Yet they worked closely with the better-educated white, middle-class Louisiana feminists, networking, devising strategies, traveling to conferences together, and forging sincere and lasting friendships. Of mixed race, they had both experienced racism and classism. Thus they could link gender to the racism and classism faced by their own constituencies (labor unions) and communities (women of color) and thereby persuade at least a portion of their audience to assist the drive for gender equality. These converts then lobbied on behalf of feminist goals, giving vital support to Louisiana's tiny and besieged independent feminist movement.[31]

Because lobbying was their job, Sibal Taylor and Fran Bussie were in Baton Rouge every day that the legislature was in session, and from that position they advocated measures sought by feminists. They brought to the task experience, continuity (a crucial asset often lacking in other feminist groups), associations, and preexisting networks. As a result, they were able to deliver two critical voting blocs in the legislature: the labor bloc and the Legislative Black Caucus. These two groups continually advanced the causes advocated by feminists in Louisiana; they wrote or sponsored bills that feminists wanted, made floor speeches on behalf of gender equality, and rounded up votes. These legislators, almost all of whom were male, were also the ones who sponsored the ERA and argued forcefully, amid heckling and cackles, on its behalf. Alphonse Jackson Jr., an African American Democrat from Shreveport, for example, was one of the bill's premier champions during the ten-year-long battle for ratification.[32]

The Louisiana AFL-CIO and the Limits of Political Power

The Louisiana AFL-CIO while under the leadership of Victor Bussie held unusual political power compared to its status in other southern states, where right-to-work (RTW) laws had long hampered union formation. With the help of Governor Earl Long, brother of Huey Long, a RTW law passed in 1954 was replaced in 1956, when the state and national AFL-CIO agreed to a compromise bill that retained the RTW law for agricultural workers but repealed its provisions for industrial workers. With the backing of powerful populist governors like Earl Long (who died in 1960) and his political heirs such as Edwin Edwards, organized labor remained a powerful presence in Baton Rouge during the heyday of the battle over the ERA. Though the percentage of Louisiana's nonagricultural workers who belonged to unions was well below the national average, it was among the highest in the South.[33] Historian Michael Martin has characterized the two decades between 1956 and 1976 as "the labor era, a time when labor and its leaders were at the center of elections and governance."[34] Louisiana was one of the last southern states to pass RTW legislation. Until that happened in 1976, labor had considerable influence in the legislature.[35]

Professors Jack Bass and Walter DeVries, while researching their book *The Transformation of Southern Politics*, interviewed Louisiana's Governor Edwin Edwards in 1973 and asked him about the unusual role played by labor: "Louisiana seems to be an exception to the political role of organized labor in most southern states. We believe organized labor has not been very effective in most southern states, but my understanding is that this is not the case here [in Louisiana]. Am I correct on that and what is the role of organized labor?"[36] Edwards replied in the affirmative, although he noted that the endorsement of the AFL-CIO had its downside, too: it cost him the support of the business community, the "country club set, the people who are anti-organized labor." Financially, the AFL-CIO was not much of an asset, according to the governor, contributing "maybe $5,000 during a campaign," but due to the influence of Victor Bussie, it had "tremendous effectiveness in the legislature." When Bass asked where the "real political power" lay in Louisiana, Edwards said the only forces worth mentioning were "to some extent Victor Bussie representing organized labor, and black groups."[37] Notably, both were allies to feminists, and both backed Edwards.

Because the national AFL-CIO limited state affiliates' ability to negotiate contracts with employers, call strikes, or organize locals, state federations concentrated on political activity. In the first volume of its newsletter in 1963, the Louisiana AFL-CIO made clear that it existed

> solely for the purpose of representing the members of local unions in Louisiana in legislative, public relations, and related services. In order to be effective in these efforts, it is essential that we succeed in political elections. Otherwise, the Legislature and the Congress will be filled with the conservative, anti-Labor men and women who will vote against the interests of workers just as they did when the Legislature was completely controlled by conservative rural interests before the days of Huey Long. If the workers in this state had to depend upon the votes from the conservative group, the benefits under unemployment and workmen's compensation laws and other beneficial laws would be much less. Also, we would have many anti-Labor laws such as right-to-work, just as Mississippi and many other southern states do.[38]

The Louisiana AFL-CIO could guarantee substantial votes to legislators who earned its endorsement. The state federation was a well-oiled political machine, financed by mandatory union dues and led by a professional staff. Hundreds of voting delegates and thousands of guests, including many powerful state and national figures, regularly attended the annual conventions, where resolutions reflecting the interests of constituent unions were debated and passed by majority vote. Not all the issues were peculiar to the needs of members of organized labor. Others, including matters such as workplace safety regulation and taxation, were of interest to "the general public," as Bussie liked to put it, by which he meant working-class folk regardless of their union affiliation. Besides tax policies, members debated labor-management laws, workers' compensation, price and credit regulations, wages and working conditions, and health and welfare benefits. The AFL-CIO also paid close attention to the political process, carefully watching for any change in the legislature's procedural rules that could potentially diminish its influence and for changes in election laws that might discourage the labor vote.

The organization's state leadership designed a pamphlet for legislators, *Political and Legislative Views of the Louisiana AFL-CIO*, informing them of the positions affirmed at the annual convention. Legislators were asked to check "yes" or "no" beside each issue and return the pamphlet to the state office. Victor Bussie and the office staff published the results of this poll of state and federal representatives in the newsletter. Though it did not tell members how to vote, the newsletter identified "friends" and "enemies" in the fight for workplace justice. It trumpeted its legislative achievements on behalf of workers and noted its successful lobbying against measures it considered regressive and detrimental to wage earners. This powerfully well-run constituency of more than 175,000 members could deliver tens of thousands of votes in any given gubernatorial election.[39]

While organized labor exercised considerable influence in Louisiana politics, legislators dismissed and mocked the beleaguered women's rights movement for at least one simple reason: there was no "women's vote." Though they tried, feminist organizers could not develop or deliver a dependable bloc of voters that they could use as leverage. Women, divided along class, racial, and religious lines, did not (and do not) vote as a bloc, in Louisiana or anywhere else. Pro-ERA activists and other progressive women wrote letters and lobbied on their own behalf, but they had nothing to offer legislators, which is why the state AFL-CIO was so important to them: it provided Louisiana feminists with access to government in a way that no other institutional network did.[40]

If the pro-feminists had difficulty organizing white women, they found it even harder to recruit black women, especially working-class black women, despite being antiracist in rhetoric as well as in action. As we have seen, some African American groups, especially those popular among middle- and upper-class blacks, endorsed the ERA and lent at least tacit support to the cause.[41] But black women had a tendency to see the ERA as a "white woman's struggle." The New Orleans African American newspaper *Louisiana Weekly* quoted Rose Loving, a member of the Orleans Parish School Board, as saying, "Black women have not traditionally felt they needed liberation because they have traditionally been heads of their households. They probably don't feel that they have a lot to gain by ERA." Melba Lemieux, managing editor of *Black Collegiate* magazine, however, explained that her sentiments had changed over time: "My initial thought of ERA was that it was a woman's lib movement and that it was a white woman's thing. But now as I see it [it] would enable black women to get equal jobs with no restrictions on race or sex."[42]

Because of the state's long history of white supremacy, most black women, especially those who were poor and worked as domestic help in white women's homes, regarded white women as the oppressors. Faced with multiple oppressions, their priorities were community activism and civil rights, not feminism.[43] As Sibal Taylor put it, they thought ERA "was about white women not wearing bras, or going into the army, or going to the bathroom with men," none of which much interested them. Furthermore, black women had never been drawn to CR sessions, which were predominately white and, if not always entirely middle class, usually were made up of college students and/or graduates who were aspiring middle class. As Wini Breines said of white women, "A common culture facilitated their closeness" and made women of color feel uncomfortable in their midst, even if this was not intended. Among other things, discussing sex or sexuality in public made black women uneasy. White Louisiana feminists, then, though they wished to include African American women, found the gulf between the races too cavernous for them to bridge on their own. But black and Hispanic women were likely to be organized and to feel safe and confident in union meetings. It is there that many white and black women seeking progressive change in Louisiana found common ground. Sibal Taylor worked hard to bring those sides together.[44]

Sibal Taylor

Sibal Taylor, born in 1946, was the fourth of five children of New Orleans native Mattheo Francisco Suarez, a descendant of a Spanish family whose roots in Louisiana stretched back nearly two centuries, and Emelda Fredericks, who was African American. She grew up in New Orleans' Seventh Ward, a mixed-race neighborhood typically identified as the Creole base. The meaning of the term "Creole" has shifted over time, but in this context it refers to people of a mixed racial background. Taylor said she has always identified as African American. She attended Corpus Christi Catholic Grammar School, a neighborhood school with a multiracial student population, but because her skin was much darker than that of her fellow students, they looked down on her. As southerners said, "white was right," and lighter skin meant status and privilege, even among people of color. Taylor remembered the sting of this ostracism her entire life.[45]

Taylor admired her older brother, Matteo (Matt) "Flukey" Suarez, who participated in voting rights drives and other civil rights initiatives even though doing so put his life in danger. White supremacists also menaced his family. "They used to call my mother and threaten to blow up the house, which I really should have taken much more seriously. And I'd just disregard it," Matt remembered years later. "I told my mother, 'Oh. Don't worry about that. They ain't going to do nothing. They're just talking.'" His mother knew better: in 1966, one of the peak years of civil rights activity, there were twenty-six bombings in New Orleans.[46]

Yet Emelda Suarez continued to support her son and his fellow movement workers, housing and feeding them. They slept on the floor of the Suarez home, exposing Sibal to the thrill of commitment to a righteous cause. Sheltering activists required great courage in the face of continual and unpredictable threats. At some point, though, Emelda Suarez decided enough was enough. She made it clear to her other children that she did not want them getting involved in "anything risky." Emboldened by the example of the activists whom she had come to know, however, Taylor said she "wanted to do something. So [she] chose the union."

Following a court decision that required Southern Bell to hire minority workers, in 1965 Sibal Taylor (Sibal Suarez at that time) was one of twenty-eight African Americans to break the color barrier at the Bell System that year. "They put me through hell" on the job, Taylor recalled. "As fast as they brought us in, they would turn us out. We didn't trust the white union officials [of the CWA] to represent us. The blacks got together and decided that we had to have some black representatives in the union," so she and another woman decided to put themselves forward, and they won.

The CWA was a powerful union not only in Louisiana but nationally. Because a large number of telephone workers were female, the CWA produced a number of powerful white women labor activists and had a representative on the federal Women's Bureau's Labor Advisory Committee. A series of strikes involving tens of thousands of Bell Telephone employees in the 1950s won some gains. Southern women, including Selina Burch, regional director of the CWA in New Orleans, waged a seventy-two-day-long strike in 1955. This strike cost the CWA about half its membership in the South, and it took years to recover its previous numbers. However, the losses also taught union officials the importance of building positive community relations, and they often hired women to help with this.[47]

With such a high percentage of women among its ranks, it is perhaps foreseeable that the CWA "voted overwhelmingly in favor" of endorsing the ERA at its national convention in 1972. The executive board, presided over by Joseph A. Beirne, issued a lengthy policy statement supporting ratification. The Louisiana chapter also endorsed the ERA, one of the few individual unions to do so on its own. The Louisiana American Federation of Teachers and United Teachers of New Orleans, also heavily female, did so as well.[48]

Taylor credited the president of her CWA local, Ejerico Fernandez, for his guidance, support, and advancement of her union career. An immigrant who had suffered discrimination because of his ethnicity and his accent, Ejerico Fernandez's background made him sensitive to discrimination of any kind. He immediately understood the similarity between gender and racial stigmatization and oppression. As president of the New Orleans CWA chapter, he pushed the phone company to integrate the workforce, but it "refused." After the Civil Rights Act of 1964 required employers to end discrimination against minorities, Fernandez said, they continued to hire "by color": the lighter a person's skin, the more likely he or she was to be hired and promoted.[49] White was still right, regardless of the law.

Bigoted employers were not the only racists Fernandez had to contend with. The union rank and file (which numbered about five thousand people in Local 3410) gave him nearly as much trouble when he attempted to integrate the New Orleans local in the 1960s. White members, raised in a racist culture, saw minorities as competitors for jobs. Though fellow workers labeled him a "radical" for his views, Fernandez did not let this deter him. To change the culture, he urged recruitment of and more prominent roles for minorities within the union. "I saw [leadership] promise in Sibal," he said, so he encouraged her to become a steward and then a delegate to the state AFL-CIO convention. He backed her decision to apply for the job as assistant to President Victor Bussie and wrote her a letter of recommendation. He was proud of her accomplishments and "never disappointed" with her efforts at the state level.[50]

Ejerico Fernandez, Sibal Taylor, Fran Martinez, and Victor Bussie grew up in different places and were of different ethnicities, but the common tie among them was that they were all raised Catholic. Bussie grew up in northern Louisiana in a working-class family. His father, once a sharecropper, went to work for the railroad company, but the family always remained marginal. After landing in Shreveport on the Red River in the northwest corner of the state, Bussie became a firefighter and in quick succession moved into the presidency of the Shreveport Firefighter's Local Union and then the Shreveport Central Trades and Labor Council. He became vice president of the Louisiana AFL in 1949. When the AFL and the CIO merged in 1956, he was elected the first president and was reelected without opposition for forty-one continuous years. Often against the wishes of some of his constituents, Bussie led the AFL-CIO to support black enfranchisement and racial integration as well as other progressive causes.[51]

Both Sibal Taylor and Fran Bussie agreed that Vic was "very supportive of women and of women's issues," at least in part because he had grown up in a household full of women whom he respected and admired. Roberta Madden, a Baton Rouge feminist leader, recognized Vic Bussie's support for women's issues at a dinner in his honor hosted in 1978 by the A. Philip Randolph Institute (APRI), a predominately African American organization. After outlining the goals of the women's movement, Madden told her audience, "Victor Bussie has always been there to help us. No one, male or female, that I know has done more to help women get equal opportunities—for jobs, for equal rights under the law, for employment training, consumer credit, battered women, homemakers displaced by divorce or widowhood and thrown into the job market without training. . . . Vic Bussie has done more to promote the ERA than most women have done." The opposition forces maligned him as a manipulative, self-interested union boss, Madden said, "but those of us in this room understand about the tremendous contribution Victor Bussie has made to our lives and to human rights."[52] The *Baton Rouge Advocate*, upon his retirement, headlined him as "a gentleman lobbyist with a white-collar suit and a blue-collar heart," an apt summary of his character.[53] When he died—ironically, on Labor Day in 2011—one of his friends and fellow firefighters eulogized him by saying that "his successful leadership abilities, which included the highest degree of honesty and integrity, earned him the respect, love and admiration of union leaders from every section of our entire state." To fellow unionists, Bussie was "the most successful, dedicated, honest and influential labor leader which this state ha[d] ever known."[54]

Vic Bussie's insistence that people should be treated fairly and equally regardless of their gender, class, or race came not only from his experiences of poverty and union activity but also from his religious convictions. Baptized a Catholic and raised in the Roman church, Bussie converted to Methodism as an adult. He and Fran found a comfortable home in the United Methodist Church because its Social Creed stood behind social, gender, and economic justice. It publicly supported ERA United, and Bussie's church, First United Methodist in Baton Rouge, was among the most progressive within the state. Indeed, the minister's wife, Ann Hearn, testified in support of the ERA in committee hearings.[55]

So, for multiple reasons, including his character, his own experiences and that of the women in his family, his intelligence, and political shrewdness, Victor Bussie welcomed participation by women on the executive council. He was thrilled when Sibal Taylor applied for the position as his assistant. Half the members of the state federation were African American, and he wanted someone on the staff who would understand the obstacles they faced.[56] When he hired her in 1975, she became the first African American paid by the Louisiana AFL-CIO, the first African American registered lobbyist in the State of Louisiana, and the first minority selected to join the executive board of any AFL-CIO in the nation. Vic charged her with acting as a liaison between the labor bloc and the Legislative Black Caucus (LBC). Taylor said later, "I was to build a relationship between labor and the black community. The black people in the legislature had a negative opinion of labor. They didn't see how voting with labor benefited them. I pointed out that labor and black people wanted the same thing: decent public schools, good jobs and good pay, quality public hospitals, housing, etc. Their plights were the same." Once she educated them about the role of organized labor in improving conditions for African Americans, the LBC became "a sure vote for labor."[57]

Taylor had been working on voter education and registration drives among African Americans since 1965, when she joined the A. Philip Randolph Institute, the organization named for the African American head of the Brotherhood of Sleeping Car Porters and former vice president of the national AFL-CIO. The APRI put into practice Randolph's philosophy that workers and their labor unions were the key forces in any political effort; he advised black people to develop political alliances with other groups that had similar aims.[58] This philosophy melded with Taylor's work as an AFL-CIO lobbyist. She was therefore in a unique position to link the African American community, labor, and the women's rights movement, and as soon as the state AFL-CIO hired her, she became chair of the ERA Coalition's legislative task force.[59]

Fran Martinez Bussie

Like Sibal Taylor, Fran Martinez Bussie learned to articulate as well as to resist multiple oppressions. She was born in New Orleans in 1935 to a Mexican father, John Martinez, and an Anglo mother, Althea Williams, of Louisiana. John Martinez had been born in Mexico but grew up on Lloyd Bentsen's family property near the Rio Grande in Hidalgo County, Texas. Lloyd Bentsen Jr., is best known as the senator from Texas who was Democrat Michael Dukakis's vice presidential running mate in 1988. His father, Lloyd Bentsen Sr., developed a huge farming and ranching enterprise that employed and sheltered a colony of Mexican political exiles. Fran's grandfather, Erasmo Martinez, a carpenter, sought refuge there when he fled Mexico after being imprisoned for political activity.[60]

The Martinezes' experience helped Fran identify with other oppressed groups. "As a Mexican," she explained in her speeches aimed at mobilizing support for the ERA, "I've been on the receiving end of racial discrimination. I know what it is to see my father hurt deeply and denied employment because of his color and the accent in his speech." This turned her into "a proponent of equal rights for all—men, women and children." Before blue-collar voters, she emphasized her class origins, too: "I'm not a professional of any type, nor do I have a college degree. I'm a Mexican-American and proud of it, even though I was blackballed from high school sororities and other organizations because of it."[61] Thus, Fran connected her working-class background to other forms of bigotry in an attempt to persuade audiences to identify with gender inequality.

Like Sibal Taylor, Fran Bussie had many years of strategic activism under her belt. She had worked with the Democratic Party since the age of six, when she accompanied her grandfather as he canvassed for the party in her neighborhood. As an adult, when her church asked for a volunteer to assist people struggling with mental illness, she raised her hand. She joined the board of the Baton Rouge Mental Health Association and did such good work as a volunteer that the board hired her on a part-time basis in 1967. From that position, she lobbied for improved treatment, better funding, and more-humane laws for the mentally ill in Louisiana. In fact, that is how Victor Bussie met Fran: Vic was the president of the statewide Louisiana Mental Health Association, and they worked together to put on the annual conference in Baton Rouge in the early 1970s. Soon Vic began to call on her to help union members who, due to sickness, unemployment, death, disability, age, or financial difficulties, needed services. Shortly after they married on September 2, 1972, this evolved into a paid position, community services officer (CSO) for the state AFL-CIO. Though designed to help union members and their families, the position always had a political element; the CSO's job description, according to the national organization, was to work with "the community's network of social agencies, especially toward developing union leadership for effective community action" on behalf of publicly funded services for working-class people. Thus, Fran Bussie's position required that she lobby the legislature for better social services for all Louisianans, but particularly those who could not afford to pay for private services.[62]

Fran Bussie sat on the board of ERA United from its inception in 1973 and served as its president in the late 1970s and early 1980s, until the final defeat of the ERA in 1982. She testified before the House Civil Law and Procedures Committee numerous times, trying to win over enough votes to move the bill out of that committee and back onto the floor for a vote. The ERA was the right thing to do for women of all classes but most especially for working women, she said. When testifying in 1974, she told legislators that it would "ensure that under the law work done by women [would] be valued on the same basis as the same work done by men; and therefore, employers could not use women as a cheap source of labor. Not only [would] it help to equalize salaries, but it [would] also guarantee equal treatment in employment opportunities, promotional rights and fringe benefits." While critics of ERA said that women had all the protection they needed as a result of the Equal Pay Act of 1963 and the Civil Rights Act of 1964, Fran Bussie countered that "federal and state legislative acts applying to equal and just employment practices [could] be repealed or amended at any time," something a constitutional amendment would prevent. To win the sympathy of pro-family advocates, she pointed out that many women in the workforce were heads of household trying to support children "left fatherless by death, divorce or separation." Because women workers earned, on average, one-third less than their male counterparts, they found it difficult to "properly raise and support their children." Appealing to those concerned about rising rates of juvenile crime and truancy, she said that if women were paid equitably, as the ERA would presumably ensure, they could better provide for their children and "give them proper supervision, thus reducing the incidence of delinquency in countless cases." Moving away from the practical issues, she made a case for gender and workplace justice: "Is not society at fault if merely because she is a woman her pay and benefits are substantially less, making it impossible for her as head of the household to provide the type of home life needed by all children?"[63]

Appealing to as broad a voting base as possible, Bussie also pointed out that, while the ERA's passage would end protective legislation that applied only to women, it could also be the means of "extending beneficial protection to men," since statutes would become gender neutral. Like all supporters of the ERA, she held that protective laws did as much harm as good for women workers. They shielded women from "higher pay and advancement in the traditional male occupations and from overtime pay." Furthermore, the laws were selectively applied and were therefore unfair: "Some states have laws which say that women cannot serve late in restaurants (when tips are higher), but they can clean offices or work for phone companies all night." Such arbitrariness hurt working-class women, Fran's constituency. Furthermore, though she did not specify race in her testimony, she made it clear that African American women suffered the most: "Protective legislation has rarely covered the poorest working women in the country, those in service occupations." No state's protective laws applied to domestics, for example, nearly all of whom were black. Finally, Fran concluded with an argument based on American liberal ideals: "We [those who supported the ERA] believe that American citizens should have equal access to whatever opportunities their abilities and choice incline them."[64]

Fran Bussie assisted the feminist movement in a number of ways. She served on the Board of the Louisiana Commission on the Status of Women and worked closely with the Women's Bureau (part of the Louisiana Department of Labor). She chaired the 1976 Governor's Conference on Women, and she and Sibal Taylor played important roles at the International Women's Year Conference in Baton Rouge. Both were also elected delegates to the national conference in Houston in 1977, where they joined in support of antiviolence efforts, reproductive freedom, lesbian rights, and rights for women of color.

As a member of many different organizations with commitments to social service, Fran Bussie was in a unique position to link the independent women's movement with other important constituencies. She held membership in National Labor for ERA; the Coalition of Labor Union Women (CLUW), where she was the ERA contact person for Louisiana; the YWCA; the Louisiana Conference of Social Welfare; the Democratic Women's Organization of Baton Rouge; and several more politically oriented groups, such as the Women's Political Caucus and the Women's Equality Action League. But her most effective organizational efforts were always through the unions. As a representative of ERA United of Louisiana and in her capacity as the community services officer for the Louisiana AFL-CIO, she called the various union offices and requested that they allow her to speak about the ERA at their local and regional meetings. Seldom did they turn her down, but they were not always a receptive audience.[65]

Just as the union members had resisted desegregation when Victor Bussie led the state federation to support civil rights, most of the rank and file initially resisted women's rights, as well. To win them over, Fran linked that issue to previous battles fought by the AFL-CIO, such as civil rights, voting rights, universal education, and Social Security. She stressed the importance of the ERA for working women and especially for minority women when addressing union audiences whom she hoped to persuade to assist her and the other feminists lobbying to move the ERA out of the house committee that kept killing it.

> It seems to me that when one segment of our society is made to suffer, we all suffer equally in one way or another. . . . There is also a long list of other issues that we as concerned, interested citizens should make our voices heard on: justice in the tax system, fair treatment of women in granting credit, social security coverage and benefits for the housewife, national health insurance, pension legislation, rising unemployment. . . . The challenge we must all answer is not to be satisfied with passage of the ERA—let's continue our interest and concern and diligently work toward wiping out all injustices which affect all men, women and children, no matter what their social or economic status, or their race, religion, color, sex or age may be.[66]

The broad social-justice ethic she expressed in that last sentence was a commonly held view among Methodists and many Catholics as well, but politics rarely moves on principles of general social welfare. Instead, it attends to the needs of particular groups, and those that express their opinions the loudest, marshal money, and turn out votes have more leverage than those who advocate ideas about the general good. To that end, both the Bussies and Sibal Taylor worked to raise the political stakes for legislators considering the bill. Taylor reached out to a constituency that still had little clout in Baton Rouge, African American women.

African American Feminists

The ERA could sometimes present a problem for African American women, Taylor noted. Black women were more concerned with economic discrimination and improvements on the job than with the abstract rights contained in the ERA.[67] Because they were often the primary breadwinners in their homes, black women also desperately needed the ability to get credit in their own names. Some were interested in welfare rights; others, if they were working and owned property, in changing the law in Louisiana that prohibited illegitimate children from inheriting from their mothers. Taylor organized talks with black women at the AFL-CIO hall in Baton Rouge or in her own home where she listened to their concerns and also educated them about how the ERA could help them. If they were married, Taylor pointed out something that few wives in Louisiana were aware of, which is that their husbands could sell the family home out from under them as a result of the head-and-master provision of Louisiana's community property law.[68]

In addition to black union members, Taylor also reached out to poor women organized into the Louisiana Welfare Rights Organization (LWRO), affiliated with the National Welfare Rights Organization (NWRO), which had begun in Los Angeles in 1963 at the instigation of Johnnie Tillmon. Tillmon described herself as a poor, black, middle-aged woman on welfare. "In this country," she told *Ms.* magazine, "if you're any one of those things, you count less as a human being. If you're all those things, you don't count at all." Tillmon had grown up in Arkansas and moved to California in 1959. She worked for years in a laundry, which eventually made her too sick to work at all. With six children, she needed AFDC. When her benefits proved inadequate, she formed an organization to help herself and the many women like her around the country.[69] Local and statewide branches of the NWRO formed nearly everywhere, although some protest groups sprang up independently and then affiliated with the NWRO. In New Orleans, women on welfare had been organizing and protesting since 1967, when they began to conduct rent strikes, file lawsuits, and stage protests and sit-ins at the state welfare office building in New Orleans. Calling themselves the New Orleans Welfare Rights Organization, local attorneys, women's liberationists, and a few representatives from the NWRO assisted them. In the end, historian Kent Germany concludes, they achieved "modest successes in preserving AFDC benefits and in publicizing the plight of welfare recipients." Radical feminists in Louisiana who believed in "wages for housework" supported the efforts of women on welfare to secure sufficient benefits. Sandy Karp, Mary Capps, and other white women on the radical left, as we have learned, tried to assist women on AFDC in New Orleans. The collaboration was short-lived, but the "welfare warriors" along with their feminist allies did help to identify welfare as a women's issue.[70]

Baton Rouge's Annie Smart served as the longtime president of the Louisiana Welfare Rights Organization.[71] Smart lived up to her name: "She had so much wisdom," Sibal Taylor recalled admiringly. Smart let Taylor know that black women receiving public assistance felt as though white women talked down to them, so it was important that the speakers at their meetings be African American and that the leaders of the welfare rights organizations be at the meetings to help drive the message home. Since union women worked outside the home, the welfare moms sensed that the union women "didn't know or understand their world."[72]

At these gatherings of black women, Taylor connected feminist goals to the priorities of workers and women of color: "I would discuss how ERA could help all of us. It was about equal job opportunities; about being equal in all aspects of life. We asked them to do group meetings in their communities to explain the issues. We asked them to call their legislators to community meetings to explain about issues of concern to women." She invited women of color on the faculty at (SUBR) to speak and encouraged the wives of black legislators to come to the meetings. "We had to convince African American legislators," she recalled. "At first ERA was a big joke to some of them." Through persistent lobbying, she and Fran Bussie converted the Legislative Black Caucus into the most reliable and consistent supporter not only of the ERA but also of other issues pushed by feminist activists. Representative Alphonse Jackson Jr., a sponsor of the bill in the house and himself African American, backed the ERA, he said, because many women of color had to support themselves and their children, and the amendment would "afford the women of this nation equality in terms of job employment."[73]

Polls revealed that African American women *and* men supported the ERA in larger numbers than did whites, and many black women joined forces with ERA United.[74] The Louisiana NAACP endorsed the ERA in 1973, and in 1974, the state field director, Harvey Britton, publicly "urged all NAACP units in Louisiana to begin ... securing support of their legislators on behalf of the proposed 26th Equal Rights Amendment."[75] Thus, African Americans were on the feminist/labor side almost from the beginning of the fight for the ERA. Though black female activists in Louisiana were often pulled in many different directions, serving as officers and on the boards of multiple nonprofit organizations and assisting their churches, they were not, as a general rule, hostile to the feminist movement.

Many of those black women were simultaneously raising large families. This was one major distinguishing factor between black and white activist women in the 1970s. Even though feminist events nearly always offered child care, and even though pro-feminist lobbyists pressed the Louisiana legislature, unsuccessfully, to provide free or subsidized day care as a part of state services, most white female progressives of the seventies generation had few or no children. In the absence of high-quality affordable day care, and in an age when men could not be expected to share the work of childcare, children seemed like a burden to white women seeking job and educational opportunities. Having children would interrupt their careers and make it difficult or impossible for them to make a political contribution themselves; thus, white feminists limited the number of children they had.[76] Although some lesbians may have had children from previous marriages, most did not, and many of the heterosexual married women had no children either. Attorney Sylvia Roberts had none, for example; Roberta Madden and Fran Bussie each had one child, and so on.

But for black women, children were a source of pride and positive identity in their neighborhoods and among their kin. Caring for children was "a central, valued component of their adult role" as socializers and educators of the next generation.[77] Indeed, concern not only for their own children but for others is what drove them into politics, whether agitating for welfare rights or for the ERA. This phenomenon, known as "othermothering," was particularly notable among educators, who often acted as extended family for their students. The "ethic of care," scholars have noted, "permeate[d] the atmosphere of HBCUs," and graduates of these schools carried it forward into their activist careers. This was certainly true of Rupert Richardson, Millie Charles, Louadrian Reed, and Dorothy Mae Taylor, all of whom lent support to the fight for the ERA.[78]

Rupert Florence Richardson Clemons, a teacher and the mother of eight, counted herself among the ranks of feminists, though she is most remembered for her work with the state and national NAACP. (Rupert was named for her mother's brother, Rupert Tecumseh Samuels; her sister was named Kermit for another relative.) Born in Navasota, Texas, in 1930, she moved to Lake Charles, Louisiana, as an infant. Her father's mother was from Washington, Louisiana, near Opelousas in the Cajun triangle, and her paternal grandfather was a native of Lake Charles. Likewise, both of her maternal grandparents were from Louisiana, mostly from the DeRidder area (a timber town not far north of Lake Charles). They, along with her parents, helped her acquire a sense of dignity and standing up for what was right from an early age.[79]

Richardson's mother, Mary, was a teacher and a principal at Cherry Street Elementary, a black school in Lake Charles; her father worked as a dry cleaner and as a labor union activist. Lake Charles, she said, "was very racist." But her parents taught her never to patronize white-owned businesses that practiced segregation and insulted black customers, for example, by requiring them to use the back door. The family would not drink from "colored" water fountains or ride city buses because they would be forced to sit in the back. Her parents instilled in her not just race consciousness but also the importance of education. Rupert attended Leland College in Louisiana, a black HBCU, until it lost its accreditation, whereupon she transferred to the public HBCU, Southern University in Baton Rouge. She worked as a substitute teacher while her children were young, but after earning a master's degree in counseling and psychology from McNeese State University in 1966, she found "employment security as a counselor. And I never went back to teaching after that," she told an interviewer in 2004.[80]

Richardson got involved with the NAACP for the first time due to the desegregation of the Lake Charles schools. Her children were among the first to integrate the all-white Lake Charles High School, "and the petty things that were happening were so bothersome that I decided to be involved," she recalled. "I went with a complaint to the branch about the way black children were being treated. And of course there was not one black teacher to whom they could go. So I showed up at the NAACP, and they took on my complaint and helped me to investigate it and to resolve it, but then, they said, 'Could you be the education chairman?' And that was in the early sixties, maybe '66, '65, and I've never looked back."[81]

Not long afterward, Richardson became the first black person hired by the Louisiana state unemployment office. Working there, she came to know firsthand the economic hardships that people of color faced. After divorcing James Clemons Jr. in 1975, she moved to Baton Rouge and took a job in the Department of Health and Hospitals (DHH). There she served as an administrator for thirty years before starting her own health-care consulting firm in 1994. A beautiful woman who looked years younger than her actual age, Richardson was known for "her elegance, grace and fanciful hats." Highly intelligent and refined, she was a talented public orator. "She could captivate any audience," her son Todd Clemons remembered. "Whether it was a one-on-one interview or before a big crowd, it came naturally to her." Leadership gifts complemented her flair for public speaking, and others quickly recognized her talents. Once in Baton Rouge, though she worked two jobs to help ensure that her children wanted for nothing, she also volunteered with the NAACP and quickly rose through the ranks. For sixteen years she was president of the Louisiana State Conference, and in 1981 she joined the national board. She served as vice president from 1984 to 1991, as national president from 1992 to 1995, and after 1999, chaired the NAACP Health Committee. When she died in 2008, at age seventy-eight, national board chairman Julian Bond referred to her as the "Grand Dame" of the NAACP. Governor Bobby Jindal, who had known her when he was head of the DHH, had so much respect for her that he offered the family the extraordinary privilege of allowing her body to lay in state at the Old State Capitol in Baton Rouge.[82]

Clemons described his mother as "passionate about equality for everyone," and her words and actions support this assertion. She did not think of equality as a zero-sum game where more opportunities for one group meant fewer for others. She saw her role as a leader in the NAACP meshing easily with her advocacy of women's liberation: "The struggles of blacks and women cannot be mutually exclusive. The NAACP is dedicated to equality for all persons. I could not choose between my identities. I'm at all times both black and female, feminist as well. The NAACP will always be a part of everyone's quest for equality." She put her considerable talents, energy, and intelligence to work on that quest: she helped to lead the Louisiana ERA effort, served on the Louisiana Task Force on the talent bank for women, chaired a session at the Louisiana IWY conference on women in the criminal justice system, and went to Houston as a delegate to the national conference. Her expansive vision, which extended the concept of equal citizenship rights to all marginalized groups, even included supporting gay rights, which in the 1980s and 1990s, especially for a devout Baptist who taught Christian education at her church, was quite extraordinary.[83]

In 1982, Richardson was asked if black women had always been powerful, emasculating matriarchs, as some people maintained. She denied that charge emphatically and in so doing explained why she felt feminism was necessary:

> Why do black men and women have to "take turns" seeking equality? Why should we compete with the men? I resent the implication that black women have always been liberated. Was it liberating to work in the fields all day and then take care of other women's babies to the neglect of your own? Was it liberating to bear children for your slave-holder? Was it liberating to work as entering professionals for a third of what white people made? Did that make black teachers liberated? I have never understood how anybody came to that conclusion and yet you hear that a lot among black people as well as white. Until all women are liberated black women cannot be liberated. Being a minority within a minority, we suffer doubly. No one ever stops to think about how we are penalized twice, for our gender as well as for our color.[84]

Though it is not clear from the interview whether she was referring to the Louisiana feminist movement in this sentence, she did note that "some black women have had unfortunate experiences within the general feminist movement, and that accounts for those that stick to civil rights and don't want to work on women's rights. Some black women felt used by the feminist movement as 'a sprinkling of color.'" If she meant the Louisiana feminist movement, she didn't consider the problem too great: "But I think that's turning around, at least in Louisiana. We have seen fairness in the way women are treated in holding offices in organizations."[85]

Richardson fits the profile of a Louisiana black woman who supported equal rights in that she was a mother and an educator dedicated to bringing about progressive changes for oppressed minorities. Millie Charles, an educator and social worker, also fits that description. Born in New Orleans in 1923, Charles attended segregated public schools and entered Dillard University at age fifteen. In 1956, she successfully challenged LSU to integrate its graduate school. "For a time, she was the only black student in LSU's School of Social Work. She later worked with the NAACP on voter registration" and assisted in the boycotts in New Orleans. She received her MSW from the University of Southern California in 1958 and went on to found Southern University–New Orleans (SUNO)'s School of Social Work in 1965. Dedicated to "empowering socially oppressed people" through education, she explained to *Louisiana Weekly* that she strongly favored equal rights for women: "When women begin to recognize and understand their oppression in society they will better recognize the oppression of black people." She was a speaker at the IWY conference, supported the ERA, and led the SUNO School of Social Work for many years.[86]

Another black educator who joined the feminist movement was Louadrian Dejoie Reed. Reed was born in 1935 in an integrated neighborhood in New Orleans to middle-class parents. Aristide Dejoie was a pharmacist, and Stella Brown Dejoie had a bachelor's and master's degree in education from Xavier. Aristide Dejoie, who got his degree from Mahary in Nashville because no pharmacy school in Louisiana at that time would admit African Americans, owned and operated the drugstore that his father had owned before him. Reed described the integrated neighborhood she grew up in as middle class, "more white than black," and without any racial trouble. She believed that this background gave her a lifelong facility for working with white people. While quite common in New Orleans, the ability to move in and out of white social and political circles with ease was unusual elsewhere in the state, where the lines of segregation were more strictly drawn.[87]

Coming from a well-educated middle-class family with some resources also cushioned the racism she encountered and assisted Louadrian Reed when she became an activist later in life. She acquired an education as a matter of course. "My friends and I all knew that we were going to college," she said. "That was just understood. There was no questioning it." She earned a degree in education from Dillard University in New Orleans. In 1957, she married Langston Reed, a dentist, and taught school for a few years, but after the children began to come along (there were five in all), it became too difficult and she left teaching in 1964.

As the family expanded, she and her husband decided to build a big house in a mostly Jewish neighborhood on Prieur Street. Only one of the neighbors seemed upset about a black family moving into the neighborhood; he tried to stop it by going to the zoning board, citing violations of zoning laws. However, the Reeds' representative on the zoning board overruled him and permitted them to proceed since they were not, in fact, in violation of any ordinance. That was the only real trouble they had, Reed later said, even though their neighbors were all white, many of them Jews. Her best friend, Grace Zelman, lived across the street. Her next-door neighbor was Judy Watts, an activist who founded Agenda for Children. Reed's children, used to being around whites, were among the first to integrate some of the nearby schools. Her oldest son, for example, integrated Holy Name of Jesus, the Catholic school behind Loyola University.

Reed got involved in women's rights when she heard someone talk about abuses of the head-and-master provision of the community property system, specifically, the Selina Martin and Barbara Hansen cases, which are discussed in the next chapter. These injustices moved her to act. "It doesn't do any good to be infuriated," she insisted. "You have to do something about it. You have to put some sweat equity into it, and I was prepared to do that." So she lobbied for reform of head and master and for the ERA. Her husband drove with her to Baton Rouge to lobby legislators. Though she did not join ERA United or any of the other pro-ERA groups, she was a member of the Women's Equality Action League, the National Women's Political Caucus (NWPC), and the Louisiana League of Good Government (LLOGG), of which she was president for a time.[88] When she joined the IWO in the early 1970s, she became one of only a handful of black members, perhaps the first one. The other black women were Gail Broussard (who remained a lifelong member), Sybil Morial, and Norma Eddington, who was also active in the NWPC.[89]

As was the case with many black change-seekers, what motivated her was her children. She explained, "I had three girls whose futures I cared about. I wanted them to have more possibilities than I did. At the time I went to college, the only careers open to me were teacher, social worker, and secretary. I wanted more for my daughters." In that, she was successful: all three of her daughters attained advanced degrees. Jennifer is a psychologist in California; Angelique is a small-claims judge in New Orleans; and the youngest, Meredith, is vice president for enrollment management at Our Lady of Holy Cross College in New Orleans and is working on her PhD. Meredith Reed has also been active with the IWO in the years since Hurricane Katrina.[90]

Louadrian Reed had more time on her hands than many African American women who had to work to supplement their husbands' meager salaries. She did not work outside the home while her children were young but returned to work in 1981 when Mayor Ernest Morial appointed her coordinator of the Women's Office, a department Morial had created in 1978. Reed stayed in that job until the administration of Sidney Barthelemy (Morial's archenemy), who abolished it. When announcing the appointment, Mayor Morial cited Reed's service as a public school teacher and member of numerous women's organizations, including being vice president of the IWO, and president and state chairperson of the NWPC in Louisiana.[91] Her job as coordinator of the Women's Office involved referring women who called for help to the appropriate agency and sponsoring seminars and workshops that encouraged women to become active in their communities on behalf of women. She was politically engaged and noted that "a lot of women from other countries came through." Interacting with women from other cultures, she came to realize how universal women's oppression was.

When asked how the ERA was received by the black community in New Orleans, particularly by black men, she said that she did not find black men resistant to it. The antis who showed up in Baton Rouge to lobby against it, she remembers, were all white women. There was no organized black opposition to the ERA. The main opponents, the Catholic Daughters of America, were white.

Most of the black women active in women's rights efforts worked in the field of education because there were so few other professional opportunities for them. For some, the Louisiana Education Association, organized in 1901 in Alexandria as the African American counterpart to white teachers' unions, was an avenue to leadership. Among the notable heads of this organization were Clarence Marie Collier, who cochaired the 1977 Louisiana International Women's Year conference, and Alphonse Jackson, an African American legislator and supporter of the ERA. The group's original name was the Louisiana Colored Teachers Association, but in 1947 members voted to change it to the Louisiana Education Association (LEA) to encompass all races, creeds, and groups. Among other things, the organization supported and encouraged salary equalization and other lawsuits, assisted by the NAACP, which opened up colleges and universities to black students.[92]

Dorothy Mae Taylor

Though Dorothy Mae Taylor did not have an education degree, she became a political figure who opened many doors for black women because of her leadership role in the Parent-Teacher Association. A talented natural leader, she parlayed her position as president of the PTA (a role considered appropriate for black women, since it was associated with black schools) into several groundbreaking "firsts" for African American women in Louisiana.

Taylor became the first African American woman, and only the second African American person, elected to the Louisiana legislature since Reconstruction when she won a special election to fill Ernest "Dutch" Morial's seat in 1971. For a couple of years, those two, successively, were the sole African Americans in the legislature. (Morial had vacated his seat to accept a judgeship.) The federal government, the Voting Rights Act, and the Census of 1970 forced a redistricting to create more majority-black districts in the early 1970s, but until then, Taylor was the lone black voice, and a female one at that. That would be enough to make anyone nervous, but Taylor's response was to charge the lion. She represented the community where she had always lived, New Orleans's Seventh Ward, a huge, integrated section of the city that Sibal Taylor and Sybil and Dutch Morial had also grown up in. A graduate of Booker T. Washington High School and a devoted member of Mount Zion United Methodist Church, where she served as president of the Women's Society of Christian Service, Taylor frequently held community meetings in both places. Both church and school had always served as safe havens for African American gatherings and thus were logical launching points for activist careers.[93]

Taylor was forty years old, married to small-business owner Johnny Taylor, and the mother of seven children aged six to twenty when she ran for Morial's seat. She was well known to those in her community because for twenty years she had been active as a member of the Urban League Board of Directors and with the PTAs associated with her children's schools. She fought racist practices in public schools and in the New Orleans Recreation Department (NORD), in both cases successfully. Taylor also gained fame by joining the fight to stop the construction of a new Mississippi River bridge that would have destroyed several historic black or lower-income neighborhoods. Hired as the director of Total Community Action's Central City Health Clinic, she there met and befriended Oretha Castle Haley, a noted civil rights leader. Haley urged her to run for office, and when Taylor agreed, Haley managed her campaign.[94]

When Taylor took her legislative seat in 1971, her first action in Baton Rouge was to introduce a resolution that vestigial Jim Crow legislation be removed from the books. Laws calling for separate restrooms, eating places, housing, swimming pools, and entrances based on race violated the Civil Rights Act of 1964 and had been declared unconstitutional. Taylor expected that her resolution would encounter little if any resistance. She was wrong. Though it eventually passed, she found to her dismay that legislators ran from it as though it were the plague.[95] That was her first lesson in realpolitik. Perhaps because she was the only African-descended legislator in the entire body, she learned to use confrontational language and tactics. Bill Rouselle, a twenty-six-year-old organizer, encouraged her to do so. Rouselle believed that there were too

few blacks in office for them to be powerful, as Taylor's first attempt at a resolution made evident. "She couldn't get a cold passed in Baton Rouge," one constituent observed. But black officials could use their offices as bully pulpits to
raise awareness by attracting media attention. "A black politician has to use the
media as a weapon," Rouselle said. Rouselle and Oretha Haley helped Taylor
organize Black Organization for Leadership Development, or BOLD, "the closest thing uptown has to a powerful organization," the *Vieux Carré Courier* proclaimed in 1973. Already-existing black voter-education organizations SOUL
(led by Taylor's friend and political adviser, attorney Nils Douglas) and COUP
came from downtown to help BOLD get started.[96]

Taylor "breathed fire" about prison conditions and other issues affecting the
poor, black and white. Angry over rapes in Orleans Parish Prison (OPP), she led
a band of irate citizens to Sheriff Louis Heyd Jr.'s house. (OPP is the prison that
was investigated by the federal Justice Department after Hurricane Katrina.
The city has been ordered to remodel the prison and to pay millions in restitu-
tion.) Other black politicians were dismayed by Taylor's braggadocio, thinking
it unseemly. They preferred the politics of respectability.[97]

Taylor understood that women and minorities brought a unique perspective
to political leadership, and black women were particularly needed in the legislature because they brought both perspectives. Like so many black women leaders, Taylor considered the people of her community her top priority, regardless of
their gender. She did not immediately identify as a feminist, though she did (like
nearly every other black legislator) support the ERA. "I believe in equality for all
people," she said, "which is what the ERA means to me." In 1977 she told *Louisiana Weekly*, "As a black woman, I do not consider the Equal Rights Amendment
as a number one priority, but it is important and it gives the opportunity for
women to exert themselves as a whole person." At the same time she was willing to speak out forcefully in support of the measure when the house committee
deliberated its fate, saying for the record, "I've been discriminated against all
my life for being black, and more so for being a woman." She became a "familiar
figure" in the "committee hearings where the Equal Rights Amendment failed
time and time again . . . urging fellow legislators to ratify."[98] The political clout of
the Legislative Black Caucus and the union bloc, however, proved insufficient.

ERA's Defeat

The rise and decline of the feminist movement roughly paralleled that of organized labor in the 1960s and 1970s. By 1976, liberalism was on the defensive
against the rising tide of the New Right. Even Governor Edwin Edwards, who
had won election with the support of organized labor, caved in to the pressure

of business interests. In July, the Louisiana legislature passed a right-to-work bill, and despite intense lobbying from the Bussies and union members, the governor signed it. When Victor Bussie announced to the thousands of supporters gathered at the capitol that they had lost the fight, Fran stood next to him, crying silently. Twenty-one years later, on the eve of his retirement as president of the AFL-CIO, Bussie characterized this as "our most devastating defeat."[99] Following the passage of the RTW and the beginning of organized labor's decline, the ERA lost any chance of getting out of committee. In 1980, while the nation elected Republican Ronald Reagan president of the United States, Louisiana voters put David Treen into the governor's mansion, the first Republican since Reconstruction. Democratic Governor Edwards had finally come out in support of the ERA, but Treen, like President Reagan, opposed it. In 1982, the congressionally imposed ratification period for the ERA expired with the amendment still three states short of the thirty-eight required for approval. Just as in the battle over right-to-work laws, capital trumped labor.

As activists began to win victories over gender discrimination through the courts and by seeking enforcement of existing federal legislation, legislators (like many in the public) increasingly saw the ERA as superfluous. Despite polls that consistently showed a majority of Louisianans in support of the ERA, legislators felt the pressure of antis and were not going to throw themselves under the bus for an amendment that had become, in their view, freighted with negative connotations and virtually meaningless in the law.

Though they were sorely disappointed by the defeat of the ERA, feminists in Louisiana benefited from ratification politics in two ways: it forced them to put aside differences of ideology, class, region, religion, and race as they focused on the shared goal; and the threat of ratification of the ERA served as a "bogeyman" that scared legislators into passing other statutory reforms, more concrete and restricted, sought by feminists.[100] They were also points of agreement for most of the women involved on both sides of the ratification fight, thus making it easier for lawmakers to support them.

Legislators were willing to pass state laws instead of ratifying a rather vague federal amendment that left interpretation up to the U.S. Supreme Court. That specter only heightened southern whites' fears of judicial activism and overweening federal power. Because of recent civil rights and other controversial decisions (e.g., *Roe v. Wade*), southern whites loathed and feared the Supreme Court.

Though second-wave feminists have taken a great deal of flak for being overwhelmingly white, their ranks in Louisiana were far more diverse ethnically, socioeconomically, and religiously than were their opponents'. White feminists and women of color in the South perhaps had an easier time finding each other than did movement women elsewhere in part because they were in constant contact, even if on an unequal basis. But whatever the reason, Louisiana women of all races and classes came together to work toward gender and economic justice in their local communities and at the state level. Organized feminism, like virtually every movement for liberal reform, required resources, free time, and networks of reform-oriented people. Thus, feminism in Louisiana, as elsewhere, was largely a movement of women who shared those essential elements. Yet, in contrast to their opponents, who had a narrow and singular view of "woman" and her proper role (a stay-at-home mom who depended on her husband to support the family), feminists sought to improve the lives of all women, not just those who looked like they did, not just their coreligionists or women of their same ethnic or class background. Their motives were both personal ("I'm oppressed") and political, in that they were grounded in a broad social justice ethic ("discrimination is unjust and must end").

To that end, change-seeking Louisiana women pushed through a Displaced Homemakers Act and, much to the delight of black and working-class women, an equal credit bill. In 1975, after intense lobbying, the Louisiana legislature passed a bill to end the standard practice of discriminating against women in lending.[101] This half a loaf was little comfort to those who had invested considerable energy and staked their identity as well as moral capital on ratification. Southern supporters of the ERA felt the sting of defeat greatly, and some have refused to give up the fight. Roberta Madden is still working for the amendment, currently serving as codirector of *RATIFY ERA-NC* from her home in Black Mountain, North Carolina.[102]

Women from diverse backgrounds also came together to support reform of the head-and-master provision of Louisiana's community property code. Ending the husband's traditional control over marital property was a long struggle that took several court decisions as well as grassroots organizing and political pressure from women attorneys to achieve. When the political system presented unflinching opposition to feminist goals, women turned to the third branch of government, the judiciary, to get results. That endeavor is the subject of chapter 9.

CHAPTER 9

"Real Progress for Women"

Attorneys and Gender Equality, 1965–1995

Baton Rouge attorney Sylvia Roberts, an asthmatic, was a tiny woman—about five feet two inches tall and ninety-two pounds. But Roberts was a mouse that roared. When it served her, she used her diminutive size to her advantage, as she did when arguing the case of *Weeks v. Southern Bell* in the Fifth Circuit Court of Appeals in New Orleans. Roberts defended a woman, Lorena Weeks, who had been denied a promotion to switchman at Southern Bell Telephone because of a rule that women could not be hired for jobs that required them to lift more than thirty pounds. To demonstrate how ridiculous the weight limitation rules were, Roberts requested that every tool involved in a switchman's job be brought into the courtroom. She proceeded to pick up each one and walk around with it while she talked. The petite attorney hoisted a forty-pound workbench on her shoulder as she pointed out that women hauled sacks of groceries and carried toddlers weighing more than thirty pounds all the time. She mentioned that women were not prevented from working as nurses even though they had to move people who may have weighed more than they did. The rules were arbitrary and discriminatory, she charged, and thus violated the law. Her arguments persuaded the court. In one of the first major victories for NOW's legal defense team, the Fifth Circuit Court ruled in 1969 that Title VII of the Civil Rights Act allowed women, not their employers, to decide whether they wanted untraditional jobs.[1]

Women who filed lawsuits against gender discrimination and the attorneys who represented them were critical to several key successes of the second wave. Like Sylvia Roberts, many of the Louisiana attorneys who won feminist victories were members of NOW. The women who founded NOW in 1966 had modeled it on the NAACP, and just as the NAACP had employed legal battles as a weapon when white-dominated legislatures proved unresponsive to civil rights concerns, NOW launched court challenges against male-controlled legislatures that resisted gender equality in the law. As the foundation of litigation, NOW attorneys seized on Title VII of the Civil Rights Act of 1964, which prohibited employment discrimination on the basis of gender as well as race, religion, and national origin, and on the Fourteenth Amendment's guarantees of due process and equal protection.

Marguerite Rawalt—the only lawyer who volunteered full-time for NOW—received hundreds of letters in the NOW headquarters in Washington, D.C., from women asking for legal help. Like Lorena Weeks, many of those who wrote complained that they were being held back by laws that prohibited women from lifting heavy objects or from working long hours. Though such laws had been passed early in the twentieth century to protect "the weaker sex" from harsh and dangerous working conditions, in reality employers used them to disqualify women from lucrative jobs and overtime pay. NOW used Title VII to help poor, minority, and lower-class women who worked because their families needed the money. The earliest such NOW-assisted lawsuits emanated from women in the South, and the first one to succeed was *Weeks v. Southern Bell.*[2]

Sylvia Roberts said she was born a feminist and had always understood instinctively that women needed to be self-supporting. The daughter of a schoolteacher and a college professor, Roberts was born in 1933 in Bryan, Texas, where her father taught at Texas A&M. She grew up in Lafayette, Louisiana, and moved to California (her mother's home turf) in 1945, where she graduated from UCLA. Finding California values not to her liking, she returned to Louisiana in 1953 and entered LSU law school, one of only three women in the entire school and the only one in her class. Even though she had never seen a woman lawyer before, she was exceedingly anxious to get a law degree. "I knew I could never work well for anybody else," she explained, "and I was no good at math or science, so by process of elimination, I decided on the law." Encountering a great deal of hostility from the male students and professors at LSU in Baton Rouge, she left after a year and went to Tulane, which she reckoned would be more accepting of female law students because "New Orleans ha[d] always been more laid back." She was right. Because there were more women in the Tulane University Law School, she "was not an object of curiosity there." She graduated in 1956, but upon learning that no law firm in Louisiana would hire a woman lawyer, she left the country to attend the University of Paris because she thought (wrongly, as it turned out) that she might encounter a more receptive atmosphere there. Coming back to New Orleans after a year in Paris, Roberts worked as a law clerk for the Supreme Court and then as a legal secretary for a firm in Baton Rouge, where she built up her own practice. When she read in the local newspaper about the formation of NOW in 1966, Roberts sent in her membership dues and was immediately asked by Marguerite Rawalt to take the case of poor Lorena Weeks.[3]

Weeks had given nineteen years of "exemplary" service to Southern Bell Telephone in Georgia as she helped to support an orphaned younger sister and brother and then, following her marriage, to help pay for her own children's expenses. She applied for the job of switchman in 1966 because it paid better than her clerical job and because she felt certain she could perform the duties with ease. She was stunned when the phone company told her the job was closed to women. When Weeks pressed the issue, Southern Bell hid behind the Georgia law that prohibited women from holding jobs that required lifting anything weighing more than thirty pounds (despite the fact that the manual typewriter she hoisted onto her desk every morning and stowed away at night weighed thirty-four pounds). Having learned about Title VII from her union newsletter, Weeks decided to sue. Though no one she knew had ever considered suing to break down a gender barrier, she was still shocked by the reaction of her friends and relatives, who did not understand why she wanted to "stir up trouble" and take a job away from a "good man." Even her husband questioned her decision. The union-provided lawyer lost the case in district court and told her she would probably lose her job, too. She was indeed suspended for a time—a blow serious enough to make her cry "all weekend"—but she was also determined not to give up. Weeks contacted Marguerite Rawalt, who told her NOW would represent her without charge if she would promise to stick it out.[4]

Sylvia Roberts happened to be the lawyer on NOW's list of volunteers who lived closest to Georgia, and she was glad Rawalt asked her to take the case. "There wasn't anybody else" to help Lorena, she said. "Her union didn't want to help her anymore. The case had been lost. I got it when she wanted to appeal." Both Rawalt and Ruth Bader Ginsburg of the ACLU collaborated with Roberts to develop the winning legal strategies. But the struggle was not over for Lorena Weeks: the telephone company dragged its heels for two years after the ruling while she plugged along at her old job, scared to death that she might be fired for any infraction. Meanwhile, her husband was severely injured in a car wreck, meaning the household income declined, and Lorena now had the additional burden of caring for a convalescing spouse as well as her three children. Finally, the judge ordered the phone company to promote her to switchman, and Weeks received $31,000 in back pay plus commuting expenses.

Years later, Lorena Weeks lauded Roberts's role in helping her make it through the stress: "Sylvia Roberts ... kept me from drowning. She's never gotten credit and she was the most wonderful thing."[5] Roberts was awarded twenty-five dollars per hour for her work on that case, even though the minimum fee for both the Georgia and the Baton Rouge bars was thirty-five dollars per hour, but more importantly, she had won the first indisputable victory for Title VII. Rawalt biographer Judith Paterson describes its impact: "The case was a death knell for labor laws that had shackled women, limiting their chances for higher wages and promotion in the name of protection."[6] *Weeks v. Southern Bell* abolished many artificial stumbling blocks to occupational advancement for women, but perhaps even more importantly, it opened space in the imagination for girls to envision different futures for themselves.

Roberts hated the idea of the dependent housewife and wanted women to understand that they must be in a position to support themselves financially. She believed that NOW could help spread that message. She and Roberta Madden established Baton Rouge NOW, and Roberts volunteered to serve as NOW's first southern regional director. In that position, she traveled around a large area covering roughly the old Confederate states, helping women organize NOW chapters. She believed firmly in grassroots feminism: "I didn't want people to think of the movement as something out of New York, as just about abortion rights and ERA. I wanted it to be meaningful to them, wanted them to use NOW to make real progress for women."[7] Eventually she also served as general counsel and then president of the NOW Legal Defense and Education Fund, where she continued to represent women in employment discrimination cases. After 1977, she focused on Louisiana family law and worked with several other lawyers to end the husband's control of the marital community property. She became heavily involved in efforts to prevent domestic violence, something that troubled her greatly because of the extremely high mortality rate. "Women die at the hands of these sadists," she told me; "we need to get to girls before they ever get into these relationships in the first place." She continued working as a lawyer full time, and for women's legal rights and personal safety in her free time, until a brief illness following a fall suddenly took her life in December 2014. Roberts was perhaps an extraordinary southern feminist and (for the most part) an unsung one, but she was typical of many female attorneys of her generation who sought to dismantle the patriarchal state.[8]

In addition to Title VII, feminist attorneys used the Fourteenth Amendment to the U.S. Constitution to assist their cause. Ratified in 1868, this Reconstruction amendment prohibited states from making laws that abridge the privileges or immunities of citizens of the United States; from depriving any person of life, liberty, or property without due process of law; and from failing to provide equal protection of the law to all citizens. Originally intended to safeguard the rights of the newly freed slaves, in the 1960s, attorney Ruth Bader Ginsburg with the ACLU and Columbia University Law School assembled a team and systematically began to push forward cases arguing that sex discrimination violated the Fourteenth Amendment just as much as Jim Crow laws did. Ginsburg argued six cases before the U.S. Supreme Court in the 1970s and won five of them, including the case of *Reed v. Reed*, in which Ginsburg represented Sally Reed, a divorced mother of a deceased son who had been denied by the Idaho Probate Court the right to administer her child's estate solely because she was a woman. Chief Justice Warren Burger ruled that Idaho's preference in favor of males was unconstitutional because women and men were equally qualified to administer estates and that the Fourteenth Amendment disallowed "unreasonable" gender bias. This was the first of many victories over male prerogative in the law won by Ginsburg, who would later be appointed to the U.S. Supreme Court. *Reed v. Reed* became the legal foundation used by feminist attorneys across the nation as they sought to end arbitrary gender classification in state laws.[9]

Ginsburg, who developed the ACLU's Women's Rights Project, was in a position to aim for national victories, but southern women, often with far fewer resources, also won significant legal victories on behalf of gender and racial justice. Virginia women, for example, fought in the courts to end pregnancy discrimination in the military, to mitigate sex discrimination against faculty and students at universities, and to end employers' practice of discriminating against women in pay, promotion, and hiring. The Virginia case that had the greatest national reach, however, was *Loving v. Virginia* (1967), which challenged the state's strict antimiscegenation law that prohibited marriage between whites and people of color. It came not from a university-educated white woman but from a humble, soft-spoken, quiet, but determined woman of mixed racial ancestry who hailed from rural Virginia. Mildred Loving contacted the ACLU in Washington, D.C., in 1964, seeking redress against the state law that refused to recognize her marriage to Richard Loving, a white man. The ACLU's lawyers agreed to take the case. Mildred Loving would probably not have called herself a feminist, but she was by all accounts the stronger personality of the pair and was willing to risk personal safety in order to preserve her marriage and the legitimacy of her three children. She understood the implications of a victory in this case and withstood threats of bodily harm to herself and her family in order to see the case through to its successful conclusion. In the end, the 1967 U.S. Supreme Court decision invalidated every antimiscegenation law in the country, a victory that ranks with other major civil rights triumphs of the era. The Lovings' marriage endured the ordeal, although Richard did not survive the trauma of a car accident in 1975, which took his life less than a decade after the momentous decision.[10]

Yet another major victory for gender justice initiated by a southern woman began when flight attendant Eulalie Cooper, living in Louisiana at the time, sued her employer, Delta, then a southern regional airline. Stewardesses—as the airlines called them in those days—had been working through their unions since the 1950s to end demeaning and sexist workplace conditions in the "friendly skies" (a United Airlines slogan). Though the regulations varied somewhat from one airline to another, it was not uncommon for airlines to fire stewardesses when they turned thirty-two or married. Airlines wanted flight attendants to be single and attractive because a high percentage of the seats were filled by businessmen. The stewardesses were sex objects and potential sexual partners for men staying the night in a hotel. Try as they might, stewardess unions made little progress against age, weight, height, dress, and "single status" requirements. When the Equal Employment Opportunity Commission opened its office in 1965, flight attendants were waiting at the door, hoping for some assistance, but it was slow going. The EEOC took racial discrimination much more seriously than gender discrimination until lawsuits made it pay attention to women's concerns.[11] Cooper was one of the first to go that route, rather than through her union (which was getting nowhere) or the EEOC (which was almost as ineffective). Cooper sued Delta because the company fired her upon discovering that she had secretly married; a Louisiana judge ruled against her, saying that Delta's rules met the standard of "bona fide" qualification for airline service. Several legal battles later, angry and desperate flight attendants won the war. In 1973, a federal court in the District of Columbia ruled that airlines could not impose any restrictions—including gender, weight, and appearance—that did not relate directly to safety duties. Cooper had helped jump-start the process. Women also fought successfully to replace the term "stewardess" with "flight attendant," a more gender-neutral term that could (and soon did) include male cabin crew.[12]

Lawsuits helped to overturn gender injustice when successful, but even when they were not, they exposed patterns of gender discrimination. Such was the case with the head-and-master provision of Louisiana's matrimonial regimes system, commonly referred to as the community property system. Louisiana was one of eight states having a system of community property that derived from Continental European principles of civil law rather than from English common law.[13] Many praised the community property system as superior to the common law principle of *couverture*, which applied in the former English colonies, because not only was the wife half owner of all property acquired during the marriage (the "community of gains"), but she also retained separate ownership of all that she brought into the marriage or received from inheritance or donation during the marriage. Such a system recognized that the wife's contribution to the marriage was equal even though she may not have contributed monetarily. As Janet Mary Riley, the Loyola law professor who spearheaded the reform, put it, the system recognized that "neither spouse earns anything alone, but each is a better earner because of the cooperation of his or her spouse." Feminists sought to preserve this principle in the new system.[14]

However, while the wife had an undivided half *ownership* of the community, she did not control the property during the marriage. Since it was first codified in 1808, Louisiana's civil law had declared the husband the head-and-master of the community, meaning that he was responsible for managing the family's property, including real estate, both spouses' earnings, and the family business (if any). The only way a wife could negate this control was if she had signed an agreement before the wedding ceremony refuting the community and specifying that she would administer her own property. She could also register intent to administer her separate property obtained by donation or inheritance. Almost no one did this, either because most did not know such a thing was possible, or if they did, they were afraid that doing so would cast aspersions upon the husband's abilities and create conflict in the marriage. Furthermore, though frequently lauded as a "protection" for wives, renouncing the community was especially damaging to those who were not employed because they had no legal entitlement to any portion of their husband's salary.[15]

The matrimonial regimes code also contained other very limited protections for a wife. To prevent the husband from selling the family home out from under her, she could file a notarized Declaration of Family Homestead that would thereafter require the signature of both spouses before the residence could be mortgaged or sold, but this restriction applied only to the family dwelling and not to any other community property. The wife could sue the head and master for mismanagement of community funds if she could prove his management was detrimental to the welfare of the community, but she bore the burden of proof. If successful, she could obtain a separation of property, but it only protected her from future mismanagement and offered no recompense for past damages. In practice, few women did this. Furthermore, since the wife was not entitled to an inventory or an accounting of the community property, mismanagement was difficult to detect until the damage was obvious and it was often too late.[16]

The community property system regulated not only married persons' affairs but also inheritance, creditors', testamentary, contractual, and judicial rights.[17] Reform would necessarily reach far and wide and would upset many interested parties beyond husbands who stood to relinquish their control. In 1974, a committee tapped by the Louisiana legislature, which included two other women and eight male attorneys in addition to Riley, the chair, devoted nearly all its time for the next three years to developing a plan for reform of this antiquated system.[18]

After researching the reforms under way in the other seven states that had community property systems as well as those in Europe, Riley found Louisiana trailing behind. In 1965, France, the mother country whose Code Napoleon served as a foundational document for Louisiana's civil code, eliminated the husband's status as head of the family and established joint management of family affairs by the two spouses. Drawing on the civil law reforms proceeding elsewhere, Riley drafted a proposal technically known as "the joint and several management plan," informally referred to as "equal management." The proposal required action by both spouses to dispose of immovable property such as real estate, land, improvements, timber and mineral rights. Joint action by husband and wife was also required for mortgaging property or leasing it, and both spouses had to agree to take action to sell movable property (such as furniture) used by the family.[19]

Robert Pascal, a conservative, vociferously opposed Riley's plan. An LSU law professor, family law specialist, and fellow member of the LSLI advisory committee, Pascal battled Riley in committee deliberations, testified against her proposal (and against the ERA) in the legislature, and gave public speeches against her plan. In a 1974 letter to Riley that expressed his outrage, Pascal referred to feminists as "mal-oriented 'women's liberation' zealots."[20] Pascal and others who sought to retain the old matrimonial regimes system based their arguments on a traditional view, often religiously informed, of the roles and rights of men and women. Pascal argued that the legal tradition that codified the position of the husband as the head and master was "consistent with societal practices that each has assigned roles." Publicly, he proclaimed that he felt "strongly that marriage ha[d] broken down into sharp definitions of individuality" and there was a "loss of love in marriages." Coequal management of assets would not work, he asserted: "We cannot have dual control or joint control in marriage. We must have one head, not a two-headed monster."[21] Pascal thus believed that the new type of marriage based on partnership and mutual equality set up a competition between spouses, a competition that did not exist in the old system. Such an opinion failed to recognize that the vaunted "cooperation" of the traditional marriage rested on an inequality that seriously disadvantaged the wife and made it highly unlikely that she would ever refute or contest the husband's control. Riley countered that the equal management plan would "encourage couples to talk things over"; after all, less suspicion about what a husband did with the money would "make for a stronger family."[22]

While Pascal was arguably the highest profile opponent of change, he certainly was not alone. Arguments against increasing women's power and participation in public life and in household financial management came from many quarters. Some Louisianans clung to the old notion of the family as a unit

represented in the world by the head, the husband. David Conroy of the Louisiana Bar Institute expressed the view of many when he declared that just as
businesses were not run with copresidents, "the overall tendency is to feel that
somebody ought to be in charge." Which somebody? Conroy answered, "Most
couples prefer the husband to be the manager of the community."[23] Devan Dag-
get, a legislator, believed that the only problem with the current law was an
"emotional" one, saying: "I think the concern is that the term head and master
has become offensive." He suggested that the only necessary change would be
to refer to the husband as the "administrator" instead of "head and master" of
the community property.[24] The business community, particularly the chamber
of commerce, went even further, arguing that equal management would give
the wife the power to stymie her husband's business dealings; commerce in
the state, it insisted, would grind to a halt.[25] Finally, defenders of existing practices regularly cited the special "protections" or "privileges" women supposedly
enjoyed and portrayed the new laws as a diminution in their status.[26]

Many women in Louisiana, however, found that the old system harmed
them far more than it helped. For some, learning about the inequities of head
and master was what brought them to feminism. One of those was Kim Gandy,
who explained that her "click" moment came when she was nineteen years old,
and she and her husband were going to work for the telephone company in
New Orleans.

> We were filling out our employment forms and they had this great deal called
> the Company Stock Option Plan where they would take three percent out of
> your paycheck and they would put it into AT&T stock and then the company
> would match it with three percent. We were sitting there side by side filling out
> our cards and when I got to the end of the card on the back, it said, "If a married
> woman, husband must sign here." I looked at that and I said, "Honey, what does
> your card say?" He opened it up and it said the same thing. He said, "well, you
> sign mine, and I'll sign yours." He was smart. I said, "No, no, no, no."[27]

Gandy asked her boss about it, and he explained that it was the result of the
head-and-master law, which, in his words, mandated that her "paycheck really
belonged to [her] husband. Therefore, that's why [she] needed his permission to
take three percent out of it. Because, otherwise, he would be getting the whole
thing, instead of only 97 percent." Gandy was horrified.[28]

> I was only nineteen and had grown up in Bossier City [in northern Louisiana]
> and then had gone to college [Louisiana Tech] in Ruston, and I have to say that I
> was not very worldly wise. But there was something about this that did not feel
> right, somehow. It was within a few weeks after that I saw Clay Latimer on tele-

vision talking about head and master. I just sat there in front of the television absolutely transfixed by this discussion among these women of what they were doing to try to get rid of this law and about something called the Equal Rights Amendment, which I had heard about in the news, but didn't really understand it. This was 1973. They were smart enough to get the telephone number and information about the NOW meeting out on the show. I wrote it down. I showed up in Gayle Gagliano's basement for a NOW meeting and presented myself, "Here I am!" Clay Latimer and Annabelle Walker and Louise Coleman welcomed me as an incredibly naïve and unknowledgeable, but willing, nineteen-year-old and gave me a chance to spend the next seven years working to get rid of head and master. And we did it![29]

Gandy, as we know, went on to become an attorney and a national figure in the women's rights movement.

Louisiana feminists used examples of women harmed by head and master to raise awareness around the state about the lopsided power arrangement within the matrimonial regime system. The cases of Barbara Bullock, Barbara Hansen, and Selina Martin showed how husbands could easily abuse their prerogative. With the assistance of local feminists, who helped her pay the fees and a lawyer, Barbara Bullock filed suit in U.S. District Court after her checking account was seized by the IRS to settle a tax debt incurred by her husband before their marriage. Despite her pleas that he sell certain property of his own to satisfy the tax obligation, he had refused. In federal court, her attorney, Anita Ganachaux, made a case that the designation of the man as head and master was unconstitutional: the automatic conferring on the husband of such broad control over community assets violated the Fourteenth Amendment because this designation was based solely on sex regardless of individual capabilities or qualities. The LWV filed an amicus brief on behalf of Bullock, but she lost in U.S. District Court, as expected, because in income tax cases, the IRS followed the laws of the state. Nonetheless, Ganachaux's arguments helped to create an appreciation of the need for reform.[30]

Barbara Hansen's situation was similarly a federal income tax case. Donald and Barbara Hansen were married for twenty-eight years and had five nearly grown children when she filed for legal separation in 1972. Donald Hansen was severely depressed, and the couple's financial situation had badly deteriorated. In her oral argument before the Fifth Circuit Court of appeals, Hansen, who represented herself because she could not afford an attorney, described her plight: "I thought I was facing the greatest challenge of my life in 1972 when I legally separated from a marriage which had become a financial disaster. I had maintained a home for my five children until they had almost finished their education. I knew this meant starting my life over again as I was 50 years old." Her husband had mortgaged her car without her knowledge, and, unable to make the payments, she lost it; she also lost the house. She finally found a job working for the telephone company making $1.85 an hour. Shortly after the separation, her husband committed suicide by jumping off a tall building in Lafayette.[31]

Hansen was proud that she had struck out on her own, that her five children were all self-supporting, and that she paid her own bills on her small salary. Then, disaster hit. In October 1975, she received a bill from the IRS for $3,064 plus $919 for penalties for negligence and failure to file because her husband had not paid income tax for the last year they were married. The letter told her that she was guilty and had the burden of proof. "Never mind that the couple had been separated, that she had no idea of his finances and saw none of his money," feminists argued on her behalf. Under head and master, she owed half of the tax because she and Don Hansen were still married when he failed to file his tax return. The IRS notified her that her wages would be garnished to satisfy the debt.[32]

Hansen's case became a cause célèbre among Louisiana feminists, who raised money and wrote letters to anyone anywhere in the country who might offer help. Ruth Bader Ginsburg let them know that Hansen did not stand a chance of winning under current law. "Legislation appears to be the only approach likely to be successful," Ginsburg wrote to Ollie Osborne, who was trying to raise enough money to hire a lawyer for Hansen. "The facts are so sympathetic, I think you could enlist support for a private bill," read Ginsburg's handwritten note at the bottom of her 1978 letter.[33] Women such as Ollie Osborne who mobilized in Hansen's defense learned a great deal about the disabilities women suffered under Louisiana law. As they wrote letters, publicized the case, and solicited funds for Hansen, they educated scores of women, many of who now became dedicated advocates of reform.

In the end, Hansen reached a compromise with the IRS, with the help of a federal tax court judge, whereby she agreed to pay $458 in return for the IRS dropping the case against her. The publicity feminists brought helped her tremendously, but the larger question had not been resolved because no decision about head and master had been reached by the courts.[34]

Selina Martin's situation was even more outrageous than Barbara Hansen's. In 1974, Martin, an African American woman, stormed into a credit union office, incredulous that officials there had given her husband a second mortgage on their home without her permission. Her husband was unemployed, and she was the only one working. They could barely pay their bills as it was. But scream, yell, and throw things though she might, she could not change the situation. Her husband, who had mortgaged the family home in order to pay his mother's debts, never made a single payment, and the credit union sought to foreclose on the house. Martin went to Louisiana NOW, which had been looking for someone to test head and master. NOW provided an attorney (Dorothy Waldrup) and assistance, but Martin lost on all counts: her case, her home, and her head and master (she filed for divorce).[35] Louisiana NOW members hosted forums and speak-outs that featured Martin and many other women who had been hurt by the head-and-master provision. These cases helped feminists build political capital around the idea that Louisiana's archaic system that put management of community property in the hands of the husband constituted unreasonable and arbitrary sex discrimination.[36]

Even though Martin lost, it was clear that the Louisiana Supreme Court wanted the legislature to move in the direction of equal management. In *Corpus Christi Parish Credit Union v. Martin*, "the Louisiana Supreme Court hinted that if the legislature did not move toward equal management the old marriage laws would be stricken as unconstitutional because they favored one spouse over another."[37] In *Kirchberg v. Feenstra*, a decision handed down in December 1979, the appellate court found Louisiana's head and master unconstitutional. Rendered moot by the new equal management law that was due to go into effect on January 1, 1980 (discussed later), it was another signal that the federal courts increasingly were indicating that the old system would not stand.[38]

Meanwhile, Janet Riley's equal management plan had garnered the support of a majority of women in the state. At the Louisiana statehouse, Riley testified on its behalf. When asked by legislators if equal management would not create the possibility of abuse of the community property by the wife (due either to revenge, extravagance, or poor judgment), she replied that husbands would "face exactly the same kinds of dangers that wives have faced since Louisiana was formed."[39]

The momentum for reform was becoming a tidal wave directed at the reluctant legislature now from both the executive as well as the judicial branches. When Ann Davenport, Governor Edwards's secretary, testified before the House Civil Law and Procedures Committee in 1978, she first issued the required disclaimer that she was "speaking as an individual and not in any official capacity," but it was clear by her appearance that the governor approved of Riley's proposal. Speaking "as a wife and as a human being asking for equity," she summed up her position by stating, "Equal management is fair, it is constitutional, and it will work."[40] The legislature passed an equal management law in the summer of 1978 but sent it to the Law Institute for further study, much to the dismay of its supporters. When a revised version came up in 1979, "women's groups from around the state mobilized to support it," Riley said later. "It was very exciting."

The Louisiana Bar Association and the Louisiana AFL-CIO also endorsed the bill, which took effect January 1, 1980, and applied to every marriage in the state after the effective date.[41]

The new law removed all sex bias from community property management. The words "husband" and "wife" were replaced with "spouse." Community *real estate* could not be sold, leased, or disposed of without consent of both spouses. *Movable property*, which must be registered when purchased, cannot be sold, leased, or mortgaged by only one spouse *if and only if* the movables were registered in both names.[42]

Another major change was that the law made possible contracts between husband and wife, strictly prohibited under the old law. This meant they could be business partners and be employed by each other. They could also sue each other. Finally, creditors could seize community property for payment of any debt—one incurred before or during the marriage. This last part helped to win the support of the credit industry for the equal management plan.

One part of the new law reflected a compromise: a provision that allowed one spouse to give the other an irrevocable waiver of his or her right to consent to the sale, mortgage, or lease of real estate and all assets of a community business. Selina Martin, Janet Riley, and others were unhappy about this, because everyone understood that it would likely always be the wife who would turn over her right in the business.[43]

Despite that setback on irrevocability, Janet Riley was generally pleased with the reform. She reflected in 1980 that the drive to end head and master "was the one issue that united all women in the state. I saw women with anti-ERA buttons sitting side by side with women wearing pro-ERA slogans. Both sides saw it as a victory for their cause when the bill passed; the anti-ERA women used it to show that states can handle women's rights locally and don't need a national ERA, and the pro-ERA women saw it as a natural step toward a national ERA. I don't know of one woman who opposed it."[44] Indeed, standing behind Governor Edwards at the bill-signing ceremony in Baton Rouge were black and white women activists who represented a variety of professions as well as organized labor. Ironically, Janet Riley was not among them; she did not have the funds to allow her to make the trip to Baton Rouge that day.[45] Yet she was proud of what she and the other women had accomplished: "It brings Louisiana into the 20th century," Riley said. "But we have to understand that it wasn't handed to us by the legislature. We fought for it every inch of the way."[46]

If overturning inequities in the management of community property was a ten-year-long uphill battle, changing the culture of sexual harassment that was common to nearly all workplaces was an even longer and tougher one. Feminists began raising the issue in New York in 1975 at Cornell University. Newspapers picked it up, and then lawyers, who began to sue under Title VII of the Civil Rights Act. Catherine MacKinnon, whose JD and PhD are from Yale, developed the idea that sexual harassment was a form of discrimination and won a substantial victory in 1986, when the Supreme Court agreed with her argument in *Meritor Savings Bank v. Vinson*.[47]

The first case to raise the issue of same-sex harassment was *Gould v. Emory*, initiated by a woman living in New Orleans at the time of the suit's filing against her former professor at Emory University, Elizabeth Fox-Genovese. Virginia M. Gould, a native of Mobile, Alabama, lived in Atlanta in the 1980s and 1990s with her husband and four children while attending Emory University, where she earned a PhD in history under renowned historian Fox-Genovese. In 1992, shortly after the Anita Hill–Clarence Thomas hearings, Gould filed a suit alleging that Fox-Genovese not only abused Gould by forcing her to do what feminists call the "shit" work that wives traditionally were expected to do (such as cleaning her house and picking up her laundry) but also sexually harassed her. The case nearly went to trial, but when Gould's lawyers lined up a half dozen or so graduate students, all female, who were prepared to offer similar testimony against the well-respected Fox-Genovese, the university settled out of court. Ironically, Elizabeth Fox-Genovese had founded the women's studies program at Emory, yet she adopted an imperious and authoritarian air with her students and abused her power as a tenured professor.[48] But Gould, a native southerner, fought back and in the end forced not just Emory but every university to confront the issue of sexual harassment, to develop better policies and procedures, and to implement faculty training.

Attorneys were important to women's advancement in the political arena as well as in the courtroom. Louisiana's Association of Women Attorneys organized in part to get women appointed to decision-making positions in the bar association, where they could introduce a female voice into what had always been a conservative old boys club. They also assisted with the Fifty States Project in the 1980s. Presented by Ronald Reagan after the ERA was pronounced dead in 1982 as an alternative to ERA, state committees evaluated state laws and their impact on women. The board made recommendations to the governor, who could then do with them whatever he wanted.[49]

Constance "Connie" Willems, a New Orleans attorney who sat on the Louisiana board of the Fifty States Project, pointed out that attorneys were "pretty independent from men because they usually make a good living."[50] Furthermore, they saw women come into their offices in desperate circumstances and with few resources, which turned them toward feminism if they were not already inclined in that direction. They often felt an obligation to help these women but found themselves hampered because the law was not on their side.

In the early 1980s, attorneys from around the state formed the Louisiana Women's Lobby Network and hired Maurice Durbin, a woman, as a lobbyist to work full-time on behalf of women's issues in Baton Rouge. Sylvia Roberts mortgaged her house and "a number of people began to hold fundraisers to help pay Maurice," Willems reported. "We got a lot of contributions from women and some men, including some female representatives."[51] The problem for women, as noted earlier, is that they lacked a firm constituency. In the halls of the capitol, lobbyists representing unions, corporations, the oil and gas industry, and other big moneyed interests got politicians' attention. But women had no ready pool of capital or a large group of voters that they could use as leverage when dealing with lawmakers. Thus these women lawyers stepped in to try to remedy the deficiency. For a time, at least, it appeared to work.

Given the recalcitrance of conservative legislators and the entrenched patriarchal privilege of male employers and coworkers, legal challenges were sometimes the only way to budge the system toward gender neutrality. Advocates for women wanted all people to be recognized and rewarded for their skill sets and not have their sex (i.e., their femaleness) be the determinant of their ability to work, administer estates, and manage capital resources. Though it took longer—perhaps a generation—to change the culture and create respect for women's abilities to do the job, that forward progress might never have occurred had it not been for women willing to sustain legal challenges that overturned old gender hierarchies.

Into the Twenty-First Century

I hope this book has shown how an overwhelmingly conservative Bible Belt
state could produce radicals within its borders who were its own best critics.
These "heroes of their own lives," to use historian Linda Gordon's phrase, braved
scorn and social ostracism to wage an uphill battle against gender inequality.[1]
They did not win every campaign, and for some, the movement disappointed.
Feeling as though they were beating their heads against a wall, they left the
South with a bitter taste in their mouths and never returned. Regardless of
where they landed, however, most continued to be warriors for the cause.
Kathy Barrett, after working with the feminist movement in New York, became
a nurse, moved west, and joined women's groups in Colorado and Michigan.
She spent the rest of her life involved in movements for peace, justice, and
human rights.

Casey Hayden, who worked in social-justice efforts throughout the South,
was never particularly happy with the antimale tone of the women's liberation
movement that she had helped jump-start. She moved to the Bay Area of California and carried on her activism as an individual, rather than as part of a
movement. She married a second time and in 1971 gave birth to her daughter at
home, adding to the critical mass of women who helped to create the natural
childbirth movement that reclaimed birth from the hands of the patriarchal
medical establishment. She moved to Arizona in 1989 and found happiness in a
Zen community there. Her third marriage was to an Episcopal priest and community organizer, Paul Buckwalter, a man who, it appears, embodies her pas-
sions for both religious ethics and social activism.[2]

Most feminists covered in this book, however, stayed in the South, if not
always in Louisiana, and carried on the fight for gender justice through their
choice of careers rather than through independent feminist organizations.

In the end, the bills must be paid. Jeannette and Ed King, members of one of the first CR groups in New Orleans, moved back to Jackson, Mississippi, and divorced in 1986. A social worker, Jeannette helped to establish the domestic violence and rape crisis services in the city.[3] Once an activist, always an activist.

Some carried on their work on behalf of women and children's rights in anti–domestic violence efforts or returned to school to become attorneys or, like Jeannette King, social workers. Lesbian feminists became therapists specializing in counseling women in same-sex relationships, or perhaps other mental health professionals, often working for nonprofit agencies. Liz Simon, a lesbian involved in antiwar and antiviolence measures, went into social work and earned her MSW because feminism taught her to help women in desperate situations. Like many others, she dedicated her life "to the cause." She explained, "It changed how I conducted my practice. Instead of going for the moneyed clients who came through the door every 45 minutes, I have worked to help poorer women."[4]

In the 1980s, Lynette Jerry, Sue Laporte, and Susan LosCalzo became record distributors for Olivia Records, the first record company that promoted lesbian music. Sue Laporte eventually began her own firm, Terpsichore Productions, and organized women's music concerts and festivals (where the artists as well as the audience members were predominately lesbian) as well as art shows.[5] Laporte is now a practicing attorney in New Orleans. In 1978, Susan LosCalzo opened a woodworking business, Lofty Notions, which built sleeping lofts in many of the high-ceilinged homes in New Orleans. In 1981, she and her partner at that time, Sherolyn Shoup, started the Women and Children's Annual Camping Party in Pensacola, Florida, an event that has continued ever since. Susan currently lives with her partner of thirty years, Kathy Nance, in Rutherfordton, North Carolina.[6]

Like Sue Laporte, many feminists became lawyers so that they could challenge patriarchy in the courts and in the halls of the legislature. They also sought to assist women who had few resources. Clay Latimer worked for decades as an attorney for the State of Louisiana in the child protection department; now retired, she devotes her energy to a variety of woman-focused and lesbian-friendly causes. Kim Gandy and Ayn Stehr, in their private practices, represented women who needed help fighting abusive partners. After leaving the presidency of NOW in 2008, Gandy served as vice president of and general counsel for the Feminist Majority Foundation and subsequently became president and CEO of the National Network to End Domestic Violence, a position she still holds.[7]

A few Louisiana feminists acquired advanced degrees in their quest to understand the nature of gender and its social construct and then entered academia. Mary Capps became a professor at Nicholls State University in Thi-bodaux, Louisiana, where she taught sociology and women's studies until her retirement in 2003. She currently resides on the Mississippi Gulf Coast with her life partner. Sandy Karp remained in New Orleans until Hurricane Katrina destroyed her home in 2005. She now resides in Massachusetts with her part-ner, Bobbie Geary, and is writing a tome on the history of feminist philos-ophy. Celeste Newbrough left the state in the mid-1970s, obtained a master's in women's studies from San Francisco State, and taught as an instructor in that field. Gayle Gagliano taught in the English and women's studies program at the University of New Orleans for many years. Now retired, she still lives in New Or-leans. Sarah Brabant, retired professor of sociology at ULL, keeps up the fight for fair treatment of women in the workforce, and Martha Ward, an anthropol-ogist and writer, created the women's studies program at UNO.

Susan Tucker earned her PhD in archival history, communication, and archivistics from the University of Amsterdam in 2009. Her latest project is *New Orleans: City of Remembering: An American History of Genealogy*, in production with University Press of Mississippi. She retired as archivist at Newcomb Col-lege Institute in May 2015 and entrusted to her successor, Chloe Raub, the New-comb Archives and Vorhoff Library's mission of collecting the papers of women on the Gulf Coast.

Several women joined the back-to-the-land movement, another form of activism in the 1970s. Born of an ecological consciousness, it was particularly popular among sexually fluid women seeking to live communally with other women. Lynn Miller and Suzanne Pharr both left New Orleans in the early 1970s and joined the great lesbian migration back to the land. Miller, exhausted and worn down from "hay fever," moved to the mountains of North Carolina, where she still lives. Suzanne Pharr, one of the editors of *Distaff*, left New Orleans after she was fired from the elite Country Day School because of her sexual orien-tation. She moved to Arkansas to live with other lesbians in an intentional community in the rural Ozarks. She helped to start the first battered women's shelter in Fayetteville and in 1980 founded the Little Rock–based Arkansas Women's Project, which focused on antiviolence efforts. She later become director of the Highlander Center (1999–2004), worked with the National Coa-lition against Domestic Violence, and became the political education coordi-nator of Southerners on New Ground, or SONG, which supports southern inter-sectional movement work.[8]

Darlene Fife, who produced *NOLA Express* with her partner, Robert Head, a Baptist preacher, abandoned the city in 1974 and went back to the land, too. She remained a lifelong friend of Barbara Scott, whose hotel in Eureka Springs, Arkansas, made that town into a gay mecca in the 1970s. Scott eventually moved

to the Gulf Coast region of Mississippi, along with many other New Orleans lesbians. Scott, who lost her house and all her documents in Hurricane Katrina,
today lives in a beautiful new home on the edge of the ocean in Pass Christian,
Mississippi, surrounded by visitors and members of her family. She remains a
committed activist, although now her causes center on older women and ger-
ontology.[9] Phyllis Parun has lived in the same home in Fauberg Marigny, a New
Orleans artists' enclave, since the 1970s. She works as an artist and a teacher of
a holistic lifestyle, including macrobiotic eating and qigong.

Corinne Barnwell, a longtime board member of Planned Parenthood, is
fighting against the state's efforts to close abortion clinics. Faced with mount-
ing opposition, Planned Parenthood of the Gulf Coast (PPGC) has again brought
together people of faith to assist them. When Governor Jindal's administration
halted construction on its new clinic in New Orleans in 2015, PPGC put together
a large new advisory committee chaired by Pamela Steeg of the NCJW. The committee includes a Muslim woman, many African Americans (among them Dr.
Eric Griggs and Carole Bebelle, head of the Ashe Cultural Arts Center on Oretha
C. Haley Boulevard in New Orleans), and Henry Hudson, rector at Trinity, the
largest Episcopal church in Louisiana. Hudson began quietly organizing Protestant clergy to overcome the opposition and ensure that construction proceeds,
which, as of this writing, it has.

Corinne Barnwell's sister, Margery, and Margery's husband, David Billings,
who for a time was pastor of St. Mark's, to this day travel the country conducting interracial training.

Mary Gehman worked for years to keep *Distaff* alive, but lack of funds finally
forced its closure in 1982. Until 2014, she ran Margaret Media, a small press
focused on publishing books about Creoles of color and women's and Louisiana history. Stranded on the interstate during Hurricane Katrina in 2005, she
lost her New Orleans home and moved to Donaldsonville, a little river community about an hour up River Road from New Orleans, where she is now retired.

Others for whom the 1970s were pivotal years became notable public figures. Bernette Johnson is the first African American woman to serve as chief
justice of the Louisiana Supreme Court. Sybal Morial returned to New Orleans
several years after Hurricane Katrina and in 2015 published her memoir, *Witness to Change: From Jim Crow to Political Empowerment.*[10] She remains active
on the board of Flint-Goodrich Hospital and in other civic causes dear to her
heart. In 1992, Lorna Bourg won a MacArthur Fellowship, commonly called the
"genius award," for accomplishments in public affairs, dedication to creative
pursuits, and capacity for self-direction. Bourg still works on behalf of farm
workers as director of the Southern Mutual Help Association, the organization
in New Iberia, Louisiana, that she helped to found.

Sibal Taylor Holt and Fran Bussie continued their activities on behalf of social and workplace justice for many years after the ERA's defeat in 1982. In 1997, Holt took over the position of secretary-treasurer of the state AFL-CIO and served in that capacity until she was elected president in 2004, whereupon she became the first African American woman ever to lead a state AFL-CIO federation. In addition to serving as president of the A. Philip Randolph Institute in Louisiana, she participated in numerous other state and community organizations. Holt currently lives in Alexandria, Louisiana, where she is owner-operator of S Holt Construction.[11] Fran Bussie retired from her position in the AFL-CIO when her husband, Vic, decided not to stand for reelection in 1997. Vic Bussie died in 2011, but Fran remains active in Methodist Church work. Though slowed down by arthritis, she is still a regular visitor to the capitol, if not an official lobbyist. In the 2013 legislative session, she attempted (unsuccessfully) to slow Republican governor Bobby Jindal's drive toward privatization of the public sector, a conservative counterrevolution that would, in her words, undo "everything we worked for."

Felicia Kahn, now in her eighties, with the help of African American veteran member Gail Broussard, revived the IWO after Hurricane Katrina and remains heavily involved in Democratic Party politics.[12] She and Clay Latimer still drive to the capital on a regular basis to lobby for women's issues and campaign for progressive candidates, assisted now by a new generation of IWO members including Julie Schwam Harris (of the Legislative Agenda for Women, or LAW) and Margaret Walker.

The IWO's membership is now almost half African American. Among those black women whose stars are on the rise are attorney Marie Bookman; Nakisha Ervin-Knott, a Civil District Court judge for Orleans Parish; and city attorney (City of New Orleans) Sharonda Williams. Some of the more veteran members include A. Lena Stewart, administrative assistant to state representative Johnny Jackson for many years; Tracie Washington, local civil rights attorney; Meredith Reed, professor and daughter of Louadrian Reed; New Orleans-area politician Cynthia Willard Lewis; Angelle Wilson-Gant, who has been a city leader in New Orleans and has worked with the Landrieus in many capacities; Yvonne Mitchell Grubb, president of the New Orleans chapter of the National Coalition of 100 Black Women; and Cynthia Hedge-Morrell, a New Orleans city council member. These women know that they stand on the shoulders of black women before them, such as Dorothy Mae Taylor, the first African American woman in the state legislature.

Taylor was not afraid of controversy. In 1986, she became the first black woman to win election to the New Orleans city council, where she gained infamy for introducing an ordinance prohibiting discrimination based on race or religion in krewes that parade on public streets. The council unanimously passed the law at the end of 1991. Rather than comply, three old-line krewes that had been around since Mardi Gras's modern origins in 1857 announced that they would cease parading. Proteus eventually returned, but Comus and Momus were never seen on the streets again. While some white people remember her only for her role as "the vixen of Mardi Gras," others think of her as a principled woman who never backed down. Term limited from the council in 1994, she remained active in her church, Mount Zion Methodist in New Orleans, until her death in August 2000. A veritable who's who of Louisiana politicians attended her funeral.[13]

It saddens me that Dorothy Mae Taylor and many other women whose stories are in this book passed on before I got a chance to talk to them. Ollie Osborne, the leader of the ERA coalition and the LWV in Lafayette, had died before I even knew she had existed. Virginia Peyton, who was first Mary Capps's and then Nikki Alexander's life partner, was in the Intensive Care Unit of New Orleans's Touro Hospital when Hurricane Katrina hit. She died at age sixty-eight when the hospital lost power on August 31, 2005, officially a "Katrina-related death."

Rupert Richardson, the woman who led the NAACP for many years and who was from my hometown of Lake Charles, died the day before I was scheduled to interview her in 2008. That was a terrible blow because she was prominent in both the black freedom movement, for which she is best known, as well as the women's rights movement. Todd Clemons and Gaynell Clemons, two of her children, filled in some of the gaps for me. George Ethel Warren and Bernardine Proctor, two more African American women whose stories bear full telling, also died before I could interview them. I learned a great deal about Warren by interviewing her daughter, Vera Warren-Williams, owner of the Afro-centric Community Book Center in New Orleans, in 2014. Vera provided me with a funeral program and a brief bio of her mother, but, like so many others, the family lost all their documents when their house in the Lower Ninth Ward was destroyed in Hurricane Katrina. Bernardine Proctor never had children, and I was unable to locate any relatives to interview.[14] Novyse Soniat, an African American woman active in the Women's Political Caucus, the IWO, the LWV, NOW, and the NAACP, also died young. In 1975, she along with Marie Galatas (another black woman activist), Celeste Newbrough, and Dorothy Taylor founded the Grass Roots Organization for Women, a short-lived feminist group dedicated to organizing poor and working-class women.[15]

I worked on this research long enough to grieve the loss of several women who passed away after I had discussed history with them, while I was still in the process of writing what turned into a much bigger project than I originally anticipated. Pat Evans, head of the Louisiana Bureau of Women for many years, died in May 2013. Her obituary accurately described her as a "pioneer in implementing and changing Louisiana laws dealing with family violence, rape, community property, equal credit and displaced homemakers." In December 2014, we lost Janet Pounds and Sylvia Roberts. I regret that they did not live to see the fruits of our collaboration make it into print.

All these women went to their graves believing that they had lived a life of good works because they sought liberation of the oppressed, including themselves. As Vera Warren said of her mother, she put community before self, but she also knew that communities improve immeasurably when women are given a chance at bettering themselves.

Louisiana feminists lost many of their battles and saw many of their earlier initiatives undermined by Governor Jindal, but they still shifted the center. None but the most reactionary would call for a return to the days when gender determined one's possibilities in life, including choices of schools and careers. As Susan Jane Allen put it proudly, "We changed the world!"

In some ways, they did. But the pull of capital is strong. The rise of the New Right and Blue Dog Democrats, with their tendencies toward privatization and subsidies and rewards to for-profit corporations, has increased economic inequality in the United States over the past forty years. This is unfortunate for those who desire systemic and long-lasting social changes aimed at ending class inequalities. As we have seen, critical backing for the women's movement came from not-for-profit entities, including from government funding (e.g., for women's shelters, women's conferences, women's bureaus, displaced homemakers centers). Many, perhaps most, liberal feminists were employed by government institutions during their activist years, by public schools, universities, and social service agencies. Eventually, a good number of the radical feminists went to work for those same institutions. The public sector provided a haven that allowed a few audacious women to challenge nineteenth-century notions of gender roles and the resultant inequalities. The danger was, as Mary Capps noted, that the state could also be disempowering and co-optive. Of course, corporations and market forces can be even more repressive, and this is probably one of the main reasons that conservative administrations like Governor Jindal's seek to privatize as many state services as possible. Once vested in a career, few people are willing to risk it by speaking truth to power too forcefully.

Given the overwhelming dominance of capital, there were limits to what movement warriors could achieve. For the most part, the successful reform was one that fit within the already-existing power structure. Economic leveling, the goal of many of the radical women, has generally been out of reach. Conservative forces overrode all attempts at getting wages for housework, and even paid maternity or family leave or state-subsidized day care is not an option for most working people. There is still little flextime on the job, and almost no onsite or subsidized day care is available in Louisiana for children under the age of four. Furthermore, in the South, conservatives simply need to raise the banner of "states' rights," and they can defeat or stymie many federal initiatives designed to help the poor. A recent example is Governor Jindal's refusal to expand Medicaid, as provided for under the Affordable Care Act (Obamacare). Jindal, a conservative Catholic and a Republican, had the backing of capital.

As we've seen, however, Catholics are not of one mind about many social issues, and the current Pope Francis, a Jesuit elected in 2013, has repeatedly denounced inequalities of wealth. For every Bobby Jindal, there is a Mary Claire Landry, former nun and current head of the Family Justice Center in New Orleans who has devoted her life to the cause of gender justice. While many progressive religions have lost members to the upstart big-box evangelistic churches that instill values of submission and obedience in women, there remain many liberal women who continue to work through the traditional mainstream denominations on behalf of gender equality. I have highlighted how religion was a powerful force for reform in Louisiana in the hope that it might inspire spiritually inclined young women and men with ideas about righting many of the wrongs that persist in American society today. The battle for social justice, after all, is never over.

People Interviewed

All interviews were conducted by the author unless otherwise noted in the text. Digital copies of author interviews conducted face-to-face are available in the Newcomb Archives, Newcomb College Institute, Tulane University, New Orleans. Author's notes from interviews done via telephone or via email are also available in the Newcomb Archives.

Alexander, Nikki
Allen, Susan Jane
Anderson, Nancy
Arceneaux, Muriel
Bajoie, Diana
Baker, Vaughan Burdin
Barnwell, Corinne
    Freeman
Barrett, Kathy
Billings, David
Billings, Margery Freeman
Blunt, Barbara
Bohlke, Mary Ann
Bourg, Lorna
Brabant, Sarah
Bussie, Fran
Cade, Cathy
Cahee, Barbara
Canaan, Andrea
Capps, Mary
Chrisco, Carla
Clemons, Todd

Clemons, Gaynell
    Veronica
Cloutman, Evelyn
Cooper, Judy
Cormier, Judith
Cotten, Geneva
Davidson, Barbara
Denton, Pat
Dobbins, Peggy
Evans, Pat
Fife, Darlene
Fossier, Mildred
Gagliano, Gayle
Gandy, Kim
Gardner, Mary Frances
Gates, Jody
Gaumer, Susan
Gehman, Mary
Hayden, Casey
Helwig, Jeanne
Henneman, Nadine
Holahan, Shawn

Holt, Sibal
Johnson, Bernette Joshua
Kahn, Felicia
Karp, Sandy
Kent, Joan
Knapp, Ann
Landry, Mary Claire
Landrieu, Mary
Laporte, Susan (Sue)
Latimer, Clay
LosCalzo, Susan
Madden, Roberta
Martin, Linda
Matthews, Regina
McConnell, Marilyn
McElroy, Meredith
Milam, Mindy
Miller, Lynn
Morial, Sybil
Newbrough, Celeste
Olivo, Darlene
O'Shaunessy, Kathy

Parks, Glenda
Parun, Phyllis
Perrilloux, Yolanda
Polak, Ann
Pottharst, Kris
Pounds, Janet
Redwine, Marguerite
Reed, Louadrian
Roberts, Sylvia
Runte, Betty
Schinderman, Jace
Schornstein, Flo

Senter, Kit
Scott, Barbara Foreman
Shirley, Eleanor
Simon, Liz
Stehr, Ayn
Stembridge, Jane
Swanson, Donna
Tierney, Karline
Trahan, Barbara
    Melançon
Tucker, Susan
Walker, Annabelle

Ward, Martha
Warren, Vera
Watts, Judy
Wells, Rebecca
White, Janelle
White, Mary Menhinick
Willinger, Beth
Wilson, Mary Ann
Woodbury, Diane
Zellner, Dorothy

APPENDIX 2

Participants in the New Orleans Women's Movement

The following people were members of the New Orleans Women's Liberation Coalition and/or were on the Women's Center mailing list, March 25, 1974.

Adams, Ann
Aime, Deanne
Alexander, Nikki
Ambrose, Moira Buckley
Anderson, Susie
Armstrong, Este
Armstrong, Moss
Baker, Lesley
Ball, Lauren
Bernard, Jean
Blair, Celeste
Bourg, Jean
Bynum, Charlotte
Canaan, Andrea
Cancelliere, Theresa
Capps, Mary
Carr, Jean
Chancey, Becky
Chancey, Susie
Charbonnet, Denise
Clark, Sheryl
Conger, Presley
Cormier, Judith
Davis, Karen

Dixon, Jo Ann
Fiser, Joan
Galmeyer, Ann
Gilbert, Jan
Giordana, Tanya
Hall, Kathy
Heuther, Sarah
Hicks, Lon
Hingle Olivo, Diane
Hugh, Bette
Jerry, Lynette
Jones, Mary
Kaplan, Julia
Karp, Sandy
Kendall, Kathy
Kidder, Janice
Kilgore, Kathy
Kohler, Jan
Laporte, Sue
Lilith, Theo
Little, Mary
LosCalzo, Susan
Lovell, Anne
Lu, Mei-Kwang

MacDonald Cupric, Janet
Malone (later Dobbins),
  Peggy
McElroy, Meredith
Mendinez, Maria Teresa
Moody, Dru
Myhre, Donna
Newbrough, Celeste
O'Neal, Maurean
O'Neil, Carl
O'Malley, Susan
Owens, Melanie
Patteson [sic], Anne
Panara, Diana
Peyton, Diane
Peyton, Virginia
Pharr, Suzanne
Prentis, Boo
Reeves, Jean
Rogers, Elizabeth
Rota, Marlene
Schroeder, Sue
Scholar, Nancy
Seidman, Evie

Shoup, Sherolyn   Smith, Joyce   Trahan, Barbara
Shroyer, Margery   Steelman, Susan   Vaughan, Beverly
Simon, Liz   Stevenson, Judi   Vanaman, Linda
Simpson, Maryann   Stimson, Sandy   Youngblood, Marty

NOTES

Introduction. "To My Yankee Friends"

1. Robin Morgan, *Sisterhood Is Powerful* (New York: Vintage, 1970); Sandra Karp, telephone interviews by the author, February 15, 2008, and August 30, 2014. Karp, ironically, was a cofounder of Tulane Women for Change. For more on this organization, see Clarence L. Mohr and Joseph E. Gordon, *Tulane: The Emergence of a Modern University, 1945–1980* (Baton Rouge: Louisiana State University Press), 404.

2. Karp interviews.

3. Tulane University is private, and the tuition is expensive. It would have been out of reach for Karp, who came from a working-class background, without the assistance of scholarships.

4. Karp received a BA from Case Western Reserve University in Cleveland, where she was active in the civil rights movement, and a masters from Brown University. She acquired a left-wing political view from her parents and grandparents, who were working-class Jews (her grandfather was a union organizer and "bona fide commie" in New Jersey).

5. Phyllis Parun, "To My Yankee Friends," typescript, Newcomb Archives, Newcomb College Institute at Tulane, New Orleans, hereinafter cited as Newcomb Archives; Phyllis Parun, interview by the author, March 20, 2014; correspondence, January 27, 2016. The 1970s use of the terms "lesbian feminist" and "woman-identified woman" were in some part devices used by activists trying to identify their place on the political spectrum at the time. For some, they became cherished lifelong labels, while for others they were temporary. The terms may not have reflected self-identity as much as they were driven by the environment of homophobic, patriarchal oppression of the 1960s and 1970s. Some people now describe their sexuality as "fluid," meaning that it changes over time and according to the situation.

6. Becky Thompson, "Multiracial Feminism: Recasting the Chronology of Second Wave Feminism," *Feminist Studies* 28 (Summer 2002): 341–42. For a southern Jewish feminist perspective on growing up different in the South, see Gayle S. Rubin, *Deviations: A Gayle Rubin Reader* (Durham, N.C.: Duke University Press, 2011), 2–5.

7. Parun, interview and correspondence.

8. The term first appeared in a *New York Times Magazine* article, "The Second Feminist Wave," in 1968. Nancy Hewitt, ed., *No Permanent Waves: Recasting Histories of U.S. Feminism* (New Brunswick, N.J.: Rutgers University Press, 2010), 2.

9. Recently, scholars have challenged the "wave" metaphor to describe the twentieth-century women's rights movement. For historiographical overviews, see Nancy Hewitt, introduction to *No Permanent Waves*, and Kathleen A. Laughlin et al., "Is It Time to Jump Ship? Historians Rethink the Waves Metaphor," *Feminist Formations* 22, no. 1 (Spring 2010): 76–135. Research showing that women remained active between the two waves goes back at least as far as Susan Lynn's excellent study *Progressive Women in Conservative Times: Racial Justice, Peace, and Feminism, 1945 to the 1960s* (New Brunswick, N.J.: Rutgers University Press, 1992).

10. Jacqueline Dowd Hall, "The Long Civil Rights Movement and the Political Uses of the Past," *Journal of American History* 91, no. 4 (March 2005): 1, 233–63. The term "long women's movement" is used by Kathleen A. Laughlin and Jacqueline L. Castledine, eds., in *Breaking the Wave: Women, Their Organizations, and Feminism, 1945–1985* (New York: Routledge, 2011), 1–8, and is now becoming standard in the field.

11. An octoroon was one-eighth black, a quadroon one-quarter black, and a mulatto half black. The term "Creole" has shifted and has been highly contested by both whites and blacks. In the colonial period, it designated someone born in Louisiana without regard to status or ethnicity. In the nineteenth century, whites sought to reclaim the term for themselves, which is why mixed-race, French-speaking Catholics began to be referred to as "creoles of color" to distinguish them from "pure" white Creoles. Today the term generally connotes a person with a French surname with mixed racial heritage. See Joseph G. Tregle Jr., "Early New Orleans Society: A Reappraisal," *Journal of Southern History* 8 (February 1952): 20–36; Virginia R. Dominguez, *White by Definition: Social Classification in Creole Louisiana* (New Brunswick, N.J.: Rutgers University Press, 1994).

12. Homer Plessy was backed by the Comité des Citoyens (Citizens' Committee), a group of professional men of color, one of whom owned a New Orleans newspaper, the *Daily Crusader*. Keith Weldon Medley, "When Plessy Met Ferguson," *Louisiana Cultural Vistas* 7 (Winter 1996–97): 52–59; and Medley, *We as Freemen: Plessy v. Ferguson* (Gretna, La.: Pelican, 2012); Rebecca J. Scott, *Degrees of Freedom: Louisiana and Cuba after Slavery* (Cambridge, Mass.: Belknap Press of Harvard University Press, 2005), esp. 88–93; and Scott, "Public Rights, Social Equality, and the Conceptual Roots of the *Plessy* Challenge," *Michigan Law Review* 106 (March 2008): 777–804.

13. Tureaud is covered in Adam Fairclough, *Race & Democracy: The Civil Rights Struggle in Louisiana* (Athens: University of Georgia Press, 1995); and Nikki Brown, "A. P. Tureaud," in *KnowLA Encyclopedia of Louisiana*, edited by David Johnson, Louisiana Endowment for the Humanities, 2010, article published March 15, 2011, http://www.knowla.org/entry/743/&view=summary. On women, see Shannon Frystak, *Our Minds on Freedom: Women and the Struggle for Black Equality in Louisiana, 1924–1967* (Baton Rouge: Louisiana State University Press, 2009); Lee Sartain, *Invisible Activists: Women of the Louisiana NAACP and the Struggle for Civil Rights, 1915–1945* (Baton Rouge: Louisiana State University Press, 2007); Leslie Gale Parr, *A Will of Her Own: Sarah Towles Reed and the Pursuit of Democracy in Southern Public Education* (Athens: University of Georgia

Press, 1998). Greta de Jong, *A Different Day: African American Struggles for Justice in Rural Louisiana, 1900–1970* (Chapel Hill: University of North Carolina Press, 2002) covers men and women in the black freedom struggle.

14. The South's protest traditions have been well documented, beginning with the works of C. Vann Woodward: *Tom Watson: Agrarian Rebel* (New York: Macmillan, 1938); *Origins of the New South, 1877–1913* (Baton Rouge: Louisiana State University Press, 1951); and *The Strange Career of Jim Crow* (New York: Oxford University Press, 1955). For Louisiana, see William Ivy Hair, *Bourbonism and Agrarian Protest: Louisiana Politics, 1877–1900* (Baton Rouge: Louisiana State University Press, 1969); Hair, *The Kingfish and His Realm: The Life and Times of Huey P. Long* (Baton Rouge: Louisiana State University Press, 1991); John C. Rodrigue, *Reconstruction in the Cane Fields: From Slavery to Free Labor in Louisiana's Sugar Parishes, 1862–1880* (Baton Rouge: Louisiana State University Press, 2001); Donna A. Barnes, *The Louisiana Populist Movement, 1881–1900* (Baton Rouge: Louisiana State University Press, 2011); and more recent biographies of Huey and Earl Long, such as Richard D. White Jr., *Kingfish: The Reign of Huey P. Long* (New York: Random House, 2006), among others.

15. Alice Kessler-Harris, *Out to Work: The History of Wage-Earning Women in the United States* (Oxford: Oxford University Press, 1982); Kessler-Harris, *In Pursuit of Equity: Women, Men, and the Quest for Economic Citizenship in 20th-Century America* (Oxford: Oxford University Press, 2001); Dennis A. Deslippe, *"Rights, Not Roses": Unions and the Rise of Working-Class Feminism, 1945–1980* (Urbana: University of Illinois Press, 2000); Dorothy Sue Cobble, *The Other Women's Movement: Workplace Justice and Social Rights in Modern America* (Princeton, N.J.: Princeton University Press, 2004); and "Labor Feminists and President Kennedy's Commission on Women," in *No Permanent Waves: Recasting Histories of U.S. Feminism*, ed. Nancy Hewitt (New Brunswick, N.J.: Rutgers University Press, 2010), 144–67; Susan Hartmann, *The Other Feminists: Activists in the Liberal Establishment* (New Haven, Conn.: Yale University Press, 1998); Nancy MacLean, "Postwar Women's History: The 'Second Wave' or the End of the Family Wage?," in *A Companion to Post-1945 America*, ed. Jean-Christophe Agnew and Roy Rosenzweig (Oxford: Blackwell, 2006), 235–59. Nancy MacLean wrote a useful summary of recent historiography of second-wave feminism in "Gender Is Powerful: The Long Reach of Feminism," in *Social Movements in the 1960s*, special issue, *OAH Magazine of History* 20, no. 5 (October 2006): 19–23.

16. Suzanne Pharr, *Homophobia: A Weapon of Sexism* (Berkeley, Calif.: Chardon Press, 1997), xiv–xv; Kim Gandy, email correspondence with the author, February 12, 2009; "Keeping the Memories: Louisianans of the 2nd Wave Feminist Movement," transcript of banquet discussion sponsored by Veteran Feminists of America, March 22, 2001, Newcomb Archives; "Voices from the Louisiana Women's Movement: First-Hand Accounts from People Who Made It Happen," 2 VHS tapes, Symposium, March 24, 2001, Newcomb Archives; Sara Evans, *Personal Politics: The Roots of Women's Liberation in the Civil Rights Movement and the New Left* (New York: Vintage Books, 1979), 133. For more on the roots of women's liberation in the South, see Stephanie Gilmore's "The Second Wave and Beyond," http://scholar.alexanderstreet.com/pages/viewpage.action?pageId=1501, accessed September 5, 2007.

17. Sarah Wilkerson-Freeman first used the term "stealth feminism" in "Stealth in the Political Arsenal of Southern Women: A Retrospective for the Millennium," in *Southern Women at the Millennium*, ed. Melissa Walker, Jeanette R. Dunn, and Joe P. Dunn (Columbia: University of Missouri Press, 2003), 42–82. For more on southerners' conservative approach to feminist reform, see Nancy E. Baker, "Hermine Tobolowsky: A Feminist's Fight for Equal Rights," in *Texas Women: Their Histories, Their Lives*, ed. Elizabeth Hayes Turner, Stephanie Cole, and Rebecca Sharpless (Athens: University of Georgia Press, 2015), 434–56.

18. Barbara Smith, "Racism and Women's Studies," *Frontiers: A Journal of Women Studies* 5, no. 1 (Spring 1980): 48–49, italics added. Smith was a member of the 1973 Combahee River Collective and coauthored the influential "Black Feminist Statement," which posited that black women suffered multiple and interlocking systems of racial, class, and gender oppressions, a concept that Kimberlé Williams Crenshaw later called "intersectionality." See "A Black Feminist Statement," in *All the Women Are White, All the Blacks Are Men, but Some of Us Are Brave: Black Women's Studies*, ed. Gloria T. Hull, Patricia Bell Scott, and Barbara Smith (Old Westbury, N.Y.: Feminist Press, 1982), 13–22; Kimberlé Williams Crenshaw, "Demarginalizing the Intersection of Race and Sex: A Black Feminist Critique of Antidiscrimnation Doctrine, Feminist Theory and Antiracist Politics," *University of Chicago Legal Forum* 1989, 139–67. See also Deborah King, "Multiple Jeopardy, Multiple Consciousness: The Context of a Black Feminist Ideology," *Signs* 14, no. 1 (1988): 42–72.

19. Not all feminists were women. Sympathetic men who were important to the movement in Louisiana are covered in chap. 8.

20. Mary King interview in Elizabeth Jacobs, "Revisiting the Second Wave: In Conversation with Mary King," *Meridians: Feminism, Race, Transnationalism* 7, no. 2 (2007): 103–5.

21. Rupert Richardson, interview by Diane Holeman, VHS tapes 21 and 22, 1984, Pat Denton Collection, Newcomb Archives.

22. Hartmann, *Other Feminists*, 177; bell hooks, *Ain't I A Woman: Black Women and Feminism* (Boston: South End Press, 1981), 187.

23. bell hooks, *Feminist Theory: From Margin to Center*, 2nd ed. (Cambridge, Mass.: South End Press, 2000), 26. The Combahee River Collective also noted that "Black, other Third World, and working women have been involved in the feminist movement from its start, but both outside reactionary forces and racism and elitism within the movement itself have served to obscure our participation." "Black Feminist Statement," 14.

24. Johnetta Betsch Cole and Beverly Guy-Sheftall, *Gender Talk: The Struggle for Women's Equality in African American Communities* (New York: Ballantine, 2003). See also Patricia Hill Collins, *Black Feminist Thought* (Boston: Unwin Hyman, 1990). Carol Giardina, in *Freedom for Women: Forging the Women's Liberation Movement, 1953–1970* (Gainesville: University Press of Georgia, 2010), also makes the case that black women's feminism preceded the women's liberation movement.

25. Benita Roth, "The Making of the Vanguard Center: Black Feminist Emergence in the 1960s and 1970s," in *Still Lifting, Still Climbing: African American Women's Contemporary Activism*, ed. Kimberly Springer (New York: New York University Press, 1999), 70–72;

Roxanne Baxandall, "Re-Visioning the Women's Liberation Movement's Narrative: Early Second Wave African American Feminists," *Feminist Studies* 27, no. 1 (Spring 2001): 225–45.

26. Kristen Anderson-Bricker, "'Triple Jeopardy': Black Women and the Growth of Feminist Consciousness in SNCC, 1964–1975," in Springer, *Still Lifting, Still Climbing*, 49–69; Clayborne Carson and Heidi Heiss, "Student Nonviolent Coordinating Committee," in Darlene Clark Hine, *Black Women in America: An Historical Encyclopedia*, 1993, available online: http://www.stanford.edu/~ccarson/articles/black_women_3.htm, accessed December 3, 2013. For Pan-Africanism, see Brenda Gayle Plummer, *Rising Wind: Black Americans and U.S. Foreign Affairs, 1935–1960* (Chapel Hill: University of North Carolina Press, 1996); Penny von Eschen, *Race Against Empire: Black Americans and Anticolonialism, 1937–1957* (Ithaca, N.Y.: Cornell University Press, 1997); Thomas Borstelmann, *The Cold War and the Color Line: American Race Relations in the Global Arena* (Cambridge, Mass.: Harvard University Press, 2001); James Meriwether, *Proudly We Can Be Africans: Black Americans and Africa, 1935–1961* (Chapel Hill: University of North Carolina Press, 2002); Giardina, *Freedom for Women*, 30–31.

27. Thompson, "Multiracial Feminism," 352n7. For histories of second-wave feminism among women of color, see Patricia Hill Collins, *Black Feminist Thought*; Beverly Guy-Sheftall, *Words of Fire: An Anthology of African American Feminist Thought* (New York: The New Press, 1999); Benita Roth, *Separate Roads to Feminism: Black, Chicana, and White Feminist Movements in America's Second Wave* (New York: Cambridge University Press, 2004); Kimberly Springer, *Living for the Revolution: Black Feminist Organizations, 1968–1980* (Durham, N.C.: Duke University Press, 2005); Winifred Breines, *The Trouble between Us: An Uneasy History of White and Black Women in the Feminist Movement* (Oxford: Oxford University Press, 2006); Hartmann, *Other Feminists*, chap. 6.

28. Alice Walker, *In Search of Our Mother's Gardens: Womanist Prose* (New York: Harcourt Brace Jovanovich, 1983), xi–xii.

29. HBCUs in New Orleans were Dillard (private historically black Protestant); Southern University in New Orleans (SUNO); and Xavier University of Louisiana (private historically black Catholic). The two HBCUs elsewhere in the state were Grambling in north Louisiana and Southern University in Baton Rouge (SUBR).

30. For more on black women and racial uplift, see Paula Giddings, *When and Where I Enter: The Impact of Black Women on Race and Sex in America* (New York: William Morrow, 1984); Darlene Clark Hine, *A Shining Thread of Hope: The History of Black Women in America* (New York: Broadway Books, 1998); Deborah Gray White, *Too Heavy a Load: Black Women in Defense of Themselves, 1894–1994* (New York: W. W. Norton, 1999). On black women in the civil rights movement, see, among others, Lynn Olson, *Freedom's Daughters: The Unsung Heroines of the Civil Rights Movement from 1830 to 1970* (New York: Scribner, 2001). For Louisiana, see Shannon Frystak, *Our Minds on Freedom: Women and the Struggle for Black Equality in Louisiana, 1924–1967* (Baton Rouge: Louisiana State University Press, 2009). On the historic confluence of race and feminism, see Kate Dossett, *Bridging Race Divides: Black Nationalism, Feminism, and Integration in the United States, 1896–1935* (Gainesville: University Press of Florida, 2008), as well as works cited earlier.

31. ERA United flyer, September 1975, Newcomb Archives; *Times-Picayune*, August 28, 1978; *Times Picayune*, June 30, 1972; Hartmann, *Other Feminists*, 177.

32. Nancy Whittier, "Persistence and Transformation: Gloria Steinem, the Women's Actions Alliance, and the Feminist Movement, 1971–1997," *Journal of Women's History* 14, no. 2 (2002): 148–50; Doug Rossinow, *The Politics of Authenticity: Liberalism, Christianity, and the New Left in America* (New York: Columbia University Press, 1998), 312; Alice Echols, *Daring to Be Bad: Radical Feminism in America, 1967–1975* (Minneapolis: University of Minnesota Press, 1989), 6.

33. For a general historiographic overview of the discipline, see Cornelia H. Dayton and Lisa Levenstein, "The Big Tent of U.S. Women's and Gender History: A State of the Field," *Journal of American History* 99, no. 3 (December 2012): 793–817, and the responses, 818–38.

34. Merril Mushroom and Rose Norman, "Notes for a Special Issue," in *Sinister Wisdom: A Multicultural Lesbian Literary & Art Journal* 93 (Summer 2014): 5. See also the web-based supplement, which includes extended interview transcripts: http://www.sinisterwisdom.org/SW93Supplement.

35. Casey Hayden, "Fields of Blue," in *Deep in Our Hearts: Nine White Women in the Freedom Movement* (Athens: University of Georgia Press, 2000), 333; Peggy Dobbins, telephone interview by the author, September 7, 2007; Giardina, *Freedom for Women*, 128.

36. In addition to widely circulated mimeographed statements, early feminist journals include *Voice of the Women's Liberation Movement* (Chicago), *Notes from the First Year* (New York), *Notes from the Second Year* (New York), *No More Fun and Games* (Boston), *Women: A Journal of Liberation* (Baltimore), *It Ain't Me Babe* (Berkeley), *Tooth and Nail* (Bay Area), *Sister* (Los Angeles), and *And Ain't I a Woman* (Seattle). Rachel Blau DuPlessis and Ann Snitow, *The Feminist Memoir Project: Voices from Women's Liberation* (New York: Three Rivers Press, 1998).

37. David Farber, review of *The Politics of Authenticity: Liberalism, Christianity, and the New Left in America*, by Doug Rossinow, *Reviews in American History* 27, no. 2 (June 1999): 298–305; Sara M. Evans, foreword to *Feminist Coalitions: Historical Perspectives on Second-Wave Feminism in the United States*, ed. Stephanie Gilmore (Urbana: University of Illinois Press, 2008), vii–viii.

38. Major monographs of national scope do not give sufficient attention to the South or to southerners at least in part because that history had not yet been written. Examples are Flora Davis, *Moving the Mountain: The Women's Movement in America since 1960* (Urbana: University of Illinois Press, 1999); Susan Brownmiller, *In Our Time: Memoir of a Revolution* (New York: Dial Press, 1999); Ruth Rosen, *The World Split Open: How the Modern Women's Movement Changed America* (New York: Viking, 2000); Sara Evans, *Tidal Wave: How Women Changed America at Century's End* (New York: Free Press, 2003); Estelle B. Freedman, *No Turning Back: The History of Feminism and the Future of Women* (New York: Ballantine Books, 2002).

39. Of the former Confederate states, only Tennessee and Texas ratified the ERA.

40. Donald G. Mathews and Jane Sherron De Hart, *Sex, Gender and the Politics of ERA: A State and the Nation* (New York: Oxford University Press, 1990).

41. Stephanie Gilmore, *Groundswell: Grassroots Feminist Activism in Postwar America* (New York: Routledge, 2013).

42. Melissa Estes Blair, *Revolutionizing Expectations: Women's Organizations, Feminism, and American Politics, 1965–1980* (Athens: University of Georgia Press, 2014).

43. Anne M. Valk, *Radical Sisters: Second-Wave Feminism and Black Liberation in Washington, D.C.* (Urbana: University of Illinois Press, 2008), 5.

44. Carol Giardina, "Origins and Impact of Gainesville Women's Liberation, the First Women's Liberation Organization in the South," in *Making Waves: Female Activists in Twentieth-Century Florida*, ed. Jack E. Davis and Kari A. Frederickson (Gainesville: University Press of Florida, 2003); Giardina, introduction to *Freedom for Women*, 31–33; *Sinister Wisdom: A Multicultural Lesbian Literary & Art Journal* 93 (Summer 2014): 17–64.

45. Joan S. Carver, "The Equal Rights Amendment and the Florida Legislature," *Florida Historical Quarterly* 60, no. 4 (April 1982): 455–81; Kimberly Wilmot Voss, "The Florida Fight for Equality: The Equal Rights Amendment, Senator Lori Wilson and Mediated Catfights in the 1970s," *Florida Historical Quarterly* 88, no. 2 (Fall 2009): 173–208.

46. Judith N. McArthur and Harold L. Smith, *Texas through Women's Eyes* (Austin: University of Texas Press, 2010). On Texas, see also Kyle Goyette, "The Good Fight: Texas Women and the Battle for the ERA, 1972–1982," *Journal of the American Studies Association of Texas* 40 (November 2009): 35–42; Baker, "Hermine Tobolowsky."

47. McArthur and Smith, *Texas through Women's Eyes*; Harold L. Smith, "Casey Hayden: Gender and the Origins of SNCC, SDS, and the Women's Liberation Movement," in *Texas Women: Their Histories, Their Lives*, ed. Elizabeth Hayes Turner, Stephanie Cole, and Rebecca Sharpless (Athens: University of Georgia Press, 2015), 359–88; Sarah Weddington, *A Question of Choice* (New York: G. P. Putnam's Sons, 1992).

48. Katarina Keane, "Second-Wave Feminism in the American South, 1965–1980" (PhD diss., University of Maryland, College Park, 2009); "From Soft-Sell to Hardball: The Evolution of the Pro-Equal Rights Amendment Campaign in South Carolina, 1972–1982" (master's thesis, University of South Carolina, 2011).

49. Janet Allured, "Arkansas Baptists and Methodists and the Equal Rights Amendment," *Arkansas Historical Quarterly* 43 (Spring 1984): 55–66; Janine A. Parry, "'What Women Wanted': Arkansas Women's Commissions and the ERA," *Arkansas Historical Quarterly* 59, no. 3 (Autumn 2000): 265–98; Anna M. Azjicek, Allyn Lord, and Lori Holyfield, "The Emergence and First Years of a Grassroots Women's Movement in Northwest Arkansas, 1970–1980," *Arkansas Historical Quarterly* 62 (Summer 2003): 153–81; Brock Thompson, *The Un-Natural State: Arkansas and the Queer South* (Fayetteville: University of Arkansas Press, 2010); *Shewolf's Directory of Wimmin's Lands and Lesbian Communities* (Melrose, Fla.: Target Blue Enterprises, 2012); Sine Anahita, "Nestled into Niches: Prefigurative Communities on Lesbian Land," *Journal of Homosexuality* 56, no. 6 (2009): 719–37; Anna Zajicek and Allyn Lord, "Women's Intentional Communities; aka Women's Land Communities," *Encyclopedia of Arkansas History & Culture*, http://www.encyclopediaofarkansas.net/encyclopedia/entry-detail.aspx?entryID=6513, accessed August 23, 2015. (Lord is at Shiloh Museum of Ozark History, and Zajicek at the University of Arkansas, Fayetteville.) The landdyke community in Oregon is probably the most famous, at least in part because *Womanspirit* magazine was published there for ten years. Pelican Lee, "Setting Up Women's Land in the 1970s: Could We Do It?" *off*

our backs, March–April 2003, 43–47; Kate Ellison, "Lesbian Land: An Overview," *off our backs*, May–June 2003, 39–41.

50. The series is "Southern Women: Their Lives and Times," http://www.ugapress.org /index.php/series/SWTLT, accessed May 28, 2015.

51. Martha Swain, "In the Mainstream: Mississippi White Women's Clubs in the Quest for Women's Rights in the Twentieth Century," in *Mississippi Women: Their Histories, Their Lives*, ed. Elizabeth Anne Payne, Marjorie Julian Spruill, and Martha H. Swain, vol. 2 (Athens: University of Georgia Press, 2010), 269–86; Marjorie Julian Spruill, "The Mississippi 'Takeover' : Feminists, Antifeminists, and the International Women's Year Conference of 1977," in *Mississippi Women: Their Histories, Their Lives* 2:287–312.

52. Marjorie Julian Spruill, "Victoria Eslinger, Keller Bumgardner Barron, Mary Heriot, Tootsie Holland, and Pat Callair: Champions of Women's Rights in South Carolina," in *South Carolina Women: Their Lives and Times*, ed. Marjorie Julian Spruill, Valinda W. Littlefield, and Joan Marie Johnson, vol. 3 (Athens: University of Georgia Press, 2012), 373–408.

53. Cynthia A. Kierner, Jennifer R. Loux, and Megan T. Shockley, *Changing History: Virginia Women through Four Centuries* (Richmond: Library of Virginia, 2013).

54. Quote from Melissa A. McEuen and Thomas H. Appleton Jr., eds., introduction to *Kentucky Women: Their Lives and Times* (Athens: University of Georgia Press, 2015), 6; John Paul Hill, "Martha Layne Collins (1936–): Textbooks, Toyota, and Tenacity," in McEuen and Appleton, *Kentucky Women*, 356–78; Carol E. Jordan, *Violence against Women in Kentucky: A History of U.S. and State Legislative Reform* (Lexington: University Press of Kentucky, 2014).

55. Hartmann, *Other Feminists*; Bettye Collier-Thomas, *Jesus, Jobs, and Justice: African American Women and Religion* (New York: Alfred A. Knopf, 2010).

56. Louise A. Tilly, "Gender, Women's History, and Social History," *Social Science History* 13, no. 4 (Winter 1989): 440–41.

57. The few academic monographs that existed when I began teaching Louisiana history in or around 2001 were Carmen Lindig, *The Path from the Parlor: Louisiana Women, 1879–1920* (Lafayette: Center for Louisiana Studies, 1986); Emily Toth, *Unveiling Kate Chopin* (Jackson: University Press of Mississippi, 1999); Leslie Gale Parr, *A Will of Her Own: Sarah Towles Reed and the Pursuit of Democracy in Southern Public Education* (Athens: University of Georgia Press, 1998); and Pamela Tyler, *Silk Stockings & Ballot Boxes: Women and Politics in New Orleans, 1920–1963* (Athens: University of Georgia Press, 1996). Thereafter, the production of scholarly books about women began to increase fairly rapidly and include Alecia P. Long, *The Great Southern Babylon: Sex, Race, and Respectability in New Orleans, 1865–1920* (Baton Rouge: Louisiana State University Press, 2004); Janet Allured and Judith Gentry, eds., *Louisiana Women: Their Lives and Times* (Athens: University of Georgia Press, 2009). Others are cited elsewhere in these notes.

58. Jean Quataert and Leigh Ann Wheeler, "Editorial Note: Individual Lives: Windows on Women's History," *Journal of Women's History* 24, no. 3 (Fall 2012): 7–12; Susan Ware, "Writing Women's Lives: One Historian's Perspective," *Journal of Interdisciplinary History* 40, no. 3 (Winter 2010): 413–35; Alice Kessler-Harris, "AHR Roundtable: Why Biography?"

American Historical Review 114, no. 3 (June 2009): 625–30; Lois W. Banner, "AHR Round-table: Biography as History," *American Historical Review* 114, no. 3 (June 2009): 579–86.

59. I am a member of the Episcopal Church of the Good Shepherd in Lake Charles.

60. Leila J. Rupp, *Worlds of Women: The Making of an International Women's Movement* (Princeton, N.J.: Princeton University Press, 1997); Grace Victoria Leslie, "United for a Better World: Internationalism in the U.S. Women's Movement, 1939–1964" (PhD diss., Yale University, 2011).

Chapter 1. "Me? A Feminist?"

1. "The Pelican," August 1976, Newcomb Archives.

2. On the BPW's role in the movement for women's equality between the waves, see the superb article by Kathleen A. Laughlin, "Civic Feminists: The Politics of the Minnesota Federation of Business and Professional Women's Clubs, 1942–1965," in *Breaking the Wave: Women, Their Organizations, and Feminism, 1945–1985*, ed. Kathleen A. Laughlin and Jacqueline L. Castledine (New York: Routledge, 2011), 11–27.

3. Susan Lynn, "Gender and Progressive Politics: A Bridge to Social Activism of the 1960s," in *Not June Cleaver: Women and Gender in Postwar America, 1945–1960*, ed. Joanne Meyerowitz (Philadelphia: Temple University Press, 1994), 105; Kathleen Laughlin, introduction to Laughlin and Castledine, *Breaking the Wave*, 4. The earliest monographs that reconceptualized women's activism "between the waves" were Leila J. Rupp and Verta Taylor, *Survival in the Doldrums: The American Women's Rights Movement, 1945–1960s* (New York: Oxford University Press, 1987); and Cynthia Harrison, *On Account of Sex: The Politics of Women's Issues, 1945–1968* (Berkeley: University of California Press, 1988).

4. For a thorough examination of the relationship between peace activism and feminism, see Harriet Hyman Alonso, *Peace as a Women's Issue: A History of the U.S. Movement for World Peace and Women's Rights* (Syracuse, N.Y.: Syracuse University Press, 1993).

5. On the woman suffrage amendment, see Elna C. Green, "The Rest of the Story: Kate Gordon and the Opposition to the Nineteenth Amendment in the South," *Louisiana History* 33 (Spring 1992): 171–89. For a history of the LWV in Louisiana, see Tyler, *Silk Stockings & Ballot Boxes*, esp. chap. 3.

6. Stephanie Coontz, in *A Strange Stirring: The Feminine Mystique and American Women at the Dawn of the 1960s* (New York: Basic Books, 2011), points out that in 1941, as the war began, 90 percent of the nation's local school districts refused to hire married women, and 70 percent required female teachers to quit when they married (60).

7. A marvelously nuanced account of the impact of *The Feminine Mystique* is Coontz's *Strange Stirring*. Betty Friedan, *The Feminine Mystique* (New York: W. W. Norton, 1963), 305–8.

8. History of the Calcasieu Women's Shelter, typescript, Oasis, accessed 2012; Evelyn Cloutman, interviews by the author, September 6, 2007, and October 19, 2012; article on Cloutman in Lake Charles's *Jambalaya*, available online at http://thejambalayanews .com/features/details.cfm, accessed October 15, 2012; Lake Charles *American Press*, September 17, 2000. The shelter's board included one black woman, Bernardine Proctor, who knew Cloutman through the League.

9. For a general history of the LWV, see Louise M. Young, *In the Public Interest: The League of Women Voters, 1920–1970* (New York: Greenwood Press, 1989). Lorraine Gates Schuyler focuses on the South in *The Weight of Their Votes: Southern Women and Political Leverage in the 1920s* (Chapel Hill: University of North Carolina Press, 2006). Other historians who have written about the LWV as a bridge organization are Jennifer A. Stevens, "Feminizing Portland, Oregon: A History of the League of Women Voters in the Postwar Era, 1950–1975," 155–72, and Catherine E. Rymph, "Exporting Civic Womanhood: Gender and Nation Building," 65–79, both in *Breaking the Wave*; Melissa Estes Blair, "A Dynamic Force in Our Community: Women's Clubs and Second-Wave Feminist at the Grassroots," *Frontiers* 30 (2009): 30–51; Blair, "Women's Organizations and Grassroots Politics: Denver, Durham, and Indianapolis 1960–1975," (PhD diss., University of Virginia, 2008); and Blair, *Revolutionizing Expectations*.

10. For the LWV in Mississippi, see Martha H. Swain, "In the Mainstream: Mississippi White Women's Clubs in the Quest for Women's Rights in the Twentieth Century," in Payne, Swain, and Spruill, *Mississippi Women*, 2:269–86, and Sarah Wilkerson-Freeman, "The Second Battle for Woman Suffrage: Alabama White Women, the Poll Tax, and V. O. Key's Master Narrative of Southern Politics," *Journal of Southern History* 68, no. 2 (May 2002): 333–74. For Tennessee, see Carole Bucy, "Martha Ragland (1906–1996): The Evolution of a Political Feminist," in *Tennessee Women: Their Lives and Times*, ed. Sarah Wilkerson-Freeman and Beverly Greene Bond, vol. 1 (Athens: University of Georgia Press, 2009), 214–42. For South Carolina, see Jennifer Black, "Harriet Simons: Women, Race, Politics and the League of Women Voters of South Carolina," 179–99, and Marjorie Julian Spruill, "Victoria Eslinger, Keller Bumgardner Barron, Mary Heriot, Tootsie Holland, and Pat Callair: Champions of Women's Rights in South Carolina," 373–408, both in Spruill, Littlefield, and Johnson, *South Carolina Women*, vol. 3. For Texas, see McArthur and Smith, *Texas through Women's Eyes*.

11. Rosa Keller, "League of Women Voters of New Orleans, History, 1942–1985," typescript, League of Women Voters Records of New Orleans, Collection 556, Louisiana Research Collection, Tulane University; *Louisiana Weekly*, June 20, 1970; Shannon Frystak, "From Southern Lady to Steel Magnolia: Newcomb Women and the Struggle for Civil Rights in New Orleans," in *Newcomb College: 1886–2006: Higher Education for Women in New Orleans*, ed. Susan Tucker and Beth Willinger (Baton Rouge: Louisiana State University Press, 2012), 320–33; Frystak, "'With All Deliberate Speed': The Integration of the League of Women Voters of New Orleans, 1953–1963," in *Searching for Their Places: Women in the South across Four Centuries*, ed. Thomas H. Appleton Jr. and Angela Boswell (Columbia: University of Missouri Press, 2003), 261–83; and Frystak, "Elite White Female Activism and Civil Rights in New Orleans," in *Throwing Off the Cloak of Privilege: White Southern Women Activists in the Civil Rights Era*, ed. Gail S. Murray (Gainesville: University Press of Florida, 2004), 186–87.

12. The LWV had active chapters in most major cities in Louisiana by the 1960s, but most appeared to be fairly new. Records for the Louisiana league are spotty and incomplete. The New Orleans League, founded in 1942, was always the largest in the state, with more than one hundred members. But even outside New Orleans, some local chapters' numbers in the 1970s approached one hundred. The Shreveport Chapter, founded in

1945, had ninety-five members in 1976. League of Women Voters Records, box 1, FF 4, LSU–Shreveport Archives and Special Collections, Noel Memorial Library, Shreveport; League of Women Voters Records of New Orleans, Collection 556, Louisiana Research Collection, Tulane University; Francine Merritt Collection, Newcomb Archives.

13. Proctor's sisters were Agnes Evans, the first black registered nurse in Lake Charles, and Beatrice Chandler, the first black public housing manager in the city. Her brothers were Clarence, a postal employee, and Louis, an instructor for the Pullman Company. Regrettably, Proctor died before I began the research for this book. As far as I'm aware, she left no personal papers in any archive. The information here is compiled from my interview with Evelyn Cloutman and from newspaper accounts: Lake Charles *American Press*, January 12, 1984, *Flair* (Special Section), and January 22, 1990.

14. Frystak, *Our Minds on Freedom*, 43–56.

15. Ibid., 71.

16. Evelyn Brooks Higginbotham, *Righteous Discontent: The Women's Movement in the Black Baptist Church, 1880–1920* (Cambridge, Mass.: Harvard University Press, 1993). Paisley Jane Harris summarizes Higginbotham's now widely used concept: "She specifically referred to African American's promotion of temperance, cleanliness of person and property, thrift, polite manners, and sexual purity. The politics of respectability entailed 'reform of individual behavior as a goal in itself and as a strategy for reform.' Respectability was part of 'uplift politics,' and had two audiences: African Americans, who were encouraged to be respectable, and white people, who needed to be shown that African Americans could be respectable." Harris, "Gatekeeping and Remaking: The Politics of Respectability in African American Women's History and Black Feminism," *Journal of Women's History* 15, no. 1 (Spring 2003): 212–20. Since Higginbotham, many scholars have found the concept of the politics of respectability useful in describing the work of male and female African American leaders in the twentieth century. Harris reviews three works that advance and challenge traditional notions of the concept: Victoria W. Wolcott, *Remaking Respectability: African American Women in Interwar Detroit* (Chapel Hill: University of North Carolina Press, 2001); Patricia Schechter, *Ida B. Wells-Barnett and American Reform, 1880–1930* (Chapel Hill: University of North Carolina Press, 2001); and E. Frances White, *Dark Continent of Our Bodies: Black Feminism and the Politics of Respectability* (Philadelphia: Temple University Press, 2001).

17. The information in this and in the following paragraphs, unless otherwise noted, is compiled from Sybil Morial, interviews by the author, January 17, 2008; October 21, 2012; November 6, 2014; Sybil Morial résumé and bio, typescript in possession of the author; the New Orleans Chapter of The Links, Inc., Amistad Research Center at Tulane University, box 3 (membership files); and *Louisiana Weekly*, July 28, 1979. For more on Ernest Morial, see Kim Lacy Rogers, *Righteous Lives: Narratives of the Civil Rights Movement* (New York: New York University Press, 1993).

18. The state passed laws in the 1950s designed to thwart any moves toward integration. Though the LWVNO tried to integrate in 1956, it had to give up when confronted by the state's massive resistance to integration. The LWVNO received permission from the national league to put off integration. Frystak, *Our Minds on Freedom*, 53–55; 81; Frystak, "'With All Deliberate Speed,'" 276–78. For more on the laws passed by the State of Loui-

siana and their effect on the NAACP in New Orleans and elsewhere, see Fairclough, *Race & Democracy*, 209–10.

19. Among the guests of honor were Constance Baker Motley and Maxine Waters.

20. *Sybil H. Morial vs. Orleans Parish School Board and State of Louisiana*; *Times-Picayune*, April 5, 1968. Virtually no historian has written about the lawsuit filed by Sybil Morial, which resulted in a ruling declaring the state's laws unconstitutional.

21. On the LWV's desegregation, see Frystak, "'With All Deliberate Speed,'" 281–82. Frystak notes that the 1965–66 membership roster of the LWVNO indicated 15 African American members out of 499 for that year.

22. Black women had been combining a public life with marriage, career, and motherhood since the late nineteenth century. See, for example, Bart Landry, *Black Working Wives: Pioneers of the American Family Revolution* (Berkeley: University of California Press, 2000). See also the extensive bibliography in Stephanie Coontz, *Strange Stirring*.

23. Ernest Morial was the first black person to receive a law degree from Louisiana State University in Baton Rouge and was a protégé and law partner of A. P. Tureaud, the chief lawyer for the Louisiana NAACP. Morial became president of the New Orleans branch of the NAACP in 1962.

24. The Morials had two sons and three daughters, the last one born in 1970. Marc Morial became mayor of New Orleans and president of the National Urban League. http://nul.iamempowered.com/who-we-are/executive-leadership/executive-staff/marc-h-morial, accessed February 19, 2014. Sybil Morial interviews; *Louisiana Weekly*, February 11, 1978; January 20, 1982; New Orleans Chapter of The Links, Inc., Amistad Research Center at Tulane University, box 3 (membership files).

25. "The League of Women Voters: Its Partisan Slip Is Showing," July 3, 1965 issue of *Human Events*, copy in Louisiana Research Collection files, and also available at the Human Events website: http://humanevents.com/.

26. The Shreveport LWV reported that its membership had dropped from ninety-five in 1976 to sixty-six in 1982, and that only a handful of members were doing all the work.

27. "Women in Politics 1971–1973," Newcomb Archives. The group predates the formation of the National Women's Political Caucus, another example of Louisiana feminists prefiguring national movements. Louisiana delegates went to the convention in Houston in 1972 when the NWPC organized.

28. Tyler, *Silk Stockings & Ballot Boxes*; and "The Independent Women's Organization," in *KnowLA Encyclopedia of Louisiana*, ed. David Johnson, Louisiana Endowment for the Humanities, 2010–, article published February 1, 2011, http://www.knowla.org/entry/862/. IWO women appeared frequently in newspaper articles and in ERA coalition documents as supporting the ERA. See, for example, *New Orleans Times-Picayune*, May 17 and 28, 1972.

29. The leaders of the YWCA sometimes referred to it as the YW because if they said only "Y," people automatically assumed they meant the YMCA. Rosemary Skinner Keller, Rosemary Radford Ruether, and Marie Cantlon, eds., *Encyclopedia of Women and Religion in North America* (Bloomington: Indiana University Press, 2006), 1033–34; Sarah Wilkerson-Freeman, "Stealth in the Political Arsenal of Southern Women: A Retro-

spective for the Millennium," in Walker, Dunn, and Dunn, *Southern Women at the Millennium*, 67.

30. Collier-Thomas, *Jesus, Jobs, and Justice*, 375; Giddings, *When and Where I Enter*, 155–58; Jacqueline Anne Rouse, *Lugenia Burns Hope—Black Southern Reformer* (Athens: University of Georgia Press, 1989).

31. Collier-Thomas, *Jesus, Jobs, and Justice*, 378; Lynn, *Progressive Women in Conservative Times*, 15, 65–66. In the South, John Egerton notes, the YWCA "generally stayed ahead of its male counterpart [the YMCA] in pressing for cooperation and equality across the barriers of race and sex," particularly in the 1930s and 1940s. John Egerton, *Speak Now Against the Day: The Generation before the Civil Rights Movement in the South* (Chapel Hill: University of North Carolina Press, 1995), 123. Likewise, in her study of Sarah Patton Boyle, a white Episcopalian who rebelled against racism in the years preceding the civil rights movement, Joanna Bowen Gillespie concludes that "during the 1940s, the YM and YWCAs were the major national white organizations promoting racial integration." Gillespie, "Sarah Patton Boyle's Desegregated Heart," in *Beyond Image and Convention: Explorations in Southern Women's History*, ed. Janet L. Coryell et al. (Columbia: University of Missouri Press, 1998), 162–63. Drawing on her experiences in the YWCA in the 1920s, Katherine Du Pre Lumpkin said that women were less bigoted than men and were more inclined to push the envelope and challenge social mores. Oral History Interview with Katharine Du Pre Lumpkin, August 4, 1974, interview G-0034, Southern Oral History Program Collection (4007) in the Southern Oral History Program Collection, Southern Historical Collection, Wilson Library, University of North Carolina at Chapel Hill. For more information, see "Southern Women, the Student YWCA, and Race (1920–1944) Collection," Sophia Smith Collection, Five College Archives & Manuscript Collections, http://asteria.fivecolleges.edu/findaids/sophiasmith/mnsss503_scope.htmlhttp://asteria.fivecolleges.edu/findaids/sophiasmith/mnsss503_scope.html

32. Judith Weisenfeld, *African American Women and Christian Activism: New York's Black YWCA, 1905–1945* (Cambridge, Mass.: Harvard University Press, 1997); Barbara Ransby, *Ella Baker and the Black Freedom Movement: A Radical Democratic Vision* (Chapel Hill: University of North Carolina Press, 2003), 71, 260–62.

33. Pauli Murray, *Pauli Murray: The Autobiography of a Black Activist, Feminist, Lawyer, Priest, and Poet* (Knoxville: University of Tennessee Press, 1989); Nancy MacLean, *Freedom Is Not Enough: The Opening of the American Workplace* (Cambridge, Mass.: Harvard University Press, 2006), 118–31; Ransby, *Ella Baker*, 71, 260–62.

34. Dorothy Height, *Open Wide the Freedom Gates: A Memoir* (New York: Public Affairs, 2003), 95–96; 114–20; and chap. 11. Collier-Thomas, *Jesus, Jobs, and Justice*, 378–82, 418–19; http://ncnw.org/about/height.htm and http://classweb.uh.edu/wims/, accessed December 2, 2014. For her role in the National Women's Political Caucus, see http://www.nwpc.org/history, accessed December 2, 2014.

35. Ollie T. Osborne, ed., *Issues and Answers: Final Report, Louisiana Women's Conference, 1977*, sponsored by National Commission on the Observance of International Women's Year, 1977, 64, Ollie Tucker Osborne Papers, Collection 93, University Archives and Acadiana Manuscripts Collection, Edith Garland Dupré Library, University of

Louisiana at Lafayette (hereinafter cited as Osborne Collection); obituary and funeral program of George Ethel Warren (1918–96), courtesy of Vera Warren-Williams; *Times-Picayune*, October 10, 1958; May 1, 1959. One Mrs. Ethel Turner, who headed the NCNW chapter in New Orleans for several years in the 1950s, was also active in the branch YW on Claiborne Street. The black YWCAs were typically called "branch" Ys because white YWCAs were considered the central institution and black ones as subsidiary branches. The only city in the United States where there were two autonomous YWCAs was Washington, D.C., where the Phyllis Wheatley YWCA (the black Y) preceded the founding of the white Y. Dorothy Height was the director of the Phyllis Wheatley Y for decades. Height, *Open Wide the Freedom Gates*, 98; Kent B. Germany, *New Orleans after the Promise: Poverty, Citizenship, and the Search for the Great Society* (Athens: University of Georgia Press, 2007), 57.

36. In New Orleans, the "Negro Branch" of the YWCA began in 1934 when Straight University, a historically black college that subsequently became Dillard University, leased the girls' dormitory to it for one dollar a year. Frystak, *Our Minds on Freedom*, 37.

37. Louadrian Dejoie Reed, interview by the author, October 30, 2013, New Orleans.

38. Frystak, *Our Minds on Freedom*, 38, 118; *New Orleans Times-Picayune* October 18, 1948; Oral History Interview with Clark Foreman, November 16, 1974, Interview B-0003, Southern Oral History Program Collection (4007) in the Southern Historical Collection, Wilson Library, University of North Carolina at Chapel Hill, http://docsouth.unc.edu /sohp/B-0003/excerpts/excerpt_2651.html, accessed November 25, 2014. The Constitutional Education League, a group of veterans of World War I, had formed in 1919 during the first Red Scare. It issued a report saying that the "114 [YWCA] national board committee memberships and headquarters staff posts are held by leaders whose Communist or Communist-front affiliation are a matter of official record in Washington." The national Y board denounced the CEL's report as nonsense.

39. Anne C. Loveland, *Remembering the Struggle: Oral Histories and Photographs of Baton Rouge Women Who Worked for Human Rights* (Baton Rouge: Baton Rouge Area Young Women's Christian Association, 1983), interviews with Earline Williams and Karline Tierney.

40. Roberta Madden, email correspondence, February 28, 2008. Madden, cofounder, with Sylvia Roberts, of the Baton Rouge chapter of NOW, was executive director of the Baton Rouge YWCA from 1980 to 1983, and worked there as the director of Public Policy and Women's Health until she retired in 2009. See also Madden interview conducted by Jennifer Abraham, February 6, 2002, Collection 4700 1564 T3137, Hill Library, Louisiana State University, Baton Rouge.

41. Hayden quote in Lynn, "Gender and Progressive Politics," 114. See also Mary King, *Freedom Song: A Personal Story of the 1960s Civil Rights Movement* (New York: Quill, William Morrow, 1987), 59, 64–66; Evans, *Personal Politics*, 98–100.

42. *New Orleans Times-Picayune*, March 15 1973; Blair, *Revolutionizing Expectations*, 45–47.

43. When the St. Bernard Street Y opened in 1967 as a fully integrated facility, the branch Y on Claiborne closed. *New Orleans City Directories*, 1965, 1967. Marguerite Redwine, interview by the author, October 8, 2013.

44. Kate Weigand, *Red Feminism: American Communists and the Making of Women's Liberation* (Baltimore: Johns Hopkins University Press, 2001), 153; Rosen, *World Split Open*, 206.

45. *Louisiana Weekly*, March 7, 1970; *New Orleans Times-Picayune*, March 5, 1970; March 5, 1971; *Vieux Carré Courier*, March 14, 1970. Roxanne Dunbar-Ortiz, a radical leftist and a visitor to New Orleans, claims to have organized the meeting. The newspapers reported that it was sponsored by the International Women's Day Committee, "a coalition of members of several different [local] organizations," black and white. Roxanne Dunbar-Ortiz, *Outlaw Woman: A Memoir of the War Years, 1960–1975* (San Francisco: City Lights Books, 2001), 164.

46. "SNCC Women and the Stirrings of Feminism," in *Circle of Trust: Remembering SNCC*, ed. Cheryl Lynn Greenberg (New Brunswick, N.J.: Rutgers University Press, 1998), 150.

47. Lynn, "Gender and Progressive Politics," 108.

48. For more on Keller and SOS, see Tyler, *Silk Stockings*, 225–29; Frystak, *Our Minds on Freedom*, 82–106; Kim Lacy Rogers, *Righteous Lives: Narratives of the New Orleans Civil Rights Movement* (New York: New York University Press, 1993); and Liva Baker, *The Second Battle of New Orleans: The Hundred-Year Struggle to Integrate the Schools* (New York: Harper Collins, 1996). Two examples of similar organizations in other southern states are the Women's Emergency Committee to Open Our Schools in Little Rock and Help Our Public Education in Atlanta.

49. *New Orleans Times-Picayune*, May 22, 1995; May 23, 1995; September 23, 2007 (Betty Wisdom obituary); Betty Wisdom, audio tape of interview, August 28, 1995, Betty Wisdom Collection, Louisiana and Special Collections Department, Earl K. Long Library, University of New Orleans.

50. African Americans Leontine Luke and Dorothy Mae Taylor both joined the PTA because they had school-aged children and wanted to ensure that black children got their fair share of resources. *Louisiana Weekly*, June 14, 2011, http://www.louisiana weekly.com/remembering-dorothy-mae-taylor-the-first-lady-of-1300-perdido-st/, accessed April 14, 2015.

51. For women with college degrees, the marriage rates were even lower. Barbara Miller Solomon, *In The Company of Educated Women: A History of Women and Higher Education in America* (New Haven, Conn.: Yale University Press, 1985), 118–22; Karen Manners Smith, "New Paths to Power: 1890–1920," in *No Small Courage: A History of Women in the United States*, ed. Nancy F. Cott (Oxford: Oxford University Press, 2000), 369.

52. Quoted in Coontz, *Strange Stirring*, 45–46.

53. Addams is widely credited with being the mother of the settlement house movement in the United States. Abbot cofounded the American Association of Schools of Social Work, and Abbot and Breckenridge cofounded the *Social Service Review* in 1927. Robyn Muncy, *Creating a Female Dominion in American Reform, 1890–1935* (New York: Oxford University Press, 1991).

54. Carolyn Kolb, "The New Deal's Progressive Roots: Harry Hopkins and the American Red Cross in New Orleans, 1918–1921" (master's thesis, Department of History, University of New Orleans, 1998).

55. Megan Elias, "'Model Mamas': The Domestic Partnership of Home Economics Pioneers Flora Rose and Martha Van Rensselaer," *Journal of the History of Sexuality* 15, no. 1 (January 2006): 65–88, provides a good discussion of why professional women, and professors in particular, sought the companionship of other professorial women. The classic article about the homosocial world of nineteenth-century women is Carroll Smith-Rosenberg, "The Female World of Love and Ritual: Relations between Women in Nineteenth-Century America," *Signs: Journal of Women in Culture and Society* 1 (1975): 1–30. See also Smith-Rosenberg, *Disorderly Conduct: Visions of Gender in Victorian America* (New York: Alfred A. Knopf, 1985). For an extensive discussion of historical same-sex relationships among women, see Lillian Faderman, *Surpassing the Love of Men: Romantic Friendship and Love between Women from the Renaissance to the Present* (New York: William Morrow, 1981); Faderman, *Odd Girls and Twilight Lovers: A History of Lesbian Life in Twentieth-Century American* (New York: Columbia University Press, 1991); and Faderman, *To Believe in Women: What Lesbians Have Done for America—A History* (Boston: Houghton Mifflin, 1999). See also John D'Emilio and Estelle Freedman, *Intimate Matters: A History of Sexuality in America* (New York: Harper & Row, 1988), 190–94; Blanche Wiesen Cook, "Female Support Networks and Political Activism: Lillian Wald, Crystal Eastman, and Emma Goldman," *Chrysalis* 3 (1977): 43–61, and Cook's two-volume history of the life of Eleanor Roosevelt.

56. Pathologizing lesbian relationships occurred with the popularization of psychology in the 1920s. D'Emilio and Freedman, *Intimate Matters*, 193–94.

57. Mary White's mother died when she was eight, and her father could not care for her. Mary Menhinick White, interview by the author, August 8, 2012; Mary White, taped interview by Susan Tucker, November 9, 2011, Newcomb Archives; Elizabeth Wisner and Florence Sytz's house was on Moss Street, which runs parallel to Wisner Boulevard and to Bayou St. John. The home still stands, though it is no longer in the family.

58. Ibid. Kit Senter, interview by the author, April 14, 2014. The Women's Pavilion of the Louisiana World Exposition (1984) nomination form of Elizabeth Wisner (who had died in 1976) contains a biographical sketch (Newcomb Archives). See also *New Orleans Times-Picayune*, March 6, 1960, for an interview with Wisner and Sytz on the one hundredth anniversary of Jane Addams's birth; Rufus Carrollton Harris, "Social Work Education and The Elizabethan Era," an address by the president of Tulane University at the alumni meeting upon the retirement of Elizabeth Wisner as dean of the Tulane School of Social Work, and a response by Wisner, May 6, 1958 (Newcomb Archives). Wisner used most of her response time to praise Florence Sytz. No correspondence between Wisner and Sytz has survived.

59. Samuel C. Shepherd, "Eleanor McMain," in *KnowLA Encyclopedia of Louisiana*, 2010, http://www.knowla.org/entry.php?rec=876, accessed December 18, 2012.

60. Samuel C. Shepherd, "In Pursuit of Louisiana Progressives," *Louisiana History* 44 (Fall 2005): 389–406.

61. Margaret M. Campbell, ed., *Making a Difference, 1914–1989: Tulane School of Social Work*, Tulane Studies in Social Welfare 18 (New Orleans: Tulane University, 1990). Several narrators, including Mary Capps and Sandy Karp, mentioned the powerful example provided by Wisner and other faculty at the School of Social Work.

62. Hugh at one point became emotionally involved with Annis Rae Reid, treasurer of the New Orleans chapter of NOW, but Fossier and Hugh, who had split for a time, eventually renewed their relationship. Hugh relocated to Atlanta after Hurricane Katrina and died there. Mildred Fossier died in 2011 in New Orleans. Regina Matthews, interview by the author, February 5, 2014. Clay Latimer, Mary Capps, and Liz Simon correspondence confirmed the partnership of Fossier and Hugh. For Mildred Fossier's public career, see Peggy Frankland with Susan Tucker, *Women Pioneers of the Louisiana Environmental Movement* (Jackson: University Press of Mississippi, 2013), 112.

63. Wilkerson-Freeman, "Stealth in the Political"; Coontz, *Strange Stirring*, 47; Leslie, "United for a Better World."

64. King interview, in Jacobs, "Revisiting the Second Wave."

65. The statistics about the percentage of women working are not broken down by race in this report: Susan Holton, "Summary of Research Completed by Susan Holton, Administrator, Louisiana Commission on the Status of Women," 1972; Holton, "Women Workers in Louisiana, 1970," typescript, Newcomb Archives. For national trends in women's labor-force participation, see Kristin A. Goss, *The Paradox of Gender Equality: How American Women's Groups Gained and Lost Their Public Voice* (Ann Arbor: University of Michigan Press, 2013), 50–51; Claudia Goldin, *Understanding the Gender Gap: An Economic History of American Women* (New York: Oxford University Press, 1990), 119–58; Kessler-Harris, *In Pursuit of Equity*, 205–6.

66. Women workers in Louisiana had median earnings of only half those of men workers in 1970, and professional careers for women were limited. For example, there were 163 women physicians in the entire state in 1960, as compared to 3,195 men. *Louisiana Women: Report of the Governor's Commission on the Status of Women*, 1967.

67. Holton, "Summary," 5–6.

68. Many of my sources were graduates of these schools. I do not have statistics for the percentage of the state's population that held college degrees in 1970, but if current statistics are any guide, it was very low. A 2013 report of the Lumina Foundation, a private organization dedicated to increasing the number of Americans with two- and four-year degrees, showed that Louisiana had a lower proportion of college graduates than any other state except West Virginia. In 2011, 27.9 percent of Louisiana adults twenty-five to sixty-four years old held degrees, as compared to Massachusetts, the highest ranking state, with 50.8 percent of its residents holding college degrees. The national average was 38.7 percent. http://www.nola.com/education/index.ssf/2013/06/louisiana _ranks_49th_in_number.html, accessed November 11, 2014.

69. Holton notes "that the main explanation of the earnings gap by sex cannot be reduced to an educational differential by sex can be implied from the fact that women 25 years of age and over had completed 10.8 median years of school and men, 10.7 years of school. Black women had median earnings of only half those of white women workers." Holton, "Summary," 6–7.

70. In 1970, about 9 percent of Louisiana's adult population was divorced, whereas in 1940 that figure was less than 3 percent. James R. Bobo, comp., *Statistical Abstract of Louisiana*, 1974 (Baton Rouge: Louisiana State University Press, 1974), 40–90; *Baton Rouge Morning Advocate*, June 12, 1975.

71. Susan Faludi, *Backlash: The Undeclared War against American Women* (New York: Crown, 1991), 19–25; Nancy Cott, *Public Vows: A History of Marriage and the Nation* (Cambridge, Mass.: Harvard University Press, 2000), 206–7.

72. FBI file of Phyllis Belle Parun, Newcomb Archives.

73. Susan Levine's study of the AAUW supports the notion that women continued their progressive activism throughout the twentieth century. Susan Levine, *Degrees of Equality: The American Association of University Women and the Challenge of Twentieth-Century Feminism* (Philadelphia: Temple University Press, 1995), 151–52.

74. Goss, *Paradox of Gender Equality*, 51–52; Levine, *Degrees of Equality*, 152; Cobble, *Other Women's Movement*, 159–61; Christine Stansell, *The Feminist Promise: 1792 to the Present* (New York: Modern Library, 2010), 200–201; Rosen, *World Split Open*, 66–70; Davis, *Moving the Mountain*, 38.

75. Goss, *Paradox of Gender Equality*, 51–52; Levine, *Degrees of Equality*, 152; Cobble, *Other Women's Movement*, 159–61; Christine Stansell, *The Feminist Promise: 1792 to the Present* (New York: Modern Library, 2010), 200–201; Rosen, *World Split Open*, 66–70; Davis, *Moving the Mountain*, 38.

76. Laughlin, "Civic Feminists," 15, 22; Goss, *Paradox of Gender Equality*, 180; "The Pelican," February 1977, Newcomb Archives; Business and Professional Women's Foundation website, accessed 1/29/2016, http://bpwfoundation.org/. Box 7 in the Muriel Arceneaux papers at the Newcomb Archives contains a directory of Louisiana state presidents and chapter presidents starting in 1919. There were too few records of the Louisiana BPW for me to reconstruct its entire history in Louisiana.

77. *New Orleans Times-Picayune*, September 15, 1964; October 27, 1966. Five commission members were also legislators, including one woman, Representative Lillian W. Walker, of East Baton Rouge Parish. These members had "the added responsibility of presenting pertinent recommendations to the next regular session of the Louisiana Legislature for consideration and possible action if the Governor so direct[ed]." *Louisiana Women, Report of the Governor's Commission on the Status of Women*, 1964, 37.

78. *Louisiana Women*.

79. Ibid.

80. Ibid.; Governor's Office on Women's Policy Annual Report 2006. The Commission on the Status of Women became a permanent advisory board, appointed by the governor and charged with developing recommendations for women in all areas addressed in the original report. See also "Fact Sheet, Louisiana Bureau on the Status of Women," FF 36-6, Ollie Tucker Osborne Collection 93, University Archives and Acadiana Manuscripts Collection, Edith Garland Dupré Library, University of Louisiana at Lafayette (hereinafter cited as Osborne Collection).

81. So far as I've been able to determine, none of the women on the CSW joined any of the self-identified feminist organizations such as NOW in Louisiana. The report's recommendations would be carried out by Pat Evans and a new wave of grassroots feminists.

82. Gertrude Bussey and Margaret Tims, *Pioneers for Peace: Women's International League for Peace and Freedom, 1915–1965* (London: WILPF British Section, 1965); Women's

International League for Peace and Freedom website, http://wilpfus.org/, accessed October 18, 2013.

83. Darlene Fife, *Portraits from Memory: New Orleans in the Sixties* (New Orleans: Surregional Press, 2000), 13.

84. For more on the International Women's Day celebration held in 1970 in New Orleans, see note 45 above.

85. D'Orlando and Smith are discussed further in chap. 2. The New Orleans chapter of the WILPF may have been short-lived, as there is no mention of it in the *New Orleans Times-Picayune* after 1966.

86. Glen Jeansonne, *Leander Perez: Boss of the Delta* (Jackson: University Press of Mississippi, 1977), 295. The federal judge in the case of *United States v. Plaquemines*, who ruled against Boss Perez, was Herbert W. Christenberry. Clay Latimer, email correspondence, June 12, 2013; Latimer, interview by the author, January 1, 2015; "Lesbian Herstory at Tulane University," March 26, 2014, Newcomb Archives; Janet Allured, "Clay Latimer," in *KnowLA Encyclopedia of Louisiana*, http://www.knowla.org/entry/1120/&view=summary, accessed October 21, 2013; Veteran Feminists of America biography, http://www.vfa.us/Clay%20Latimer.htm, accessed November 25, 2014.

87. Frystak, *Our Minds on Freedom*, 46; Tyler, *Silk Stockings & Ballot Boxes*, 115; http://ourfamilybios.com/mathilde/MathildeMendelsohnSchwabDreyfous-a.pdf, accessed January 2, 2015.

88. Latimer interviews.

89. Andrea Estepa, "Taking the White Gloves Off: Women Strike for Peace and 'the Movement,' 1967–73," in Gilmore, *Feminist Coalitions*, 84.

90. Ibid., 85.

91. Quoted in Rosen, *World Split Open*, 99.

92. CWLU Herstory Project, A History of the Chicago Women's Liberation Union, document posted on archive web page, http://www.cwluherstory.org/CWLUArchive /natconference.html, accessed September 5, 2007. On the conflict between older and younger members of WSP and the resulting split with the women's liberationists in 1968, see Evans, *Tidal Wave*, 27–28. Barrie Thorne, a member of the draft resistance movement in Boston and of Bread and Roses, a feminist-socialist organization formed in part by women who had been active in the antidraft movement, examines the connection between the two movements in "Women in the Draft Resistance Movement: A Case Study of Sex Roles and Social Movements," *Sex Roles* 1, no. 3 (1975): 179–95.

93. Alonso, *Peace as a Women's Issue*, 225.

Chapter 2. "In the Eyes of God"

1. Fran Bussie, speech delivered at the Second Women's Conference, YWCA, Shreveport, La., December 13, 1980, accession no. N 97–7, box 1, Division of Archives, Records Management and History (Louisiana State Archives), Baton Rouge. Bussie was a lobbyist for the Louisiana AFL-CIO. Her full biography is discussed in chap. 8.

2. Kath Kern, *Mrs. Stanton's Bible* (Ithaca, N.Y.: Cornell University Press, 2002), 1.

3. Elizabeth Cady Stanton, Susan B. Anthony, and Matilda Joslyn Gage, eds., *History of Woman Suffrage* (1881–1922; reprint, New York: Arno Press, 1969). For an analysis of the role of religion in Stanton's thought, see Vivian Gornick, *The Solitude of Self: Thinking about Elizabeth Cady Stanton* (New York: Farrar, Straus & Giroux, 2005).

4. Ann Braude, "Religions and Modern Feminism," in Keller, Ruether, and Cantlon, *Encyclopedia of Women and Religion*, 18.

5. Mary J. Henold, *Catholic and Feminist: The Surprising History of the American Catholic Feminist Movement* (Chapel Hill: University of North Carolina Press, 2008), 17.

6. Carol Ochs, *Women and Spirituality*, 2nd ed. (New York: Rowman & Littlefield, 1997), 11.

7. Sara Evans, *Personal Politics: The Roots of Women's Liberation in the Civil Rights Movement & the New Left* (New York: Vintage Books, 1980), 29.

8. Constance Curry et al., *Deep in Our Hearts: Nine White Women in the Freedom Movement* (Athens: University of Georgia Press, 2000).

9. http://archives.livedtheology.org/node/1193, accessed January 28, 2014.

10. C. McLeod Bryan, *These Few Also Paid a Price: Southern Whites Who Fought for Civil Rights* (Macon, Ga.: Mercer University Press, 2001), 95–98.

11. Hartmann, *Other Feminists*, 93.

12. Janet Allured, "The Women of the Temple: Jewish Women in Lake Charles and Shreveport," in *Religion in Louisiana*, ed. Charles E. Nolan, vol. 19 of *The Louisiana Purchase Bicentennial Series in Louisiana History* (Lafayette: Center for Louisiana Studies, 2004), 539–48.

13. James Calhoun, ed., *Louisiana Almanac, 1979–1980* (Gretna, La.: Pelican Publishing, 1979), 465–68; Edwin Adams Davis, *Louisiana: A Narrative History*, 3rd ed. (Baton Rouge: Claitor's Publishing Division, 1971), 382–83; Allured, "Women of the Temple."

14. Collier-Thomas, *Jesus, Jobs, and Justice*, 465. Methodism claimed the largest number of adherents in the United States in 1920, but they were spread out among several denominations. Black Methodists might belong to the MEC, the African Methodist Episcopal Church (AME, established in 1797), or the African Methodist-Episcopal Church Zion (AMEZ, established in 1821 in Harlem, N.Y.). After the Civil War, white members of the MECS were unwilling to allow newly freed slaves into those churches, so they helped foster the establishment of the Colored Methodist Episcopal Church denomination, today called the Christian Methodist Episcopal Church (CME). The MEC and the MECS reunited in 1939 to form the Methodist Church; the reunion occurred through a concession to segregationists that placed all African American congregations and clergy in a separate jurisdiction so that black bishops would never oversee white clergy. This segregation into a separate jurisdiction persisted until the 1968 merger of the Methodist Church with the Evangelical United Brethren, which created the United Methodist Church (UMC). Ellen Blue, email correspondence, January 2013; February 15, 2014; Keller, Ruether, and Cantlon, *Encyclopedia of Women and Religion*, 225, 997; Reginald Hildebrand, *The Times Were Strange and Stirring: Methodist Preachers and the Crisis of Emancipation* (Durham, N.C.: Duke University Press, 1995); Gary B. Nash, *Forging Freedom: The Formation of Philadelphia's Black Community, 1720–1840* (Cambridge, Mass.: Harvard University Press, 1988); AMEZ website, http://www.amez

.org/index.php?option=com_content&view=article&id=512&Itemid=97, accessed February 16, 2014.

15. Women's divisions or departments had different names, according to the denomination, and sometimes the names changed over time. In the MECS, the institutional church to which most southern white women belonged, it was the Women's Division of the Board of Global Ministries; for women of the Colored Methodist Episcopal Church, it was the Women's Missionary Society. On missions established among the Cajuns, see Janet Allured, "'Holy Boldness': Feminist Methodist Women in the South, 1960–1980," forthcoming in *Methodist Journal*.

16. John Patrick McDowell, *The Social Gospel in the South: The Woman's Home Mission Movement in the Methodist Episcopal Church, South, 1886–1939* (Baton Rouge: Louisiana State University Press, 1982), 20–30; Shepherd, "In Pursuit of Louisiana Progressives," 402; Carmen Lindig, *Path from the Parlor*.

17. McDowell, *Social Gospel in the South*, 108; Collier-Thomas, *Jesus, Jobs, and Justice*, 321–23.

18. Andrew M. Manis, "'City Mothers': Dorothy Tilly, Georgia Methodist Women, and Black Civil Rights," in Glenn Feldman, ed., *Before Brown: Civil Rights and White Backlash in the Modern South* (Tuscaloosa: University of Alabama Press, 2004), 125–56; Jacquelyn Dowd Hall, *Revolt against Chivalry: Jessie Daniel Ames and the Women's Campaign against Lynching*, rev. ed. (New York: Columbia University Press, 1993), 94.

19. Lugenia Burns Hope was married to John Hope, president of historically black Morehouse College and a founder of the Niagara Movement. He was one of several black men to lead the CIC.

20. Mary E. Frederickson, "'Each One Is Dependent on the Other': Southern Churchwomen, Racial Reform, and the Process of Transformation, 1880–1940," in *Visible Women: New Essays on American Activism*, eds. Nancy A. Hewitt and Suzanne Lebsock (Urbana: University of Illinois Press, 1993), 297–98.

21. Ibid., 306; Jean Miller Schmidt and Sara J. Myers, "Methodist Women," in Keller, Ruether, and Cantlon, *Encyclopedia of Women and Religion*, 319–26; also introduction to *Encyclopedia of Women and Religion*, xxxvii, xxxix.

22. Ellen Blue, *St. Mark's and the Social Gospel: Methodist Women and Civil Rights in New Orleans, 1895–1965* (Knoxville: University of Tennessee Press, 2011); Collier-Thomas, *Jesus, Jobs, and Justice*, 318.

23. Evans, *Personal Politics*, 30; "Ruth Harris" and "Charlotte Bunch," in *Journeys That Opened Up the World: Women, Student Christian Movements, and Social Justice, 1955–1975*, ed. Sara M. Evans (New Brunswick, N.J.: Rutgers University Press, 2003), esp. 29–39, 136. Caroline Merrick is discussed in Lindig, *Path from the Parlor*.

24. Barbara J. Love, ed., *Feminists Who Changed America, 1963–1975* (Urbana: University of Illinois Press, 2006), 347; Osborne biography, in *KnowLA Encyclopedia of Louisiana*, http://www.knowla.org/entry/851/, accessed October 17, 2013. See also Ollie Tucker Osborne Papers, Collection 93, University Archives and Acadiana Manuscripts Collection, Edith Garland Dupré Library, University of Louisiana at Lafayette.

25. Osborne Collection. Osborne became a member of the Mayor's Commission on the Needs of Women when it was founded in the mid-1970s. The University of Louisiana

at Lafayette (ULL) has undergone numerous name changes since it began functioning in 1901 as the Southwestern Louisiana Industrial Institute. In 1960, the school added graduate programs and changed its name to the University of Southwestern Louisiana. It became the University of Louisiana at Lafayette in 1999. To avoid confusion, I will refer to it by its current name throughout the book.

26. Collier-Thomas, *Jesus, Jobs, and Justice*, 465.

27. *The Church, Religion, and the Equal Rights Amendment*, a joint project of the Women's Division of the Board of Global Ministries and the Board of Church and Society of the United Methodist Church, ERA Support Project, Service Department, 100 Maryland Ave., N.E., Washington, D.C., 2002, Newcomb Archives.

28. *Louisiana Weekly*, June 14, 2011, http://www.louisianaweekly.com/remembering -dorothy-mae-taylor-the-first-lady-of-1300-perdido-st/, accessed April 14, 2014.

29. Rose M. Harris, "Dorothy Mae Taylor (1928–2000), Louisiana's First African American Political Woman," unpublished paper in the author's possession. Quotes are from *New Orleans Times-Picayune*, April 30, 1994. See also http://www.npr.org/templates /story/story.php?storyId=5235456.

30. Cheryl Townsend Gilkes, *"If It Wasn't for the Women..."* (Maryknoll, N.Y.: Orbis Books, 2001), 5.

31. Kingsley House was established by Trinity Episcopal Church's Rev. Beverley Warner, a graduate of Princeton and a native of New Jersey. Kingsley House website, http:// www.kingsleyhouse.org/about/history/, accessed December 23, 2012; Samuel C. Shepherd, "Eleanor McMain," in *KnowLA Encyclopedia of Louisiana*, 2010, http://www.knowla .org/entry.php?rec=876, accessed December 18, 2012.

32. Gillespie, "Sarah Patton Boyle's Desegregated Heart," 161.

33. Keller, Ruether, and Cantlon, *Encyclopedia of Women and Religion*, 175.

34. Other Episcopalian social activists were Thurgood Marshall, the first African American Supreme Court justice; Miriam Van Waters (1887–1974), who pushed for reform in women's prisons; Cynthia Clark Wedel (1909–86), the first woman president of the National Council of Churches and president of the World Council of Churches; and Anne and Carl Braden, who established a civil rights organization called the Southern Conference Education Fund. Sarah Patton Boyle, daughter of an Episcopal clergyman in Virginia, began writing and acting against white racist culture in the early to mid-1950s. Though her activism caused her to lose many white friends in her church and community, *The Desegregated Heart*, published in 1962, won her the Dr. Martin Luther King Jr. Award from the Southern Christian Leadership Conference. Gillespie, "Sarah Patton Boyle," 161; Edward W. Rodman, "Soul Sisters: The Emergence of Black Women's Leadership," in *Deeper Joy: Lay Women and Vocation in the 20th Century Episcopal Church*, ed. Frederica Harris Thompsett and Sheryl Kujawa-Holbrook (New York: Church, 2004), 220–21; Elaine Allen Lechtreck, "Southern White Ministers and the Civil Rights Movement" (PhD diss., Union Institute and University, 2008), 59, 72, 92, 155, 181; Catherine Fosl, *Subversive Southerner: Anne Braden and the Struggle for Racial Justice in the Cold War South* (New York: Palgrave Macmillan, 2002).

35. *Catholic World*, January 1971, 177–83.

36. Janet Pounds, email correspondence, February 3, 2008.

37. Kim Gandy, email correspondence, February 12, 2009; "Keeping the Memories: Louisianans of the 2nd Wave Feminist Movement," transcript of banquet discussion sponsored by Veteran Feminists of America, March 22, 2001, Newcomb Archives; Love, *Feminists Who Changed America*, 166.

38. Gandy, email correspondence, February 12, 2009.

39. Corinne Barnwell, interview by the author and email correspondences, October 2013. Corinne graduated from Radcliffe in 1958 with a degree in history.

40. Ibid.; Sarah Hart Brown, *Standing against Dragons: Three Southern Lawyers in an Era of Fear* (Baton Rouge: Louisiana State University Press, 1998), 242.

41. Blue, email correspondence and review of original draft, January, 2013.

42. Ellen Blue, communications, 2008–13. For a complete history of St. Mark's, see Blue, *St. Mark's*, and Blue, "True Methodist Women: Reflections on the Community of St. Mark's," in Allured and Gentry, *Louisiana Women*, 215–36. Margery Freeman and David Billings, telephone interview by the author, February 18, 2008. The board of directors, which had ultimate responsibility for running St. Mark's, remained all female during Billings's directorship.

43. Blue, *St. Mark's*, 213.

44. The name of the lounge is variously written as Upstairs, UpStairs, Up-Stairs, and Up Stairs. Clayton Delery-Edwards provides evidence that it was two words in his award-winning book, *The Up Stairs Lounge Arson: Thirty-Two Deaths in a New Orleans Gay Bar, June 24, 1973* (Jefferson, N.C.: McFarland, 2014).

45. The mayor's appointees were Rev. Lucien Baril, who took over the MCC ministry after Bill Larson's death in the fire; Bill Rushton, a journalist for the *Vieux Carré Courier* who had been critical of both the mayor and the archbishop; and Celeste Newbrough, director of research for Total Community Action. Delery-Edwards believes that Hannon, despite his denials, did issue those instructions. See his *Up Stairs Lounge Arson*, 66–67; 144–45, http://exhibits.lgbtran.org/exhibits/show/upstairs-lounge-fire, accessed September 22, 2015; *New Orleans Times-Picayune*, June 24, 1993; *Vieux Carré Courier*, July 6–12, 1973; Blue, *St. Mark's*, 215.

46. *Vieux Carré Courier*, July 6–12, 1973; Louisiana Conference of the United Methodist Church, history of St. Marks, http://www.la-umc.org/churchhistorydetail/849603, accessed September 2, 2015.

47. Lyn Diane Franks, "Torchbearers and Front Runners: The Daughters of Bilitis and Women's Rights" (master's thesis, Murray State University, 2011); Clay Latimer, interview by the author, January 1, 2015. Latimer and her then-partner Diane Clabaugh joined the DOB (as it is often called) in the late 1960s. Two excellent histories of the DOB are Marcia Gallo, *Different Daughters: A History of the Daughters of Bilitis and the Rise of the Lesbian Rights Movement* (New York: Carrol & Graf, 2006); and Martin Meeker, *Contacts Desired: Gay and Lesbian Communications and Community, 1940s–1970s* (Chicago: University of Chicago Press, 2006).

48. Rayne Memorial United Methodist Church and Parker Memorial United Methodist Church, both in Uptown New Orleans, voted to become reconciling congregations in 2012. Ellen Blue, correspondence, January 2013.

49. Blue, *St. Mark's*, 214.

50. Cynthia Grant Tucker, "Women in the Unitarian Universalist Movement," in Keller, Ruether, and Marie Cantlon, *Encyclopedia of Women and Religion*, 380–88; Sheila L. Skemp, *First Lady of Letters: Judith Sargent Murray and the Struggle for Female Independence* (Philadelphia: University of Pennsylvania Press, 2009).

51. Katherine (Kit) Senter, interviewed by Susan Tucker, August 3, 2012, Newcomb Oral History Project, Newcomb Archives; Cathy Cade, telephone interview by the author, September 6, 2007; Roberta Madden, interview by the author, October 2007.

52. Rogers, *Righteous Lives*, 157–59. Church website, http://firstuuno.org/j15/index .php?option=com_content&view=article&id=26&Itemid=36, accessed September 10, 2013.

53. Susan LosCalzo, email correspondence, March 22, 2014; Love, *Feminists Who Changed America*, 285.

54. Mary Gehman, email correspondence, September 2013; Barbara Scott, interview by the author, December 4, 2013. Scott's campaign is discussed more fully in chap. 7.

55. Many women's rights activists of varied backgrounds and racial identities donated their time and talents to keep *Distaff* in production, including Darlene Olivo, Ann Wakefield, and Suzanne Pharr. Newcomb Archives contains a full run of *Distaff*.

56. Walther League, *Bridge* (Chicago), July 1971.

57. New Walther League Manifesto, "We Will Answer—Now!" (Chicago, 1968); Susan R. Laporte et al., *Youth Power Strategy Manual* (Chicago: Walther League, 1970).

58. Laporte's grandfather, Michael LeCron, was raised in a German orphanage in New Orleans. He died before she was born, but the family stayed centered around the Ninth Ward church. Laporte, interview by the author, June 4, 2014. Herbek later worked for Kennedy's Peace Corps.

59. Walther League appointment and agreement letter signed by Dean Kell and Susan R. Laporte, March 30, 1970, Newcomb Archives. The league also agreed to pay her travel expenses.

60. This and all following citations regarding Sue Laporte come from correspondence with Sue Laporte, May 30, 2014, and a follow-up interview by the author, June 4, 2014.

61. Walther League, *Bridge*, July 1971.

62. *The Lutheran Witness*, 91, no. 15, Southern District Edition, St. Louis, Mo., November 26, 1972.

63. Correspondence with Sue Laporte, May 30, 2014.

64. See note 60.

65. Sisters helping Sisters is discussed in chap. 5. Laporte interview, September 25, 2007, and email correspondence, January 31, 2008; May 30, 2014. I conducted follow-up interviews with Laporte during my year-in-residence at Newcomb College Institute, 2014–15. The Lutheran Church in America and the American Lutheran Church began ordaining women in 1970, relatively early compared to many other denominations. Keller, Ruether, and Cantlon, *Encyclopedia of Women and Religion*, 15.

66. Email correspondence with Sue Laporte, May 30, 2014.

67. Marguerite Redwine, interview by the author, October 8, 2013.

68. Henold, introduction to *Catholic and Feminist*.

69. Henold, *Catholic and Feminist*, 38–39; Mary Daly, *The Church and the Second Sex*, 2nd ed.(1968; New York: Harper Colophon Books, 1975); Daly, *Beyond God the Father: Toward a Philosophy of Women's Liberation* (Boston: Beacon Press, 1973).

70. Rosemary Radford Ruether, "Is Roman Catholicism Reformable?," *Christian Century* 83 (1965): 1152–54; Ruether, *New Woman, New Earth: Sexist Ideologies and Human Liberation* (New York: Seabury Press, 1975); Ruether, "Women's Liberation in Historical and Theological Perspective," *Soundings* 53 (1970): 363–73. Ruether's work provided a foundation for a separatist movement that originated in the 1970s called "Women-Church." See Ruether, *Women-Church: Theology and Practice of Feminist Liturgical Communities* (San Francisco: Harper & Row, 1985).

71. Henold, *Catholic and Feminist*, 7, 87–88. In the late 1960s, as part of their desire to be less obedient to the church fathers, women who had taken vows of poverty, chastity, and obedience switched from using the terms "nun" and "sister" to the more modern "women religious." Technically, nuns were cloistered and sisters had active ministries, but in common usage the terms were typically used interchangeably. Even though they had taken vows, nuns were considered laywomen, but I will use the term "laywomen" here to refer to Catholic women who had not taken vows.

72. Sister Fara Impastato résumé, in author's possession, courtesy of Barbara Jo Brothers. She described the order she joined as "a small maverick Roman Catholic religious community."

73. Henold, *Catholic and Feminist*, 95–99; *New Orleans Times-Picayune*, October 11, 1999; *Humanities Interview* (Oklahoma Foundation for the Humanities), Spring 1988; Impastato résumé (photocopy in the author's possession, courtesy of Barbara Brothers).

74. Transcript of Fara Impastato, OP, formerly Sister Mary Lucia, Saint Mary's College, Notre Dame, Indiana, 1952; obituary, *New Orleans Times-Picayune*, May 13, 2014, http://obits.nola.com/obituaries/nola/obituary.aspx?pid=171009153, accessed September 21, 2015; http://www.clarionherald.info/clarion/index.php/news/obituaries/3425-sister-fara-impastato-op-93; program, Tenth Anniversary of Women's Studies at Loyola University New Orleans, October 15, 1998, sponsored by the Women's Studies committee, Barbara C. Ewell and Leslie Parr, chairs.

75. Henold, *Catholic and Feminist*, 95–99; *New Orleans Times-Picayune*, October 11, 1999; "Humanities Interview"; Impastato résumé.

76. Lindy Boggs, interview on NPR's *Morning Edition*, "Remembering Former Rep. Lindy Boggs," http://www.npr.org/2013/07/29/206677780/fresh-air-remembers-former-louisiana-congresswoman-lindy-boggs, accessed July 29, 2013.

77. Riley left a bequest to the New Orleans Ursulines in her will in addition to a bequest to the society. Shawn Holahan, great-niece of Janet Mary Riley, interview by the author, July 18, 2011.

78. Letter from Janet Mary Riley to Kathleen Lilly, November 12, 1962, Janet Mary Riley Papers, Monroe Library Archives and Special Collections, Loyola University of the South, New Orleans, hereinafter cited as JMR papers.

79. Vaughan Baker, interview by the author, November 20, 2013.

80. This and all following quotes about her life come from Vaughan Baker interviews, November 20, 2013, and February 28, 2015. R. Bentley Anderson covers the controversy surrounding the admission of black students to the College of the Sacred Heart in *Black, White, and Catholic: New Orleans Interracialism, 1947–1956* (Nashville: Vanderbilt University Press, 2005), 108–10.

81. Jeansonne, *Leander Perez*, 258–60.

82. Lorna Bourg, interview by the author, January 6, 2014; Lorna Bourg papers, Newcomb Archives; National Commission on the Observance of International Women's Year, *The Spirit of Houston: The First National Women's Conference; An Official Report to the President, the Congress and the People of the United States* (Washington, D.C.: U.S. Government Printing Office, 1978), 88.

83. Henold, *Catholic and Feminist*, 20–22.

84. Keller, Ruether, and Cantlon, *Encyclopedia of Women and Religion*, 17, 205–9; Henold, *Catholic and Feminist*, 95–99.

85. Keller, Ruether, and Cantlon, *Encyclopedia of Women and Religion*, 18. National NOW established its Task Force on Women and Religion, chaired by Episcopalian feminist Georgia Fuller.

86. Baton Rouge NOW newsletter, December 1971, LSU Library Special Collections. The religious orders to which they belong are not given.

87. Henold, *Catholic and Feminist*, 1–8, 20–23.

88. Mary Fainsod Katzenstein, "Discursive Politics and Feminist Activism in the Catholic Church," in *Feminist Organizations: Harvest of the New Women's Movement*, ed. Myra Marx Ferree and Patricia Yancey Martin (Philadelphia: Temple University Press, 1995), 37–38.

89. Clay Latimer interviews.

90. Brochure published by the Society of Our Lady of The Way, in author's possession, acquired from Mary Ann Tady, of Cleveland, Ohio, one of the ten remaining members of the society when I interviewed her in July 2009. Quote is from telephone interview with Tady, July 21, 2009.

91. For more on Riley, see Janet Allured, "Janet Mary Riley (1915–2008): An Angel with Teeth," *Louisiana Women: Their Lives and Times*, vol. 2, ed. Shannon Frystak and Mary Farmer-Kaiser (Athens: University of Georgia Press, 2015), 41–62.

92. United States Conference of Secular Institutes, http://www.secularinstitutes.org /index.htm, accessed July 6, 2011. See also B. M Ottinger and A. S. Fischer, eds., *Secular Institutes in the Code of Canon Law: A New Vocation in the Church*, rev. ed. (Washington, D.C.: U.S. Conference of Secular Institutes, 2008).

93. Janet Mary Riley, "Analysis of the 1980 Revision of the Matrimonial Regimes Law of Louisiana," *Loyola Law Review* 26 (1980): 456–57.

94. Wisdom's obituary, *New Orleans Times-Picayune*, September 23, 2007; audiotape interview, Betty Wisdom Collection 272-1, Earl K. Long Library, Louisiana and Special Collections Department, University of New Orleans. Nationally famous Jewish feminist leaders include Betty Friedan, Gloria Steinem, and Bella Abzug.

95. Many founders of the women's liberation movement were red diaper babies. See Evans, *Personal Politics*, 116–25; Giardina, *Freedom for Women*, chap. 3; and Weigand, *Red Feminism*.

96. Debra L. Schultz, *Going South: Jewish Women in the Civil Rights Movement* (New York: New York University Press, 2001), 141, 194; Dottie Zellner, interview by the author, September 5, 2007; Zellner, "My Real Vocation," in *Hands on the Freedom Plow: Personal Accounts by Women in SNCC*, ed. Faith S. Holsaert, Martha Prescod, Norman Noonan, Judy Richardson, Betty Garman Robinson, Jean Smith Young, and Dorothy M. Zellner (Urbana: University of Illinois Press, 2010), 313.

97. A Tulane political science professor concluded that powerful Jews in New Orleans had an aristocratic mentality. They were, he said, "as much in the don't-rock-the-boat syndrome as the gentile community." Statement attributed to Dr. Charles Y. Chai, in Eli N. Evans, *The Provincials: A Personal History of Jews in the South* (New York: Simon & Schuster, 1997), 215. Evans does not provide a date for Chai's study, but it was likely in the late 1960s or early 1970s, before the original copyright date of *The Provincials* (1973).

98. National Council of Jewish Women, Greater New Orleans Section Records, 1894–1986, box 135, FF 3, Louisiana Research Manuscript Collection 667, Tulane University, hereinafter cited as NCJW records; Allured, "Women of the Temple"; Irwin Lachoff and Catherine C. Kahn, *The Jewish Community of New Orleans* (Charleston, S.C.: Arcadia, 2005). For a history of the NCJW, see Faith Rogow, *Gone to Another Meeting: The National Council of Jewish Women, 1893–1993* (Tuscaloosa: University of Alabama Press, 1993).

99. Keller, Ruether, and Cantlon, *Encyclopedia of Women and Religion*, 536, 538, 547, 591–92, 900, 960, 1033, 1102, 1120–25; Rogow, *Gone to Another Meeting*, 190. The literature on the ERA and on the National Women's Party, which first sponsored the amendment, is voluminous. For a short version, see Amy Dru Stanley, "Protective Labor Legislation," in *The Reader's Companion to U.S. Women's History* (Boston: Houghton Mifflin, 1998), 482.

100. NCJW records.

101. Ibid. In 1989, Dryades Street was renamed in honor of New Orleans CORE leader and civil rights activist Oretha Castle Haley.

102. Kahn was born in 1926 in New Orleans and graduated from Newcomb in 1948. She served as a delegate to the Democratic National Convention in 1980, 1984, and 1992 and ran unsuccessfully for the Louisiana House of Representatives in 1975 and 1979. Her papers are deposited in the Newcomb Archives. See also Love, *Feminists Who Changed America*, 242.

103. Florence Schornstein, telephone interview by the author and email correspondence, 2008, 2012.

104. Rupert Richardson, interview by Diane Holeman, VHS tapes 21 and 22, 1984, Pat Denton Collection, Newcomb Archives; Gaynell Veronica Clemons (Richardson's daughter), correspondence, August 28, 2015, and interview by the author, September 2, 2015; Vera Warren-Williams, interview by the author, March 20, 2014, Newcomb Archives. Tulane Memorial Baptist Church is at 3601 Paris Avenue. For a discussion of the historical and organizational differences between the Baptist and the Methodist churches,

see Allured, "Arkansas Baptists and Methodists." See also Higginbotham, *Righteous Discontent.*

105. Barbara Trahan, telephone interview by the author, June 3, 2014.

106. Braude, "Religions and Modern Feminism,"19; Luisah Teish, *Jambalaya: The Natural Woman's Book of Personal Charms and Practical Rituals* (New York: Harper Collins, 1985).

107. Martha C. Ward, interview by the author, October 22, 2013, New Orleans; Carolyn Morrow Long, *A New Orleans Voudou Priestess: The Legend and Reality of Marie Laveau* (Gainesville: University Press of Florida, 2007); Martha C. Ward, *Voodoo Queen: The Spirited Lives of Marie Laveau* (Jackson: University Press of Mississippi, 2004); Ina Fandrich, *The Mysterious Voodoo Queen, Marie Laveaux: A Study of Powerful Female Leadership in Nineteenth-Century New Orleans* (New York: Routledge, 2005). For an in-depth look at the life and work of a contemporary voodoo priestess, see Karen McCarthy Brown, *Mama Lola, a Vodou Priestess in Brooklyn* (Berkeley: University of California Press, 2001; 2nd ed. 2010). After immersing herself in the family life and voodoo practices of Mama Lola, Brown, a white anthropologist, was initiated as a priestess herself.

108. Probably the most famous contemporary voodoo priestess in New Orleans is Sallie Ann Gleasman, a Jew from Maine. Voodoo practitioners in New Orleans who are African-descended are from outside the United States, typically from Caribbean islands. African Americans in Louisiana today regard voodoo in much the same way that Christians have always viewed it: as heretical black magic. African American women in Louisiana, if they are churched, are most likely Baptist, Methodist, or Catholic.

Chapter 3. "Their Courage Inspired Me"

1. A mimeograph machine, which allowed multiple copies to be made from one original, was the standard way of reproducing self-published material before photocopy machines and personal computers became common.

2. Kathy Barrett, interviews by the author and email correspondence, December 5, 2007; December 9, 2013; January 21, 2015 (hereinafter cited as personal communications); Cathy Cade, interviews by the author, August 8 and September 6, 2007. I attempted to find a roster of attendees at the Waveland meeting by interviewing Mary King and Casey Hayden, as well as by researching King's papers, available online at https://search.library.wisc.edu/catalog/999465378102121. Unfortunately, no such roster exists.

Most histories of the second wave credit the King-Hayden memo for sparking the grassroots women's liberation movement, but because the movement was so decentralized and informal groups did not keep records, it was easy to overlook the networks forming in the South in the immediate aftermath of the Waveland meeting. With few exceptions, movement histories typically locate the first CR sessions in the North as late as 1967. See, for example, Roxanne Baxandall, "Re-Visioning the Women's Liberation Movement's Narrative: Early Second Wave African American Feminists," *Feminist Studies* 27, no. 1 (Spring 2001): 229.

3. Andrew W. Kahrl, *The Land Was Ours: African American Beaches from Jim Crow to the Sunbelt South* (Cambridge, Mass.: Harvard University Press, 2012), chap. 2. Mary

King says in her autobiography that Gulfside was the only place in Mississippi where an integrated group could have met without triggering violence. However, she may have been unaware of other such places, almost all associated with liberal Christian denominations. Rust College, a black Methodist institution; Tougaloo, a black Episcopalian-supported college; and Mary Holmes Junior College, a Presbyterian college for women in West Point, Mississippi, had all held interracial meetings in the 1950s and early 1960s. Jane Schutt, an Episcopalian who headed Church Women United in Jackson, organized interracial prayer meetings at a black Baptist church and at (white) Galloway Methodist Church. Providence Farm in the Mississippi Delta, which had started in 1936 as an integrated community for sharecroppers, also hosted integrated meetings. Leesha Faulkner, interview with Jane Schutt, University of Southern Mississippi Digital Collections, http://digilib.usm.edu/cdm/ref/collection/coh/id/6235, accessed December 5, 2013. See also the Gulfside website, http://www.gbgm-umc.org/gulfsideassembly/history.html, accessed December 5, 2013.

4. Kahrl, *Land Was Ours*, 58–62. Kahrl's is an excellent study of Jones as well as of the phenomenon of blacks acquiring and then losing beachfront property in the face of white intimidation. He also covers Gulfside's obliteration by Hurricane Katrina (244–45).

5. Kahrl, *Land Was Ours*, 75, 217.

6. Barrett personal communications.

7. For the Christian-Faith-and-Life-Community, see Rossinow, *Politics of Authenticity*, esp. chap. 2, "Breakthrough." Mark C. Taylor, "Kierkegaard, Søren," in *Encyclopedia of Religion*, ed. Lindsay Jones, 2nd ed., vol. 8 (Detroit: Macmillan Reference, USA, 2005), 5140–43, Gale Virtual Reference Library, http://ezproxy.mcneese.edu:2092/ps/infomark.do?eisbn=9780028659978&userGroupName=lln_louis&prodId=GVRL&action=interpret&type=aboutBook&version=1.0&authCount=1&u=lln_louis, accessed January 30, 2014. Kierkegaard influenced Jean-Paul Sartre, Simone de Beauvoir's lifelong companion.

8. Not only does existentialism have no agreed-upon body of doctrine, there is also disagreement about who is an existentialist philosopher and who is not. John MacQuarrie, "Existentialism," in Jones, *Encyclopedia of Religion*, 2924–27.

9. I am indebted to Harold L. Smith for sharing with me an advance copy of his essay "Casey Hayden."

10. Bonhoeffer, a Lutheran pastor, studied at Union Theological Seminary in New York City with Reinhold Niebuhr. He then returned to Berlin to teach and was quickly caught up in the struggle against the nazification of the churches and the persecution of the Jews. Bonhoeffer and three members of his family were executed by the Nazis in 1945 for their resistance. Eberhard Bethge, "Bonhoeffer, Dietrich," in Jones, *Encyclopedia of Religion*, 1016–17. Niebuhr joined the faculty of Union Theological Seminary in 1928. He founded the Fellowship of Socialist Christians (1930) and was active in countless organizations involving labor unions, tenant farmers, and liberal or leftist causes. In 1940 he resigned from the Socialist Party and in 1941 helped to organize the liberal anti-Communist Union for Democratic Action. Roger Lincoln Shinn, "Niebuhr, Reinhold," in Jones, *Encyclopedia of Religion*, 6611–14.

11. Hayden, "Fields of Blue," 339.

12. Smith, "Casey Hayden," 364; Rossinow, *Politics of Authenticity*, 75–77. Camus won the 1957 Nobel Prize in Literature and died in a car crash in 1960.

13. Smith, "Casey Hayden," 365.

14. Ibid., 367–372.

15. Ibid., 372; Casey Hayden and Mickey Flacks interviews, in Ben Agger, *The Sixties at 40: Leaders and Activists Remember and Look Forward* (Boulder, Colo.: Paradigm, 2009), 169–71; Mickey Flacks interview, in Wesley C. Hogan, *Many Minds, One Heart: SNCC's Dream for a New America* (Chapel Hill: University of North Carolina Press, 2007), 111–12; Hayden, "Fields of Blue," 348.

16. Smith, "Casey Hayden," 372–73; Giardina, *Freedom for Women*, 92, 161; King, *Freedom Song*, 162, 448, 462; Hayden, "Fields of Blue," 365.

17. King, *Freedom Song*, 76–78; Mary Ann Wilson, "State of the Studies Talk: Women's Studies in Louisiana," talk delivered at the Ernest J. Gaines Center, February 7, 2013, ULL, copy in author's possession. Barbara Scott and Darlene Fife both said that Beauvoir and Lessing were important influences on them, too. Fife, *Portraits From Memory*; Scott interview. Stephanie Gilmore found only one person in the three cities she studied (Memphis, Columbus, and San Francisco) who said that reading *The Feminine Mystique* brought her to feminism. Gilmore, *Groundswell*, 89.

18. Gayle Greene, *Doris Lessing: The Poetics of Change* (Ann Arbor: University of Michigan Press, 1997), 14.

19. Mary Ann Wilson, email correspondence, January 19, 2013.

20. Fresh Air archives, 1982 and 1992 interviews with Terry Gross. Lessing, who died in 2013, remained virulently anticolonial her entire life.

21. Deirdre Bair, "Introduction to the Vintage Edition," in Simone de Beauvoir, *The Second Sex* (repr., New York: Vintage Books, 1989), xiv–xv. Bair is sympathetic toward Parshley. In *Simone de Beauvoir: A Biography* (New York: Touchstone, 1990), 433–37, Bair notes that Parshley repeatedly requested that Beauvoir assist him in deciding where to make cuts to the original, but she refused. Margaret A. Simons offers a more critical appraisal of the translation in chap. 5 of *Beauvoir and The Second Sex: Feminism, Race, and the Origins of Existentialism* (New York: Rowman & Littlefield, 1999), originally published as "The Silencing of Simone de Beauvoir: Guess What's Missing from *The Second Sex*," *Women's Studies International Forum* 6 (1983): 559–64. Simons says that Parshley's cuts were effectively sexist.

22. Algren died in 1981 and left his voluminous correspondence with Beauvoir to Ohio State University Library. Quote is from a letter Beauvoir wrote to Algren in 1947, reprinted in Simons, *Beauvoir and The Second Sex*, 170–71.

23. Simons, *Beauvoir and The Second Sex*, chap. 11, "Richard Wright, Simone de Beauvoir, and The Second Sex," originally published in 1997.

24. King, *Freedom Song*, 456; Giardina, *Freedom for Women*, 31, chap. 4. In 1986, the Redstockings, a radical feminist group in New York City, sponsored a memorial for Simone de Beauvoir two weeks after her death, at which many organizers testified to her significance. Copies of the testimonials are available from Redstockings Women's Liberation Archives for Action, www.redstockings.org.

25. Mary King, interview in Elizabeth Jacobs, "Revisiting the Second Wave: In Conversation with Mary King," *Meridians: Feminism, Race, Transnationalism* 7, no. 2 (2007): 103–5.

26. Smith, "Casey Hayden," 378–79; King, *Freedom Song*, 448, 460–62; Hayden, "Fields of Blue," 365. Belinda Robnett provides a nuanced discussion of the memo's context and its reception among African American women in *How Long? How Long? African American Women in the Struggle for Civil Rights* (New York: Oxford University Press, 1997), 119–39.

27. King, *Freedom Song*, 462.

28. Anderson-Bricker, "'Triple Jeopardy,'" 53; Breines, *Trouble Between Us*, 33–35.

29. Smith, "Casey Hayden," 381; King, *Freedom Song*, 458.

30. Smith, "Casey Hayden," 381; Casey Hayden and Mary King, "Sex and Caste: A Kind of Memo," *Liberation* 10 (April 1966): 35. The full text is also reprinted in King, *Freedom Song*, appendix 2; Evans, *Personal Politics*, appendix; in *Meridians*, 113–16; and online, http://crmvet.org/docs/snccfem.htm, accessed December 3, 2013.

31. Hayden and King, "Sex and Caste," 36.

32. King, *Freedom Song*, 468; Casey Hayden, interview in Agger, *Sixties at 40*, 259; King, "Fields of Blue," 374.

33. Clayborne Carson, *In Struggle: SNCC and the Black Awakening of the 1960s* (Cambridge, Mass.: Harvard University Press, 1981), 32.

34. Hanisch was a native of Iowa who had worked in the Voter Registration Project in Mississippi in 1964. Bob Zellner worked with Sam Shirah as a field staff member in SNCC. Zellner and Shirah were both sons of Methodist ministers in the Alabama-West Florida Conference. Zellner had gone to Huntingdon, a Methodist College in Alabama. After SNCC expelled all whites, Dottie and Bob Zellner and Carol Hanisch went to work for the SCEF. Evans, *Journeys That Opened Up the World*, 162; Schultz, *Going South*, 141; Hayden, "Fields of Blue," 333, 371. "The Personal Is Political" is available at truthtellers@hvi.net. For its origins in discussions with Zellner, see Hanisch's introduction on the same website, January 2006. Hanisch's original title in February 1969 was "Some Thoughts in Response to Dottie's Thoughts on a Women's Liberation Movement." Zellner confirmed this in a telephone interview, September 5, 2007. See also Giardina, *Freedom for Women*, 128 and n. 13.

35. Copies of New Orleans Women's Liberation Coalition papers, Newcomb Archives; New Orleans and Baton Rouge NOW newsletters.

36. Kathy Barrett, email correspondence, January 21, 2015.

37. Marilyn Boxer lists the course offered by Cade and Dobbins as one of the first three women's studies courses in the United States—all offered for the first time in 1966. Marilyn Boxer, "For and About Women: The Theory and Practice of Women's Studies in the United States," *Signs* 7, no. 3 (1982): 663. Love, *Feminists Who Changed America*, 67–68, 120.

38. Clark A. Pomerleau, *Califia Women: Feminist Education against Sexism, Classism, and Racism* (Austin: University of Texas, 2013), 21–23.

39. Katherine Mellon Charron, *Freedom's Teacher: The Life of Septima Clark* (Chapel Hill: University of North Carolina Press, 2009), 2.

40. In Louisiana as in many other southern states, laws passed by the all-white state legislature required an applicant to pass inscrutable tests that had been specifically designed to ensure that blacks failed. Many questions on Louisiana's "citizenship test" had no right answer. There were no standards, rubrics, or keys that gauged what constituted a correct response. The "grade" was determined by the registrar, who was always white. Registrars could ask almost any question they could imagine and sometimes included questions that had nothing to do with citizenship, such as "How many bubbles are in a bar of soap"? The process was not only undemocratic; for many uneducated or poorly educated people, it was insurmountable. Though the federal Voting Rights Act of 1965 banned all tests for voting, many southern registrars were slow to give up their old ways, and newly registering blacks still needed tutoring and encouragement to go through the process. For more information, see, e.g., Fairclough, *Race & Democracy*, and Frystak, *Our Minds on Freedom*.

41. Quote from Joe Street, "Reconstructing Education from the Bottom Up: SNCC's 1964 Mississippi Summer Project and African American Culture," *Journal of American Studies*, 38, no. 2 (August 2004): 274–75, who cites John Dittmer, *Local People: The Struggle for Civil Rights in Mississippi* (Urbana: University of Illinois Press, 1994), 242–314. See also Charles M. Payne, *I've Got the Light of Freedom: The Organizing Tradition and the Mississippi Freedom Struggle* (Berkeley: University of California Press, 1995), 300–311.

42. Matt Fleischer-Black, "Free Universities," in *American Countercultures: An Encyclopedia of Nonconformists, Alternative Lifestyles, and Radical Ideas in U.S. History*, ed. Gina Misiroglu, vol. 1 (Armonk, N.Y.: Sharpe Reference, 2009), 285–86.

43. Barrett personal communications. Jeannine and Matt Herron moved to Jackson, Mississippi, in 1963, with their two small children, to work in the civil rights movement. In 1964, they moved to New Orleans. http://www.takestockphotos.com/pages/herron .html, accessed January 30, 2014. Because of Ed King's activism, the president of Tougaloo was forced to resign, and King eventually lost his position there. In 1967, Jeannette and Ed King and their two daughters moved to New Orleans, where they spent two years. Bryan, *These Few Also Paid a Price*, 19–26.

44. Cathy Cade, "Caught in the Middle," in Holsaert et al., *Hands on the Freedom Plow*, 195–96; Echols, *Daring to be Bad*, 73; Brownmiller, *In Our Time*, 19.

45. Barrett, personal communications.

46. Ibid.; Peggy Dobbins, interview by the author, September 18, 2007; Cade interviews, August 8, 2007, September 6, 2007; Echols, *Daring to be Bad*, 94–96; Evans, *Personal Politics*, 208; Evans, *Tidal Wave*, 94. Carol Hanisch also joined NYRW.

47. The first two national women's liberation meetings held after the Waveland meeting both took place at religious encampments. In 1968, a group of radical women met at a Quaker camp in Sandy Springs, Maryland. About 150 radical women from all over the United States attended the next meeting, held at a YWCA retreat center outside Chicago (Lake Villa, Illinois), in 1969. Giardina, *Freedom for Women*, 141; CWLU Herstory Project, A History of the Chicago Women's Liberation Union, document posted on archive web page, http://www.cwluherstory.org/CWLUArchive/natconference.html, accessed September 5, 2007.

Chapter 4. "To Empower Women"

1. Jean S. Kiesel, *Images of America: Lafayette* (Charleston, S.C.: Arcadia, 2007), 7–8. The growth of the petrochemical industry in the 1970s is one reason for the rise of the Republican Party in a once-solidly Democratic state.

2. *Daily Advertiser*, April 29, 1973; Sarah Brabant, Judith Gentry, and Della Bonnette, interview by the author, June 2, 2015.

3. Nancy Levit and Robert R. M. Verchick, *Feminist Legal Theory* (New York: New York University Press, 2006), chap. 8, "Sex and Violence."

4. Davis, *Moving the Mountain*, 308–13.

5. Estelle B. Freedman, *Redefining Rape: Sexual Violence in the Era of Suffrage and Segregation* (Cambridge, Mass.: Harvard University Press, 2013), 2, 276–78.

6. Ibid., 6.

7. Hall, *Revolt against Chivalry*.

8. Danielle L. McGuire, *At the Dark End of the Street: Black Women, Rape, and Resistance—A New History of the Civil Rights Movement from Rosa Parks to the Rise of Black Power* (New York: Alfred A. Knopf, 2011).

9. Maria Bevacqua, *Rape on the Public Agenda: Feminism and the Politics of Sexual Assault* (Boston: Northeastern University Press, 2000), 50; Darlene Clark Hine, "Rape and the Inner Lives of Black Women in the Middle West: Preliminary Thoughts on the Culture of Dissemblance," *Signs: Journal of Women in Culture and Society* 14 (1989): 912–20.

10. White feminist writer and poet Ruth Herschberger explored the issue of rape and "laid much of the groundwork for the 1970s feminist conceptualization of rape as a problem rooted in male dominance" in her collection of essays published in 1948, says Maria Bevacqua, in *Rape on the Public Agenda*, 26. See Ruth Herschberger, *Adam's Rib* (New York: Pellegrini & Cudahy, 1948).

11. Freedman, *Redefining Rape*, 277–78; Brownmiller, *In Our Time*, 195–205; Bevacqua, *Rape on the Public Agenda*, 55.

12. Freedman, *Redefining Rape*, 278; Susan Brownmiller, *Against Our Will: Men, Women and Rape* (New York: Bantam Books, 1975), 244–58.

13. *Vieux Carré Courier*, October 25–31, 1973.

14. Ibid.

15. The HRC had been initiated by Mayor Victor Schiro in 1969. *New Orleans Times-Picayune*, August 15, 1977.

16. District Attorney's Office files, Sex Crimes Unit, box 2, City Archives, New Orleans Public Library.

17. *Vieux Carré Courier*, October 25–31, 1973.

18. Bevacqua, *Rape on the Public Agenda*, 47; testimony of "Madelyn," speak-out sponsored by Women against Violence against Women, held November 14, 1977, at the Salvation Army Citadel in New Orleans, Nikki Alexander Collection, Newcomb Archives, and in possession of the author.

19. "Madelyn's" rape had occurred in New Orleans in 1974.

20. *Vieux Carré Courier*, October 25–31, 1973.

21. Echols, *Daring to Be Bad*, 16.

22. Freedman, *Redefining Rape*, 278; Bevacqua, *Rape on the Public Agenda*, discusses the spread of rape crisis hotlines in the first two chapters and includes a timeline in the appendix. However, she makes no mention of antirape efforts in the South.

23. Bevacqua, *Rape on the Public Agenda*, 75–77; Mary Capps, curriculum vita and email correspondence, November 22, 2013; *New Orleans Times-Picayune*, August 9, 1974.

24. Mary Capps email correspondence, January 29–30, 2015. YWCAs all over the country almost simultaneously became loci for their areas' first antirape and antiviolence programs. See, for example, Jordan, *Violence against Women in Kentucky*, 40–41; Blair, *Revolutionizing Expectations*, 59; Pomerleau, *Califia Women*, 78.

25. Marguerite Redwine, "History of YWCA Rape Crisis," written October 8, 2013, Newcomb Archives; Marguerite Redwine interview by the author and email correspondence, October–November, 2013; Rape Task Force, 1975, National Council of Jewish Women, Greater New Orleans Section Records, 1894–1986, box 135, FF 3, Louisiana Research Manuscript Collection 667, Tulane University (hereinafter cited as NCJW records).

26. *Distaff*, September 1974.

27. Johnson, who later joined the Louisiana Supreme Court, served as an attorney in New Orleans and participated in the "Women and Work" session at Louisiana's International Women's Year conference in Baton Rouge, 1977. Ibid.; Osborne, *Issues and Answers*, 76.

28. *Louisiana Weekly*, August 3, 1974.

29. *Distaff*, September 1974.

30. "Foundations of Feminist Organizing: Radical Women's Movement," VHS (2 tapes) recorded by Roberts Batson, UNO panel discussion, 1997, Newcomb Archives. See also Mary Capps Collection, Newcomb Archives.

31. Mary Capps, interview by the author, September 26, 2007, and email correspondence; Mary Capps and Donna Myhre, draft, "Safe Space: A Strategy for Ending Violence against Women," Newcomb Archives, and in author's possession. Published in *Aegis* ca. 1983. Brooks had been raised in the Methodist Church and then joined the United Church of Christ as an adult. On Brooks, see Pomerleau, *Califia Women*, 35–37, 77–79. Brooks first developed the self-defense courses in 1973. Though she was not the first in that area to offer such courses, hers were the most far-reaching.

32. Bevacqua, *Rape on the Public Agenda*, 26; Celeste Newbrough announcement, NCJW records.

33. Celeste Newbrough, telephone interview by the author, September 9, 2008; *New Orleans Times-Picayune*, September 6, 1970. The paper reported that the New Orleans Chapter of NOW organized August 26, 1970, the fiftieth anniversary of female suffrage (now called Women's Equality Day). The elected officers were Celeste Newbrough, president; Gayle Gagliano, vice president; Pat Kearns, secretary; and Sheila Breaux, treasurer.

34. Nikki Alexander, email correspondence, January 15, 2015.

35. *Distaff*, September 1974 and December 1979; Nikki Alexander, interview with Donna Myhre, April 29, 1980, typescript, Donna Myhre papers, in author's possession.

36. Mary Capps interview, 2007; Latimer correspondence.

37. Janelle L. White, telephone interview by the author, June 3, 2015; "Survivors of African Descent," *Calcasa* (photocopy in author's possession); Janelle White, "Our Silence Will Not Protect Us: Black Women Confronting Sexual and Domestic Violence," (PhD diss., University of Michigan, 2005).

38. Mary Capps, email correspondence, January 26, 2015; *New Orleans Times-Picayune*, four-part series on rape, August 11–15, 1977, quoted Mary Capps, Nikki Hufford, Donna Myhre, and Betty Spencer.

39. Sarah Brabant and Margaret Ritchey, letter to the Mayor's Commission on the Needs of Women, May 12, 2015; Sarah Brabant, interview by the author, May 12, 2015.

40. *Lafayette Daily Advertiser*, June 9, 1978; Sarah Brabant, telephone interview by the author, May 5, 2015. Brabant biography on Veteran Feminists of America website, http://www.vfa.us/SARAH%20BRABANT.htm, accessed April 18, 2015.

41. Bevacqua, *Rape on the Public Agenda*, 83.

42. Brabant interview. The RCS was eventually taken over by the DA's office because it began to serve children who had been molested, not just adult women. It is now called Hearts of Hope.

43. *New Orleans Times-Picayune*, August 15, 1977.

44. "Foundations of Feminist Organizing."

45. NCJW records, box 135, FF 3.

46. Bevacqua, *Rape on the Public Agenda*, 96; Freedman, *Redefining Rape*, 279.

47. NCJW records, box 135, FF 3.

48. *New Orleans Times-Picayune*, July 5, 1975.

49. Freedman, *Redefining Rape*, 281.

50. Gail Collins, *When Everything Changed: The Amazing Journey of American Women from 1960 to the Present* (New York: Little, Brown, 2009), 322.

51. NCJW records, box 135, FF 3.

52. *Distaff*, June 1975; *Louisiana Weekly*, May 31, 1975; *Lafayette Daily Advertiser*, August 17, 1975; *New Orleans Times-Picayune*, September 16, 1975.

53. Quoted in Keane, "Second-Wave Feminism in the American South," 239.

54. Holley G. Haymaker, email correspondence, April 1, 2015.

55. Dorothy Mae Taylor (New Orleans) was elected in 1971 to fill the unexpired term of Dutch Morial. She served for five years and decided not to run for reelection. Virginia Shehee (Shreveport) was elected to the state senate in 1975 and served a single term (she stepped down in 1980).

56. Mary Landrieu, interview by the author, April 9, 2015. Lowenthal served two terms in the state house from 1980 to 1987. Lowenthal obituary, *Lake Charles American Press*, July 23, 2003. Bajoie won her first seat in the house in 1975, the second female to be elected from New Orleans in modern history (Landrieu was the third). After one term in the house, she served seventeen years in the Louisiana senate.

57. Diana Bajoie, interview by the author, New Orleans, September 9, 2009. See also *Louisiana Weekly*, December 20, 1975, and *Baton Rouge State-Times*, June 8, 1976.

58. Diana E. H. Russell, *Rape in Marriage*, expanded rev. ed. (Bloomington: Indiana University Press, 1990), 379, citing RSA § 14.41–43. Ayn Stehr, interview by the author, January 23, 2015.

59. Mary Capps and Donna Myhre, "Conferences We Have Known," *Feminist Alliance against Rape Newsletter*, May/June 1977.

60. Capps and Myhre, "Safe Space."

61. Bevacqua, *Rape on the Public Agenda*, 77–78; 199–200; Amy Fried, "'It's Hard to Change What We Want to Change': Rape Crisis Centers as Organizations," *Gender and Society* 8, no. 4 (December 1994): 567–69; Nancy A. Matthews, *Confronting Rape: The Feminist Anti-Rape Movement and the State* (New York: Routledge, 1994), xii, 12, 58–59, 160; Sandra Morgen, "The Dynamics of Cooptation in a Feminist Health Clinic," *Social Science and Medicine* 23, no. 2 (February 1986): 201–10; Judith Ezekiel, *Feminism in the Heartland* (Columbus: Ohio State University Press, 2002), 138–41; Keane, "Second-Wave Feminism in the American South," 197.

62. Flyer for Take Back the Night March, produced by Women against Violence against Women, announcing a community meeting, December 5, 1979, held at Kingsley House in New Orleans, Nikki Alexander Collection, Newcomb Archives. On the speak-out, see *Louisiana Weekly*, November 19, 1977. Others who assisted or participated in these actions were Virginia Peyton, Judith Stevenson, Andrea Canaan, Diana Panara, Lucy Gallese, and Eddy Marshman. Mary Capps, email, November 2013.

63. Freedman, *Redefining Rape*, 279; Bevacqua, *Rape on the Public Agenda*, 71–72; *Louisiana Weekly*, January 26, 1980; Yolanda Perrilloux, interview by the author, June 2, 2015.

64. Judith Cormier, interview by the author, May 7, 2014, Newcomb Archives.

65. *Louisiana Weekly*, February 2, 1980; *New Orleans Times-Picayune*, January 26, 1980.

66. *Louisiana Weekly*, February 2, 1980.

67. Judith Cormier, interview, May 7, 2014, Newcomb Archives.

68. LAFASA website, http://www.lafasa.org/, accessed December 6, 2013.

69. Testimony of "Laura," speak-out sponsored by Women against Violence against Women, 1977, Nikki Alexander Collection, Newcomb Archives.

70. Pharr, *Homophobia*, 14.

71. Elizabeth Pleck, *Domestic Tyranny: The Making of American Social Policy against Family Violence from Colonial Times to the Present* (New York: Oxford University Press, 1987), 183, 188; Kathleen J. Tierney, "The Battered Women Movement and the Creation of the Wife Beating Problem," *Social Problems* 29, no. 3 (February 1982): 207.

72. Pizzey's confrontational nature led to several fissures in the movement in Great Britain. A power struggle, which Pizzey lost, erupted over leadership and control of the money. Embittered, she publicly attacked her opponents and wrote an extremely controversial piece (and later a book) that claimed that domestic violence was reciprocal, that women and men were equally responsible, and that some women were "violence prone," meaning they sought out abusive relationships. Lois Yankowski, "Pizzey Stirs Controversy," *Feminist Alliance against Rape* (May/June 1977), 26–27; Pizzey and Jeff Shapiro, *Prone to Violence* (Feltham, England: Hamlyn, 1982). Pizzey has said that she "loathed feminism," at least in Great Britain, and believed it would destroy the family, http://www.erinpizzey.com/index.html, accessed November 18, 2013.

73. Pleck, *Domestic Tyranny*, 187–89; Evans, *Tidal Wave*, 49; Del Martin, *Battered Wives* (New York: Pocket Books, 1976); Ann Jones, "Battered Women," in *The Reader's Companion to U.S. Women's History*, ed. Wilma Mankiller et al. (Boston: Houghton Mifflin, 1998), 608–9.

74. Latimer interviews.

75. Redwine interview, 2013; *New Orleans Times-Picayune*, November 9, 1977.

76. Jan Logan to Rep. John Breaux, June 14, 1978, box 2026, Collection 1000, Louisiana Research Collection, Tulane University, New Orleans (hereinafter cited as Boggs papers); Rosary Nix Hartel, letter to the editor, *New Orleans Clarion Herald*, November 23, 1978; *New Orleans Times-Picayune*, April 30, 1987.

77. Lindy Boggs, speech on domestic violence, April 15, 1978, Boggs papers.

78. Osborne, *Issues and Answers*, 66–67.

79. Ibid.

80. The one-thousand-dollar grant sponsored a panel in November 1977. Latimer interviews; Osborne, "Issues and Answers," 66–67, 89.

81. Tierney, "Battered Women Movement," 207–8; *Clarion Herald*, August 11 1977.

82. *New Orleans Clarion Herald*, June 22, 1978.

83. Thomas Ferrell and Judith Haydel, "Hale and Lindy Boggs: Louisiana's National Democrats," *Louisiana History: The Journal of the Louisiana Historical Association* 25, no. 4 (1994): 399; Boggs papers.

84. Newspaper clipping, Boggs papers.

85. Lindy Boggs to James W. Sanderson, November 16, 1979, Boggs papers; Cheryl Q. W. Cramer, Chairperson, Social Action Committee, Central Congregational United Church of Christ, Letter, Boggs papers; *New Orleans Times-Picayune*, November 9, 1977.

86. Capps and Myhre, "Safe Space."

87. Pharr, *Homophobia*, 14–19.

88. Pleck, *Domestic Tyranny*, 194.

89. Ayn Stehr and Kim Gandy interviews and correspondence.

90. *New Orleans Times-Picayune*, November 2, 1980.

91. Pleck, *Domestic Tyranny*, 196–97; *New Orleans Times-Picayune*, November 9, 1977; January 29, 1978; September 22, 1978; Corinne "Cokie" Roberts, email correspondence, February 12, 2015; box 2023, Boggs papers.

92. *New Orleans Times-Picayune*, January 29, 1978; September 22, 1978; Ferrell and Haydel, "Hale and Lindy Boggs," 399; Mary Claire Landry, interview by the author, December 9, 2014. Landry is the director of the Family Justice Center, which replaced Crescent House after it was destroyed in Hurricane Katrina. I'm grateful to Landry for giving me access to the oral history published in the *Domestic Violence Handbook*, 2010, in the Family Justice Center. In this oral history, recorded in 2009, Songy said that after being approached by Boggs, she went to see Archbishop Hannan, who offered her the building and helped her get an audience with Governor Edwards, and within a short time, she and a few assistants had secured a $250,000 grant to act as a catalyst for the new program. This conflicts somewhat with reports in the newspapers at the time and with Pat Evans's account of how Crescent House began. What funding materialized when is unclear from the extant record.

93. Boggs papers; *New Orleans Times-Picayune*, January 29, 1978; September 22, 1978.

94. *Louisiana Weekly*, March 18, 1978; *Baton Rouge Morning Advocate*, April 7, 1978. According to the *Morning Advocate*, the report showed that about one thousand women reported battery to the police in Baton Rouge alone. The actual number of incidents was probably far higher, since most women did not report such attacks.

95. Archdiocese of New Orleans, letter dated September 19, 1979, FF Domestic Violence, box 2028, Boggs papers; *New Orleans Times-Picayune*, November 18, 1979; March 27, 1981; Pat Evans speech given at Newcomb College Symposium, March 24, 2001, handwritten copy in author's possession; videotape of speech, "Voices from the Louisiana Women's Movement: First-Hand Accounts from People Who Made It Happen," Newcomb Archives. The $110,000 grant came from the Louisiana State Department of Health and Human Resources. Governor Edwards was raised Roman Catholic, but at one point in his life he converted to Pentecostalism. He later returned to Catholicism, but he was never a particularly dutiful churchgoer.

96. Jace Schinderman, telephone interview by the author, December 17, 2013. Schinderman returned to Tulane while employed at Crescent House and earned an MBA. She then worked at Tulane and subsequently at other universities, including Columbia University, always with community services. Like many other feminists, she connected her avocation and her vocational life. She married at age fifty-six, retired from Columbia, and began a consulting business working for a nonprofit to eradicate child poverty.

97. Songy oral history.

98. *New Orleans Times-Picayune*, January 20, 1980; La. R.S. 46:2126; Ayn Stehr, email correspondence, March 19, 2015.

99. LSA-R.S. 46:2122; Schinderman, telephone interview; Ann Polak, former director of the Calcasieu Women's Shelter, interviews and email correspondence, January–February, 2013, February 8, 2015; Sami Riley, executive director, Chez Hope Family Crisis Center, interview, January 25, 2013. In 2013, there were eighteen shelters in the state of Louisiana.

100. Ayn Stehr, biography, copy in author's possession; Ayn Stehr interviews by author, January 18, 2014; February 10, 2015; and June 1, 2015. Edith L. Batz, director, Battered Women's Program, Baton Rouge, La., to Lindy Boggs, September 14, 1979; and reply from Lindy Boggs, October 12, 1979, Boggs papers; memo for files, March 7, 1980, Boggs papers.

101. Chennault leased the land from St. Patrick's Hospital. Ann Polak interviews.

102. "History of the Calcasieu Women's Shelter" and other materials, Oasis, A Safe Haven for Survivors of Domestic and Sexual Violence (formerly Calcasieu Women's Shelter); Mrs. J. C. (Lloyd Gaudet) Barras, obituary, *Lake Charles American Press*, September 11, 1994. Other members of the founding board were Mary Kordisch, Elsie Whitman, Betty Runte (another LWV member who attended the IWY convention), Russell Bello, and Shirley Riff (a member of Temple Sinai).

103. Ann Polak, interviews, February 18, 2–15; March 12, 2015.

104. Ibid.; "History of the Calcasieu Women's Shelter." Polak and the board raised the money entirely from donors. No government funds or grants were used to build the new shelter.

105. White, "Survivors of African Descent."

106. Barbara Cahee, interview by the author, August 13, 2015.

107. Stehr became director of the Capital Area Family Violence Intervention Center (now the Iris Domestic Violence Center) in 1982. Stehr biography and interviews.

108. In 1977, Oregon became the first state to enact mandatory arrest legislation for domestic violence. Maurice Durbin Collection, 2007-40, n.d., Newcomb Archives.

109. Leigh Goodmark, *A Troubled Marriage: Domestic Violence and the Legal System* (New York: New York University Press, 2012), 16.

110. In a letter to the editor of the *New Orleans Times-Picayune*, March 23, 1982, Michael Groetsch, director of probation, decried the unnamed state representative's comments.

111. *New Orleans Times-Picayune*, April 26, 1984.

112. Connie Willems, interview by A. Van Heel, March 30, 1985, Friends of the Cabildo Oral History Program, copy in New Orleans Public Library and Newcomb Archives. Willems was born in Utrecht, Holland, in 1942, and graduated with a JD from Tulane University in 1977.

113. Pleck, *Domestic Tyranny*, 198; Jan Schoonmaker, Lindy Boggs's former staffer, email correspondence, February 23, 2015.

114. Fred Strebeigh, *Equal: Women Reshape American Law* (New York: W. W. Norton, 2009), 351.

115. Congress reauthorized VAWA in 2013. See Freedman, *Redefining Rape*, 286–88. Besides VAWA and the Family Violence Prevention and Services Act, shelters in Louisiana receive funding from the United Way, the Louisiana Commission on Law Enforcement, Louisiana Bar Foundation community service funds, the Department of Housing and Urban Development (a federal agency), the state general fund, and Temporary Assistance to Needy Families.

116. Goodmark, *Troubled Marriage*, 83.

117. Ayn Stehr, telephone interview by the author, June 1, 2015.

118. Ibid.

119. Protection from Dating Violence Act, 2001.

120. In 1998, Stehr developed the Legal Services Component at the Baton Rouge program and served as its director until March 2012, after which she began training law students, lawyers, and judges on domestic, dating, and family violence. Stehr interviews.

121. Ibid.

122. Ann Polak and Ayn Stehr interviews; Ayn Stehr biography.

123. Kimberlé Williams Crenshaw, "Mapping the Margins: Intersectionality, Identity Politics, and Violence against Women of Color," *Stanford Law Review* 43, no. 6 (1991): 1241–99; Natalie J. Sokoloff and Ida Dupont, chap. 1, in *Domestic Violence at the Margins: Readings on Race, Class, Gender, and Culture*, ed. Natalie J. Sokoloff with Christina Pratt (New Brunswick, N.J.: Rutgers University Press, 2005), 2–3; Beth E. Richie, "A Black Feminist Reflection on the Antiviolence Movement," in Sokoloff with Pratt, *Domestic Violence at the Margins*, 50–55.

124. Yolanda Perrilloux, telephone interview by the author, June 2, 2015.

125. Ibid.; Cahee interview.

126. Barbara Parmer Davidson and Pamela J. Jenkins, "Class Diversity in Shelter Life," *Social Work* (November 1989): 491–94; Ann Polak interviews; *History of the Louisiana Coalition against Domestic Violence: A Timeline*, received from Sheila Cole, LCADV project coordinator, March 15, 2013.

127. Jordan, *Violence against Women in Kentucky*, 3.

128. Pleck, *Domestic Tyranny*, 199; Ann Polak interviews; *New Orleans Times-Picayune*, November 2, 1980. Among the female attorneys who were pioneers in the anti–domestic violence movement in Louisiana was Debra Henson, who had once been a counselor at the New Orleans YWCA program.

Chapter 5. "Murder or Mercy?"

1. Dr. Sidney Knight, quoted in the same article, said he knew of several doctors who did abortions "in their offices or in apartments" for anywhere from three hundred to five hundred dollars. The *New Orleans States-Item*, January 18, 1971; Leslie J. Reagan, *When Abortion Was a Crime: Women, Medicine, and Law in the United States, 1867–1973* (Berkeley: University of California Press, 1997).

2. *New Orleans States-Item*, January 11, 1971; *Vieux Carré Courier*, April 7–13, 1972.

3. *New Orleans Times-Picayune*, October 29, 1995, contains the obituary of Albert Destrehan Harvey. Albert Harvey, Rose Mary Harvey Charbonnet, and Horace H. Harvey Jr. (father of H. Hale Harvey III) were children of Capt. Horace Hale Harvey, "whose family owned Destrehan Plantation House and engineered the construction of the Harvey Canal and the Harvey Locks." H. Hale Harvey III was born in 1931.

4. Horace Hale Harvey III, "Decision Theory in the Good Life: Mathematical, Logical, Ethical and Other Tools and Techniques as Aids for Making Ethical-Moral Decisions" (PhD diss., Tulane University; submitted, 1969; copyright, 1970), available via ProQuest and microfilm.

5. Howard Moody and Arlene Carmen, *Abortion Counseling and Social Change* (Valley Forge, Pa: Judson Press, 1973), 73; Bernard N. Nathanson, MD with Richard N. Ostling, *Aborting America* (Garden City, N.Y.: Doubleday, 1979); Cynthia Gorney, *Articles of Faith: A Frontline History of the Abortion Wars* (New York: Simon & Schuster, 1998), 34. The phrase "moral pioneers" was first used by Rayna Rapp in *Testing Women, Testing the Fetus: The Social Impact of Amniocentesis in America* (New York: Routledge, 1999) and applied to physicians by Leslie J. Reagan in *Dangerous Pregnancies: Mothers, Disabilities, and Abortion in America* (Berkeley: University of California Press, 2010), 5.

6. The *New Orleans States-Item* series started on January 11 and ran through January 19, 1971.

7. This and the information in the paragraphs that follows is taken from histories of abortion in the United States. In addition to Reagan, *When Abortion Was a Crime*, see James Mohr, *Abortion in America: The Origins and Evolution of National Policy, 1800–1900* (Oxford: Oxford University Press, 1978); Janet Farrell Brodie, *Contraception and Abortion in Nineteenth-Century America* (Ithaca, N.Y.: Cornell University Press, 1994); Andrea Tone, ed., *Controlling Reproduction: An American History* (Wilmington, Del.: Scholarly Resources, 1997); David J. Garrow, *Liberty and Sexuality: The Right to Privacy and the Mak-*

ing of Roe v. Wade (New York: Macmillan, 1994); Linda Greenhouse and Reva B. Siegel, *Before Roe v. Wade: Voices That Shaped the Abortion Debate before the Supreme Court's Ruling* (New York: Kaplan, 2010).

8. Innocent or even therapeutic work became suspect as a result of these laws, and doctors ceased researching or publishing information about reproductive health because medical journals went through the U.S. mail. Should Anthony Comstock determine that the article was "obscene," the doctor/authors faced criminal penalties. Not wanting to risk their license or professional careers, physicians erred on the side of caution. As a result, as late as the 1930s, medical professionals still were unclear about how a woman's reproductive cycle worked. In addition to sources already cited, see Nanette J. Davis, *From Crime to Choice: The Transformation of Abortion in America* (Westport, Conn: Greenwood Press, 1985), chap. 5.

9. Reagan, *When Abortion Was a Crime;* Gorney, *Articles of Faith,* 34.

10. Numerous reports of arrests and prosecutions for criminal abortion appear in Louisiana newspapers. See, for example, *New Orleans Times-Picayune*, March 18, 1964, which reported that three "Negroes" and one white man, probably the boyfriend of the victim, were arrested for criminal abortion after the woman died. The abortionist, Mrs. Frances Welch ("Negro"), according to the newspaper, had been arrested many times but had never been convicted.

11. *New Orleans Times-Picayune*, August 9, 1946.

12. *New Orleans States-Item,* January 11, 1971; Dixie (insert in *New Orleans Times-Picayune*), September 4, 1972, 12; John Montjoy, "Abortion and the Law: A Proposal for Reform in Louisiana," *Tulane Law Review* 43 (1969): 847–49.

13. Davis, *From Crime to Choice*, 89; quote is from Grace Lauer Warolin, interview by Corinne Barnwell, February 22, 2003, Newcomb Archives. For views of pre-Roe abortions as relatively safe, see Rickie Solinger, *Beggars and Choosers: How the Politics of Choice Shapes Adoption, Abortion, and Welfare in the United States* (New York: Hill & Wang, 2001), 51–52, 57; Carole Joffe, *Doctors of Conscience: The Struggle to Provide Abortion before and after "Roe v. Wade"* (Boston: Beacon Press, 1995); and Reagan, *When Abortion Was a Crime*, chap. 5. My survey of the *New Orleans Times-Picayune* and the *Lake Charles American Press* since 1945 revealed that among those arrested for criminal abortion were midwives, pharmacists, and a lab technician at Touro Infirmary in New Orleans.

14. Conversations with women in New Orleans who wish to remain anonymous; Dr. Mary Frances Gardner, interview by the author, April 7, 2015. Gardner, like all who got their medical degrees from the LSU medical school in New Orleans, trained at Charity. This phenomenon has been corroborated in many other cities by others, e.g., Davis, *From Crime to Choice*, 90–96.

15. *New Orleans States-Item,* January 12, 1971.

16. Montjoy, "Abortion and the Law," 836.

17. Martha C. Ward, *Poor Women, Powerful Men: America's Great Experiment in Family Planning* (Boulder, Colo.: Westview Press, 1986), 15. Ward cites a study by Carl L. Harter and Joseph D. Beasley, "A Survey concerning Induced Abortions in New Orleans," *American Journal of Public Health* 57 (11): 1847–48.

18. Gabriela Noa Betancourt, "Uncovering the Story of June Emily Wall," *Newcomb College Institute Research on Women, Gender, & Feminism* 1, no. 2 (2014), available on-line at https://library.tulane.edu/journals/index.php/NAJ/index.

19. *New Orleans Times Picayune*, October 27, 1955.

20. See, for example, *New Orleans Times-Picayune*, May 26, 1951; *Lake Charles American Press*, July 3, 1964, and those sources noted earlier.

21. *New Orleans States-Item* January 11, 1971.

22. Ibid.

23. Moody and Carmen, *Abortion Counseling and Social Change*, 14.

24. Gorney, *Articles of Faith*, 170; Garrow, *Liberty and Sexuality*, 275–77; Davis, *From Crime to Choice*, 4–5. By the early twenty-first century, abortion was eleven times safer than childbirth.

25. Tom Davis, *Sacred Work: Planned Parenthood and Its Clergy Alliances* (New Brunswick, N.J.: Rutgers University Press, 2006), 135–41.

26. Greenhouse and Siegel, *Before Roe v. Wade*, 24. The twelve states that adopted reforms were California, Colorado, Delaware, Georgia, Kansas, Maryland, Mississippi, New Mexico, North Carolina, South Carolina, and Virginia. On the ALI, see Garrow, *Liberty and Sexuality*, 277.

27. Greenhouse and Siegel, *Before Roe v. Wade*, 31; Rickie Solinger, "Abortion," 3–7; Carol Downer, "Abortion Self-Help Movement," 7, and Julie Burton, "Pro-Choice and Antiabortion Movements," 474–78, both in Mankiller et al., *Reader's Companion to U.S. Women's History*.

28. Montjoy, "Abortion and the Law," 888–89.

29. N. E. H. Hull and Peter Charles Hoffer, *Roe v. Wade: The Abortion Rights Controversy in American History* (Lawrence: University Press of Kansas, 2001), 100; Gorney, *Articles of Faith*, 51,

30. Reagan, *Dangerous Pregnancies*.

31. Greenhouse and Siegel, *Before Roe v. Wade*, 207–10.

32. Jennifer Nelson, *Women of Color and the Reproductive Rights Movement* (New York: New York University Press, 2003); Reagan, *When Abortion Was a Crime*, 234; Loretta J. Ross, "African American Women and Abortion," in Rickie Solinger, *Abortion Wars* (Berkeley: University of California Press), 161–207.

33. Greenhouse and Siegel, *Before Roe v. Wade*, 207.

34. Quote is reprinted in Ross, "African American Women and Abortion," 183.

35. Nelson, *Women of Color*, 69–70.

36. Susan Jane Allen, interview by the author, February 13, 2014, and email correspondence, April 15–16, 2014.

37. Melissa Flournoy, Louisiana state director, Planned Parenthood, personal communication, March 2015. Sister Song website, http://www.sistersong.net/.

38. *Tuscaloosa (AL) News*, January 1, 1978; Ward, *Poor Women, Powerful Men*, 136.

39. Ward, *Poor Women, Powerful Men*, 28–29, 142; *Shreveport Times*, October 22, 1972.

40. Ward, *Poor Women, Powerful Men*, 28–29, 142.

41. Ibid.

42. Ibid., 21, 95–96.

43. Ward, *Ibid.*, 136.

44. Margarete Sandelowski, review of *Reproduction, Medicine and the Socialist State*, by Alena Heitlinger; *The Regulation of Sexuality: Experiences of Family Planning Workers*, by Carol Joffe. *Poor Women, Powerful Men: America's Great Experiment in Family Planning*, by Martha Ward, in *Signs* 13, no. 4 (Summer 1988): 853.

45. http://www.vitals.com/doctors/Dr_Joseph_Beasley.html, accessed February 16, 2015.

46. Susan Jane Allen, email correspondence, April 17, 2014.

47. Paul R. Ehrlich, *The Population Bomb* (New York: Ballantine Books, 1968); NPR story, http://www.npr.org/blogs/money/2013/12/31/258687278/a-bet-five-metals-and -the-future-of-the-planet, accessed April 15, 2014.

48. Sometimes called "the Rockefeller Commission," the report is available online at http://www.population-security.org/rockefeller/001_population_growth_and_the _american_future.htm, accessed September 25, 2015.

49. The *New Orleans Times-Picayune* carried announcements of the Louisiana ZPG chapter's meetings. See, for example, July 24, 1970, and September 6, 1970. Letter to the editor published March 22, 1971.

50. Montjoy, "Abortion and the Law," 850–53.

51. *Dixie*, September 24, 1972.

52. Laura Kaplan, *The Story of Jane: The Legendary Underground Feminist Abortion Service* (Chicago: University of Chicago Press, 1995); Gorney, *Articles of Faith*, 210–14; Suzanne O'Dea Schenken, *From Suffrage to the Senate: An Encyclopedia of American Women in Politics* (Santa Barbara, Calif.: ABC-CLIO, 1999), 5.

53. Rosen, *World Split Open*, 158; *Ms.*, Spring 1972, preview issue, 34–35. The French-women's statement had been published in *Le Nouvel Observateur* on April 5, 1971. Simone de Beauvoir was among the most famous signers, but what she did not reveal at the time is that she had never had an abortion. She simply wanted to protest the law. Bair, *Simone de Beauvoir*, 547.

54. *New Orleans States-Item*, January 11, 1971.

55. NOW Bill of Rights, reprinted in Greenhouse and Siegel, *Before Roe v. Wade*, 38.

56. Garrow, *Liberty and Sexuality*, 349–50.

57. Gorney, *Articles of Faith*, 83; Lawrence Lader, "The Scandal of Abortion Laws," *New York Times Magazine*, April 25, 1965.

58. Greenhouse and Siegel, *Before Roe v. Wade*, 38.

59. In 1965, the United States Supreme Court struck down all remaining state anti-contraceptive laws in *Griswold v. Connecticut*, when it ruled that banning the use of con-traceptives violated the constitutional right to privacy.

60. Greenhouse and Siegel, *Before Roe v. Wade*, 69–79.

61. Ibid., 207–10.

62. *New Orleans States-Item*, January 14, 1971.

63. Davis, *Sacred Work*, Chapter 7; Greenhouse and Siegel, *Before Roe v. Wade*, 69-79.

64. Moody was influenced by Lawrence Lader, who lived a few subway stops away from Moody's church and who had called for a clergy consultation service on abortion in the first of his three books on this subject, *Abortion* (Indianapolis: Bobbs-Merrill, 1966).

Lader's second book, *Abortion II: Making the Revolution* (Boston: Beacon Press, 1973), is his account of the growth of the abortion rights movement and the founding of the Clergy Consultation Service.

65. Anna Lou Pickett and Rev. Howard Moody, interviews, "Judson Memorial Church and the Reproductive Rights Movement," accessed April 8, 2014: http://voicesofjudson .blogspot.com/2008_12_01_archive.html; Davis, *Sacred Work*, 5, 128; David P. Cline, *Creating Choice: A Community Responds to the Need for Abortion and Birth Control, 1961–1973* (New York: Palgrave Macmillan, 2006), part 3; Joshua D. Wolff, "Ministers of a Higher Law: The Story of the Clergy Consultation Service on Abortion," (honors thesis, Amherst College, 1998), 162.

66. Wolff, "Ministers of a Higher Law," 144, 160.

67. Davis, *Sacred Work*, 127–37; Gorney, *Articles of Faith*, chap. 3; Cline, *Creating Choice*, covers the CCS in Western Massachusetts in part 3.

68. Weddington, *Question of Choice*, 33.

69. Howard Moody, Judson Memorial Church blogspot, http://voicesofjudson .blogspot.com/2008/12/reverend-howard-moody.html.

70. National Council of Jewish Women, Greater New Orleans Section Records, 1894–1986, Collection 667, Louisiana Research Collection, Tulane University, New Orleans (hereinafter cited as NCJW records). The following is a roster of the participating clergy in Louisiana:

New Orleans
Rev. Roy B. Nash, Methodist Campus Minister, Tulane
Rev. Robert Dodwell, St. Anna's Episcopal, Esplanade
Rev. James Jones, Community Unitarian
Rev. Jerry Fuller, Elysian Fields Methodist
Rev. Carole Cotton, Aurora Methodist
Rev. Albert D'Orlando, First Unitarian
Rev. William London, Metropolitan Ministries of NO
Rev. George Duerson, Kenner United Methodist
Rev. Don Rogers, Baptist Campus Minister, UNO
Rev. Milton Gutierrez, St. Matthews United Methodist, Metairie
Rev. John Schaeffer, Touro Infirmary
Rev. Russell Pregean, Rayne Memorial United Methodist, St. Charles Ave.
Rabbi Hillel A. Fine, Campus Rabbi, Tulane
Rabbi Murray Blackman, Temple Sinai
Rabbi Victor Hoffman, Conservative Synagogue
Rev. John Winn Jr., Gentilly United Methodist
Rev. Dalton R. Burch, Westside Christian
Rev. Pelham Mills, St. Paul's Episcopal, Canal Blvd., New Orleans
Rev. James O. Evans, St. Bernard's United Methodist, Chalmette
Baton Rouge
Rev. Wallace Blackwood, Francis Asbury United Methodist
Rev. Keith A. Mills, Trinity Episcopal
Rev. William D. Peoples, St. John's United Methodist

Rev. William M. Finnin, United Campus Ministry, LSU
Alexandria
Rev. Noland Pipes, St. James Episcopal
Rev. James Adams, Episcopal Church
Hammond
Rev. Brady Forman, Wesley Foundation
Rev. Richard Massey, First Presbyterian
Lake Charles
Rev. Joe Doss, Church of the Good Shepherd
Lafayette
Rev. Robert Luckett, Church of the Ascension
Monroe
Rev. David Carter, First Christian
Rev. Ted E. Edwards, Messiah Lutheran
Shreveport
Rev. James M. Poole, St. Luke's United Methodist

71. Wolff, "Ministers of a Higher Law," 161.

72. Rogers, *Righteous Lives*, 157–59; Corinne Barnwell, email correspondence, February 18, 2015; First Unitarian Universalist Church website, http://firstuuno.org/j15/index.php?option=com_content&view=article&id=26&Itemid=36, accessed September 10, 2013.

73. *Vieux Carré Courier*, April 7–13, 1972.

74. *New Orleans States-Item*, July 11, 1971.

75. Richard Brown, president, and Victor L. Hoffman, rabbi, February 18, 1972, letter asking for money to support the service, addressed to NCJW president. Attached to the letter is the Louisiana Clergy Consultation Service Statement of Intention. NCJW records.

76. *New Orleans States-Item*, January 14, 1971.

77. Louisiana Clergy Consultation Service Statement of Intention.

78. Brown and Hoffman letter, February 18, 1972.

79. NCJW records.

80. *New Orleans States-Item*, January 19, 1971.

81. Joffe, *Doctors of Conscience*; Reagan, *When Abortion Was a Crime*, 158–59.

82. Schenken, *From Suffrage to the Senate*, 5; NCJW records.

83. *Vieux Carré Courier*, April 7–13, 1972.

84. Gorney, *Articles of Faith*, 197–99.

85. Gardner interview. Claiborne Towers housed many LSU medical students and Tulane students. Located on the corner of Canal and Claiborne Streets, it was torn down to make way for the new medical complex currently under construction in New Orleans.

86. Moody and Carmen, *Abortion Counseling and Social Change*, 72–73; Davis, *Sacred Work*, 134.

87. Wolff, "Ministers of a Higher Law," 110; Moody and Carmen, *Abortion Counseling and Social Change*, 73.

88. Sandy Stimpson, interview by the author, March 24, 2014. Stimpson, now a union organizer living in Atlanta, sang Harvey's praises. Phyllis Parun, who worked for Harvey

as a counselor, seconded the opinion. Parun, interview by the author, March 20, 2014; Wolff, "Ministers of a Higher Law," 189.

89. Bernard Nathanson, who worked with Harvey at the New York clinic, later became a high-profile critic of abortion, famous for his 1984 video *The Silent Scream*, but even he praised Harvey as an empathetic physician who truly cared about the welfare of his patients. Nathanson, *Aborting America*, 94–95.

90. Pyle website, http://www.barbarapyle.com/profile/summary/, and http://barbarapylefoundation.org/ accessed September 16, 2013. Barbara Pyle Collection, Newcomb Archives; Nathanson, *Aborting America*, 96; Wolff, "Ministers of a Higher Law," 108.

91. Barbara Pyle, quoted in Wolff, "Ministers of a Higher Law," 190.

92. Nathanson, *Aborting America*, 120; Wolff, "Ministers of a Higher Law," 201–9; Parun interview. Born in 1931, Harvey still lives on the Isle of Wight. Before his mother died, he occasionally traveled to the United States to visit her in Covington, Louisiana, but has not returned since about 2007. Gardner interview.

93. Pyle Collection, Newcomb Archives.

94. Gorney, *Articles of Faith*, chap. 5.

95. Hull and Hoffer, *Roe v. Wade*, 130–33. The ruling was issued on August 7, 1970.

96. Ann Richards had been active in Texas Democratic politics since 1950. When Sarah Weddington ran for a seat in the Texas legislature in 1972, Richards helped run her campaign and, after Weddington won, served as her legislative staff director. Ann's daughter Cecile Richards currently serves as head of the Planned Parenthood Federation of America. *Our Bodies, Ourselves* first appeared in mimeographed form in 1970. For the case fought by David Richards on behalf of the *Rag*, see *New Left Education Project v. The Board of Trustees of the University of Texas*.

97. Weddington, *Question of Choice*, 25–30.

98. Ibid., 26.

99. Ibid., 45–47.

100. McArthur and Smith, *Texas through Women's Eyes*, 212.

101. Megan Shockley, in *Changing History*, discusses lawsuits launched by Virginia women in the post-1945 era. Kierner, Loux, and Shockley, *Changing History*, final chapter.

102. Greenhouse and Siegel, *Before Roe v. Wade*, 209–10, 226–28.

103. Leslie J. Reagan, review of *Doctors of Conscience*, *Bulletin of the History of Medicine* 71 (Fall 1997): 559–60. Causeway Clinic is not to be confused with Causeway Medical Suite, which had a different provider who was not well respected in the abortion services community.

104. Allen, interview and email correspondence. Allen reports that the owners were L. T. Brinkley and Mel Sol.

105. *New Orleans States-Item*, May 20, 1974; March 8, 1980.

106. *New Orleans Times Picayune*, May 3, 1973; August 14–15, 1974; *New Orleans States-Item*, May 20, 1974; March 8, 1980; Allen interview; Brown, *Standing Against Dragons*, 23.

107. *New Orleans Times Picayune*, May 11, 1973; *Louisiana Weekly*, March 24, 1973; June 7, 1975; *New Orleans States-Item*, May 20, 1974.

108. Rape crisis training handbook, NCJW records.

109. Corinne Barnwell and Martha Ward interviews; Planned Parenthood records in Newcomb Archives. Laura's husband, John Williams, was the architect of the Planned Parenthood clinic on Claiborne Avenue. Construction stopped several times because of threats to the clinic and to authorities involved with allowing it to move forward. Williams lost millions of dollars in business, and the couple received death threats.

110. Darlene Olivo, correspondence, April 14, 2015; Susan Jane Allen, correspondence, April 15, 2015.

111. http://rhrealitycheck.org/article/2014/02/18/louisiana-abortion-providers-allege -harassment-intimidation-health-officials/ accessed May 22, 2014.

112. Email correspondence, Choice Louisiana, May 21, 2014; Rh Reality Check (Reproductive & Sexual Health and Justice News, Analysis & Commentary), http://rhrealitycheck .org/article/2014/05/21/louisiana-legislature-sends-omnibus-anti-abortion-bill-gov -jindal-reproductive-rights-advocates-call-boycott/, accessed May 22, 2014.

113. In January 2016, federal district judge John deGravelles struck down as unconstitutional the requirement that doctors who provide abortions must have admission privileges at hospitals within thirty miles. The Louisiana Attorney General announced that he will appeal the ruling. *Lake Charles American Press*, January 27, 2016.

Chapter 6. "Cherchez Les Femmes?"

1. Vaughan Baker, interviews by the author, November 20, 2013; February 28, 2015.

2. Boxer, "For and About Women," 665; Mary Ann Wilson, interview by the author, May 12, 2015.

3. Marilyn Jacoby Boxer, *When Women Ask the Questions: Creating Women's Studies in America* (Baltimore: Johns Hopkins University Press, 1998), 2.

4. Wilson interview.

5. Judith Gentry, Sarah Brabant, and Della Bonnette, interview by the author, June 2, 2015; *Lafayette Advertiser*, June 29, 1976; October 5, 1977.

6. Baker interviews. To accompany the exhibit Baker wrote *Becoming Woman: A Sequence of Louisiana Portraits* (Louisiana Endowment for the Humanities, 1978). Baker's other publications include *Louisiana Tapestry: Ethnicity in St. Landry Parish*, ed. with Jean T. Kreamer, published with a grant from the U.S. Department of Education, 1983; and *Women in Louisiana History: Sources and Resources*, Louisiana Library Association Special Publication no. 2 (1981).

7. LSU professor E. A. Davis had been editing and managing the journal. When he retired from the faculty, he offered the editorial position to Glenn Conrad, a native of New Iberia, Louisiana. Vaughan Baker, "Glenn Conrad: Mentor, Friend," *Louisiana History* 47, no. 1 (Winter 2006): 27–37.

8. Baker interview. Baker was one of several Newcomb alums on the faculty at ULL. The university library is named for another one, Opelousas native Edith Garland Dupré (NC '09). "After graduating from Newcomb College in New Orleans, she joined the faculty at the Southwestern Louisiana Industrial Institute before the opening of its first session. She remained at SLII (later SLI) for her entire professional career, retiring in 1944.

Miss Dupré is best known as an English professor, but she also served in many other capacities including registrar and librarian. She was also chair of the library committee for many years. After retirement she managed the Sans Souci Bookstore in Lafayette. . . . Family, church, and the education of youth were very important to her." Dupré's papers are deposited in the archives at the library that bears her name. Bio: http://library .louisiana.edu/Spec/COL/043.shtml#D, accessed December 1, 2013.

9. Baker's course was Women in Western Society; Gentry's was History of Women in the United States. Gentry and others on the board of SAWH encouraged members to begin offering women's history courses at their respective universities. Judith Gentry, interview by the author, December 2, 2013.

10. Baker does not remember the year of the OAH conference. Scott's first book was *The Southern Lady: From Pedestal to Politics, 1830–1930* (Chicago: University of Chicago Press, 1970). Lerner published two in 1971, *The Grimke Sisters from South Carolina: Pioneers for Women's Rights and Abolition* (New York: Schocken Books, 1971), and *The Woman in American History* (Menlo Park, Calif.: Addison-Wesley, 1971).

11. Vaughan B. Baker, "Cherchez Les Femmes: Some Glimpses of Women in Early Eighteenth-Century Louisiana," *Louisiana History* 31 (Winter 1990): 21–37; email correspondence, September 26, 2015.

12. Sarah Brabant, interview by the author, May 12, 2015; *Lafayette Advertiser*, December 2, 1977.

13. Brabant interview; *Lafayette Advertiser*, December 12, 1977. The resolution was formally adopted by the city council on October 19, 1976.

14. Sarah Brabant and Margaret Ritchey, letter to the Lafayette Commission on the Needs of Women, May 12, 2015, copy in author's possession. *Lafayette Advertiser*, December 2, 1976; March 13, 1977; March 7, 1980. The Lafayette parish battered women's shelter, at least initially, was funded by the parish and the city. This presented a problem because women who lived in surrounding parishes were not allowed to use the facility.

15. Baker interview; Vaughan Baker c.v., in author's possession. Brabant interview, and Sarah Brabant biography, Veteran Feminists of America, http://www.vfa.us/SARAH %20BRABANT.htm

16. Richard Florida, *The Rise of the Creative Class* (New York: Basic Books, 2002). Marjorie Spruill found feminists in Mississippi in larger cities and university towns, too; this was likely also true in other southern states. Marjorie Julian Spruill, "The Mississippi 'Takeover': Feminists, Antifeminists, and the International Women's Year Conference of 1977," in Payne, Spruill, and Swain, *Mississippi Women: Their Histories, Their Lives*, 2:289.

17. In addition to Tulane, UNO, Dillard, Loyola and Xavier, New Orleans was also home to LSU Medical Center, New Orleans Baptist Theological Seminary, Notre Dame Seminary, Our Lady of Holy Cross College, and St. Mary's Dominican College.

18. Jeffrey Alan Turner, *Sitting In and Speaking Out: Student Movements in the American South, 1960–1970* (Athens: University of Georgia Press, 2010), 8; Mohr and Gordon, *Tulane*; Fife, *Portraits from Memory*; Kim Gandy, email correspondence, February 12, 2009. Kathy Barrett, Kim Gandy, and Clay Latimer studied at Loyola; Cathy Cade, Peggy Dobbins, Suzanne Pharr, Mary Capps, and Sandy Karp were graduate students at Tulane.

19. Judy Cooper, interview by the author, October 24, 2013; "Judy Cooper," in *KnowLA Encyclopedia of Louisiana*, article published September 12, 2012, http://www.knowla.org /entry/1148/.

20. For more on BOLD, SOUL, and COUP, see Germany, *New Orleans after the Promise*, 251–57.

21. Rosen, *World Split Open*, 292.

22. Osborne, *Issues and Answers*, 80–83.

23. Evans, *Tidal Wave*, 140–41.

24. Tucker and Willinger, *Newcomb College*, 1–3.

25. Radcliffe had been founded as the Harvard "Annex" in 1879. Students who completed the four-year course of study received certificates, not degrees, until a new charter establishing Radcliffe College in 1894 authorized the awarding of degrees. The diplomas were countersigned by the president of Harvard, just as Newcomb students received diplomas signed by both Newcomb College and Tulane University officials.

26. Sally J. Kenney, preface, in David Conradsen et al., *The Arts & Crafts of Newcomb Pottery* (New York: Skira Rizzoli in Association with the Newcomb Art Gallery, Tulane University, New Orleans, 2013), 9.

27. Tucker and Willinger, *Newcomb College*, 11–12.

28. Ibid., 18; Lynn D. Gordon, *Gender and Higher Education in the Progressive Era* (New Haven, Conn.: Yale University Press, 1990), 169.

29. Tucker and Willinger, *Newcomb College*, 8.

30. Kenney, preface, 11. In addition to explanatory articles, extraordinary full-page, full-color images of artwork created by Newcomb women is in Conradsen et al., *Arts & Crafts of Newcomb Pottery*, produced to accompany "Women, Art & Social Change: The Newcomb Pottery Enterprise," an exhibit of Newcomb arts organized by the Newcomb Art Gallery at Tulane University and the Smithsonian Institution Traveling Exhibition Service.

31. Kenney, preface, 11; Tucker and Willinger, *Newcomb College*, 18.

32. Mohr and Gordon, *Tulane*, 131–34. The bequests of both Paul Tulane and Josephine Louise Newcomb restricted the use of their donations to whites. The state charter establishing Tulane also made it a whites-only institution.

33. Tucker and Willinger, *Newcomb College*, 272.

34. Beth Willinger, "Changing Newcomb into a College for the Education of Women: Centering Women's Lives," in Tucker and Willinger, *Newcomb College*, 244–47.

35. Willinger, "Changing Newcomb," 255.

36. "Loyola Opens Women's Center," *Distaff*, April–May, 1975; Geneva Cotton, interview by the author, September 5, 2007; *Vieux Carré Courier*, February 12–18, 1976, listed upcoming course offerings. Loyola website, http://www.loyno.edu, accessed September 7, 2012.

37. Fairclough, *Race & Democracy*, 173.

38. Ruth A. Wallace, "Joseph H. Fichter's Contributions to Feminism," *Sociology of Religion* 57, no. 4 (1996): 359–66; Father George Lundy, SJ, email correspondence, January 3, 2008; Kathy Barrett, email correspondence, December 5, 2007.

39. Thomas Becnel, *Labor, Church, and the Sugar Establishment: Louisiana, 1887–1976* (Baton Rouge: Louisiana State University Press, 1980), 112, 162.

40. The 1973 series, for example, was held at the Junior League Building twice a week, once during the day and once in the evening so that working women could attend. Gayle Gagliano, telephone interview by the author, September 5, 2007; Lundy email; *Louisiana Weekly*, March 10, 1973; *Distaff*, March 1973; Charlotte Hays, "Sisters: Some Sketches of the Women's Movement," *Metro New Orleans*, November 1974; Jo Ann Canaday, "A Study of Five Politically Active New Orleans Women's Organizations," July 31, 1975, typescript, appendixes F ("Interview with Sue Keever"), L ("Interview with Gayle Gagliano"), and O ("Interview with Clay Lattimer [*sic*]"), Newcomb Archives.

41. Susan O'Malley and Sue Keever, both early feminists, were on the faculty at UNO. Canaday, "Study of Five."

42. UNO history, http://www.uno.edu/about/history.aspx, accessed November 12, 2013. The name change from LSUNO to UNO occurred in 1974, by which time UNO was the second largest university in the state. Martha Ward, interview by the author, November 8, 2013.

43. Roberta Madden, interview by Jennifer Abraham, February 6, 2002, Collection 4700 1564 T3137, Hill Library, LSU; LSU Women and Gender Studies Program website, http://uiswcmsweb.prod.lsu.edu/hss/wgs//, accessed March 30, 2015.

44. Rebecca Wells, phone interview by Mary Ann Wilson, August 7, 2011, cited in "Rebecca Wells (1952–): Her Divine Saga Deep in the Heart of Louisiana," in Frystak and Farmer-Kaiser, *Louisiana Women*, vol. 2, 254–73; Roberta Madden files, membership survey, 1971, Newcomb Archives.

45. Madden files, membership survey; "Keeping the Memories: Louisianans of the 2nd Wave Feminist Movement," transcript of banquet discussion sponsored by Veteran Feminists of America, March 22, 2001, Newcomb Archives. Pinkie Lane died in a car accident in 2008.

46. *Lafayette Sunday Advertiser*, August 27, 1978. Rosie Roy was state coordinator of the Louisiana NOW at the time of the newspaper story.

47. "Keeping the Memories"; Madden files; author interviews.

Chapter 7. "We Are All Sisters"

1. Lynn Miller, interview by the author, September 10, 2007, and email correspondence, August 8, 2008; Susan LosCalzo, interview by the author, September 5, 2007. For a full list of WLC members, see appendix 2. Radical and socialist feminist organizations favored an umbrella structure, evident in the name "coalition," because it "allowed the same individuals to work on multiple projects in different member groups." Nancy Whittier, *Feminist Generations: The Persistence of the Radical Women's Movement* (Philadelphia: Temple University Press, 1995), 35.

2. Women's Liberation position paper rebutting Roxanne Dunbar and "severing relations with her," typescript, December 4, 1971, Newcomb Archives. The fight between Dunbar and the local women concerned ideology and tactics, but the disagreement came to a head because of office equipment that Dunbar had left behind when she fled New Or-

leans. The office equipment supported the activities of the Women's Center, but Dunbar
wanted it back and claimed the women had "stolen" it.

3. Dunbar-Ortiz, *Outlaw Woman*, 236, 257–65, 360; *Mobile Register*, March 7, 1975;
Vieux Carré Courier, February 27–March 5, 1975; Mary Capps and Sandra Karp correspondences; FBI file of Phyllis Belle Parun, May 2, 1973, Newcomb Archives.

4. Roberta Salper, "U.S. Government Surveillance and the Women's Liberation Movement, 1968–1973: A Case Study," *Feminist Studies* 34, no. 3 (Fall 2008): 431–55; David Cun-
ningham, *There's Something Happening Here: The New Left, the Klan, and FBI Counterintelligence* (Berkeley: University of California Press, 2004), 6.

5. Sandra Karp, interviews and correspondence; LosCalzo interview. Documentary
evidence of the clash comes in part from the FBI mole who had infiltrated the group and
who reported on a meeting in which the members soundly criticized Dunbar's position
paper, "Female Liberation as a Basis for Social Revolution," published in *Sisterhood Is
Powerful* and widely circulated via mimeograph. Dunbar-Ortiz subsequently rejected
her position in that paper. FBI file of Phyllis Belle Parun, Newcomb Archives.

6. Following the successful Chicago women's liberation conference in 1968, the SFRU
organized a similar conference in Atlanta in February 1969, but almost nothing has been
written about it. Dunbar-Ortiz discusses outsiders like Sue Munaker and Dottie Zellner
in her memoir but mentions only three native Louisianans, none of whom were integral
to the movement in New Orleans. Dunbar-Ortiz, *Outlaw Woman*, chaps. 5–7; 164.

7. Whether to allow the male children of female members was an extremely contentious issue in many other lesbian-only communities and separate spaces. The New Orleans WLC members avoided that collision by agreeing early on that sons of members
could come with them to meetings.

8. Statement of the Women's Liberation Coalition of New Orleans, December 10, 1970,
typescript, Newcomb Archives.

9. Jeffrey A. Turner describes New Orleans as a "pocket of openness" in an otherwise
conservative and mostly conformist state. Turner, *Sitting In and Speaking Out*, 8. See also
Kevin Gotham, *Authentic New Orleans: Tourism, Culture and Race in the Big Easy* (New
York: NYU Press, 2007); John Shelton Reed, *Dixie Bohemia: A French Quarter Circle in the
1920s* (Baton Rouge: Louisiana State University Press, 2012).

10. Richard Dennis Clark, "City of Desire: A History of Same-Sex Desire in New Or-
leans, 1917–1977" (PhD diss., Tulane University, 2009); Frank Perez and Jeffrey Palmquist,
In Exile: The History and Lore Surrounding New Orleans Gay Culture and Its Oldest Gay Bar
(Hurlford, Scotland: LL Publications, 2012), introduction.

11. Among the preservationists who saved the Quarter were William Ratcliffe Irby
(1860–1926), a wealthy tobacco company executive, banker, and philanthropist in New
Orleans, and Lyle Saxon, a journalist and writer. Saxon was part of a circle of gay men
who settled in the Quarter in the 1920s and 1930s. Wealthy women such as Elizabeth
Werlein, wife of New Orleans music publisher Philip Werlein, decided to plant them-
selves in the way of the planned destruction. Werlein and others bought homes in the
Quarter with the express purpose of raising property values and revivifying the area.
They helped prevent the plan to raze the Quarter and replace it with developers' generic
American-style buildings. The French Quarter is an example of women's historic pres-

ervation efforts throughout Louisiana and indeed all over the country. In addition to Reed, *Dixie Bohemia*, see Anthony Stanonis, "'A Woman of Boundless Energy': Elizabeth Werlein and Her Times," *Louisiana History* 46 (Winter 2005): 5–26.

12. Perez and Palmquist, *In Exile*, Introduction, 141–43, 198. The Louisiana Gay Political Action Caucus formed in 1980, and the Forum for Equality established a chapter in New Orleans in 1989. Delery-Edwards, *Up Stairs Lounge Arson*, 146.

13. Latimer correspondence.

14. LA. REV. STAT. ANN § 14:89 (2012); Andrea J. Ritchie, "Crimes against Nature: Challenging Criminalization of Queerness and Black Women's Sexuality," *Loyola Journal of Public Interest Law* (March 1, 2013): 355.

15. *New Orleans Times-Picayune*, September 12, 1973; Perez and Palmquist, *In Exile*, 96–97.

16. Lyn Diane Franks, "Torchbearers and Front Runners: The Daughters of Bilitis and Women's Rights" (master's thesis, Murray State University, 2011); Clay Latimer, interview by the author, January 1, 2015.

17. Franks, "Torchbearers and Front Runners," 67, 87.

18. Lynn Miller, telephone interview by the author, September 10, 2007, and email correspondence, August 8, 2008; Richard Dennis Clark, email correspondence, September 17 and 19, 2007; GLF's newsletter, *Sunflower*, Newcomb Archives; Roberts Batson's article on Lynn Miller, *Southern Voice*, July 5, 2001. For more on gay culture in New Orleans, see Sarah Wilkerson-Freeman, "Fat Tuesday at Dixie's: Jack Robinson's New Orleans Mardi Gras Photographs, 1952–1955," *Southern Cultures* 12, no. 1 (Spring 2006): 42–63.

19. Scott was the only child of cotton farmers in northern Mississippi. She traveled to Japan for a year when she was eighteen, an experience she described as eye-opening. She attended Newcomb until her junior year, when she dropped out to get married. She and her husband lived for a few years in California before returning to New Orleans in 1962. Barbara Scott, interview by the author, December 4, 2013.

20. Scott interview; Scott campaign flyer, Newcomb Archives.

21. Thompson, *Un-Natural State*, 167–68; Scott interview.

22. A newspaper story about the hotel hit the national wire services in 1976 and showed up in newspapers all over the country. See, for example, *San Francisco Examiner*, March 10, 1976. Frank Perez, *Ambush Magazine*, April 22–May 5, 2014, 10, http://www.ambushmag.com/is814/images/814main6–10.pdf, accessed April 25, 2014.

23. *Distaff*, April–May, 1975; "Nowletter," Baton Rouge Chapter of NOW newsletter, July 1971; Helen Wheeler to Roberta Madden, 1972–74, Newcomb Archives.

24. "Keeping the Memories: Louisianans of the 2nd Wave Feminist Movement," transcript of banquet discussion sponsored by Veteran Feminists of America, March 22, 2001, Newcomb Archives.

25. Karline Tierney Collection, Newcomb Archives; ERA files of Roberta Madden, Newcomb Archives.

26. Linda Martin, email correspondences, 2008–13; Love, *Feminists Who Changed America*, 300.

27. Muriel Arceneaux Collection, Newcomb Archives; Veteran Feminists of America biography, http://www.vfa.us/MURIEL%20ARCENEAUX.htm, accessed November 15, 2013.

28. Nadine Henneman, telephone interview by the author, January 17, 2008; Liz Simon Facebook posting, October 27, 2013; Love, *Feminists Who Changed America*, 209.

29. Clay Latimer, email correspondence, February 1, 2008.

30. Celeste Newbrough, telephone interview by the author, September 9, 2008; Gayle Gagliano, telephone interview by the author, September 5, 2007.

31. Mary Gehman, "New Orleans Women's Movement: A Comprehensive Herstory," *Distaff*, October 1973–March 1974; Clay Latimer, interview by the author, August 19, 2007.

32. Diane Clabaugh, email correspondence, January 3, 2014; Canaday, "Study of Five."

33. Maryann Barakso, *Governing NOW: Grassroots Activism in the National Organization for Women* (Ithaca, N.Y.: Cornell University Press), 50.

34. Stephanie Gilmore, *Groundswell: Grassroots Feminist Activism in Postwar America* (New York: Routledge, 2013), 64.

35. Author interviews and email correspondence with Sandy Karp, Sue Laporte, Nadine Henneman, and Mary Capps; *Voices from the Louisiana Women's Movement* and *Origins of Gay Liberation in Louisiana*, VHS/DVDs of panel presentation held at UNO in 1997, featuring Donna Myhre, Sandy Karp, Clay Latimer, and Sue Laporte, recorded October 10, 1997, by the Bienville Foundation, Newcomb Archives.

36. "Lesbian Resolution," written by Dianne Clabaugh and Clay Latimer, presented June 25, 1974. Transcribed by Clay Latimer from a VHS recording cited above because the New Orleans NOW chapter records were lost in the flood following Hurricane Katrina. Clay Latimer recalls that there were about one hundred women in attendance at the meeting in New Orleans and that the resolution was generally well received.

37. Spruill, "Mississippi 'Takeover'," 2:287–312; Clay Latimer, interviews.

38. Discussing the gay-straight split, Ruth Rosen posits, "Only in small cities or less-urban settings did gay and straight feminists continue to cling together, given the common enmity they faced." *World Split Open*, 172. While neither New Orleans nor Baton Rouge is a small town, Louisiana is not a densely populated state. Nancy Whittier also notes, "There were some tensions between lesbians and heterosexual feminists, to be sure, but the 'gay-straight split' in Columbus was much less intense than the conflicts other authors have described." *Feminist Generation*, 20.

39. Pat Denton, email correspondence, February 10, 2008.

40. Miller, email correspondence, August 8, 2008.

41. Ibid.

42. The Women's Center moved several times. Lynn Miller correspondence, August 5, 2008. Mary Capps donated the tape of that interview to the Newcomb Archives. I listened to it in the spring of 2015 before turning it over to the archives. Unfortunately, when the archivists attempted to make a digital copy of the tape, it broke.

43. Suzanne Pharr interview, "Voices of Feminism Oral History Project," 2005, Knoxville, Tenn., Sophia Smith Collection, Smith College, Northampton, Mass., http://www.smith.edu/libraries/libs/ssc/vof/transcripts/Pharr.pdf, accessed November 14, 2013; Azjicek, Lord, and Holyfield, "Emergence and First Years." Repeated requests to Suzanne Pharr for comment have gone unanswered.

44. Saralyn Chesnut and Amanda C. Gable, "'Women Ran It': Charis Books and More and Atlanta's Lesbian-Feminist Community, 1971–1981," in *Carryin' On in the Lesbian and*

Gay South, ed. John Howard (New York: New York University Press, 1997), 253. About Columbus, Ohio, Nancy Whittier concludes: "Feminist organizations of varying ideological slants cooperated on specific issues far more extensively than a simplistic 'two-wing' model of the women's movement implies." *Feminist Generations*, 45.

45. Sandy Karp correspondences.

46. Mary Capps and Sue Laporte interviews.

47. Mary Capps, interview by the author, September 26, 2007; Celeste Newbrough interview.

48. Mary Gehman, "New Orleans Women's Movement: A Comprehensive Herstory," *Distaff*, October 1973–March 1974.

49. Miller correspondence.

50. Pat Denton, email correspondence, February 10, 2008. See also *New Orleans Times-Picayune*, June 30, 1985.

51. Perez and Palmquist, *In Exile*, 136–38; appendix E contains a list of gay activists and their organizational "firsts."

52. Sandra Karp, email correspondence, September 9, 2007.

53. For additional insights on this phenomenon, see Jane Mansbridge and Aldon Morris, eds., *Oppositional Consciousness: The Subjective Roots of Social Protest* (Chicago: University of Chicago Press, 2001); Stephanie Gilmore and Elizabeth Kaminski, "A Part and Apart: Lesbian and Straight Feminist Activists Negotiate Identity in a Second-Wave Organization," *Journal of the History of Sexuality* 16, no. 1 (January 2007): 95–113; Laurel A. Clark, "Beyond the Gay/Straight Split: Socialist Feminists in Baltimore," *NWSA Journal* 19, no. 2 (Summer 2007): 1–31; and Jo Reger, "Organizational Dynamics and Construction of Multiple Feminist Identities in the National Organization for Women," *Gender and Society* 16, no. 5 (October 2002): 710–27.

Chapter 8. "I Wanted More for My Daughters"

1. Francis and Victor Bussie, interview by the author, July 8, 2008. After Victor Bussie (pronounced with a long "u," as in Byou-see) died in September 2011, I conducted additional interviews with Fran Bussie.

2. The best source for Senator Ervin's arguments against the ERA remains Mathews and De Hart, *Sex, Gender and the Politics of ERA*. Louise Johnson's papers are at Louisiana Tech University Special Collections, M-134.

3. Jane J. Mansbridge, *Why We Lost the ERA* (Chicago: University of Chicago Press, 1986), 4–5, 15–16; Neil J. Young, "'The ERA is a Moral Issue': The Mormon Church, LDS Women, and the Defeat of the Equal Rights Amendment," *American Quarterly* 59, no. 3 (September 2007): 623–44; Committee of Concerned Citizens ad, n.d., Karline Tierney Collection, Newcomb Archives.

4. Louisiana AFL-CIO newsletter, May 25, 1964, Louisiana and Special Collections Department, Earl K. Long Library, University of New Orleans (hereinafter cited as New Orleans AFL-CIO Collection), Collection 101, box 59.

5. "STOP" was an acronym for Stop Taking Our Privileges. Schlafly held the first national conference of STOP ERA in St. Louis on September 26, 1972. Representing

Louisiana was Charlotte Felt, a member of the Women's Auxiliary of the New Orleans Chamber of Commerce. Donald T. Critchlow, *Phyllis Schlafly and Grassroots Conservatism: A Woman's Crusade* (Princeton, N.J.: Princeton University Press, 2005), 219; Nancy MacLean, *Freedom Is Not Enough: The Opening of the American Workplace* (Cambridge, Mass.: Harvard University Press, 2006), 246.

6. *Farm Bureau News*, April 1979.

7. Guarisco quote, undated newspaper clipping, source unknown; *Baton Rouge Sunday Advocate* May 2, 1973 (?); *Baton Rouge State Times*, May 9, 1977; *New Orleans Times Picayune*, May 24, 1972; June 19, 1972.

8. *Baton Rouge Sunday Advocate*, March 10, 1974.

9. Erin M. Kempker writes about right-wing women and their ideology in "Battling Big Sister Government: Hoosier Women and the Politics of International Women's Year," *Journal of Women's History* 24, no. 2 (Summer 2012): 144–70.

10. *Farm Bureau News*.

11. Virtually all newspaper stories about the ERA ratification effort in Louisiana reported on both supporters and opponents. Johnson quote: *New Orleans Times-Picayune*, April 22, 1973; February 19, 1974. Charlotte Felt of the Women's Auxiliary of the New Orleans Chamber of Commerce was a spokesperson for Women Opposed to ERA. See, for example, *New Orleans Times-Picayune*, February 3, 1977.

12. Johnson quote, *New Orleans Times Picayune*, May 22, 1972; Louise Johnson to Mrs. Dayton C. Woolie, March 23, 1973, Tierney Collection, Newcomb Archives.

13. Mansbridge, *Why We Lost the ERA*, 175, observed the same phenomenon in her home state, Illinois. She was working on the proratificationist side in the Illinois state capitol when she became aware that the fundamentalist churches were busing in women. The churches had an advantage over the pro-ERA side, she noted, because "they had preexisting meetings places, buses, and claims on their members' time and money."

14. National Board of the Catholic Daughters of America, statement opposing the Equal Rights Amendment, Osborne Collection; *New Orleans States-Item*, May 30, 1972; Joan Kent, telephone interview by the author, February 25, 2009. In addition to the groups listed, there were many other ad hoc groups that opposed the ERA, with names such as HA, Home Administrators, and Louisiana Women Opposed to ERA. Ollie Osborne and Karline Tierney both maintained files on the opposition.

15. *New Orleans Clarion Herald*, July 22, 1976. Schlafly flew into the state to address gatherings of conservatives on many occasions, the first time in 1973. See, for example, *New Orleans Times-Picayune*, April 27, 1973; May 7, 1977.

16. ERA United of Louisiana, "Louisiana Groups Supporting Passage of the Equal Rights Amendment," September 1975, lists the Catholic Human Relations Committee, New Orleans; the Executive Board, National Assembly of Women Religious, Lafayette; and Sisters Senate, Catholic Dioceses of Baton Rouge among its supporters. Newcomb Archives.

17. *Baton Rouge Sunday Advocate*, May 13, 1979.

18. Henold, *Catholic and Feminist*, 223; Mansbridge, *Why We Lost the ERA*, 15.

19. *New Orleans Clarion Herald*, May 16, 1974.

20. *New Orleans Clarion Herald*, May 16 and May 23, 1974.

21. Richard L. Camp, "From Passive Subordination to Complementary Partnership: The Papal Conception of a Woman's Place in Church and Society since 1878," *Catholic Historical Review* 76 (1990): 521–23.

22. *New Orleans Clarion Herald*, August 31, 1978.

23. The national AFL-CIO adopted a resolution supporting the ERA at its Tenth Biennial Convention in 1973.

24. https://en.wikipedia.org/wiki/Sidney_Barthelemy, accessed Sept. 28, 2015.

25. *Baton Rouge Morning Advocate* May 2, June 8, and June 30, 1972; *Baton Rouge Sunday Advocate*, March 10, 1974. The votes were reported in the *Morning Advocate*, May 22, 1972, and *Baton Rouge State-Times*, January 7, 1975.

26. Latimer interviews; Fran Bussie interviews.

27. *New Orleans Times-Picayune*, June 30, 1972; May 12 1974; May 6, 1975; *Baton Rouge State-Times*, January 6, 1979; *Lake Charles American Press*, April 4, 1979; ERA United flyer, "Louisiana Groups Supporting Passage of the Equal Rights Amendment," September 1975, Tierney Collection, Newcomb Archives. For an analysis of why the polling data could be misleading, see Mansbridge, *Why We Lost the ERA*, chap. 3, "Rights versus Substance."

28. ERAmerica Political Analysis of Unratified States, dated October 1977, noted that in Louisiana "there is no strong support [for the ERA] from any visible source." The report estimated that twenty votes in the senate were needed to ratify and only nine were lined up; fifty-three needed in house and only twenty to twenty-five lined up. "Likelihood of Ratification by 1979: unlikely." RG9–003 Civil Rights Department, box 34, folder W10, George Meany Memorial Archives (hereinafter GMMA), Silver Spring, Maryland.

29. Susan M. Hartmann contends that "no factor carried as much force in shaping an organization's feminist agenda as a prior commitment to civil rights." Hartmann, *Other Feminists*, 6.

30. During the 1970s, Sibal used her first husband's surname, Taylor. Following her second marriage, she took the name Holt and today goes by Sibal S. Holt. However, because documents of the 1970s always refer to her as Sibal Taylor, that is the name I use when discussing her activities during those years. To distinguish Fran from her husband, Victor Bussie, I use both names.

31. On the phenomenon known as "labor feminism," see Kessler-Harris, *Out to Work*; Kessler-Harris, *In Pursuit of Equity*; Deslippe, *"Rights, Not Roses"*; Cobble, *Other Women's Movement*; Hartmann, *Other Feminists*; MacLean, "Postwar Women's History"; Robert Rodgers Korstad, *Civil Rights Unionism: Tobacco Workers and the Struggle for Democracy in the Mid-Twentieth-Century South* (Chapel Hill: University of North Carolina Press, 2003).

32. Fran and Victor Bussie interview, 2008; Sibal Taylor Holt, telephone and in-person interviews, July 30, 2008, through May 10, 2013.

33. Charles Thomas Fagan, "Labor Union Membership Estimates for Louisiana 1971–1974" (master's thesis, Louisiana State University, 1976); William Canak and Berkeley Miller, "Gumbo Politics: Unions, Business, and Louisiana Right-to-Work Legislation," *Industrial and Labor Relations Review* 43, no. 2 (January 1990): 258–71. Canak and Miller's

chart of labor union membership in the South (261) shows that the percentage of Louisiana's nonagricultural workforce that was unionized ranged from a low of 9.8 percent in 1939 to a high of 19.8 in 1975, the year before the RTW legislation passed. No southern state ever went above 25 percent. Alabama in 1953 and Kentucky in 1960 both topped out at 25 percent.

34. Michael S. Martin, "The Battle over the 'Right to Work': Vetoes and Votes in Post–World War II Louisiana," paper delivered at the Louisiana Historical Association Annual Conference, 2010, courtesy of the author. Martin, director of the Center for Louisiana Studies at the University of Louisiana at Lafayette, based this paper in part on Victor Bussie's papers deposited in the University of Lafayette Special Collections.

35. Becnel, *Labor, Church, and the Sugar Establishment*, chap. 9. Despite the powerful presence of the AFL-CIO in Louisiana politics, relatively little has been published by academic historians, although Alan Draper, in *Conflict of Interest: Organized Labor and the Civil Rights Movement in the South, 1954–1968* (Ithaca, N.Y.: ILR Press, 1994), covers Louisiana in some parts. For statistics, see Bernard A. Cook and James R. Watson, *Louisiana Labor: From Slavery to "Right-to-Work"* (Lanham, Md.: University Press of America, 1985). The George Meany Archive in Silver Spring, Maryland, has the published proceedings of the state conventions through 1958.

36. Edwin Edwards, interview by Jack Bass and Walter DeVries, September 25, 1973, interview A-85 (A), transcribed as typescript, Southern Oral History Program, 4007, Southern Historical Collection, Wilson Library, University of North Carolina at Chapel Hill, accessed April 6, 2013.

37. Ibid.

38. "News from Louisiana AFL-CIO," November 1963, New Orleans AFL-CIO Collection; Gary M. Fink, ed., and Mary Mills, comp., *State Labor Proceedings: A Bibliography of the AFL, CIO, and AFL-CIO Proceedings, 1885–1974, Held in the AFL-CIO Library* (Westport, Conn.: Greenwood Press, 1975), xi.

39. Pamphlets, New Orleans AFL-CIO Collection, Collection 135, box 3. At the 1966 convention, for example, 336 organizations sent 896 delegates, and more than 3,000 guests attended.

40. Fran Bussie, Testimony before the Louisiana Legislative Committee, May 28, 1974, typescript, Osborne Collection. The Louisiana AFL-CIO resolution followed the text of the national AFL-CIO. ERA United of Louisiana newsletter of 1974 noted that the AFL-CIO had sent "110% of fair share" to the group. The 1983 *Autumn Report* of the Louisiana Women's Political Caucus, contains a half-page advertisement on p. 12 stating, "The Louisiana Women's Political Caucus appreciates the support of the Louisiana AFL-CIO." Newcomb Archives.

41. ERA United of Louisiana, "Louisiana Groups Supporting Passage of The Equal Rights Amendment," flyer dated September 1975, lists seventy-two groups, including the Louisiana AFL-CIO. Those groups that were entirely or predominantly African American were the National Association of College Women, Southern University Branch; the Louisiana League of Good Government; the Welfare Rights Organization; the Negro Chamber of Commerce, Shreveport; Links, Inc., the NAACP; and the Council of Black Women (a New Orleans political action group).

42. *Louisiana Weekly*, November 12, 1977.

43. In addition to the academic works on the civil rights movement already listed, for black women's community activism in New Orleans, see Germany, *New Orleans after the Promise*.

44. Quote is from Sibal Taylor Holt interview. For the historic antagonism between whites and blacks in the movement, see Breines, *Trouble between Us*; and Roth, *Separate Roads to Feminism*. Breines discusses the problems with CR sessions on 94–95.

45. All information about Sibal Taylor Holt comes from personal interviews and correspondence between July 2008 and May 2013 unless otherwise noted.

46. Matt "Flukey" Suarez, Oral History, March 2000, conducted at Tougaloo College as part of the Civil Rights Documentation Project. Transcript available at http://www.crmvet.org/nars/suarez.htm, accessed April 10, 2013.

47. Cobble, *Other Women's Movement*, 129; Thomas R. Brooks, *Communications Workers of America: The Story of a Union* (New York: Mason/Charter, 1977), chap. 11.

48. "Louisiana Groups Supporting Passage of the Equal Rights Amendment," September 1975; "The Equal Rights Amendment," ERA United of Louisiana flyer issued by the national CWA under the presidency of Joseph A. Beirne, box 39, FF 15, Osborne Collection. The CWA first went on record in support of the ERA in March 1972.

49. Ejerico Fernandez, telephone interview by the author, March 29, 2009.

50. Ibid.

51. Alan Draper, in *Conflict of Interest*, makes a case that the AFL-CIO leaders supported civil rights and especially voting rights for blacks because they saw African Americans as allies against the white conservatives who continuously opposed them in their state legislatures. See chap. 4, "In Search of Realignment." Also Patrick J. Maney, "Hale Boggs, Organized Labor, and the Politics of Race in South Louisiana," in *Southern Labor in Transition, 1940–1995*, ed. Robert H. Zieger (Knoxville: University of Tennessee Press, 1997), 230–50.

52. Roberta Madden, speech in honor of Victor Bussie, typescript, Newcomb Archives; *New Orleans Times-Picayune*, May 24 and 28, 1976.

53. Fran Bussie, interview by the author, April 14, 2013; *Baton Rouge Advocate*, clipping, n.d.; Charles George, president emeritus of Firefighters Local 561 and the Professional Firefighters Association of Louisiana, Lake Charles, letter to the editor, *Lake Charles American Press*, September 18, 2011.

54. George, letter to the editor, September 18, 2011.

55. Fran Bussie interview, April 14, 2013. The principle of gender equality is in the Book of Discipline of the United Methodist Church under "Rights of Women."

56. Fran Bussie interview, April 14, 2013. African Americans were heavily represented in unions of government workers, including postal workers, the American Federation of State, County, and Municipal Employees—which included groundskeepers and sanitation workers—hotel workers, and a schoolteachers' union, the Louisiana Federation of Teachers, which organized university professors from the historically black colleges and universities as well as elementary and secondary school teachers.

57. Louisiana Senate Resolution no. 166, sponsored by Senators Bajoie, Murray, Jones, and Nevers, Regular Session, March 7, 2005.

58. Cobble (*Other Women's Movement*, 55) points out that labor feminists often were active in mixed-sex reform organizations as well, such as the NAACP, the National Council of Negro Women, and Democratic Party politics, thus extending their reach. Within these groups, they advanced feminist goals. The APRI encouraged black voter registration, among other goals. The resolution passed by the Louisiana senate in 2005, cited above, said that Holt was responsible for "an astounding 70,000 new voters for Louisiana."

59. ERA United Newsletter, October 1975.

60. Fran Bussie interview, April 14, 2013; Michael L. Collins, "Lloyd Bentsen Jr.," in *Profiles in Power: Twentieth-Century Texans in Washington*, ed. Kenneth E. Hendrickson Jr., Michael L. Collins, and Patrick Cox (Austin: University of Texas Press, 1993), 256.

61. Fran Bussie, remarks to CLUW, 1975, "Women in the Labor Force," accession no. N 97-7, box 1, Division of Archives, Records Management and History, Louisiana State Archives, Baton Rouge.

62. It was becoming increasingly common for women to fill this type of position in unions. Description of services: Proceedings of the Fifteenth Constitutional Convention of the AFL-CIO, New York, New York, November 14–20, 1963 (copy in UNO Public Library); Fran Bussie, vita, 27–21, Osborne Collection; Lucretia M. Dewey, "Women in Labor Unions," *Monthly Labor Review*, February 1971, GMMA.

63. Fran Bussie, testimony before Louisiana Legislative Committee, 1974.

64. Ibid.

65. Fran Bussie, vita, 1980; speeches in box 1, Division of Archives, Records Management and History, Louisiana State Archives, Baton Rouge.

66. Fran Bussie, "Women in the Workforce," 1972.

67. Hartmann, *Other Feminists*, 204.

68. Janet Allured, "Janet Mary Riley: Angel with Teeth," in Frystak and Farmer-Kaiser, *Louisiana Women*, 2:41-62.

69. *Ms.*, Spring 1972, preview issue.

70. Eartha St. Ann, Shirley Lampton, Audrey Delair, Clementine Brumfield, and Monica Hunter were leaders in the welfare rights movement in New Orleans. Premilla Nadasen, *Welfare Warriors: The Welfare Rights Movement in the United States* (New York: Routledge, 2005), 221–22; Germany, *New Orleans after the Promise*, 225.

71. Annie Smart of Baton Rouge represented the LWRO at the International Women's Year Conferences in 1977. She is identified in the Louisiana report as president of the Louisiana Welfare Rights Organization and southern regional representative, National Welfare Rights Organization, in *Issues and Answers: Final Report, Louisiana Women's Conference, 1977*, sponsored by National Commission on the Observance of International Women's Year, ed. Ollie T. Osborne (1977), 82.

72. For more on the national welfare rights movement, see Annelise Orleck, *Storming Caesars Palace: How Black Mothers Fought Their Own War on Poverty* (Boston: Beacon Press, 2005).

73. *Louisiana Weekly*, May 20, 1974.

74. ERA United flyer, "Louisiana Groups Supporting Passage of the Equal Rights Amendment," September 1975; *New Orleans Times-Picayune*, August 28, 1978; *New Orleans Times Picayune* June 30, 1972.

75. *Louisiana Weekly*, May 20, 1974.

76. Baxandall, "Re-Visioning the Women's Liberation Movement's Narrative," 238–39; Rivka Polatnick, "Diversity in Women's Liberation Ideology: How a Black and a White Group of the 1960s Viewed Motherhood," *Signs* 21, no. 3 (Spring 1996): 679–706; and M. Rivka Polatnick, "Poor Black Sisters Decided for Themselves: A Case Study of 1960s Women's Liberation Activism," in *Black Women in America*, ed. Kim Marie Vaz (Thousand Oaks, Calif.: Sage, 1995), 126–27. It was not unusual for the earlier generation of white feminists like Evelyn Cloutman to have raised a houseful of baby boomers, but the white women born in the 1940s and 1950s took advantage of new methods of contraception that became widely available after the 1965 Supreme Court decision in *Griswold v. Connecticut*.

77. Polatnick, "Diversity in Women's Liberation Ideology," 684.

78. Collins, *Black Feminist Thought*, 115–23; Tamar Carroll, "Unlikely Allies: Forging a Multiracial, Class-Based Women's Movement in 1970s Brooklyn," in Gilmore, *Feminist Coalitions*, 196–99; Breines, *Trouble between Us*, 92.

79. "Rupert Richardson," interview in *Untold Glory: African Americans in Pursuit of Freedom, Opportunity, and Achievement*, ed. Alan Govenar (New York: Harlem Moon, 2007), 309–24.

80. Ibid.

81. Ibid.

82. Todd Clemons (Richardson's son), interview by the author, August 26, 2015; Gaynell Veronica Clemons (Richardson's daughter), correspondence, August 28, 2015, and interview by the author, September 2, 2015; Richardson obituary, *Lake Charles American Press*, January 30, 2008; NAACP press release upon her death, http://www.naacp.org/press/entry/naacp-mourns-passing-of-rupert-richardson-past-president—amp—national-board-member, accessed August 28, 2015.

83. Richardson was raised in Evergreen Baptist Church in Lake Charles and joined Shiloh Baptist Church in Baton Rouge after moving there. Gaynell Veronica Clemons interview; Richardson, tapes 21 and 22, Pat Denton Collection, Newcomb Archives.

84. Richardson, tapes 21 and 22

85. Richardson, tapes 21 and 22; Richardson obituary.

86. *Louisiana Weekly*, November 12, 1977; Frystak, *Our Minds on Freedom*, 113; Millie Charles bio, provided by her daughter, Hrimgalah M. Amen. Millie Charles's records, housed at SUNO, were destroyed in the flood associated with Hurricane Katrina in 2005.

87. Reed was born and raised on Coliseum Street in uptown New Orleans. Unless otherwise noted, all information about Louadrian Reed comes from author's interview, October 30, 2013. Reed lost all her documents in Hurricane Katrina. A short interview with her appears in Canaday, "Study of Five," Appendix N.

88. *Louisiana Weekly*, November 1, 1975.

89. *Louisiana Weekly*, May 15, 1971.

90. Meredith Reed, email correspondence, October 1, 2013.

91. *Louisiana Weekly*, March 7, 1981; Barthelemy was mayor of New Orleans from 1986 to 1994.

92. *Louisiana Weekly*, November 21, 1970.

93. Taylor won a special election in March 1971. She won reelection in 1972 and served a total of five years. Joan Kent, "Focus: Rep. Taylor Today," *New Orleans States-Item*, January 29, 1976.

94. *Louisiana Weekly*, December 19, 1970; Germany, *After the Promise*, 255.

95. *Vieux Carré Courier*, January–February 1973.

96. Ibid.

97. United States Department of Justice website announcing consent decree regarding Orleans Parish Prison, http://www.justice.gov/opa/pr/justice-department -announces-consent-decree-regarding-orleans-parish-prison-new-orleans, accessed January 26, 2016.

98. *Louisiana Weekly*, November 12, 1977; *Baton Rouge Morning Advocate*, June 12, 197?; Kent, "Focus."

99. *Baton Rouge Morning Advocate*, July 9, 1976; March 2, 1997.

100. Mathews and De Hart, *Sex, Gender and the Politics of ERA*, 209.

101. *Baton Rouge Morning Advocate*, June 12, 1975; *Louisiana Weekly*, August 9, 1975.

102. For a succinct overview of Supreme Court rulings that struck down discriminatory legislation in the 1970s, see Mary Frances Berry, *Why ERA Failed: Politics, Women's Rights, and the Amending Process of the Constitution* (Bloomington: Indiana University Press, 1986), chap. 8.

Chapter 9. "Real Progress for Women"

1. *Baton Rouge Advocate*, June 2, 2008; Sylvia Roberts, interview by the author, September 28, 2007, Newcomb Archives; Collins, *When Everything Changed*, 91–92.

2. Rosen, *World Split Open*, 81; Collins, *When Everything Changed*, 87; MacLean, *Freedom Is Not Enough*, 127–32.

3. Roberts interview.

4. Collins, *When Everything Changed*, 91; MacLean, *Freedom Is Not Enough*, 123; Judith Paterson, *Be Somebody: A Biography of Marguerite Rawalt* (Austin, Tex.: Eakin Press, 1986), 184.

5. Collins, *When Everything Changed*, 92–94; Paterson, *Be Somebody*, 196–97; Stansell, *Feminist Promise*, 297–98; MacLean, *Freedom Is Not Enough*, 123–24.

6. Paterson, *Be Somebody*, 196–97.

7. Roberts interview.

8. Ibid.

9. MacLean, *Freedom Is Not Enough*, 133–34; Strebeigh, *Equal*, chap. 2. Ginsburg was appointed to the court by President Bill Clinton and took the oath of office in August 1993. She is the first Jewish female member of the court.

10. Mildred Loving died in 2008. Kierner, Loux, and Shockley, *Changing History*, chap. 7; Peter Wallenstein, *Tell the Court I Love My Wife: Race, Marriage and Law—An American History* (New York: Palgrave Macmillan, 2004); Phyl Newbeck, *Virginia Hasn't Always Been for Lovers: Interracial Marriage Bans and the Case of Richard and Mildred Loving* (Carbondale: Southern Illinois University Press, 2004).

11. Davis, *Moving the Mountain*, chap. 1.

12. Collins reports, "To add insult to injury, the Louisiana Unemployment Compensation Board denied Cooper benefits on the grounds that she had left her job 'voluntarily.'" Collins, *When Everything Changed*, 266–67; *Cooper v. Delta Air Lines*; MacLean, *Freedom Is Not Enough*, 124–25.

13. The other states were Texas, New Mexico, Arizona, Idaho, Nevada, California, and Washington. Janet Mary Riley, ed., *Louisiana Community Property: Cases and Materials on Louisiana Property Law of Marriage*, 2nd ed. (Baton Rouge: Claitor's Publishing Division, 1981), A-2. The exact origin of Louisiana's Civil Code has been a subject of debate for decades, with some legal scholars emphasizing the Spanish roots while others point to French sources. See, for example, Rodolfo Batiza, "Actual Sources of the Marriage Contract Provisions of the Louisiana Code of 1808: The Textual Evidence," *Tulane Law Review* 54 (1979): 77–116.

14. Janet Mary Riley, "Women's Rights in the Louisiana Matrimonial Regime," *Tulane Law Review* 50 (1976): 560; *Louisiana Community Property Law and How Its Effects Can Be Changed by Contract: A Pamphlet for Louisiana Citizens about to Marry and for Married Persons from Other States Who Come Here to Live*, January 1977, published by the Louisiana Department of Justice. The pamphlet notes that "not all property owned by the husband or the wife is community property. Property owned by the man or the woman before their marriage, gifts made to the husband or to the wife alone, and property inherited by the husband or the wife alone are separate property. Income from separate property, however, is usually community property." Clay Latimer, email correspondence, March 3, 2010.

15. People who had married outside Louisiana and moved here had one year to file an agreement. See *Legal Rights of Louisiana Women* (NOW Legal Defense and Education Fund, 1972). No author is indicated, but the pamphlet was likely written jointly by Marguerite Rawalt and Sylvia Roberts.

16. *Louisiana Community Property Law*.

17. *Baton Rouge Morning Advocate*, June 15, 1974, reprint of an address to the Law Institute by Mack E. Barham, associate justice, Supreme Court of Louisiana.

18. In addition to Riley, who was technically known as the reporter, the committee consisted of Thomas A. Casey, Katherine Brash Jeter, Helen Kohlman, Thomas B. Lehmann, Max Nathan, Robert A. Pascal, Eric O. Person, Robert Roberts III, and Wayne S. Woody. Katherine S. Spaht, "Background of Matrimonial Regimes," *Louisiana Law Review* 39 (1979): 325.

19. Janet Mary Riley, "A Revision of the Property Law of Marriage—Why Now?" Louisiana Bar Journal (1973): 37–41; and Riley, "Women's Rights," 557.

20. Robert A. Pascal to Janet Mary Riley, chair of the LSLI Matrimonial Regimes Reform Project, cc'd to the entire committee, October 17, 1974, JMR papers.

21. Cynthia Woody, "The Family as Legal Entity: Consideration of Changes," *Baton Rouge State-Times*, February 2, 1974.

22. *New Orleans Clarion Herald*, June 17, 1976.

23. Deidre Cruse, "Work Begins on Community Property Equal Management Plan," *Baton Rouge Morning Advocate*, October 27, 1977.

24. Ibid.

25. Deidre Cruse, "Community Property Bill Said Equitable, Workable Plan; Bankers Fear Harm to Commerce," *Baton Rouge State-Times*, June 7, 1978.

26. Ibid.

27. "Keeping the Memories: Louisianans of the 2nd Wave Feminist Movement," transcript of banquet discussion sponsored by Veteran Feminists of America, March 22, 2001, Newcomb Archives.

28. Ibid.

29. Ibid.

30. *Barbara Bullock vs. Edwin Edwards et al.*, U.S. District Court, Eastern District of Louisiana, no. 74-3149, decided November 11, 1975. Judgment stored at the National Archives, Fort Worth, Texas. *Distaff*, March 15–April 15, 1975.

31. *Barbara M. Hansen v. Commissioner of Internal Revenue*, "Oral Argument," United States Court of Appeals, Fifth Circuit, November 9, 1978, typescript, Barbara Hansen Collection, Edith Garland Dupré Library, University of Louisiana at Lafayette.

32. *Lafayette Daily Advertiser* March 11, 1980; Barbara Hansen Collection.

33. Ruth Bader Ginsburg to Ollie Tucker Osborne, October 24 1978, Barbara Hansen Collection.

34. *Lafayette Daily Advertiser*, March 11, 1980.

35. The U.S. Supreme Court declined to hear the case. Spaht, "Background of Matrimonial Regimes Revision," 338–40; *New Orleans Times-Picayune*, December 9, 1979, "Dix" (special insert), 10. Waldrup was a native of Gadsden, Alabama, and lived in New Orleans from 1974 to 2002. Dorothy Waldrup obituary, *New Orleans Times-Picayune*, June 23, 2012.

36. *Distaff*, April–May 1975.

37. *Corpus Christi Parish Credit Union v. Martin*; *New Orleans Times-Picayune*, June 23, 1979.

38. *Kirchberg v. Feenstra v. Edwin Edwards and State of Louisiana, Third Party*, U.S. Court of Appeals, Fifth Circuit, no. 77-1991, December 12, 1979.

39. *Baton Rouge Morning Advocate*, October 27, 1977.

40. "Statement of Ann Davenport to House Civil Law and Procedure Committee, May 1978," typescript, Newcomb Archives; *Baton Rouge Morning Advocate*, June 7, 1978.

41. *New Orleans Times-Picayune*, June 23, 1979.

42. *Distaff*, December 1979; Revised Statute §§2831 to 2856 Repealed by Acts 1979, no. 709, §5, eff. January 1, 1980.

43. That provision would be changed by the legislature within a few years to place a three-year time limit on the irrevocability of the renunciation. "Legislative update" by Maurice Durbin, n.d., probably 1988; Act 554, SB 365; Kelly, in JMR papers.

44. *Distaff*, January 1980.

45. Those pictured were Corinne Maybuce, Jean Reeves (LWV), June Rudd, Katherine Spaht, Pat Evans, Susan Hymel, Mildred Clark, Roberta Madden (WIP and Common Cause), Felicia Kahn (LWPC), Fran Bussie, and Sibal Taylor.

46. *Distaff*, January 1980.

47. Evans, *Tidal Wave*, 134.

48. Jon Wiener, *Historians in Trouble: Plagiarism, Fraud, and Politics in the Ivory Tower* (New York: New Press, 2005), chap. 1, "Feminism and Harassment: Elizabeth Fox-Genovese Goes to Court"; Virginia L. Gould, email correspondence, January–June, 2013.

49. Connie Willems, interview by A. Van Heel, March 30, 1985, Friends of the Cabildo Oral History Program, copy in New Orleans Public Library and at Newcomb Archives. Willems and her husband, Casey Willems, a potter, moved to New Orleans in 1972.

50. Ibid.

51. Ibid.; Maurice Durbin Collection, Newcomb Archives. Eventually, Durbin went to work for Mary Landrieu, the first female elected to the U.S. Senate from Louisiana. Senator Landrieu lost her bid for reelection to Republican Bill Cassidy in 2014.

Epilogue. Into the Twenty-First Century

1. Linda Gordon, *Heroes of Their Own Lives: The Politics and History of Family Violence—Boston, 1880–1960* (New York: Viking, 1988).

2. Smith, "Casey Hayden," 383; Casey Hayden interview, in Agger, *Sixties at 40*, 259.

3. Jeannette King, "Inside and Outside of Two Worlds," in Holsaert et al., *Hands on the Freedom Plow*, 223–30.

4. Liz Simon, Lesbian Herstory event at Newcomb College Institute, March 26, 2014.

5. Susan Laporte, interview by the author, September 25, 2007; Susan LosCalzo, interview by the author, September 5, 2007.

6. Laporte interviews; Susan LosCalzo, email correspondence, March 22, 2014.

7. http://nnedv.org/about/staff/65-staff/89-kgandy.html, accessed September 30, 2015.

8. Miller interviews; SONG website, http://www.southernersonnewground.org; interview with Suzanne Pharr, http://www.smith.edu/libraries/libs/ssc/vof/transcripts /Pharr.pdf. "Lesbian-Only 'Intentional Community' Outlasts Others," *Northwest Arkansas Democrat-Gazette*, August 31, 2015, http://www.nwaonline.com/news/2015/aug/31 /lesbian-only-intentional-community-outl-1/, accessed Sept. 4, 2015.

9. Fife, *Portraits from Memory*; Barbara Scott, interview by the author, December 4, 2013.

10. Sybil Morial, *Witness to Change: From Jim Crow to Political Empowerment* (Winston-Salem, N.C.: John F. Blair, 2015). Morial's memoir appeared too late to use as a source in this book. I relied instead on interviews and newspaper accounts to tell her story.

11. Louisiana Senate Resolution, March 7, 2005.

12. Fran Bussie interview, April 14, 2013.

13. Taylor obituary, *New Orleans Times-Picayune*, August 24, 2000; *Louisiana Weekly*, June 14, 2011; Carol Flake, *New Orleans: Behind the Masks of America's Most Exotic City* (New York: Grove Press, 1994).

14. Vera Warren-Williams, interview by the author, March 20, 2014, Newcomb Archives.

15. Canaday, "Study of Five," appendix P; *Louisiana Weekly*, September 20, 1975, and October 3, 1975.

CPSIA information can be obtained
at www.ICGtesting.com
Printed in the USA
LVOW08*0255270517
536040LV00005B/276/P